Hiking
Southern
New England

by
Rhonda and George
Ostertag

FALCON™

Falcon Press® Publishing Co., Inc.,
Helena, Montana

©1997 by Falcon Press Publishing Co., Inc.
Helena and Billings, Montana.

All black-and-white photos by authors.
Cover photo by George Ostertag

Library of Congress Cataloging-in-Publication Data
Ostertag, Rhonda   1957-
　　Hiking Southern New England / by Rhonda and George Ostertag.
　　　　p.　cm.
　　Includes bibliographical references.
　　ISBN 1-56044-507-6 (pbk.)
　　1. Hiking—New England—Guidebooks.　2.　Trails—New England—
-Guidebooks.　3.　New England—Guidebooks.　I.　Ostertag, George,
1957- 　.　II.　Title.
GV199.42.N38078　1997　　　　　　　　　　　　　97-627
796.5'1'0974—dc21　　　　　　　　　　　　　　　CIP

CAUTION

Outdoor recreational activities are by their very nature potentially hazardous. All participants in such activities must assume the responsibility for their own actions and safety. The information contained in this guidebook cannot replace sound judgment and good decision–making skills, which help reduce risk exposure, nor does the scope of this book allow for disclosure of all the potential hazards and risks involved in such activities.

Learn as much as possible about the outdoor recreational activities in which you participate, prepare for the unexpected, and be cautious. The reward will be a safer and more enjoyable experience.

♻ Text pages printed on recycled paper.

CONTENTS

CONTENTS

Central Massachusetts Trails

Eastern Massachusetts Trails

Western Connecticut Trails

CONTENTS

ACKNOWLEDGMENTS

We would like to acknowledge the work of the trail associations and individual volunteers who help blaze and maintain Southern New England's trails, the efforts of the preservationists who work to save the area's landscape and history, and the generosity of landowners who have allowed the tri-state trail system to grow and endure.

We would also like to thank the individuals who helped with our research and volunteered their ideas or faces to this book, and our east and west coast base camps for freeing us to do our work.

OVERVIEW MAP – LOCATION OF HIKES

A. Western Massachusetts
B. Central Massachusetts
C. Eastern Massachusetts
D. Western Connecticut
E. Eastern Connecticut
F. Rhode Island

N

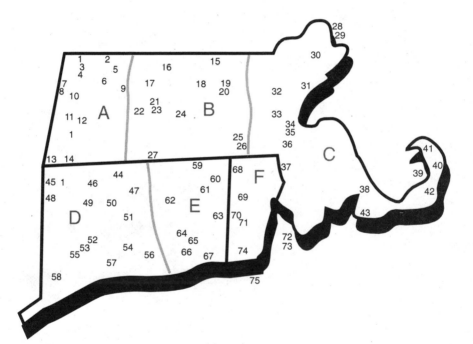

LEGEND

Interstate	95	Wetland	
U.S. Highway	101	Campground	
State or County Road		Picnic Area	
Paved Road		Trail Shelter	
Gravel Road		Bridge	
Unimproved Road		Building	
Trailhead/Parking	P	Cemetery	
Described Trail		Mine/Quarry	
Alternate Trail		Viewpoint	
Brook		Point of Interest	
River		Powerline	
Body of Water		Lookout Tower	
Summit	2,477ft.	Railroad	
Waterfall		Scale	0 0.5 1 Miles
Dam		Spring	

INTRODUCTION

The trails of Massachusetts, Connecticut, and Rhode Island weave an intriguing tapestry that invites exploration. Hundreds of trail miles entice hikers to lace on their boots to experience tours ranging from short nature walks to rugged skyline hikes to wilderness beach strolls. Trails wandering through natural areas and extensive forested reaches offer a winning diversity, rich in geologic and cultural history.

The trails in this book explore many of Southern New England's premier parks, forests, peaks, coastal flatlands, swamps, beaches, and private reserves and sanctuaries. Travel past charming waterfalls and daunting cliffs, revel in summit views and wilderness solitude, shuffle across the leafy carpet of autumn-blazed woods, and dig your toes into clean white sand. Turtle, fish, salamander, deer, raccoon, porcupine, eagle, hawk, warbler, and gull share these byways with human visitors.

While traveling the trails, flip through the pages of history. Discover dinosaur tracks and Native American graves, see where the Pilgrim's first tasted the sweet water of the New World, make a pilgrimage of your own to a sacred Shaker Society hilltop, and unravel the story of colonial settlement and the Industrial Revolution. Then, when your boots are worn and your soul is primed, walk in the footsteps of Henry David Thoreau.

This guidebook features a region-wide sampling of nature walks, a full range of day-length hikes, and, where available, backpacking trips. The collection serves as a launch pad to both the sport of hiking and to the foot-travel possibilities that lay ahead.

WEATHER

Southern New England offers fairly reliable three-season hiking, with days of no or minimal snow extending the season into winter. Several trails also serve as winter cross-country ski or snowshoe routes. Spring and fall offer the preferred mix of mild temperatures and low humidity levels, while summer can bring extremes in both categories.

TERRAIN

Glaciers sculpted the face of Southern New England, grinding down ridges, broadening valleys, and depositing rocky glacial debris. The tri-state area offers hikers a landscape of outcrop vistas and traprock ridges, tranquil waterfalls, broad rivers and clear-coursing streams, reservoirs, beaver ponds, swamps, rolling hardwood forests, and exquisite coastal sands.

LAND OWNERSHIP

While this book concentrates primarily on public land offerings, trails also cross private, utility, trustee, Audubon sanctuary, and conservancy lands.

1

Junction sign, Norman Bird Sanctuary, RI.

Eastern forest, Chatfield Hollow State Park, CT.

Hikers assume full responsibility for their own well-being when traveling on private lands, and implicitly consent to abide by posted rules. Stay on designated trails, leave gates as you found them, and pick up and pack out litter left by other trail users as well as your own trash. "Pack it in, pack it out."

We make every effort to indicate if and where a trail traverses or abuts private land. Occasionally, land ownership changes or a landowner may withdraw the privilege of thru-travel; respect such closures.

Publicly held lands. Trails traveling lands managed by state, local, and federal agencies are the core of this book.

State Parks typically show greater grooming and development and possess more facilities. At most state parks, expect to pay a seasonal entrance fee.

State Forests, *Reservations*, and *Management Areas* account for much of the region's open space. These minimally-developed woodland sites typically offer a wilder experience, with few or no facilities. Some may charge a seasonal or campground fee.

Public *Wildlife Management Areas* and *National Wildlife Refuges* primarily promote and sustain waterfowl and wildlife populations, with hunting and fishing, bird watching, and hiking allowed as compatible recreations.

Privately held lands. The privately held lands of *The Trustees of Reservations* in Massachusetts offer outstanding hiking opportunities. The Trustees, a nonprofit entity and the world's oldest land trust (founded in 1891), purchases and preserves properties of exceptional scenic, historic, and ecological value throughout Massachusetts for public use and enjoyment. Their

3

Southford Falls, Southford Falls State Park, CT.

mission is supported by membership dues, contributions, admission fees, and endowments. When visiting The Trustees sites, obey the posted rules that protect the unique qualities of each property, confine your visits to daylight hours, and keep vehicles on designated roads.

The Nature Conservancy (TNC), an international nonprofit organization devoted to the protection of biodiversity, opens its trails to the public for hiking, nature study, and photography. Please note that straying from the trails, hiking with pets, collecting, smoking, picnicking, camping, building fires, swimming, and bicycling are forbidden activities.

TNC extends hiking privileges only where and when compatible with their primary mission of conserving and preserving the land, its habitats, and inhabitants. Donations defray the cost of maintaining existing preserves and acquiring new ones.

National and state *Audubon Society* lands welcome travelers, but visitors must hold Audubon membership or pay a visitor fee. Respect the posted rules and any closures designed to protect the wildlife and natural habitat. Picnic only at established sites, leave pets at home, travel by foot only—no mountain bikes, and no collecting.

White Memorial Foundation, in Litchfield, Connecticut, maintains a remarkable 4,000-acre gift from a farsighted brother and sister committed to preserving nature and its tranquillity, and to providing future generations the opportunity to enjoy and explore the land. The site promotes conservation, research, education, and compatible forms of recreation in a natural arena. Heed trail use restrictions. No collecting.

TRAIL MARKINGS

Decades or centuries of use, rather than planned cutting, have created most trailbeds in the tri-state area. The predominance of leafy woods (which often obscure trails) make necessary some manner of trail blazing (paint, diamond, or disk markers) to guide hikers. A double blaze typically warns of a change in direction with the top blaze offset in the direction of the turn.

While the intervals between blazes can vary greatly from trail to trail, the spacing on a particular trail often has a consistent rhythm. If you note the frequency of blazes along a trail, an uncommonly long lapse between blazes can warn that you have strayed from course. In autumn be especially alert, as fallen leaves can conceal the tracked path.

The Connecticut Forest and Park Association marks its 600-odd miles of forest, park, and private land trails with a blue-paint blaze; side trails typically bear a colored dot within the blaze.

The Appalachian National Scenic Trail brands its route with white blazes as it slices across the northwest corner of Connecticut and through western Massachusetts.

On Massachusetts Audubon lands, find letter- and number-coded junction and site markers with orientation arrows keyed to the area map. You may also find a directional blazing scheme that uses blue blazes to indicate travel away from the trailhead or nature center and yellow blazes for travel toward the trailhead or nature center.

On private lands, consult a mapboard or flyer before plotting your course, as some trails are marked for one-way travel only. Following these trails in

Tyler Swamp Loop, Savoy Mountain State Forest, MA.

reverse, without aid of markers, could result in hikers becoming lost.

THE VOLUNTEER COMPONENT

Devoted, energetic volunteers and established hiking organizations, such as the Appalachian Mountain Club, help maintain, promote, and expand the regional trail system. Hikers can encourage and support this work by becoming members of these groups and by purchasing their maps and materials. The maps produced and sold by the volunteer organizations are often the best and most current available, containing up-to-date information on the lay of the trail, land ownership, shelters, facilities, and obstacles.

Hikers are likewise indebted to the private landowners who allow trails to cross their lands. Many trails would not exist without their cooperation.

Within this recreation dynamic, trail users have an obligation to use the land responsibly and to protect and preserve trails and the landscape they traverse. Respect switchbacks, contours, and other design features intended to retain the integrity of the land. Remember, one's adventure should not come at the price of the land or the enjoyment of the trails by future generations.

HOW TO USE THIS GUIDE

To help you decide which trails you would like to hike, we have grouped the trails into six geographic regions and provided a trail-at-a-glance summary at the head of each write-up.

Summary entries provide a character sketch of the trail, its general location, special attractions, length, elevation change, difficulty, available maps, special requirements or concerns, season, and an information resource. (You can find contact information for each listed resource in Appendix D.) At the end of the summary, you will find detailed directions to the trailhead.

"The hike" component of the write-up describes the progress of the trail, drawing attention to special features and alerting readers to obstacles and potentially confusing junctions. Habitat changes, seasonal surprises, sidelights, and unusual discoveries flesh out the tour description. Where appropriate, we mention flaws and disappointments for a balanced view.

The maps in this book are not intended to replace the more detailed agency maps, road maps, state atlases, and/or topographic maps, but they do indicate the lay of the trail and the site's attractions, helping readers visualize the tour.

AN EXPLANATION OF SUMMARY TERMS

Listed distances represent pedometer readings. Backpacking excursions—sometimes dictated by distance, sometimes by attraction—are left to the hiker's judgment and the rules of the appropriate agency.

The assignment of a subjective classification of"easy," "moderate," or "strenuous" considers overall distance, elevation change (the difference between the trail's elevation extremes), cumulative elevation (how rolling a trail is), trail surface, obstacles, ease of following, and its relative difficulty to other hikes in the book.

We do not estimate hiking times, as personal health, party size, the interest of the trail, the weather, and the trail's condition, all can influence the time needed to complete a hike. Instead, gain a sense of your personal capabilities and hiking style and judge the time for yourself based on the distance, the elevation change, the difficulty rating, and what you glean from the text. Customize the hike to fit your needs; you need not continue just because a description does, nor must you stop where the description stops. Interlocking loops, side trails, and alternative destinations may await.

GLOSSARY

Car-shuttle hikes. Typically, these are linear routes which require a drop-off and pick-up arrangement, spotting a second vehicle at trail's end, or hiking back to the trailhead you started from.

Corduroy. This side-by-side alignment of logs, boards, or branches provides dry passage over soggy trail segments or delicate meadow sites.

Forest lanes, carriageways, or cart paths. These routes typically are narrower than a woods road, yet wider than a trail, serving foot and horse travelers.

Jeep trails. These doubletrack routes typically serve foot and horse travelers. Most are no longer drivable.

Service roads. These routes carry minimal traffic, allowing official vehicles only.

Woods roads. These dirt, grass, or rocky routes are abandoned logging, farm, and town roads that have been reclaimed as trails. Most are closed to vehicle travel, although some may allow snowmobile or mountain bike use. We alert readers if we are aware of vehicle use or illegal vehicle use.

OUTDOOR PRIMER

Whether wilderness trekking is a revitalizing experience or an ordeal depends largely on preparation. Nature is not without inherent risks and discomforts, but learning to anticipate and mitigate them smoothes the way to great outdoor fun.

PREPARATION

Ten Essentials. Outdoor experts recommend "Ten Essentials" for safe backcountry travel. They are

(1) extra food,
(2) extra clothing,
(3) sunglasses,
(4) knife,
(5) candle or chemical fuel to ignite wet wood,
(6) dry matches,
(7) first-aid kit and manual,
(8) flashlight with bulb and batteries,
(9) maps for the trip, and
(10) compass.

Dress. The amount and types of clothing worn and carried on a hike depend on the length of the outing, the weather, and one's personal comfort. Layering is the key to comfort and well-being; select items that can serve more than one purpose. A long-sleeve shirt may be layered for warmth, lends sun protection, hinders mosquitoes, and protects against ticks. A lightweight raincoat may double as a windbreaker.

Choose wool or good quality synthetic fleece for cold, wet, or changeable weather conditions; these fabrics retain heat even when wet. Choose cotton for dry summer days. For their weight, hats play an invaluable role, shielding eyes, face, and top of the head, and preserving body heat.

Footgear. While sneakers may be passable for nature walks, for long hikes and uneven terrain, wear boots for both comfort and protection. Sock layering, with a light undersock worn next to the foot and a second wool sock worn atop, helps prevent rubbing, cushions the sole, and allows absorption of perspiration. Avoid socks with a large cotton content, as they are cold when wet and slow to dry.

Food. Pack plenty: Hiking demands a lot of energy. Pack foods that will not spoil, bruise, or break apart in the pack. Maximize the energy value for the weight, particularly when backpacking. Food fends off fatigue, a major contributor to accidents on the trail.

Equipment. The quantity and variety depend on the length and nature of the hike and on the season (Appendix A offers a checklist of commonly carried items), but a good pack for transporting the gear is essential. A day pack with padded straps, a reinforced bottom, and side pockets for water bottles works for most short outings. For overnight trips, select a backpack that has a good frame and balance and supports the weight without taxing hips, neck, or shoulders.

As backpacks represent a major investment, newcomers should first try renting a backpack. One cannot evaluate a pack in the store with only a few sandbags for weight. A trail test delivers a better comfort reading, plus it demonstrates how well the unit packs with one's personal gear. Many backpacking stores with a rental program will allow the rental fee to be applied to the purchase of a new pack; ask the manager.

Map and Compass. All hikers should learn to read maps in conjunction with a compass. Maps provide orientation to an area, suggest alternative

Lily pads, Miles Standish State Forest, MA.

routes, and aid in planning and preparation for the journey.

Become familiar with the United States Geological Survey (USGS) topographic maps. While most of these quads for Southern New England are too dated to show the current lay of the trail, they provide information about the steepness of the terrain, the vegetation (or lack of it), the course of waterways, and the location of man-made structures. The USGS offers topo maps at two scales: 7.5-minute and 15-minute series.

Remember when using a compass that true north does not equal magnetic north. For the region, the mean declination is about 14 degrees west. Search the map border for the specific declination.

TAKING TO THE TRAILS

Pacing yourself. Adopt a steady, comfortable hiking rhythm, take in the surroundings, and schedule short rests at regular intervals to guard against exhaustion.

Wading streams. Cross at the widest part of a watercourse, where the current is slower and the water shallower. Sandy bottoms suggest a barefoot crossing; fast, cold waters and rocky bottoms require the surer footing of boots. For frequent stream crossings or for hiking stream beds, lightweight sneakers earn their passage.

Hiking cross-country. For safe cross-country travel, one must have good map and compass skills, good survival skills, and good common sense. Steep terrain, heavy brush, and downed timber physically and mentally tax hik-

Trailhead information board, Bald Hill Reservation, MA.

10

ers, increasing the potential for injury. This, of all hiking, should not be attempted alone. Even know-how and preparation cannot fully compensate for nature's unpredictability and human fallibility.

Hiking with children. For young children, choose simple destinations and do not insist on reaching any particular site. Allow for differences in attention span and energy level. Enjoy the scenery, and share and encourage children's natural curiosity. Come prepared for sun, mosquitoes, and poison ivy, and discuss what to do should you become separated. Even small ones should carry a pack with some essential items: a sweater, water bottle, and food.

A WILDERNESS ETHIC

Trails. Keep to the path. Shortcutting, skirting puddles, and walking two abreast all contribute to erosion and the degradation of trails. Report any damage.

Permits and Registration. In sensitive areas, land agencies may require trail or camp permits to help monitor and manage the sites and minimize over-use. To protect the integrity of the wild, keep party size small.

At trail registers, take the time to sign both in and out and to comment on the condition of the trail and its markings. The collected information affects the allotment of funds and labor for trail improvement and expansion.

For designated backpacking trails in Connecticut, hikers must request camping permits in writing two weeks before an overnight stay. The permit request letter should list the camp area(s), the date(s), the name and address of the leader, and the number and ages of the group's members. Limit camping to a one-night stay per location, and leave pets at home. For a list of backpacking trails, or to submit a permit request, contact the Connecticut Department of Environmental Protection, Bureau of Outdoor Recreation, State Parks Division; the address is in Appendix D.

Pets. Owners should strictly adhere to posted rules for pets. Controlling your animal on a leash is not just a courtesy reserved for times when other hikers are present; it is a responsibility to protect the wildlife and ground cover at all times.

Camping. Low-impact camping should be everyone's goal. Camp only where it is allowed. Select an established campsite and do not alter the ground cover, bring in logs for benches, bang nails into trees, or dig drainage channels around tents. Leave no (or few) clues that a hiker has passed this way.

Where no established campsite exists, select a site at least 200 feet from the water and well removed from any trail. Avoid delicate meadow and alpine environments, and do not camp at lakeshores, waterfalls, overlooks, or other prized sites.

Reduce comforts (as opposed to necessities). Carry a backpacker's stove for cooking; when a campfire is unavoidable, keep it small. Snags and live trees should never be cut.

Outcrop passage, Westwoods Preserve, CT.

Garter snake, Macedonia Brook State Park, CT.

Sanitation. For human waste disposal, select a site well away from the trail and at least 300 feet from any water body. Dig a hole 8 inches deep in which to bury the waste. This biologically active layer of soil holds organisms that can quickly decompose organic matter. If the ground prohibits digging a hole of the specified size, dig as deep a hole as possible and cover well with gravel, bark, and leaves.

Use tissue sparingly, and for day excursions, carry a zip-seal plastic bag for packing out soiled tissue. Burying often results in the tissue becoming nest-building material for rodents or unsightly garbage scattered by salt-seeking deer.

Litter. "Pack it in, pack it out." This includes aluminum foil, cans, orange peels, peanut shells, cigarette butts, and disposable diapers. It takes nature six months to reclaim an orange peel. A filter-tip cigarette butt takes ten to twelve years to decompose, and disposable diapers have become an incredible nuisance and contaminant in the wild. Burying is not a solution.

Washing. Washing of self or dishes should be done well away from the lake or stream. Carry wash water to a rocky site and use biodegradable suds sparingly, remembering that even these soaps can degrade water quality.

SAFETY

Water. Water is the preferred refreshment; carry a reserve of safe water at all times, as wilderness sources often dry up or become fouled. Know that caffeine and alcohol are diuretics which dehydrate and weaken.

All wilderness water (even from the most pristine-appearing streams) used for drinking, food preparation, and washing dishes should be treated to remove or destroy *Giardia lamblia* (a water-borne protozoan causing stomach and intestinal discomfort) and other disease-causing organisms.

Water purification systems that remove both debris and harmful organisms offer the most common and satisfactory treatment for natural water sources. The alternative is to bring the water to a full boil for at least five minutes. Iodine tablets do not protect against *Giardia*, do not fully protect against other water-born diseases and are not considered safe for pregnant women.

Getting Lost. Prior to departure, notify a responsible party of your intended destination, route, and time of return. Then keep to it and notify them upon your return.

If lost, sit down and try to think calmly. No immediate danger exists, as long as one has packed properly and followed the notification procedure. If hiking with a group, stay together. Short outward searches for the trail, returning to an agreed-upon, marked location if unsuccessful, is generally considered safe. If near a watercourse, following it downstream typically delivers a place of habitation or a roadway, where help may be sought. Aimless wandering is a mistake.

Blowing a whistle or making loud noises in sets of three may summon help. If late in the day, prepare for night and try to conserve energy. Unless one has good cross-country navigational skills, efforts are best spent conserving energy and aiding rescuers by staying put and hanging out bright-colored clothing.

Leaf litter, Wachusett Mountain State Reservation, MA.

Hypothermia. This dramatic cooling of the body occurs when heat loss surpasses body-heat generation. Cold, wet, and windy weather command respect. Attending to the Ten Essentials, eating properly, avoiding fatigue, and being alert for hypothermia's symptoms—sluggishness, clumsiness, and incoherence—among party members remain the best protection. Should a party member display such symptoms, stop and get that member dry and warm. Dry clothing, shared body heat, and hot fluids all help.

Heat Exhaustion. Strenuous exercise combined with summer sun can lead to heat exhaustion, an over-taxation of the body's heat regulatory system. Wearing a hat, drinking plenty of water, eating properly (including salty snacks), and avoiding fatigue are safeguards.

Poison ivy and poison sumac. The best way to avoid contact with these and other skin irritating plants is to learn what they look like and in what environments they grow. Consult a good plant identification book. Vaccines and creams have yet to conquer these irritating plant oils. If you suspect you have come in contact with one of these plants, rinse off as soon as possible and avoid scratching, as it spreads the oils.

Ticks, stings, and bites. Again the best defense is knowledge. Learn about the habits and habitats of snakes, bees, wasps, ticks, and other "menaces" of the wild and how to deal with the injuries they may cause. Also become aware of any personal allergies and sensitivities that you or a party member might have.

Lyme disease, transmitted by the tiny deer tick, has become a serious concern in the East, but it need not deter you from the outdoors. Hikers come into contact with ticks amid grasses and shrubs; the ticks do not drop from trees. Wear light-colored long pants and long-sleeved shirts, and keep your layers tucked into one another. This will help you identify any ticks and keep them on the outside of your garments. While hiking, make frequent checks for the unwanted hitchhiker. When at home, shower and search skin surfaces thoroughly and launder hiking clothes directly.

Should a tick bite and become anchored in the skin, remove the tick by drawing evenly on its body, disinfect the site with alcohol, and monitor over the next few weeks. Look for a red bull's-eye swelling at the site of the bite; also be alert to inexplicable muscle pain, tiredness, or flu-like symptoms. Consult a physician immediately should any kind of symptom occur.

Bears. The black bears in the East represent more nuisance than threat. Use common sense; do not store food near camp, and especially not in the tent. If clothes pick up cooking smells, suspend them along with the food from an isolated overhanging branch well away from camp. Sweet-smelling creams or lotions should be avoided.

Hunting. Although most public lands open to hunters do not prohibit hiking during hunting season and few have any record of conflict, we would still advise fall hikers to point their boots toward lands and trails where hunting is not allowed. If you hike where hunting occurs, wear bright orange clothing and keep to the trail. Rhode Island law demands each hiker wear a fluorescent orange hat or vest from October 1 through February 28.

Poison ivy, Vin Gormley Trail, Burlingame State Park, RI.

Trailhead Precautions. Unattended hiker vehicles are vulnerable to break-ins, but the following steps can minimize the risk:

Whenever possible, park away from the trailhead at a nearby campground or other facility.

Do not leave valuables in the car. Place keys and wallet in a button-secured pocket or remote, secure compartment in the pack where they will not be disturbed until your return.

Do not leave any visible temptations; stash everything in the trunk, and be sure any exposed item advertises it has no value.

Be suspicious of loiterers and do not volunteer the details of your outing.

Be cautious about the information you supply at the trailhead register. Withhold information such as license plate number and duration of stay, until you are safely back at the trailhead. Instead, convey that information to a responsible party back home.

Backcountry travel includes unavoidable risks that every traveler assumes and must be aware of and respect. The fact that a trail or an area is described in this book is not a representation that it will be safe for you. While the book attempts to alert users to safe methods and warn of potential dangers, it is limited. Time, nature, use, and abuse can quickly alter the face of a trail. Let independent judgment and common sense guide you.

For more detailed information about outdoor preparedness, consult a good instructional book or enroll in a class on outdoor etiquette, procedure, and safety. Even an outdoor veteran can benefit from a refresher.

WESTERN MASSACHUSETTS TRAILS

Western Massachusetts encompasses the attractions of the Berkshires and Taconics, boasting the highest peaks in the three-state region of Southern New England. Hike through northern hardwood forest and enjoy rare pockets of boreal evergreens and mountain ash at the highest elevations. Southern hardwoods in the lower foothill and valley realms produce a salute to autumn that is among the nation's finest. Trails explore skyline ridges, tag vista points, and journey along brooks and picturesque mountain ponds, delicate waterfalls, an attractive skyline war memorial, a rare cobble, and blueberry patches season travel. Scenic river valleys and pockets of population part the steep-sided ridges of the region.

1 APPALACHIAN NATIONAL SCENIC TRAIL

General description: This 2,155-mile national scenic trail, journeying from Springer Mountain, Georgia to Mount Katahdin, Maine, traverses the northwest corner of Connecticut and western Massachusetts, touring forest, field, and mountain top. It offers various tour options for round-trip, shuttle, and thru-trail hikes.

General location: Northwest corner of Connecticut through the Berkshires of western Massachusetts.

Special attractions: Vistas, ponds, waterfalls, the Housatonic River, hardwood and boreal forests, spring blooms, fall foliage.

Length: 138 miles one-way (53 miles in Connecticut; 85 in Massachusetts).

Elevation: Travel between a low point of 250 feet along the Housatonic River and a high point of 3,491 feet at Mount Greylock in Massachusetts. The high point for the trail in Connecticut is 2,330 feet at Bear Mountain.

Difficulty: Strenuous.

Maps: Appalachian Trail Conference maps, Appalachian Trail Guide to Massachusetts-Connecticut.

Special requirements: Thru-hikers must plan how to pick up supplies along the route and what to do in case of emergency. They also need to arrange for transportation at the end of the trail. The trail is rocky and difficult in spots, and hikers should have strong map and compass skills.

Season and hours: Spring through fall.

For information: Appalachian Trail Conference.

Finding the trailhead: The Appalachian Trail crosses many Connecticut and Massachusetts state routes and traverses several state parks and state forest lands. Find the southernmost road access to the Connecticut-Massachusetts segment along Connecticut 55 at the New York-Connecticut border. The northernmost road access lies along Massachusetts 2 in North Adams.

The hike: The first trail in the nation to win national scenic trail designation, the Appalachian Trail (AT) passes through the mountain wilds of fourteen eastern states. Conceived in the early 1920s, the ribbon of the AT rolls atop the ancient Appalachian Mountains, dipping to cross the important eastern river valleys. Most of the AT greenway has received permanent public protection; some 4,000 volunteers along with 200 public agencies maintain and oversee the trail.

In Connecticut and Massachusetts, the AT rolls along the Housatonic River Valley, up and down the peaks of northwestern Connecticut and through the forests of the southern Berkshires. The tour concludes with rigorous climbs and descents, traversing the high peaks of northwestern Massachusetts.

A boreal complex crowns Mount Greylock, but hardwood forests are the norm on this hike. Swamps, fields, streams, lakes and ponds, the Housatonic River, and picturesque Southern New England villages complement the tour. Ledges and clearings regularly reward with views.

Open to hiking only, the white-blazed AT advances primarily via foot trail, with some sections of abandoned woods road. In rare places, it travels developed roads, including a 2-mile stretch between CT 4 and Falls Village. The terrain can be rocky and steep, so expect to use your hands occasionally for steadying, climbing, and easing yourself over rocks. Stay on the trail to avoid straying onto private land, as the protected greenway is often quite narrow.

Some fifteen lean-tos and shelters lie along or just off the AT, providing

Appalachian Trail sign, MA.

convenient, dry overnight waysides, but, since they cannot be reserved, a tent should be standard equipment. Gambling that you will arrive early enough to claim a lean-to for the night is an unwise and unnecessary wilderness risk. Camp in established sites to minimize environmental harm to this prized national trail.

From south to north, the Connecticut-Massachusetts leg of the AT sashays back and forth between New York and Connecticut for the first 7 miles, then settles in Connecticut for the next 46 miles. From the Housatonic River Valley, the trail mounts a ridge, where ledges provide a raven's-eye view of the river.

The tour crosses Caleb's Peak and passes the renowned St. Johns Ledges, popular for rock climbing. Red pines add to the oak-deciduous tour. Where the trail drops from the ridge, it follows the west bank of the Housatonic River for a 5-mile stretch—one of the longest river segments on the entire AT.

The trail returns to the ridge, overlooking the river, crossing Sharon Mountain, and passing through Housatonic State Forest. A 2-mile road stretch interrupts the reverie of the trail, where the AT twice crosses the river, the second crossing occurring in Falls Village.

The tour then passes from the Housatonic Valley floor over Prospect Mountain to tag the southern end of the Taconic Range. Some brook crossings mark off distance. Atop Bear Mountain (the highest peak in Connecticut), a tower, now half its original size, provides an exciting 3-state panorama. Side trails branch off to visit waterfalls as the trail resumes its rolling rhythm.

Sages Ravine Brook, just across the Connecticut-Massachusetts line, delights with cascades, waterfalls, and towering trees. Where the trail again rolls skyward, Race Mountain and Mount Everett reward with vistas.

From the mountains, the AT dips once more to the Housatonic Valley, touring a flat stretch, sometimes on road, passing through pasture, field, and swamp. Stone walls recall the early settlers of the valley.

The tour now stays mainly in forest, touring ridge and summit for frequent vistas. Where the AT crosses MA 23, an area of snapped trees commemorates the spring 1995 tornado that swept through Great Barrington. The storm cut a broad path of destruction, a testament to Nature's power. To the north, the AT traverses Beartown State Forest, passing again through tranquil hardwood-conifer forests and skirting Benedict Pond. Beaver ponds likewise mark the tour.

The trail passes briefly through the valley of Hop Brook, passing more areas impacted by beaver. At Lower and Upper Goose Ponds, hikers may want to adjust the day's planned mileage to allow for a long stop. A rolling tour through October State Forest follows. Where a long forested ridge then advances the trail, you'll find but a few views. The occasional stone wall or swampy passage provide visual interest.

Near Gore Pond, the AT passes from the Housatonic to the Hoosic River drainage. This more demanding section travels to the top of Mount Greylock. At the summit find rustic stone-and-wood Bascom Lodge (the Appalachian

APPALACHIAN NATIONAL SCENIC TRAIL

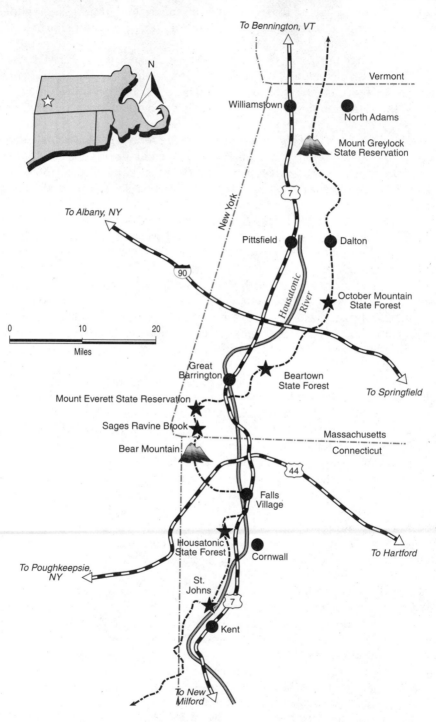

Mountain Club lodge) and the inspiring War Memorial. Greylock's chiseled drainages and steep plunging flanks add to its commanding presence in northern Massachusetts. Seldom reaching this far south, a boreal forest of fir and spruce engages trekkers.

The trail continues north along Mount Greylock's summit ridge eventually dropping to cross MA 2 in North Adams. For the final miles, the trail parallels a brook north to ascend East Mountain. Soon after tagging the quartzite outcrop of Eph's Lookout, the AT leaves Massachusetts to enter Vermont.

Thru-trail travelers and hikers planning short excursions along the AT should contact the ATC for its official maps and guides. Entire books have been devoted to this premier hiking trail and to the Massachusetts-Connecticut component alone. They are likely available at your local library, bookstore, or backpacker/outfitters supply store.

2 MONROE STATE FOREST

OVERVIEW

This 4,321-acre Massachusetts State Forest in the northern portion of the Hoosac Range features the beautiful mixed woods along Dunbar Brook and the enfolding rounded hills. Remote, sparkling and pristine, Dunbar Brook hosts the best brook hike in the entire three-state area. Elsewhere, trails travel hill, ridge, and hollow.

General description: Two short hikes explore brook and summit and may be combined for a single long tour. Brookside campsites and a trail shelter provide overnight accommodations.
General location: In Monroe and Florida, Massachusetts.
Special attractions: Beautiful energetic brook, rich mixed woods, scenic big boulders, woods flora, fall foliage.
Length: Dunbar Brook Trail, 5.6 miles round-trip; Spruce Mountain Trail, 3.2 miles round-trip.
Elevation: Dunbar Brook Trail, 700-foot elevation change; Spruce Mountain Trail, 1,000-foot elevation change.
Difficulty: Both, moderate.
Maps: State forest map.
Special requirements: Heed posted trailhead hours for the lower trailhead: 6 a.m. to 9:30 p.m. Backpackers, park at the Raycroft Trailhead. With a recent decline in maintenance, trail and junction markings have become unreliable.
Season and hours: Spring through fall.
For information: Monroe State Forest.

Finding the trailhead: From Massachusetts 2 in Florida, turn north on Florida-Monroe Road/Main Road, and go 3.9 miles to find the upper trailhead, turning right (south) on Raycroft Road, an unmarked dirt road opposite North Road. Locate the trails and parking for a handful of vehicles on either side of the Dunbar Brook bridge. Although Raycroft Road continues south through the forest, drive no farther than the south side of the bridge without a 4-wheel-drive vehicle.

For the lower trailhead, remain on Florida-Monroe Road another 2 miles and turn right on Kingsley Hill Road. In 1.2 miles, meet and bear right on River Road. Find the trailhead parking lot on the right in another 1.7 mile; New England Power maintains the site. Locate the power company's Bear Swamp Visitor Center another 0.7 mile south on River Road.

For an alternative approach to the lower trailhead, turn north off MA 2 on Zoar Road at the east end of the Mohawk Indian Bridge (2 miles west of Charlemont). Go 2.4 miles and turn left at the T-junction, following the Deerfield River north via River Road. Reach Bear Swamp Visitor Center in another 7.4 miles, the lower trailhead 0.7 mile farther north.

The hikes: From the River Road trailhead, ascend the service road near the utility line to begin **Dunbar Brook Trail**. Hike the south shore upstream, paralleling a boardwalk that leads to a small dam. Dunbar Brook feeds into the Deerfield River, a critical water in this power company corridor. Initially, overlook a deep, narrow reservoir shaped by the dam; the wild brook awaits upstream.

By 0.25 mile, travel a steep bank 15 feet above the natural brook; hardwoods and evergreens cloak the slope. In autumn, eddies along the brook lasso the colored leaves into scenic pools. The trail rolls, contouring upstream. Descend to a small camp flat at 0.5 mile; there enjoy overlooks of the sterling brook, its cascades and pools. Ahead moss-and-fern decorated boulders claim the slope.

At 0.7 mile, the **Raycroft Trail** charges uphill to the left to reach **Smith Hollow Trail** and Raycroft (Hunt Hill) Lookout. Bear right to cross the footbridge, continuing the Dunbar Brook Trail; beware of broken planks.

Continue upstream along the north bank, passing three desirable brook campsites to ascend amid a woods showing large spruce and pine. Find more birch and a tilted footbridge over Haley Brook, as the trail approaches the overnight shelter (1.2 miles). The lean-to sleeps five and has a wooden floor, fire ring, grill, and privy in disrepair.

At the left side of the lean-to, veer right, hiking past the privy, to resume the tour; avoid a tracked path that follows Haley Brook downstream. Find a steady ascent through mostly deciduous woods, passing under a utility line at 1.5 miles. While markers are rare, the trail remains followable.

Dip and rise at a deep drainage lined by birch. Farther upstream, travel a scenic hemlock stand where the forest floor seemingly erupts with mossy boulders. Cross a large side brook via stone, log, or wading at 1.8 miles and traverse a woods flat within feet of Dunbar Brook.

MONROE STATE FOREST

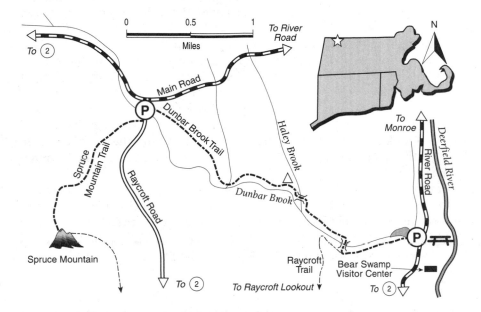

Enjoy a series of picture-pretty cascades, riffles, boulders, and window-clear pools. Hobblebush, striped maple, and ferns contribute to the under-story. Proceed along or just above the brook, touring a brief swampy area with remnant corduroy. The trail slowly climbs; where it plateaus at 2.1 miles, watch for red, yellow, or blue blazes indicating a sharp right turn. Ascend away from the brook, contouring northwest uphill, zigzagging amid some gargantuan boulders.

At the upper slope, bear left continuing northwest, well removed from the brook. The path broadens to a woods road; the rushing sound of the brook still carries up slope. Descend, again gaining filtered looks at the prized waterway. Cross a side brook atop slippery rocks, pass a pair of 6-foot-high mossy rock walls, and watch for blue blazes, as the hike follows a faint, rolling trail to Raycroft Road, 2.8 miles.

Backtrack, or bear left, cross the bridge, and follow Raycroft Road uphill, reaching Spruce Mountain Trail on the right (3 miles). From the bridge, admire the energetic wild, clear water coursing over gneiss-schist outcrop and boulders.

Find the blue-blazed **Spruce Mountain Trail** heading right off Raycroft Road, 0.1 mile south of the Dunbar Brook bridge. Be alert for its start. Look for a large roadside boulder and downed trail post.

Ascend steeply via a charming foot trail framed by fern, aster, and club moss. A vibrant tapestry of fall color and shape may regale the eye. The ascent briefly levels at 0.25 mile and then resumes amid fern-dressed rocks and ledges. Black cherry, birch, maple, beech, striped maple, and hobblebush contribute to the mix. At 0.7 mile, meander through a scenic log-strewn woods.

With a sudden climb, contour the slope, finding spruce. At times, eyes must strain for the next marker. Quartzite appears in some of the rock; a grouse sounds in the distance. Ascend steadily as the midstory vegetation frisks passersby.

At 1.6 miles, find a trail fork atop Spruce Mountain (elevation 2,730 feet). The right fork (straight ahead) leads to an outcrop in 150 feet for limited seasonal looks and an ending point to the tour. While the destination no longer affords open views, it still offers a tranquil retreat. Return as you came.

Alternatively, the left fork continues across Spruce Mountain ridge and descends southeast to Raycroft Road, the Raycroft (Hunt Hill) Lookout, Smith Hollow, and ultimately Raycroft Trail and Dunbar Brook. This 9- to 10-mile loop travels trail and drivable dirt road. Before attempting, inquire about trail conditions and the reliability of trail markings.

3 MOUNT GREYLOCK STATE RESERVATION, NORTH

OVERVIEW

In the northern Berkshires of Massachusetts, this 12,500-acre reservation protects the state's highest peak, Mount Greylock (elevation 3,491 feet) and its mostly wild flank. The mountain, topped by an inspirational 100-foot-tall stone war memorial, commands the setting for miles in any direction. The Appalachian Trail travels the spine, serving as a critical link for loop hikes. Centuries-old spruce, five-state panoramas, and wilderness challenges and reverie call hikers to the mountain. Fifty miles of interlocking trail explore wooded flank, razorback side ridges, and wind-tortured summit.

General description: Two summit tours and a short hike to a waterfall represent the hiking in the northern reservation.
General location: Midway between Lanesborough and North Adams, Massachusetts.
Special attractions: Historic war memorial and Bascom Lodge, a 100-mile, 360-degree tower vista, waterfalls, boreal and northern hardwood forests, spring and summer wildflowers, fall foliage.
Length: Appalachian Trail (AT) to Mount Williams, 5.2 miles round-trip;

MOUNT GREYLOCK STATE RESERVATION, NORTH

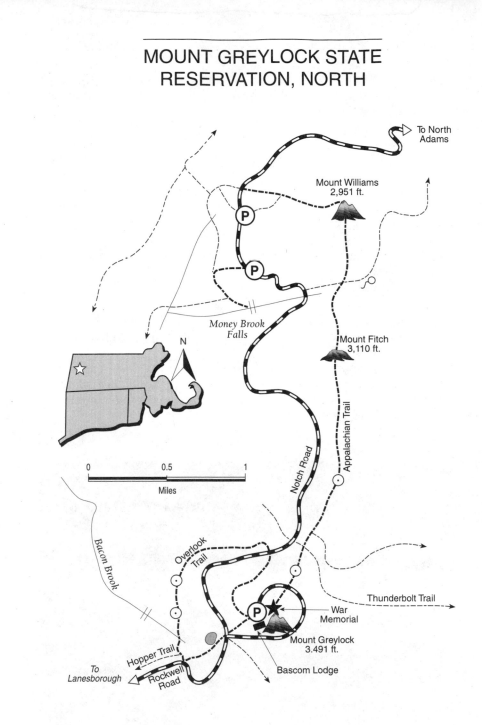

To North Adams

Mount Williams
2,951 ft.

Money Brook Falls

Mount Fitch
3,110 ft.

N

Appalachian Trail

Notch Road

0   0.5   1
Miles

Bacon Brook

Overlook Trail

Thunderbolt Trail

War Memorial

P

Mount Greylock
3.491 ft.

Hopper Trail

To Lanesborough

Rockwell Road

Bascom Lodge

AT-Overlook Loop, 2.4-mile loop; Money Brook Falls Hike, 1 mile round-trip.

Elevation: AT to Mount Williams, 790-foot elevation change; AT-Overlook Loop, 600-foot elevation change; Money Brook Falls Hike, 300-foot elevation change.

Difficulty: All moderate.

Maps: State reservation map.

Special requirements: White blazes indicate the AT, blue blazes all other trails.

Season and hours: Spring through fall for hiking. Day-use: 7 a.m. to 8 p.m.; Visitor Center: 9 a.m. to 5 p.m. daily; Bascom Lodge: 7 a.m. to 10 p.m. daily, mid-May through mid-October (reservations required for rooms and meals); War Memorial: 10 a.m. to 5 p.m. summer weekends.

For information: Mount Greylock State Reservation; Appalachian Mountain Club, Bascom Lodge.

Finding the trailhead: Find the southern approach through Lanesborough, Massachusetts. From the center of town, go 1.2 miles north on U.S. Highway 7 and turn right on North Main Street, following signs. In another 0.7 mile, bear right onto Rockwell Road. Find the visitor center on the right in 1 mile; reach the summit in another 8 miles.

For the northern approach, from the Massachusetts 2-Massachusetts 8 junction in North Adams, go 1.1 miles west on MA 2 and turn south on Notch Road at the sign. In 1.2 miles, turn left, staying on Notch Road. Reach the summit in another 7 miles.

War memorial, Mount Greylock State Reservation.

The hikes: Start the **AT to Mount Williams** at the summit; look for the painted AT crosswalk on the park road near Bascom Lodge. Follow the AT northbound, as it heads east on a gravel walk to the War Memorial. A moving tribute to Massachusetts's war dead, this 100-foot-tall stone tower holds skyward an attractive spire-topped sphere of metal and glass. When open, ascend the tower steps to attain a grand 360-degree view.

The AT then rounds the memorial and veers left, touring the summit. At 0.1 mile, find a sign for the AT at the north end of the parking lot. Descend sharply via shrub-clad outcrop and loose rock, crossing Summit Road.

Views pan east, overlooking the community of Adams. Small aspen, birch, fir, bramble, and hobblebush frame the tour. The path remains steep and eroded, with broad fern shoulders. Look for the occasional white blaze. At 0.4 mile, a blue-blazed cut-off trail heads left to Notch Road, and 20 feet farther north the breakneck **Thunderbolt Trail** plunges right. Watch for the AT to bear left, entering a high-elevation woodland, where the blue-blazed **Bellows Pipe Trail** descends east 1 mile, reaching a lean-to.

At 0.5 mile, bear right, crossing seasonal wet spots atop hewn logs, and pass from boreal fir-spruce forest to northern hardwoods. As the AT rolls along a thin ridge, pass a ledge outcrop with an eastern perspective, before descending to a moist saddle or col.

Return to the ridge, now touring the east shoulder of Mount Fitch (elevation 3,110 feet). Where the AT next descends reach a trail intersection, 2.4 miles. Here a steep 0.2-mile descent to the right leads to an unreliable spring; the path to the left descends 0.3 mile to Notch Road, passing an old chimney from the Williams College Outing Club Cabin. The AT proceeds ahead to Mount Williams.

Ascend steadily and moderately, topping Mount Williams (elevation 2,951 feet) at 2.6 miles. Gradually descend and bear right, skirting a vernal pond, to reach a register and vista outcrop. Overlook the Hoosic River Valley, the ridges rolling east, and the peaks of New England, before backtracking to the Mount Greylock summit (5.2 miles). Alternatively, hikers may continue north on the AT as it descends amid hardwood and spruce forests, reaching Notch Road in another 0.7 mile.

For the **AT-Overlook Loop**, again start at the summit crosswalk near Bascom Lodge and the War Memorial, but follow the AT south. Pass a flagpole, snaring nice over-the-shoulder looks at the memorial, dazzling when framed by blue sky or storm-blackened cloud. Follow a wide, trimmed track across the summit meadow and descend the paved driveway toward the radio tower building. Below the building, locate the marked **Overlook Trail** and follow it right.

Come around below the building and the fenced radio tower, descending a tight fir-spruce corridor, absent of views. The firs show the protective skirts of a high-elevation forest. In places, the thin rocky soil has worn away, revealing bedrock.

Cross Notch Road (0.5 mile) and settle into a contouring course, with gentle rolls. At 1.2 miles, a spur to the right reaches a clearing at the edge of the slope, serving up a U-shaped view of "the Hopper," a glacial carved ravine harboring old-growth spruce. The Hopper bears "Unique Natural Area" distinction. Panning west, find valley farms, the Taconics with Petersburg Pass, and the distant Adirondacks—a view applauding the terrain of Massachusetts, New York, and Vermont.

Resume the Overlook Trail, encircling the upper reaches of Mount Greylock. Hewn logs ease passage over soggy reaches. At 1.6 miles, cross the headwaters of Bacon Brook, which spills to the March Cataract. Now ascend relatively steeply to meet the **Hopper Trail**. To the right lies the campground; go left to complete the summit loop.

Bear left as the trail nears Rockwell Road and continue bearing left, touring boreal forest en route to the summit. At 1.9 miles, go left on the **AT**, following its white blazes past a small pond. Cross over the park road at the juncture of Summit, Notch, and Rockwell roads, closing the loop near the memorial, 2.4 miles.

For the **Money Brook Falls Hike**, start at the parking turnout on the west side of Notch Road, 3 miles north of the Rockwell-Notch Road junction; 5 miles south of MA 2; parking accommodates 4 vehicles.

Follow the blue-blazed trail leaving the north side of the turnout, passing amid birch, large-diameter ash, black cherry, both sugar and striped maples, beech, and hobblebush. The root-bound and rock-studded trail initially parallels Notch Road, before descending steeply away.

At 0.2 mile, meet the actual **Money Brook Trail** and follow it left toward the falls. Contour the slope, entering Money Brook drainage. There descend steeply, watching your footing. A few azalea dot the tour.

At 0.4 mile, reach Money Brook; the main trail continues right. Go left, ascending stone steps for a square-on view of the falls, located 100 feet upstream of the spur's end. The highest falls in the reservation, 40-foot Money Brook Falls dances over sheer black rock before racing downstream through a rock jumble. Return as you came.

OVERVIEW

In the northern Berkshires, stretching some 11 miles north to see Greylock (elevation 3,491 feet) reigns over the neighboring landscape, inspiring hiker, poet, author, and one of the earliest conservation movements in the state of Massachusetts. Beginning in 1898, the state set aside great portions of this mountain to be kept wild. Today, the reservation encompasses more than 12,500 acres and 50 miles of trail, with 1,600 acres recognized as a National Natural Landmark. At the summit find a war memorial tower and rustic stone lodge, both dating to the 1930s. Old-growth spruce, stirring vistas, and wilderness escape recommend the mountain.

General description: A blueberry patch/vista outcrop tour, ridge circuit, and pair of waterfall hikes depict the offering found in the southern extent of the reservation.

General location: Midway between Lanesborough and North Adams, Massachusetts.

Special attractions: Historic war memorial and Bascom Lodge, vistas, waterfalls, boreal and northern hardwood forests, blueberry patch, a 1945 airplane crash site, fall foliage.

Length: Rounds Rock Trail, 1 mile round-trip; Ridge Circuit (linking the CCC Dynamite Trail, Jones Nose Trail, Appalachian Trail (AT), and Old Adams Road), 6.4 miles round-trip; Deer Hill Falls Hike, 0.8 mile round-trip; March Cataract Trail, 1 mile round-trip.

Elevation: Rounds Rock Trail, Deer Hill Falls Hike, and March Cataract Trail, each show between 180 and 200 feet in elevation change; the Ridge Circuit shows an 800-foot elevation change.

Difficulty: Rounds Rock Trail, easy; Ridge Circuit, strenuous; Deer Hill Falls Hike and March Cataract Trail, both moderate.

Maps: State reservation map.

Special requirements: Challenging terrain. Note: white blazes indicate the AT, blue blazes all other trails.

Season and hours: Spring through fall for hiking. Day-use: 7 a.m. to 8 p.m.; Visitor Center: 9 a.m. to 5 p.m. daily; Bascom Lodge: 7 a.m. to 10 p.m. daily, mid-May to mid-October (reservations required for rooms and meals); War Memorial: 10 a.m. to 5 p.m. summer weekends.

For information: Mount Greylock State Reservation; Appalachian Mountain Club, Bascom Lodge.

Finding the trailhead: Find the southern approach through Lanesborough, Massachusetts. From the center of town, go 1.2 miles north on U.S. Highway 7 and turn right on North Main Street, following signs. In another 0.7 mile, bear right onto Rockwell Road. Find the visitor center on the right in 1 mile; reach the summit in another 8 miles.

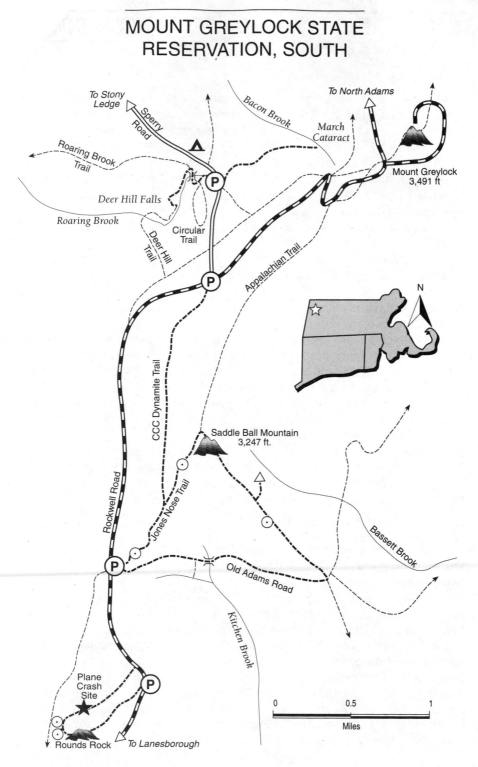

MOUNT GREYLOCK STATE RESERVATION, SOUTH

To Stony Ledge

Sperry Road

Roaring Brook Trail

Bacon Brook

To North Adams

March Cataract

Mount Greylock
3,491 ft

Deer Hill Falls

Roaring Brook

Deer Hill Trail

Circular Trail

Appalachian Trail

N

CCC Dynamite Trail

Saddle Ball Mountain
3,247 ft.

Jones Nose Trail

Rockwell Road

Bassett Brook

Old Adams Road

Kitchen Brook

Plane Crash Site

Rounds Rock

To Lanesborough

0   0.5   1
Miles

For the northern approach, from the Massachusetts 2-Massachusetts 8 junction in North Adams, go 1.1 miles west on MA 2 and turn south on Notch Road at the sign. In 1.2 miles, turn left, staying on Notch Road. Reach the summit in another 7 miles. Descend south from the summit on Rockwell Road for the visitor center.

Locate all trails off Rockwell Road between the visitor center and summit (find specifics within the trail write-up).

The hikes: Find trailhead parking for **Rounds Rock Trail** 3 miles north of the visitor center on the right (east) side of Rockwell Road. Locate the southern end of the trail, another 200 feet north on the left; the hike concludes on the left 0.1 mile north of the parking turnout.

Start at the southern terminus, following a moderate grade foot trail uphill through northern hardwood forest, followed by a shrub-meadow complex and an open blueberry patch mazed by side trails. The first spur to the left leads to Rounds Rock, as indicated by a survey marker. The bare outcrop overlooks the leafy crowns of the immediate woods.

Resume touring the broad hilltop, passing a 1912 pillar indicating the New Ashford-Cheshire town line. From there, descend into a spruce stand. At 0.4 mile and again at 0.5 mile, spurs lead left to scenic overlooks, featuring the Taconics, Catskills, and Berkshires, with reservoirs to the south. Cairns and blazes point the way over outcrop and through berry patch.

The tour concludes passing amid maple, black cherry, beech, ash, and birch. At 0.7 mile, pass a rusty steel frame and small wooden cross hinting

Mark Noepel Shelter, Mount Greylock State Reservation, MA.

at a 1945 plane crash site. Beautiful 4-foot-tall interrupted ferns adorn the woods. Meet Rockwell Road and turn right for the parking lot, 1 mile.

For the **Ridge Circuit**, start at the CCC Dynamite Trailhead for a 6.4-mile hike, beginning and ending with a scenic woods amble. Locate the trailhead on the east side of Rockwell Road, opposite Sperry Road (the campground access). For a 3.9-mile loop alone, start at the Old Adam's Road/ Jones Nose Trailhead, east off Rockwell Road, 3.7 miles north of the visitor center, 3.3 miles south of Notch Road.

The 1.25-mile **CCC Dynamite Trail** offers one of the easiest tours in this landscape of distinct ups and downs. Enjoy a scenic rolling meander through northern hardwoods, with hobblebush, fern, bramble, sarsaparilla, and whorled aster adorning the deck. At 0.1 mile, pass an old storage box that contained the dynamite for road building in the 1930s. Hewn logs cross sodden stretches; large sugar maples enrich the tour.

At 1 mile, stone-step over a brook, and at 1.25 miles meet the **Jones Nose Trail**. Follow it left for a clockwise tour of the Ridge Circuit.

Find a fairly steep ascent amid black cherry, maple, and beech trees. Soon after traverse an area of rock outcrops clad with low, dense spruce and mountain ash. A 30-foot spur to the left offers a 90-degree southwestern view, featuring the Taconics and Catskills. Now stair-step up the schist outcrop to meet and follow the **AT** south (right) at Saddle Ball Mountain (1.75 miles). Northbound, the AT reaches the summit, Bascom Lodge, and the War Memorial in another 2.6 miles.

Stay with the Ridge Circuit, following the AT south, coming upon a blue-blazed spur to a former vista mostly stolen by enfolding conifer. Enjoy a rich tour often through boreal forest, a rarity this far south.

Find a steady descent, showing less gradient than the Jones Nose Trail; schist continues to make up the trailbed. At 2.5 miles, a 0.1-mile spur leads left to the Mark Noepel Shelter at Bassett Brook. A luxury lean-to that can sleep a dozen hikers, this site offers a table, fire ring, usable privy, and nearby water source (purify all natural sources).

Resume the AT south, still descending. A spur to the right at 2.9 miles offers a grand look out the Kitchen Brook drainage, especially appealing when splashed with autumn red and orange. Where the descent eases, round a large boulder with an overhang shelter, weaving amid more fractured boulders.

Pass amid tall spruce and travel logs over muddy areas, reaching the **Old Adams Road Trail**. Turn right on this single-lane dirt road (now mountain-biking trail), for Jones Nose Parking; leafy branches overlace the route. Keep descending along the main woods road.

After crossing a small drainage, find beech trees replacing the spruce. At 4.1 miles, cross the bridge over upper Kitchen Brook; jewelweed and bramble dress the drainage. At the 4.25-mile junction, turn right to avoid private land. The route now ascends, with aspen and black cherry filling out the ranks. In 200 feet, bear right, passing amid shrubs. At 4.65 miles, round a gate reaching the Old Adams Road/Jones Nose parking area.

Resume the tour, following the **Jones Nose Trail**, heading right. Ascend the ridge, passing through woods and a broad mountain meadow, reaching the junction with the **CCC Dynamite Trail** at 5.15 miles. Retrace the dynamite trail left, ending at 6.4 miles.

For the **Deer Hill Falls Hike** and **March Cataract Trail**, start in Sperry Campground. Find day-use parking on the left, 200 feet past the fee station. For Deer Hill Falls, hike deeper into the campground, taking the first left past the day parking area; watch for a trail sign. The hike begins near site 5. For March Cataract, hike east back toward the fee station and turn left (north) per the sign. Reach the marked trailhead where the road curves left for the group sites.

For the **Deer Hill Falls Hike**, leave the campground, immediately cross a footbridge over a headwater fork of Roaring Brook, and turn right, descending amid hardwoods. At 0.1 mile, bear right re-crossing the brook; the **Circular Trail** heads left just prior to the bridge. In another 50 feet, follow the **Deer Hill Trail** downhill to the left, as the **Roaring Brook Trail** continues forward. Find all junctions well-marked.

The Deer Hill Trail descends, briefly pulling away from the brook only to switchback toward it. At 0.4 mile, arrive at the falls spur; the Deer Hill Trail proceeds downhill. The 30-foot spur leads to the base of this weeping garden-like falls with ledges of moss, fern, wildflower, and grass. From the serene falls, the water threads amid schist slabs, dropping steeply away. Return as you came.

For the **March Cataract Trail**, hike a narrow, rocky footpath angling uphill to the right where the campground road curves left toward the group campsites. In 50 feet, a little-tracked 0.2-mile **Nature Trail** journeys left through woods and fern pockets, arriving at campsite 16 (an alternative start/return for campers).

A full, rich forest enfolds the cataract trail. Ascend crossing a rocky drainage to tour a narrow wooded terrace. At 0.25 mile, earthen steps quicken the descent. At the base of the first set of stairs find a mammoth yellow birch. At the base of the second set, switchback right to cross a pair of hewn logs over a steep, pinched gulch.

Contour the slope, weaving amid rocks and boulders and passing beneath large maples. Reach the base of March Cataract on Bacon Brook, at 0.5 mile. The water streaks and skips over a sheer dark outcrop, broadening at the base; small ledges redirect flow. After plummeting 30 feet, the water tumbles through a steep rocky cataract. The return is as you came.

5 MOHAWK TRAIL STATE FOREST

OVERVIEW

In the northern Berkshires of Massachusetts, this 6,457-acre state forest presents steep-sided mountains, rich hardwood forest, abundant mountain laurel, deep ravines, and a historic Indian trail. The Cold River bisects the property, while the Deerfield River flows along the northeast boundary. Trout and Wheeler brooks drain the hillsides. Despite the key role of water in this terrain, hikes focus travel on mountain flank and crest, with only limited overlooks of the drainages.

General description: Three short hikes of varying difficulty attain vantages and present the forest offering.
General location: 4 miles west of Charlemont, Massachusetts.
Special attractions: Outcrop vistas, mountain laurel, relaxing hardwood forest, fall foliage, wildlife encounters.
Length: Indian Trail, 4.5 miles round-trip (visiting both Todd and Clark mountains); Thumper Mountain Trail, 0.5 mile round-trip; Totem Trail, 2.2 miles round-trip.
Elevation: Indian Trail, 600- to 800-foot elevation change (depending on selected turnaround points); Thumper Mountain Trail, 100-foot elevation change; Totem Trail, 700-foot elevation change.
Difficulty: Indian Trail, strenuous; Thumper Mountain Trail, easy; Totem Trail, moderate.
Maps: State forest map (generally available at site).
Special requirements: Admission fee. Portions of the first 0.5 mile of the Indian Trail are exceedingly steep; expect to use hands.
Season and hours: Spring through fall.
For information: Mohawk Trail State Forest.
Finding the trailhead: From the junction of Massachusetts 2 and Massachusetts 8A South (0.4 mile west of Charlemont), go west on MA 2 for 3.5 miles, and turn north for the state forest campground and Indian and Thumper Mountain trails. Find day-use parking near the headquarters.

Continue west on MA 2 for 0.7 mile to find the Totem Trail as it heads south off MA 2 at a monument. Locate the picnic area turnoff 0.1 mile farther west on the north side of the highway. Park there and cross the road for Totem Trail.

The hikes: For the **Indian Trail**, from the day-use parking at the headquarters, hike the park road northwest for 0.6 mile, finding the marked trailhead on the north side of the road where it curves left for campsites 36-56.

Log-reinforced steps ascend the slope. Hemlock, ash, birch, oak, maple, striped maple, witch hazel, and mountain laurel enfold the tour. Contour

MOHAWK TRAIL STATE FOREST

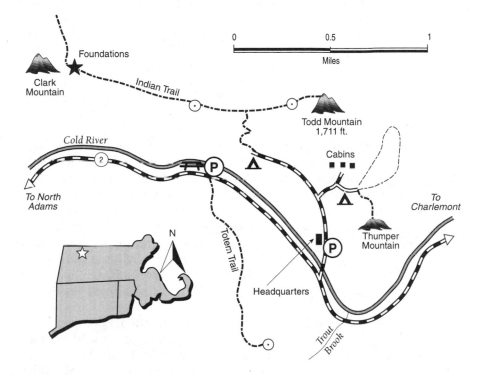

the base of the slope, bearing right in 250 feet. The trail now charges steeply uphill. The Cold River rushes in the basin below. Markers are few, but the trail well-worn.

Before long, rock outcrops dot the slope and trail, with natural rock steps advancing the tour. A few orange ribbons hint at the route. Scramble up the crevice of a canted sheer outcrop. Lichens encrust the rock and nearby oak trunks, as the trail continues to display its steep intent.

Top the saddle at 0.5 mile, arriving at a T-junction. To the right (east) lies Todd Mountain with its tree-framed vistas in 0.75-mile. To the left (west), find a gentler tour to Clark Mountain, which the trail rounds but does not top. Westbound, the trail halts in a mile, at an open field.

First, hike east along the ridge for Todd Mountain. The trail rolls along the crest, and then ascends passing between and over rocks; be careful when wet or overlain with leaves and pine needles. Pass a scenic congregation of rocks with peeks south. Snare better outward looks en route to the summit (elevation 1,711 feet). Here views pan south and east; overlook the Cold River drainage, the opposite steep-sided ridge, and rural valley of MA

35

2. Quartzite veins riddle some rocks, while reindeer lichens accent others.

Return to the T-junction and descend to camp for a 2.5-mile round-trip or add the westbound tour to Clark Mountain. An aisle of mountain laurel ushers hikers west on this rolling ridge tour. A gap in 0.2 mile offers a look across the Cold River drainage.

Amid a hemlock flat, the trail widens to carriage width. Where the ridge sags, reach another flat just below the summit. Here a pair of stone foundations, semi-masked by ferns, marks a potential ending (0.75 mile). The shady stroll continues, rounding the north flank of Clark Mountain, ending at an open field edged by picturesque birch (1 mile). Return to the T-junction and descend to camp for a total 4.5-mile round-trip. Exercise caution on descent.

For **Thumper Mountain Trail**, go 0.4 mile northwest from the headquarters and turn north for the cabins and group campsites. The trail starts at the end of the road in another 0.2 mile. Look for a post indicating "trail" east beyond the group campsites; a nature trail heads north at the gate. Periodic markers point the way; some have ambiguous placement.

Hemlock, white pine, hardwood, and laurel frame the tour. In 250 feet, bear right, ascending and traversing a ledge. In another 0.1 mile, climb steeply left. As the outcrop destination comes into view, bear right contouring to its top. Find a framed view south-southwest looking across the Cold River drainage at a wooded skyline knoll. Noise from MA 2 carries to the site. Return as you came.

The **Totem Trail** leads to Totem Viewpoint elevation 1,500 feet; a few blue and orange markers assist hikers. Ascend south at a roadside monument noting the establishment of the forest in 1921. In 100 feet turn left crossing a broad rocky drainage. A foot trail now contours east uphill. Birch, small beech, maple, and a bounty of fern weave an eye-pleasing tour.

Ascend steadily; a few rocks and roots foul footing. At 0.25 mile, meet a former woods road and follow it east still enwrapping the slope. Cross a rocky drainage at 0.6 mile, regaining both rocks and incline. The tour remains along a drainage cut for the next 0.4 mile.

At 1 mile, follow a faint foot trail, contouring and descending east. Where it rolls uphill, reach the vista site (1.1 mile), a scooped and canted outcrop overlooking Trout Brook to the east and the Cold River drainage to the north. The neighboring wooded ridges especially enchant when awash with fall color. Return as you came.

6 NOTCHVIEW RESERVATION - WINDSOR STATE FOREST

OVERVIEW

In the northwest corner of Massachusetts, the adjoining lands of Notchview Reservation (a property of The Trustees of Reservations) and Windsor State Forest throw open the gates to the tranquillity of the Hoosac Range. Rich hardwood forests and pine and spruce plantations enfold the area. Sparkling Steep Bank Brook ties together the reservation and state forest, ushering hikers between the two sites. Within the state forest, Windsor Jambs Scenic Area spotlights a small gorge and energetic rush of water.

General description: This day hike travels between the two properties. Tour mixed woods, plantations, and wet meadow bottoms, crisscrossing Steep Bank Brook to visit the rocky gorge of Windsor Jambs.
General location: 20 miles northeast of Pittsfield, Massachusetts.
Special attractions: Tranquil woods; rocky brooks; cascades; gorge; wildlife sightings of turkey, porcupine, and deer.
Length: 10.1 miles round-trip, but the hike readily breaks into shorter hikes and lends itself to a car-shuttle tour.
Elevation: Find a 1,000-foot elevation change, with the low point located on the Jambs Trail, the high point at Judges Hill (elevation 2,297 feet).
Difficulty: Moderate; strenuous and treacherous when streamed rocks and mosses are wet.
Maps: Reservation and state forest trail maps (generally available at the respective sites).
Special requirements: Privately owned Notchview Reservation suggests a per-hiker donation, while the state forest charges a parking fee. Reservation travel is at your own risk; obey posted rules.
Season and hours: Spring through fall for hiking. Reservation: 8 a.m. to dusk; Windsor Jambs Scenic Area: 8 a.m. to 8 p.m.
For information: The Trustees of Reservations, Western Regional Office; Windsor State Forest.
Finding the trailhead: To reach the reservation, from Massachusetts 9, 2 miles east of Windsor, turn north at the sign for Notchview Reservation. Go 0.2 miles to reach the Colonel Arthur Budd Visitor Center and trailhead parking area.

For the state forest, from MA 9, 6 miles east of Windsor, turn north on West Main for West Cummington and Windsor State Forest. In 0.7 mile, turn right on River Road; reach the campground, picnic area, and headquarters in another 2.9 miles. From the headquarters area, follow graveled Lower Road southeast to reach the turn for Windsor Jambs Scenic Area.

NOTCHVIEW RESERVATION
WINDSOR STATE FOREST

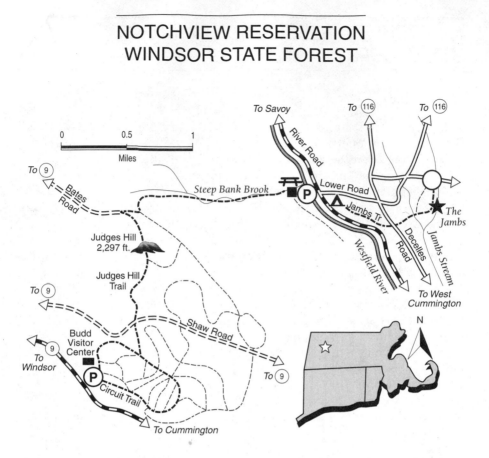

The hike: On a west-to-east tour, travel the reservation's **Circuit and Judges Hill trails**, the jointly-held **Steep Bank Trail**, and the state forest's **Jambs Trail**. Look for yellow markers and signed junctions along the reservation trails; blue markers indicate the state forest trails.

From the Budd Visitor Center at Notchview Reservation, hike the mowed track beginning to the left of the trail information board. Pass north between a set of fences and pass **Kinder Loop**, coming the junction of the **Circuit** and **Spruce Hill trails** in 250 feet. Go left for a clockwise tour of the **Circuit Trail**, traveling a time-healed woods roads with a cushiony grass and needlemat surface. The Circuit Trail serves as a hub for the reservation trail system and doubles as a winter cross-country ski trail.

On the left at 0.3 mile, pass an unusual beech tree displaying long, low, outward spreading branches. Past **Anthill Trail**, turn left on **Judges Hill Trail** to reach Windsor Jambs; the Circuit Trail turns right.

Follow a grassy woods corridor, soon crossing dirt Shaw Road. Pass from ash swale to planted spruce, again touring an old woods road; footboards and logs ease passage over wet areas. By 1 mile, find steady ascent amid mixed hardwoods. The grade steepens drawing away from the marked **Windsor Trail** junction; stay the Judges Hill Trail.

At 1.4 miles, top Judges Hill; the rockwork from an old picnic shelter and a stand of beautiful small- to mid-sized beech trees claim the summit. A quick descent to Bates Road (1.7 miles) follows. Turn right on this former stagecoach route to find the **Steep Bank Trail**, descending left in 0.1 mile.

This trail escapes much of the area boot traffic for a pleasing woods and brook meander, but stay alert for the faint trail markers; a few red Trustees' disks help point the way. Descend through a maple woodland with a lush green understory, crossing over and pursuing the thin side drainages downstream.

Along a rock wall, curve right, cross a side brook, and follow the south (right) bank of Steep Bank Brook downstream. Big birch, smaller beech, and hemlock frame this tannin-colored water punctuated by mossy boulders and 1-foot-high cascades. Various ferns accent the tour. Find the first stone-hopping crossing at 2.1 miles. Thirteen more follow, so be alert.

At times, the brook's trademark steep banks or downfalls push hikers higher up the slope. Spruce fill out the shady complex, and a few skewed state forest triangles mark or confuse the way. With the fourteenth crossing, return to the south bank and continue downstream, following a woods road contouring the slope above the brook. Turn right to reach the bathhouse at Windsor State Forest Headquarters, 3.2 miles.

Traverse the parking lot, cross River Road, and pass south through the campground, finding the **Jambs Trail** near the restroom building. A simple sign indicates "trail."

Blue markers and blazes now guide hikers through a dark hemlock-birch complex and plantations of spiny spruce. Where the soft earthen bed grows soggy, jewelweed, clintonia, and mayflower make a spotty appearance. After a slow ascent, head left on a woods road to cross dirt Decelles Road (3.8 miles) and angle left through another plantation.

Where footboards cross a wet site, find a marked junction. To the left lies Upper Jambs, but for best gorge viewing, go right as indicated for Lower Jambs. Tour hemlock-hardwood forest, following and crossing a side drainage to arrive at the mouth of The Jambs (the gorge on Jambs Stream), 4.4 miles.

Follow the left shore upstream, separated from the gorge by a mesh fence. Massive green-stained rock slabs litter the watercourse, as 50-foot cliffs pinch the 15-foot-wide tannin-steeped brook. The racing water cascades, riffles, and sheets over and around the rock, with the largest cascades plunging 12 feet. An early morning chill often hangs in the gorge. At 4.7 miles, reach The Jambs Scenic Area parking lot, the ending for shuttle-tour hikers.

Round-trip hikers backtrack, returning to the **Circuit Trail** at Notchview Reservation (8.8 miles). Continue straight on the woods road to complete a

Windsor Jams, Windsor State Forest, MA.

clockwise tour. Pass amid spruce plantation and hardwoods. Avoid the outward radiating side trails to skirt a weathered-board garage, orchard, and field. A stately staircase to nowhere hints at an earlier time when these woods supported family farms. Proceed back to the visitor center, now within sight, ending at 10.1 miles.

7 PITTSFIELD STATE FOREST

OVERVIEW

Situated along the Taconic ridgeline, this state forest covers nearly 9,700 acres and offers 35 miles of marked trail and woods road for exploration, with designated routes for hiking, mountain biking, all-terrain-vehicle driving, nordic skiing, and snowmobiling. Tranquil woods, skipping brooks, a unique hilltop azalea grove, ponds, and limited vistas vary travel. Bird and wildlife sightings introduce surprise. Two long-distance trails, the Taconic Crest and Taconic Skyline, traverse the forest; the latter allows all-terrain vehicles.

General description: Three self-guiding nature trails and a pair of hiker-only loops sample the area's best.
General location: 6 miles west of Pittsfield, Massachusetts.
Special attractions: Evergreen-hardwood forests, scenic brooks, early-June azalea blooms, fall foliage.
Length: Tranquility Trail, 0.5-mile loop; Woods Ramble, 0.6-mile loop; Berkshire Hill Ramble, 0.5 mile round-trip; Honwee Loop, 3.5-mile loop; Hawthorne-Parker Brook Loop, 4.5-mile loop.
Elevation: Tranquility Trail, virtually flat; Woods Ramble, 60-foot elevation change; Berkshire Hill Ramble, 30-foot elevation change; Honwee Loop, 900-foot elevation change; Hawthorne-Parker Brook Loop, 1,000-foot elevation change.
Difficulty: Tranquility Trail, Woods Ramble, and Berkshire Hill Ramble, all easy; Honwee Loop, moderate; Hawthorne-Parker Brook Loop, moderate to strenuous.
Maps: State forest map; request interpretive brochures/flyers for the self-guiding nature trails at the forest headquarters.
Special requirements: Keep dogs leashed at all times.
Season and hours: Year-round, spring through fall for hiking. Day-use ends at 8 p.m.
For information: Pittsfield State Forest.
Finding the trailhead: From the U.S. Highway 7 - U.S. Highway 20 junction in Pittsfield, go west on U.S. 20 for 2.4 miles and turn right on Hungerford/ Forthill Avenue at a sign for the state forest. Negotiate a series of turns,

following the marked route to enter the forest in 3.8 miles. Bear right to reach the headquarters in 0.2 mile. Continue north from the headquarters on Berry Pond Circuit Road, finding Honwee Loop on the right in 0.5 mile, Berkshire Hills Ramble on the left in 2.5 miles.

For the Tranquility, Woods Ramble, and Hawthorne-Parker Brook hikes, go left at the entrance fork; all begin on the west side of the road in 0.2 mile. Find parking on the right.

The hikes: The wheelchair-accessible **Tranquility Trail** and the earthen **Woods Ramble** share a common marked trailhead; obtain the appropriate self-guiding brochure or tape before starting. For each, the interpretive numbers suggest counterclockwise touring.

Hike west, crossing the bridge over Parker Brook coming to a junction. Where the paved Tranquility Trail arcs right, the dirt Woods Ramble continues forward. Both loops explore mixed forest, introducing the tree and plant species and the forest history: farmed and grazed in the Colonial period, logged in the 1800s for charcoal, and reforested in the 1930s. Cutoff spurs allow hikers to shorten the Tranquility Trail.

As ski and hiking trails branch from the Woods Ramble, be alert for the interpretive numbers. Pass a cross-country ski trail on the left to reach the loop junction (0.1 mile); bear right. At 0.2 mile and again at 0.25 mile, bear left as an unmarked trail and the **Hawthorne Trail** head right. The ramble twice crosses Hawthorne Brook before closing the loop and returning to the trailhead (0.6 mile).

Toad, Pittsfield State Forest, MA.

PITTSFIELD STATE FOREST

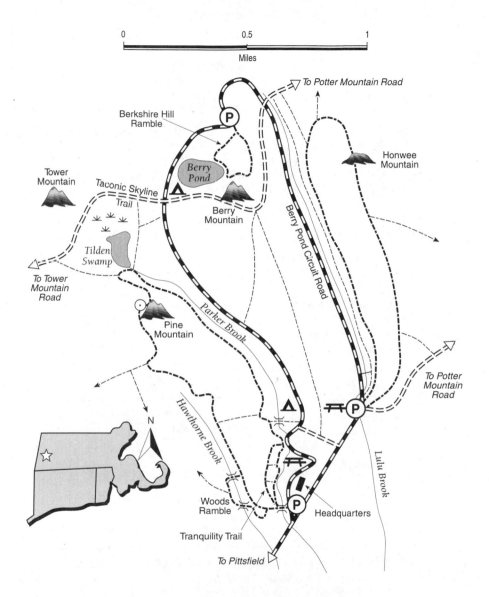

0   0.5   1

Miles

To Potter Mountain Road

Berkshire Hill Ramble

Berry Pond

Honwee Mountain

Tower Mountain

Taconic Skyline Trail

Berry Mountain

Berry Pond Circuit Road

Tilden Swamp

To Tower Mountain Road

Pine Mountain

Parker Brook

To Potter Mountain Road

Hawthorne Brook

Lulu Brook

N

Woods Ramble

Headquarters

Tranquility Trail

To Pittsfield

The **Berkshire Hill Ramble** explores the habitat of Berry Mountain and Pond, sites named for William Berry. In 1777, George Washington deeded this land to Berry as payment for his heroism during the Battle of Bennington in the Revolutionary War. Arrows, blue markers, and interpretive numbers point the way.

Edge a rare spring-fed 20-acre summit azalea field; travel amid a transition shrub complex, mixed hardwoods, and plantations of red pine, balsam fir, and spruce; and visit the shore of Berry Pond (elevation 2,150 feet), the highest natural pond in Massachusetts. Deer, frog, grouse, rabbit, and hummingbird may contribute to the 0.5-mile tour.

Find the marked trailhead for the **Honwee Loop** opposite Lulu Brook Picnic Area, 100 feet south of the bridge. It parallels Lulu Brook north upstream, contouring the hillside above the **Lulu Brook Trail**, a rolling streamside trail, now mostly cross-country in nature, overgrown, with forced detours up and downhill to link its visible trail segments. In places, it crowds to the Honwee Loop.

The Honwee Loop travels a woods road closed to vehicles. A diverse leafy canopy overlaces the straight-forward tour; a few hemlock intersperse the hardwoods. Although the whisper of Lulu Brook provides a soothing backdrop, glimpses are few. Yellow or orange triangles periodically mark the tour. At 1.25 miles, the Honwee Loop swings right, while the path straight ahead leads to the **Taconic Skyline Trail** in 0.25 mile.

Go right continuing the clockwise loop, still ascending, now with a steeper gradient. The woods road becomes more unevenly worn and pierced by roots. Maple, oak, beech, and striped maple still shade the way. At 1.5 mile, the **Churchill Brook Trail** heads left; continue forward for the loop. Find a few azalea dotting the understory.

Attain the broad summit plateau of Honwee Mountain, where beautiful black cherry trees join the big oaks and maples. By 1.9 miles, the trail descends steeply, and spurs branch left to all-terrain-vehicle routes. At the road fork at 3.25 miles, bear left; at the 3-way junction at 3.4 miles, take the center fork, coming out at the park road. Turn right to close the loop (3.5 miles).

The **Hawthorne-Parker Brook Loop** follows steep-sided drainages to top Pine Mountain and visit Tilden Marsh.

Retrace the first 0.25 mile of the **Woods Ramble** and ascend right on the **Hawthorne Trail**, traveling a woods lane parallel to the gulch of Hawthorne Brook. Beech, birch, maple, oak, and witch hazel dress the slope.

At 0.5 mile, turn right on a footpath veering away from the drainage, and in another 150 feet, bear left. Blue "H", arrow, and triangle markers guide the way, as do signs with misspellings of "Hawthorne." Azalea find a niche, while winds aloft excite the canopy. Climb steeply, following a meandering line up Pine Mountain.

Along the ridge, the gradient eases and more sunbreaks mark the tour. White pines intermix with the oaks of the upper canopy. At 0.95 mile, continue forward as a second trail descends left. In 200 feet, return to the original woods lane, following it right. The route then tapers to a hiker trail.

At 1.2 miles, meet the **Pine Mountain Trail** and follow it right. Cob webs ensnare early morning hikers. At 1.5 miles, pass the stone obelisk for the Pittsfield/Hancock town line. The trail then arcs right, touring the broad summit flat of Pine Mountain. At 1.75 miles, reach a northern vista cut, overlooking Tilden Swamp and Pond, with Berry Mountain rising to the east. A few azalea and mountain ash accent the cut.

A quick descent follows, interrupted by a scenic woods flat, lush with ferns. Where the descent resumes, find a T-junction. A left leads to Tower Mountain, a right leads to Tilden Swamp. Go right, reaching the Tilden Swamp beaver dam and **Parker Brook Trail**, at 2.4 miles.

The beaver-expanded pond reveals an impressive convex dam as well as current and abandoned lodges. Lily pads, arrowhead, and jewelweed accent the pond. Resume the hike following the outlet (Parker Brook) downstream, contouring the steep-sided drainage. Beech, birch, oak, and maple trees shade the trail. Following rains, tiny toads bounce along the trail.

At 3.1 miles, draw well above the brook. At times, hikers may glimpse the line of the park road on the opposite slope. In another 0.25 mile, veer right as the brookside path quickly becomes impassable. Continue downstream, now on a woods lane.

An uphill spur to the right at 3.9 miles leads to the **Hawthorne Trail**; stay the woods road, reaching a junction. To the left, a footbridge spans Parker Brook, leading to the campground; the path straight ahead continues the tour, still descending. At 4.3 miles, reach the paved **Tranquility Trail** at the park road. Turn right, hiking either trail or road, to close the loop (4.5 miles).

scription: Constructed and maintained by the Boy Scouts of America, this circuit travels wooded, stream, and hilltop sites key to a 19th-century Shaker society. The tour visits an area that held a Shaker family residence, farm and pasture, mills, waterworks, and two holy summits; plaques identify the points of archaeological and historical note.

General location: 5 miles west of Pittsfield, Massachusetts.

Special attractions: National Historic Trail with religious and historical sites, rock walls, mixed woods, fall foliage.

Length: 6.5 miles round-trip.

Elevation: From a trailhead elevation of 1,170 feet, top Mount Sinai (now Shaker Mountain) at 1,845 feet; Holy Mount at 1,927 feet.

Difficulty: Moderate.

Maps: Pittsfield State Forest brochure.

Special requirements: As this trail passes through the private Hancock Shaker Village (a not-for-profit museum village), hikers must first check in at the visitor center to secure a free hiker pass. Pass directly through the property to the trail, avoiding all fee attractions: buildings, lectures, and demonstrations. Hikers interested in these attractions may instead purchase a village admission ticket. No smoking and no pets within the village.

Season and hours: Spring through fall; visitor center: 9:30 a.m. to 5 p.m., April through November.

Stone wall on Holy Mount, Pittsfield State Forest, MA.

For information: Hancock Shaker Village; Pittsfield State Forest.

Finding the trailhead: From the junction of U.S. Highway 20 and U.S. Highway 7 in Pittsfield, go west on U.S. 20 for 4.5 miles. Find visitor parking for Hancock Shaker Village on the south side of the highway. Park, check-in, and cross U.S. 20 at the crosswalk.

The hike: White circles within green triangles guide hikers into the past for a glimpse at the world of an 1845 Shaker community. While woods now conceal much of the story, some of the remaining stonework, fruit trees, and cellar holes help one visualize the area. The trail tags two holy summits: Mount Sinai chosen by the Hancock Shakers; Holy Mount chosen by the Shakers of Mt. Lebanon, New York.

Commitment to a common religion, culture, and lifestyle united the Shaker members into a cohesive community, isolated from the outside world. Hancock represents one of the earliest Shaker communes formed in the United States. The trail holds the distinction of being the first National Historic Trail in Massachusetts; pass gently and respectfully.

From the crosswalk, follow the grassy track north past a small garden plot and through a field. Looks west find an elevated reservoir first used in 1790. At 0.25 mile, bear right, passing the rusty remains of a steam boiler left over from a Shaker textile mill. At 0.3 mile, again bear right, entering the woods on the historic road to the North Family residence; six such families made up Hancock.

The road travels upstream along the west shore of Shaker Brook, reaching the remnants of Lower Dam at 0.5 mile. This straight-built dam supplied power to the community. Built of rock slabs, it stands between 5 and 10 feet tall. While some of the cap rock has collapsed into the stream, it remains in remarkably fine shape. Just upstream lies the footbridge marking the start of the loop; cross, delaying a visit to High Dam until the end of the tour.

Now, proceed downstream along the east shore, again overlooking Lower Dam. A spur to the right reveals the stone foundation of the carding/fulling, grist, and saw mills. At 0.75 mile, signs to the right indicate where the North Family residence stood, now an overgrown flat and cellar depression. Although the loop now turns left for the ascent of Mount Sinai, a 0.5-mile round-trip detour straight ahead adds looks at a scenic rock wall, cornfield, and ancient maples and ash, for a sense of the land's historical use.

Resume the tour to Mount Sinai at 1.25 miles, touring a trail of cart-path width that mirrors and in places, utilizes segments of the historic route. Find a steady, moderate grade winding skyward to the hallowed ground. A mixed forest of white pine, maple, birch, ash, oak, hickory, and beech enfolds the tour. Sarsaparilla, club moss, chestnut, striped maple, and fern contribute to an understory profusion.

Twice the trail passes under a power line. Blackened earth hints at former charcoal pits; look for many more along the end of the tour. At 2.1 miles, reach and cross the summit Holy Ground, abandoned to nature. Ferns and

HANCOCK SHAKER VILLAGE TRAIL

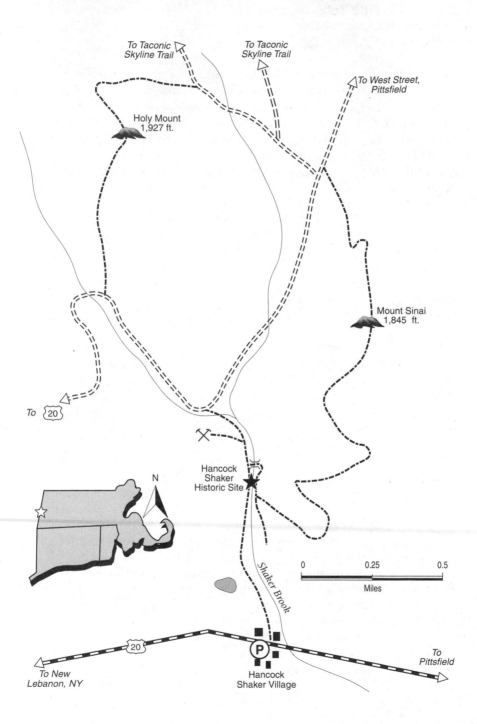

To Taconic Skyline Trail

To Taconic Skyline Trail

To West Street, Pittsfield

Holy Mount
1,927 ft.

Mount Sinai
1,845 ft.

To ⟨20⟩

N

Hancock Shaker Historic Site

Shaker Brook

0   0.25   0.5

Miles

⟨20⟩

To New Lebanon, NY

P

Hancock Shaker Village

To Pittsfield

young trees hint at the open flats of ceremony and worship. At the high point (2.25 mile), find a wooden bench.

A wooded descent follows, reaching what Shaker diaries refer to as the "great gulf" between the holy summits (2.9 miles). Here off-road-vehicle tracks scar the trail as it meets a multi-use forest road. Turn left for the loop, bearing right at the immediate road fork. Be alert for the familiar green-and-white markers.

Beautifully constructed rock walls now line the trail, as the loop arcs west to ascend Holy Mount. These walls formerly marked the north boundary of the Hancock Shaker property. Moss and lichen accent the flat rock slabs.

At 3.3 miles bear left, following a narrower, less-trafficked multi-use route through a mixed-age deciduous woods. The trail rolls and dips, crossing a side brook. At 3.8 miles, go left for a hiker-only tour snaking to the summit. Black cherry and white pine contribute to the woods, as do a few fruit trees.

A breach in the summit rock wall (4 miles) provides access to the Sacred Lot; stone walls and foundations hint at the lay of the site. Curve right, following signs south off Holy Mount.

Low, multi-trunked pines initially frame the descent, grading into a forest of oak and beech. Find a few steep pitches and canted trail segments, before ascending amid maple and birch. At 4.75 miles, turn left again following a multi-use road, now paralleling a side brook downstream.

At the fork at 5.2 miles, go right to continue the loop on a hiker-only road. After a couple of side-brook crossings, vehicle use again mars the tour. At 5.5 miles, a 0.3-mile round-trip detour right finds a limestone quarry first used in 1785. Dense ferns now mask the quarry depressions. Similar maidenhair ferns cued the brethren to the likelihood that limestone lay beneath the surface.

At 5.8 miles, resume the loop, soon turning right to travel the road downstream alongside Shaker Brook. In 100 feet on the left, find the remains of convex-shaped High Dam, circa 1810. Close the loop at 6 miles, reach the village 6.5 miles.

9 D.A.R. STATE FOREST

OVERVIEW

The Daughters of the American Revolution (D.A.R.) State Forest occupies 1,635 acres in the east-central Berkshires, serving up tranquil woods, two large lakes, and a fire tower delivering a five-state vista. The featured 5-mile tour ties together nearly all of the site's designated hiking trails; another 10 miles of bridle trail extend the exploration.

General description: This relaxing hike travels the northwest quadrant of the forest, visiting lakeshore, marshy drainage, mixed woods, and Goshen Fire Tower.

General location: 4 miles northwest of Williamsburg, Massachusetts.

Special attractions: Quiet lakeshore, summit vistas, hemlock-hardwood forest, stone walls and ruins, mountain laurel and spring wildflowers, fall foliage.

Length: Lake-Tower Hike, 5 miles round-trip.

Elevation: The trail shows a 250-foot elevation change.

Difficulty: Moderate.

Maps: State forest map.

Special requirements: Fee admission site.

Season and hours: Year-round, spring through fall for hiking.

For information: D.A.R. State Forest.

Finding the trailhead: From the junction of Massachusetts 9 and Massachusetts 112 north of Goshen Center, follow MA 112 north for the state forest. Go 0.6 mile and turn right (east), reaching the beach/day-use parking (trailhead) in 0.3 mile.

The hikes: This tour travels a portion of the self-guided **Nature Trail**, the **Long Trail**, and the **Darling Trail**.

From the day-use parking on the south shore of Upper Highland Lake, hike the footpath east along shore, cross an earthen dam, and traverse a small undeveloped beach, entering a woods of hemlock, white pine, and birch. Where the trail rounds a small point (0.2 mile), find a log gazebo overlooking boot-shaped Upper Highland Lake; the still waters reflect the rimming trees and low terrain.

Continue the pleasant lake-woods stroll, touring a cushiony woods path. At 0.5 mile, turn left on the park road to resume the shoreline tour at the boat launch; a blue arrow points the way. With gas-powered boats prohibited, enjoy a peaceful tour. A few spruce, black cherry, and towering oaks complete the woods. Above a small beachfront at 0.7 mile, a sign indicates the **Long Trail** now hosts the tour.

Pass through a gap in a stone wall, gaining a mountain laurel midstory. Some beautiful big trees punctuate the dark woods. Where the slope steep-

D.A.R. STATE FOREST

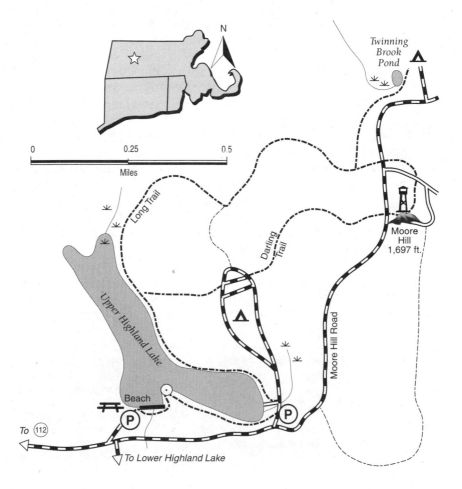

ens and the trail rolls, find a superb corridor of the 10-foot-tall laurel. At 1 mile, reach the loop junction and bear left; to the right lies the campground (0.2 mile).

A few azalea accent the shore where the Long Trail curves away from the open lake at a marshy inlet cove. Follow the inlet brook upstream; paired logs, corduroys, and stones cross the wet reaches. At 1.9 miles, another spur branches right to the campground; continue forward. The woods remain lush, green, and marshy.

Slowly ascend, touring hardwood forest with interspersed pine and spruce; blue markers aid travel. From 2.3 to 2.5 miles, travel atop a low, bumpy ridge with a few outcrop ledges and boulders. A tumbled sign reads "Great Ant Hills."

Curve away left taking either trail fork, as they again merge. Pass through a stone wall and over a drainage, finding the junction for Twinning Brook Group Camp (2.75 miles). A 0.25-mile spur heads left for the camp, descending alongside a thin drainage, with remnant stone walls and bountiful ferns. Locate the camp above a tiny dammed pond.

For the Lake-Tower Hike, continue forward crossing over paved Moore Hill Road and dirt Oak Hill Road, ascending through low-stature forest to reach the tower atop Moore Hill (elevation 1,697 feet) at 3 miles. Locate the return trail to your right as you reach the tower.

The public may ascend this 9-story tower, but the lookout loft remains closed. Views pan the Berkshires, Taconics, and Holyoke Range, with the farthest bumps on the horizon representing New York, Vermont, New Hamp-

Upper Highland Lake, D.A.R. State Forest, MA.

shire, and Connecticut. The 360-degree view applauds a broad sweep of the wooded Massachusetts terrain, resplendent in fall.

Now follow the unmarked **Darling Trail** as it descends steeply away, passing beneath a utility line to the fire tower. Cross Moore Hill Road and descend amid shoulder-high shrubs, laurel, goldenrod, and small oaks and maples. Cross a boardwalk and pass an old stone cellar, returning to forest. The width of the trail fluctuates but remains easy to follow.

Stone walls parallel the trail as it approaches the campground at 3.6 mile. Hike the paved campground road ahead, passing a utility shed, site 47, and a restroom facility to resume the foot trail (3.7 miles). It leaves the campground at a road juncture; look for blue markers. Close the loop at 4 miles, and retrace the trail left to the trailhead (5 miles).

10 CANOE MEADOWS SANCTUARY

OVERVIEW

At this tranquil 262-acre retreat along the Housatonic River, hardwood forest, meadow, riparian corridor, pond, field, and swamp woodlands contribute to varied travel and fine wildlife watching. Two short hikes introduce the area.

Wolf pine, Canoe Meadows Sanctuary, MA.

CANOE MEADOWS SANCTUARY

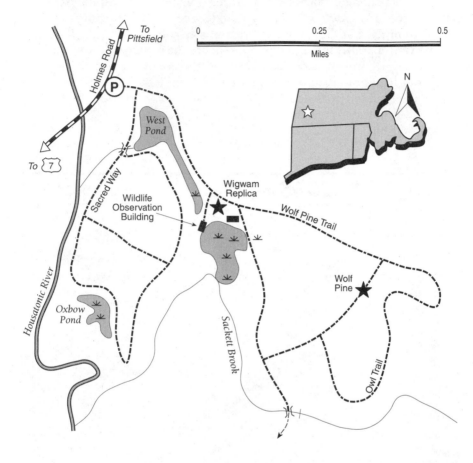

General description: Sacred Way (a pond-and-river circuit) and Wolf Pine Trail (a woodland tour) explore the sanctuary.

General location: In Pittsfield, Massachusetts, 1 mile from center.

Special attractions: Bird watching, canoeing, enclosed blind, replica wigwam, a unique pine, wildflowers, fall foliage.

Length: Sacred Way, 1.2 miles round-trip; Wolf Pine Trail, 1.5 miles round-trip (1.9 miles round-trip, adding the Owl Trail spur).

Elevation: Sacred Way, flat. Wolf Pine Trail, less than a 40-foot elevation change.

Difficulty: Both easy.

Maps: Sanctuary trail map.

Special requirements: A per-person admission fee or Massachusetts Audubon membership required. No dogs or bikes. Find privies near trailhead and wildlife observation building.

Season and hours: Year-round, spring through fall for hiking; 7 a.m. to dusk, daily except Tuesdays.

For information: Massachusetts Audubon Society, Berkshire Sanctuaries.

Finding the trailhead: From Interstate 90, take exit 2 for Lee. From the town green in Lee, go 6.9 miles north on U.S. Highway 20 West, which merges with U.S. 7 North. Turn right on Holmes Road, go 2.5 miles, and turn right for Canoe Meadows.

The hikes: These relaxing strolls invite leisurely touring with binoculars and identification guidebooks in hand.

For **Sacred Way**, hike east on either the service road or the mowed track entering a pocket of shrubs to the right of the kiosk and bear right to round West Pond, a small wildlife pond. Bramble and goldenrod claim its immediate bank, with a dense row of pines along the opposite shore.

Across the small concrete bridge, find the loop junction. Go right for a counterclockwise tour, paralleling the thickety shore of West Pond outlet downstream to the Housatonic River. An untamed field of tall grasses and milkweed sweeps away to the left. The wide mowed track offers easy walking.

At 0.25 mile, a cut-across path heads left; continue forward along the river amid a bottomland of dogwood, bramble, and woody shrubs. Oak, mixed maples, black cherry, elm, and cottonwood claim the skyline. River glimpses (best in fall) admire the 50-foot-wide smooth-flowing ribbon.

Soon, the open pools and interlocking marsh of Oxbow Pond replace the flowing river. Look for ducks, geese, Northern waterthrush, alder flycatcher, muskrat, and beaver. Mature oaks and maples preside trailside, as does a grove of sinewy-trunked hornbeam.

At 0.6 mile, overlook Sackett Brook, before drifting away from the waterways, touring woodland. Beyond the trees to the right stretches the floodplain of Sackett Brook. At 0.8 mile, the cut-across arrives on the left; follow the boardwalk ahead through swamp woodland and floodplain forest; alder, willow, and dogwood dominate. From the end of the boardwalk (1 mile), swing left along the shore of West Pond. Close the loop and return to the trailhead, 1.2 miles.

For **Wolf Pine Trail**, hike the service road as it passes through a field, skirts West Pond, and trends southeast along the watery link between West Pond and the wildlife observation pond. Maple, elm, and wild grape interweave the roadway's pine corridor. Stay southeast on the main service road, coming to a fork. To the right find the wildlife observation building, replica wigwam, and a dug-out canoe.

A boardwalk leads to the doorway of the enclosed wildlife viewing facility. Sliding Plexiglas windows on two sides present the area, keeping the elements out, while allowing photographers a clean "shot" at their subject.

Clumps of bog grass, drilled snags, and a long barn to the left contribute to the view.

Resume southeast on the service road. Near the barn find the first marked junction for the Wolf Pine Trail. Forgo taking it, staying on the service road for a counterclockwise tour. Pine stands, bog ponds coated in duckweed and rimmed by cattail, marshy woods, and hemlocks vary the tour. Blue herons commonly draw attention.

At 0.6 mile, reach the second Wolf Pine trail junction. A left continues the loop, although a brief detour southeast along the service road offers a look at Sackett Brook and its small dam washed by a 3-foot cascade. Signs caution that PCBs pollute this stream; avoid contact with water, fish, frog, and turtle.

Resume the loop at 0.75 mile, touring a scenic lane framed by hemlock, birch, beech, maple, oak, pine, and aspen. At 0.9 mile, the blazed **Owl Trail** heads right, offering an opportunity to lengthen the tour. It travels similar woods with a few smaller examples of the tour's signature "wolf pine"; continue forward to admire the featured pine.

In 100 yards near post 6, a crescent spur veers right for an audience with the starring wolf pine, a huge candelabra-shaped multi-trunked pine amid an entourage of maple. It requires no introduction. Upon resuming the loop, find the other end of the Owl Trail (on the right), offering a second chance to view its woods. Bear left, descending to the main service road (1.3 miles). Turn right to return to the parking area at 1.5 miles.

---

11 MONUMENT MOUNTAIN RESERVATION

OVERVIEW

At this 500-acre mountain preserve owned by The Trustees of Reservations, visit a peak that not only inspired Nathaniel Hawthorne, Herman Melville, and William Cullen Bryant, but a peak rich in Indian lore. A stone cairn marks the eastern precipice, the legendary site where a love-forsaken Indian maiden hurled herself from the cliff. From the cairn comes the name "Monument Mountain," from the maiden, the name "Squaw Peak."

General description: A circuitous tour passes through mixed forest, topping Squaw Peak for stirring looks at the site's sheer quartzite cliffs and southern Berkshire neighborhood.

General location: 4 miles north of Great Barrington or 3 miles south of Stockbridge, Massachusetts.

Special attractions: Vistas, white cliffs, historic literary landmark, Inscription Rock, seasonal waterfall, mountain laurel, fall foliage.

Length: 2.6 miles round-trip.

Elevation: Travel from a trailhead elevation of 900 feet to a summit elevation of 1,640 feet.

Difficulty: Moderate, with a difficult summit stretch.

Maps: Reservation map.

Special requirements: Donation appreciated. Obey posted rules.

Season and hours: Spring through fall, dawn to dusk.

For information: The Trustees of Reservations, Western Regional Office.

Finding the trailhead: From the junction of U.S. Highway 7 and Massachusetts 41 in Great Barrington, go north on U.S. 7 for 3.5 miles. Find a half-moon dirt parking lot, picnic tables, and a trailhead on the left. Look for the green Trustees sign.

The hike: From the kiosk, hike north following the white-blazed footpath of the **North Trail** as it disappears into the red pine-deciduous woods at the foot of the slope; the return is via the **South Trail**. The needle-strewn footpath broadens into a pleasant hiking lane, passing amid woods of white pine, oak, striped maple, beech, birch, viburnum, sarsaparilla, and fern. Small boardwalks span the seasonally muddy segments. Where a side trail from a rest area on U.S. 7 arrives on the right, look for the serious ascent to begin.

Despite a fairly steep incline, diagonal drainages maintain the integrity of the trail. Pockets of big hemlocks and 3-foot-tall mountain laurel decorate the woods. Round a bouldery slope and follow a steep drainage channel upstream, bypassing an abandoned side trail on the left. Cross a footbridge over the drainage and ascend the opposite bank.

A seasonal 12-foot waterfall marks the drainage, pretty when flowing; other times, the cliff overhang and a 5-foot-deep hollow intrigue travelers. Round to the top of the falls, again crossing the drainage to follow the path curving east to the rocky summit crest. At 0.6 mile, the loop arcs right, following South Trail off the mountain. Postpone taking the loop, to visit the summit and overlook the eastern precipice.

Proceed forward, finding Inscription Rock 25 feet from the junction. Beautifully etched and brushed with fine sand, the inscription relates how Rosalie Butler gifted the mountain to the people in 1899, through the agency of The Trustees. Maple, birch, oak, chestnut, laurel, and witch-hazel interweave the natural outcrops.

Ahead the trail grows steep and eroded. Early views pan east-northeast, overlooking Monument Mountain Regional High School, a marsh, and valley farmland. Pitch pine, huckleberry, and small oak continue to intersperse the rocks. The rough quartzite supports lichen, while the smooth breaks, slick like soapstone, steal footing. Exercise care when scrambling south over the rocks, gathering views.

At 0.75 mile, tag the high point. At 0.9 mile reach the end of the summit trail, finding a spectacular view overlooking the stunning eastern cliffs and the broken pinnacle of Devil's Pulpit. The skyline pines and enfolding wooded

MONUMENT MOUNTAIN RESERVATION

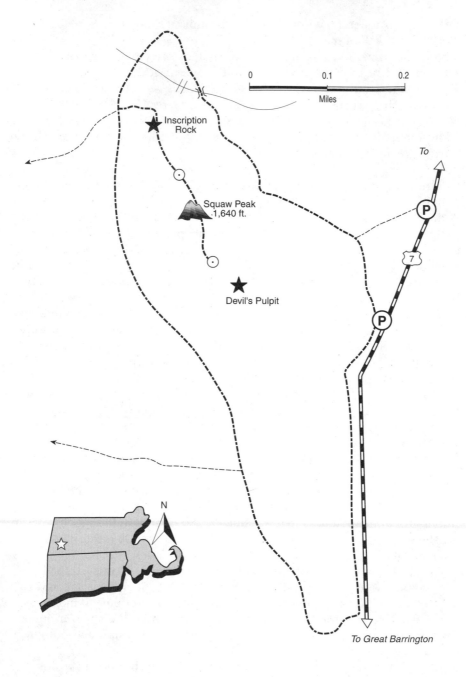

Inscription
Rock

Squaw Peak
1,640 ft.

Devil's Pulpit

To

P

7

P

0   0.1   0.2
Miles

N

To Great Barrington

terrain amplify the whiteness and precipitous drop of the cl:
and ravens ride thermals; peregrines once nested on the site's
The Housatonic River Valley stretches south, completing th'

Return as you came, passing Inscription Rock, to reach the ισ.
(1.2 miles). Turn left on **South Trail**, following this sharply pitching
woods lane off the mountaintop. Bear left at the upcoming junction, continuing the descent. Hardwoods shade the trek, joined by a few hemlock
and pines. Before long, the grade eases for a relaxing stroll.

At the 1.7-mile trail fork, take either path as they soon merge; to the
right, the trail follows an old ditch. Amid a hemlock grove at 2 miles, bear
left, avoiding the less-trafficked trail to the right. Skirt a low rock wall and
keep left, soon passing a gate. Now parallel U.S. 7 north to the trailhead,
weaving amid the quartzite boulders of the lower slope. Although U.S. 7
proves a loud neighbor, the woods remain scenic. End the tour at 2.6 miles.

12 BEARTOWN STATE FOREST

OVERVIEW

Snuggled in the southern Berkshires, Beartown represents the third largest Massachusetts state forest, encompassing more than 10,500 acres. The
site features rolling hills, mixed woods, a scenic pond, beaver-flooded bot-
tomlands, and miles of foot, bridle, and all-terrain-vehicle trails. The Appalachian Trail slices south to north through the forest, passing two lean-tos
during its Beartown sojourn.

General description: A comfortable pond loop and challenging, often tricky-
to-follow bridle trail loop explore the scenic woodland of this state forest.
General location: 8 miles east of Great Barrington, Massachusetts.
Special attractions: Benedict Pond, beaver ponds and swamps, rich
deciduous forest, limited vista, flowering shrubs and wildflowers, wildlife
discovery, fall foliage.
Length: Benedict Pond Loop, 3.2-mile loop, including Appalachian Trail
spur; Bridle Trail, 11.5 miles round-trip.
Elevation: Benedict Pond Loop, 300-foot elevation change; Bridle Trail, 450-
foot elevation change.
Difficulty: Benedict Pond Loop, easy; Bridle Trail, moderate.
Maps: State forest map.
Special requirements: Day-use fee.
Season and hours: Spring through fall for hiking, day-use: 8 a.m. to sunset.
For information: Beartown State Forest.
Finding the trailhead: From the Massachusetts 23 - U.S. Highway 7 junction
in Great Barrington, go east on MA 23 for 5.1 miles and turn north on Blue

Road. Follow it 2.1 miles, and turn right on Benedict Pond Road. Reach the day-use parking/trailhead at the pond in 0.5 mile.

The hikes: Start **Benedict Pond Loop** at the bathhouse/restroom and head right (counterclockwise) around the ladle-shaped pond, first touring its lightly developed shore. As several impostor paths thread this area, keep toward the pond; the true path reveals itself at the boat launch.

Hemlock, maple, oak, mountain laurel, azalea, and highbush blueberry dress the shore. A vulture often soars through the dip of the opposite ridge, while a raven speaks in hysterics. Some roots and rocks erupt in the path. Outcrops invite anglers and dreamers aside.

At 0.5 mile, the **Appalachian Trail (AT)** merges on the right, just as the pond trail crosses a boggy inlet via planks and hewn logs. A small rocky point next engages with a length-of-the-pond vista. Striped minnows and bluegill swim in the clear water. After crossing the main inlet bridge (0.7 mile), the AT departs to the right; the loop continues forward.

Briefly follow the AT to view a beaver swamp and obtain a southern vantage. With a moderate climb, passing amid big birch, outcrops, and mountain laurel, top a ridge (1 mile); a few steps forward finds the beaver dam, pond, and swamp. Cross the footbridge to the right and negotiate some stepping stones through a sulfurous reddish-brown ooze to reach the vista in another 0.2 mile. The tiered outcrop looks out at Livermore Peak, Mounts Everett and Darby, and a reclaimed beaver pond.

Return to Benedict Pond (1.7 miles) and turn right, traveling an old woods road above shore. Wild geraniums spangle the woods floor. At 2 miles, descend left on footpath, passing below a canted outcrop and hemlocks. At the wide end of the pond, drift away from shore, touring corduroys through soggy reaches. Next round a beaver extension, returning to the pond. Cross a footbridge, turn uphill, and pass the **Ski and Bridle Trail** on the right to cross the campground road. Soon afterward, cross the pond outlet to end the hike at 3.2 miles.

For the **Bridle Trail**, hikers should have a sense of adventure, good map and trail skills, and be willing to do some sleuthing; otherwise the hike will only frustrate. The forest supervisor has slated this trail for clearing and marking, which should ease travel.

Start by hiking clockwise on the pond loop, touring along the outlet and crossing over the campground road to take the Ski and Bridle Trail left at 0.3 mile. At the loop junction at 0.5 mile, again bear left for a clockwise tour. Red efts may animate the trail; a few orange markers point the way; and an explosion of green characterizes the multi-story forest. At 1 mile, angle left on a paved road to pick up the bridle trail on the opposite side.

An overgrown 2-track that can weight boots with mud next leads the way. Reach a dirt jeep road and follow it right. Then at 1.2 miles, hike the overgrown foot trail uphill to the right; a left leads back to Benedict Pond. Generally, one can discern the underlying trail beneath the mesh of vegetation; waist-high ferns at times claim the ascending trail.

BEARTOWN STATE FOREST

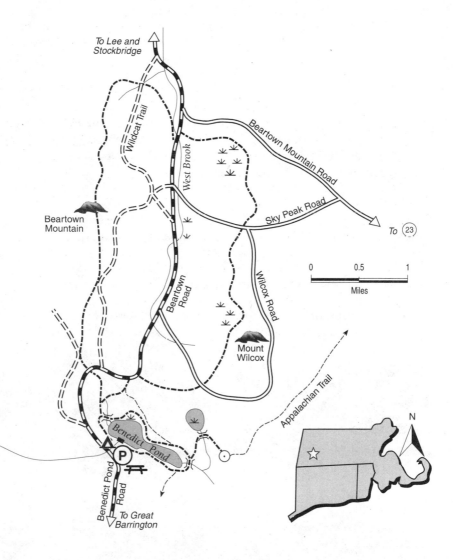

To Lee and Stockbridge

Wildcat Trail

Beartown Mountain Road

West Brook

Beartown Mountain

Sky Peak Road

To (23)

0   0.5   1
Miles

Beartown Road

Wilcox Road

Mount Wilcox

Appalachian Trail

Benedict Pond

P

Benedict Pond Road

To Great Barrington

N

At 1.6 miles, reach Wildcat Snowmobile Trail, turn left on it, and quickly turn left again re-entering woods. By 2 miles, travel a low wooded bench above a drainage, again finding laurel and hemlock. Woodpeckers, songbirds, and deer may add to the trek. Lady slipper and azalea decorate the woods. A couple of drainage crossings mark off distance.

At 4.5 miles, turn right onto Wildcat Snowmobile Trail, cross its bridge, and turn left following a grassy lane framed by big maples. Where the trail passes through a white pine grove, enjoy a cushiony needlemat trailbed. At 5.4 miles, go left on a dirt road reaching Beartown/Benedict Pond Road. Turn left on this lightly trafficked road, cross its bridge, and resume the overgrown bridle trail on the right. A few more faint markers aid travelers.

At 5.8 miles, go left for a re-route around a beaver flood. A few small ribbons, cut branches, and disturbed leaf mat cue the way. Hike through forest, pass an old bed frame, and then swing right, climbing away from a boggy drainage to meet the original trail at 6.1 miles. Stay left to resume the loop. Soon after the route changes to a time-healed woods road, look for the path of the bridle trail to bear right. The path then curves left, crosses a drainage, and charges straight up a rocky slope; midway up, the path becomes more apparent. Continue contouring and climbing right.

At 7.3 miles, cross gravel Wilcox Road. After a couple of drainage crossings, the bridle trail ascends to contour the slope above the road. While somewhat overgrown, the trail is better worn. At 8.4 miles, descend amid a lush bed of ferns, before finding another beaver-marsh pass. Bear left through woods, cross a drainage, and turn right viewing the beaver dam and lodge. Now follow the original trail left through stands of pine and spruce.

Benedict Pond, Beartown State Forest, MA.

Cross Wilcox Road a second time (9.9 miles) for a straight-fo
descent to Beartown/Benedict Pond Road at 10.3 miles. Tur
Benedict Pond, hike downhill 0.2 mile, and bear left on a gat
road. In 100 feet, the bridle trail resumes on the right. Alth
defined, it still shows soggy reaches. Close the loop at 11 miles, anu
the first 0.5 mile, returning to the bathhouse area at Benedict Pond (11.5
miles).

13 ALANDER MOUNTAIN LOOP

General description: In Mount Washington State Forest, this demanding
all-day or overnight loop with side spurs travels the South Taconics, passing
between Massachusetts and New York, gathering grand views.

General location: The southwest corner of Massachusetts on the tri-state
border of Massachusetts, Connecticut, and New York.

Special attractions: A springtime showcase for mountain laurel and azalea; fountains of fern; multistate views; fall foliage; sightings of beaver, frog,
red eft, and wild turkey.

Length: 15 miles round-trip (12.8-mile loop, 2.2 miles of round-trip side
spurs).

Elevation: Find an elevation change of 1,000 feet, with the low point at Lee
Pond Brook, the high at Mount Frissell (elevation 2,453 feet).

Difficulty: Strenuous.

Maps: Mount Washington State Forest trail map (generally available at
trailhead information board); New York-New Jersey Trail Conference map,
South Taconic Trail.

Special requirements: Permit and fee required for overnight camping in
the backcountry campsites of Mount Washington State Forest; pre-register
at headquarters (located at trailhead).

Season and hours: Year-round; portions of the tour double as winter cross-
country ski routes.

For information: Mount Washington State Forest.

Finding the trailhead: From the junction of Massachusetts 23 and Massachusetts 41 in South Egremont, take MA 41 south for 0.1 mile and turn right
on East Street. At its junction with Jug End Road in 1.7 miles, a sign indicates drivers stay on East Street for Mount Washington State Forest. In another 6.8 miles (having passed turns for Mount Everett State Reservation
and Bash Bish Falls), turn right for headquarters and trail.

    The hike: From the information board, follow the sign for **Alander
Mountain Trail**, passing through field and conifer-hardwood forest for the
first 0.5 mile. After the footbridge crossing of Lee Pond Brook, pass the

.rcoal Pit Trail to reach the loop junction at 0.8 mile. For a clockwise
.ur, follow the **Ashley Hill Trail** left, closing the loop via Alander Moun-
ain Trail (straight ahead). Either way reaches the numbered backcountry
campsites.

The woods road shows a modest ascent, contouring the slope above rushing Ashley Hill Brook; blue triangles and paint blazes point the way. Hemlock, maple, birch, and beech throw a pleasing shade. At 1.5 miles, a side
trail descends right, reaching the campsites and Alander Mountain Trail;
stay left for the loop.

Black oaks join the mix as a fern sea holds the eyes transfixed. After the
overgrown Charcoal Pit Trail arrives on the left, find a precarious crossing
of a side drainage. By 2.4 miles, enjoy an almost imperceptible incline, paralleling upstream along Ashley Hill Brook. A half dozen beaver dams punctuate the 10-foot-wide brook.

A stone-hopping crossing offers an alternative to the decrepit footbridge
at 3 miles. At the upcoming junction, stay left on Ashley Hill Trail as it
becomes more trail-like, climbing in pulses. At a clear-spilling headwater
(3.5 miles), fill water bottles for the dry tour ahead; purify natural sources.

Tall, full mountain laurels wrap the trail in bloom mid-June through early
July. Azaleas add their signature bloom a few weeks earlier. Past a Massachusetts-New York state line marker, reach a red-blazed trail junction (4.5
miles). Turn left for the **Mount Frissell Trail** and Tri-State Point; turn right
to reach the **South Taconic Trail** and continue the loop.

A detour left follows foot trail through a low-stature woods, ascending
over bedrock. Past another Massachusetts-New York state line marker, dated
1898, the climb steepens. Over-the-shoulder glimpses find Brace Mountain
and Riga Lake. At 5 miles, a simple cairn marks Tri-State Point, the highest
point in Connecticut.

Soon after, views expand sweeping from South Brace Mountain in New
York to Mount Plantain in Massachusetts, with Connecticut's Round, Gridley,
and Bear Mountains. The top of Mount Frissell lies 0.2 mile farther, but the
rimming 15-foot-high oaks steal any views.

Back at the 4.5-mile junction (5.9 miles), ascend the rock-studded red-
blazed trail to a ridge junction with the white-blazed **South Taconic Trail**,
6.2 miles. From the intersection, a detour south adds an 0.8-mile round-trip
visit to the summit of Brace Mountain; the loop follows the white blazes
north.

For the Brace Mountain detour, follow the woods road south, bearing
right at the fork. An open, shrubby complex enfolds the moderate-grade
trail. At 6.6 miles, a spur left tops Brace Mountain (2,311 feet), where a 5-
foot cairn puts an exclamation mark on the tour. Views sweep the tri-state
area.

Back on the loop at 7 miles, hike north along the rolling open ridge,
traversing lichen-etched outcrops and overlooking rural New York toward
Fox Hill. In 0.2 mile, a woods road, decorated with azalea and lady slipper,
continues the tour.

ALANDER MOUNTAIN LOOP

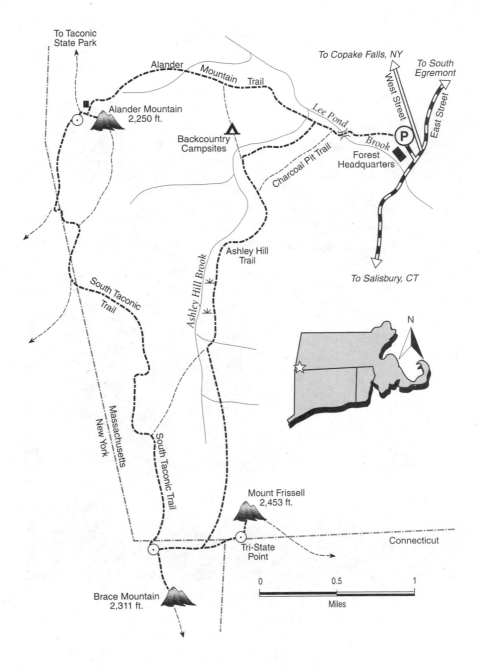

To Taconic State Park

Alander Mountain Trail

To Copake Falls, NY

To South Egremont

West Street

East Street

Alander Mountain 2,250 ft.

Lee Pond

P

Backcountry Campsites

Brook

Forest Headquarters

Charcoal Pit Trail

To Salisbury, CT

Ashley Hill Trail

Ashley Hill Brook

South Taconic Trail

N

Massachusetts

New York

South Taconic Trail

Mount Frissell 2,453 ft.

Connecticut

Tri-State Point

Brace Mountain 2,311 ft.

0   0.5   1

Miles

Fern meadow, Mount Washington State Forest, MA.

Past a blue trail, the South Taconic Trail briefly veers left from the woods road, passing amid low shrubs and outcrops for limited western views. Laurel again explodes. Elsewhere, rock walls or waist-high ferns decorate the going.

After the woods road bottoms out at a rocky drainage, the white-blazed South Taconic Trail turns right on a steeply-charging foot trail. Mixed deciduous trees dress the slope. Views build, climaxing in a 270-degree view, encompassing Mount Frissell, Alander, Brace, and Round mountains.

Atop Alander Ridge, go past the concrete platform of a former lookout tower, keeping an eye out for a faintly painted blue blaze on the open rock at 11.3 miles. This signals where the loop leaves the South Taconic Trail to again follow the **Alander Mountain Trail**.

Descend right, following the blue blazes to a saddle (0.1 mile). Here find a quaint, tight-roofed cabin, offering a dry overnight wayside on a first-come, first-serve basis. Early-summer azalea and mountain laurel fancy it up.

For the loop, descend past the cabin; to add another summit conquest, follow the blue trail ascending east. It tops Alander Mountain (2,250 feet) in 0.2 mile for an open view from New York's Brace Mountain to Massachusetts's Mount Darby. Backtrack to the saddle (11.8 miles) and descend through Mount Washington State Forest on Alander Mountain Trail.

Sometimes rocky, sometimes muddy, the trail parallels a small drainage, crossing feeder streams. Glorious waist-high fern attract the eye, while oak, maple, birch, and beech weave a rustling canopy. Despite the few and faint markers, the trail remains well-trampled.

At 12.5 miles, bear right. Before long, darker blazes, a milder grade, and a defined woods road, all ease travel. At the 13.3-mile junction, continue straight ahead to close the loop; to the right lie the campsites.

The loop now contours and mildly descends, reaching a rock-hopping crossing of Ashley Hill Brook, just upstream from its confluence with Lee Pond Brook. Ascend from the crossing (14.1 miles) to return to the loop junction at 14.2 miles. Retrace the first 0.8 mile to the vehicle.

14 BARTHOLOMEW'S COBBLE

OVERVIEW

Cobble knolls of limestone and marble formed 500 million years ago, one of the greatest concentrations of fern diversity in North America, diverse conifer-deciduous forests, grassland, pasture, and the sidewinding Housatonic River make this Berkshire reservation an exciting place to visit. Such natural attributes also won the Cobble (a property of The Trustees of Reservations) recognition from the National Park Service as a National Natural Landmark.

Spring and summer wildflowers and the fall hawk migration prove seasonal draws. The site's Bailey Natural History Museum displays letters of praise from distinguished naturalists, while the reservation's Colonel Ashley House, built 1735, holds the honor of being the oldest dwelling in Berkshire County. Weatogue Road partitions the 277-acre reservation into east-west halves.

General description: Three hikes present this outstanding property. Explore cobble, river, meadow, and woods.
General location: 10 miles south of Great Barrington, Massachusetts.
Special attractions: Cobble outcrops; bird and wildlife watching; nature study; flowering trees, shrubs, and annuals; fall foliage; museums.
Length: Eaton Trail, 0.2-mile loop; Ledges-River Hike, 2.5 miles round-trip; Hurlburt's Hill Hike, 2 miles round-trip.
Elevation: Eaton Trail, 50-foot elevation change; Ledges-River Hike, less than a 100-foot elevation change; Hurlburt's Hill Hike, a 320-foot elevation change.
Difficulty: All easy to moderate.
Maps: Reservation map; The Ledges Trail brochure.
Special requirements: Admission fee, with a separate admission charged at the Colonel Ashley House. Find signs at the key junctions and white blazes through the wooded stretches, but carry a map to sort out trails.
Season and hours: Reservation: Mid-April through mid-October, 9 a.m. to 5 p.m.; Bailey Natural History Museum: 9 a.m. to 5 p.m. Wednesday through Sunday. Colonel Ashley House: summers 1 p.m. to 5 p.m. Wednesday through Sunday and holidays.
For information: The Trustees of Reservations, Western Regional Office.
Finding the trailhead: From the center of Sheffield, Massachusetts, go south on U.S. Highway 7 for 1.5 miles and continue south on U.S. 7A for another 0.5 mile. Turn right on Rannapo Road. At its junction with Cooper Hill Road in 1 mile, a right leads to the Colonel Ashley House in 0.2 mile. To access the trails, continue straight, taking a quick right on dirt Weatogue Road. Find parking on the left in 0.1 mile; signs aid travelers in finding the reservation.

BARTHOLOMEW'S COBBLE

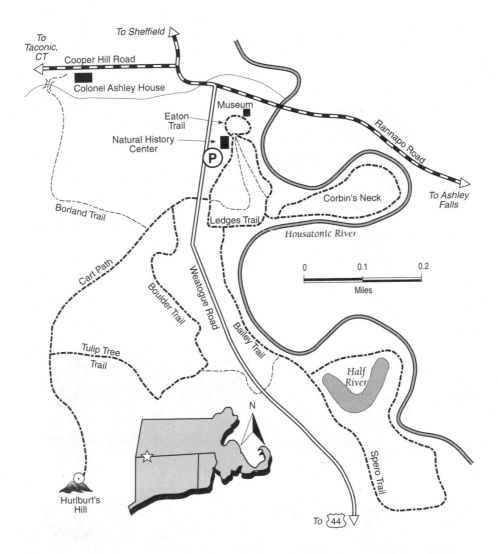

The hikes: Start all hikes from the Cobble parking lot, east off Weatogue Road. Find the trailhead kiosk and fee station to the left of the soon-to-open Natural History Center.

For the sun-drenched **Eaton Trail**, bear left (north) ascending a dirt trail framed by cedar and goldenrod to encircle and top the northern cobble. A lofty wooden bench overlooks a horseshoe bend on the Housatonic River and the grassy peninsula of Corbin's Neck. The folded, pitted, and ledged outcrop supports fern niches and caps, lichen and moss, and alkaline-loving plants and wildflowers.

Where the trail descends, pass Bailey Museum, a rustic wooden building ringed by sweet pepperbush, wild grape, and mountain laurel. Inside find a wealth of natural history information. Bear right upon leaving the museum to return to the trailhead; find the restrooms below the museum.

On the left side of the kiosk, follow the hiker path heading east (straight) for the **Ledges-River Hike**. Pass the spur to Bailey Museum, quickly reaching a 3-way junction; go left for **The Ledges Trail** (a 0.5-mile interpretive loop). The prongs for **Craggy Knoll and Cedar Hill trails** welcome alternative looks at the limestone-marble outcrop.

The Ledges Trail rounds a scenic cobble knoll, passing amid hemlocks and overlooking the Housatonic River. Admire the weathered and polished rock, worn niches, hollows, overhangs, and cavities. Even the untrained eye can detect an uncommon variety of ferns (best seen in June and July). At times, crickets enliven the air.

Guided walk, Bartholomew's Cobble Reservation, MA.

The trail rolls between the outcrop's waistline and the river level. Where it dips, expect rough footing. Oak, basswood, hophornbeam, maple, and ash contribute to a varied canopy; the silk nests of the webworm ensnare a few leafy branches. Keep to The Ledges Trail.

At 0.2 mile, detour left through a hiker stile to stroll the open grazed pasture of Corbin's Neck for a 0.5-mile circuit along the river. The muddy banks of the peninsula may reveal signs of otter, muskrat, and mink or host wading birds. Pass quietly.

Resume The Ledges Trail at 0.7 mile, ascending reinforced steps. As the trail enwraps the outcrop, a wide travel lane replaces the footpath. Red cedars grow amid the more exposed rock. At 0.8 mile, again depart The Ledges Trail, bearing left to follow the **Bailey** and **Spero trails** for a rolling tour south along the Housatonic River.

Enjoy a rare opportunity to explore the grassland and riparian woodland of the river floodplain, habitats often privately owned and closed to the hiking public. While river views are few and filtered, chance bird and wildlife sightings exist. Enjoy the diversity of the riparian woodland, including elm, ash, willow, box elder, cottonwood, and silver maple, and the richness of the thick grass meadows interlaced with nettle, jewelweed, milkweed, joe-pyeweed, and goldenrod.

At 1.2 miles, beside a colossal cottonwood, measuring 6 feet in diameter, the Spero Trail swings a generous lasso around Half River, a shallow oxbow pond. Clockwise, travel floodplain, a deciduous rise with jumbles of gneiss, and a dark hemlock woods. The loop concludes traveling a boardwalk, skirting a north-shore wetland of Half River. Retrace the Spero and Bailey trails to rejoin The Ledges tour at 2.3 miles; turn left.

Round the cobble knoll, viewing overhangs, a glacial erratic atop the rim, and quartzite seams. At 2.4 miles, bypass a hiker stile leading to Weatogue Road and the western half of the reservation. Round the knoll, finding the last interpretive post below a cave-like opening. Complete the tour (2.5 miles).

For the **Hurlburt's Hill Hike**, follow the unmarked trail heading south (right) from the kiosk, retracing the end of The Ledges Trail. Pass behind the Natural History Center and the parking area and turn right. Exit a hiker stile and cross Weatogue Road to enter the western part of the reservation.

Bear right following a mowed cart path across the small field, passing under an elm to ascend amid woodland. At the 0.3-mile junction, the **Borland Trail** heads right to Colonel Ashley House; keep to the cart path for Hurlburt's Hill.

Pass through field and mixed woods of maple, hickory, ash, birch, black cherry, witch-hazel, aspen, and hophornbeam. Squirrels leap through the rustling canopy. At 0.5 mile, the **Tulip Tree Trail** heads left for a loop; remain on the cart path ascending the high pasture for a hilltop vantage.

At 0.7 mile, reach the reservation high point (elevation 1,050 feet) and a north-facing bench for a grand 180-degree view of the Berkshire-Housatonic neighborhood. Mid-September into October, the fall hawk migration draws enthusiasts for a skywatch. The site also applauds the autumn fanfare.

Now descend the pasture slope and hike east on the **Tulip Tree Trail**. Pass mainly through leafy woods with small field breaks; a tree identification book earns its way. Beyond the hiker stile, hemlocks dominate. At 1.2 miles, pass beneath a 3-foot-diameter tulip tree, one of a few lending the trail their name. Deer sometimes startle, darting to safety.

A big boulder marks the junction where the loop turns left on the **Boulder Trail**. More boulders punctuate the hemlock woods. Mixed fern, doll's-eye baneberry, and hog peanut spot the forest floor. Pass beneath another tulip tree and through a hiker stile, touring amid mixed deciduous woods to emerge at the small field along Weatogue Road. Turn right for the hiker stile, cross the road, and bear left to return to the trailhead, 2 miles.

CENTRAL MASSACHUSETTS TRAILS

This region boasts ancient mountain features, including monadnocks (erosion-resistant isolated peaks) and the northern traprock ridges (the elongated cliff-sided mountains rising from the Connecticut River Valley). In many ways, the abrupt ridges and lone-standing peaks afford some of the state's finest panoramas. In spring and especially in fall, watch for the hawk migration, with impressive groupings or "kettles" of broadwings. Bald eagles find habitat at Quabbin Reservoir. Mountain woodland, meadow, swamp, pond, and an intriguing rock chasm further characterize the area. Find historic industrial river towns and the rural charm of church steeples and silos punctuating this central Massachusetts landscape.

15 MOUNT WATATIC LOOP

General description: Near the Massachusetts-New Hampshire border, this hike combines parts of the Wapack and Midstate trails for a loop topping Mount Watatic and Nutting Hill.
General location: 6 miles north of Ashburnham, Massachusetts.
Special attractions: Summit vistas, a watch site for the fall hawk migration, summit engravings that date to the mid-1800s, colorful fall foliage.
Length: 3.7 miles round-trip.
Elevation: Find a 570-foot elevation change, with the high point atop Mount Watatic, elevation 1,832 feet.
Difficulty: Moderate.
Maps: Ashburnham and Peterborough USGS quads. The Friends of the

Wapack put out a map and guide to the entire Wapack Trail. Send a self-address stamped envelope to the Friends for information on how to order the set (their address is in Appendix D).

Special requirements: None.

Season and hours: Spring through fall.

For information: Friends of the Wapack.

Finding the trailhead: From the junction of Massachusetts 12 and Massachusetts 101 in Ashburnham, go north on MA 101 for 3.9 miles and turn west on MA 119. Go 1.4 miles and turn right, entering a trailhead parking lot for a dozen vehicles.

The hike: Focal point of this tour, Mount Watatic occupies the southern terminus of the Wapack Range, rising above Ashburnham State Forest and the Watatic Mountain Wildlife Area. Although the abandoned fire tower is in disrepair and can no longer be mounted safely, panoramic viewing from the bald outcroppings of this twin-bump summit amply reward the effort of a climb.

Both the **Wapack and Midstate trails** start at the north end of the parking lot; round the gate, following a cart road overlaced by maple, birch, oak, and hemlock. Yellow triangles mark the route, while stone walls line the corridor. A small drainage and pond give rise to tall ferns. At 0.2 mile, the **Wapack Trail** turns right, while the Midstate Trail continues forward. Go right for a counterclockwise loop, crossing through a gap in a rock wall to a mapboard.

Round the base of Mount Watatic, touring amid mature white pines, maple, and birch; roots and rocks riddle the foot trail. Cross a drainage and pass between the split halves of a 9-foot-tall boulder for a steep assault up the south face of Mount Watatic. Hemlocks now dress the slope.

At 0.8 mile, rock outcrops serve up preview looks at the immediate neighborhood and Wachusett Mountain. Next, contour and ascend amid hemlock-spruce forest, coming to an overnight shelter in minor disrepair (1 mile). Resume the ascent, skirting the front of the shelter.

Top Mount Watatic near the abandoned tower at 1.1 miles; its open outcrop delivers a 270-degree view, lacking only looks to the northwest. Admire the Wapack Range and Mount Monadnock in New Hampshire, the twin knobs of Watatic, Wachusett Mountain, and the neighboring lakes and rolling woods, with clear-day views adding the skyrises of Boston.

Cross to the lower summit knoll (East Watatic), finding a 180-degree southern perspective, a survey marker, and the etched notations of summit travelers from the mid-1800s. During the climax of the fall hawk migration (mid-September), a thousand hawks may soar over the summit in a single day.

Return to the north side of the tower, locating a rock with a painted notice for "119" and an arrow. Just downhill, find a second painted notice, indicating "NH." Follow this arrow pointing the way to New Hampshire, heading northwest on an old dirt road. In 1.25 mile, turn left, passing the

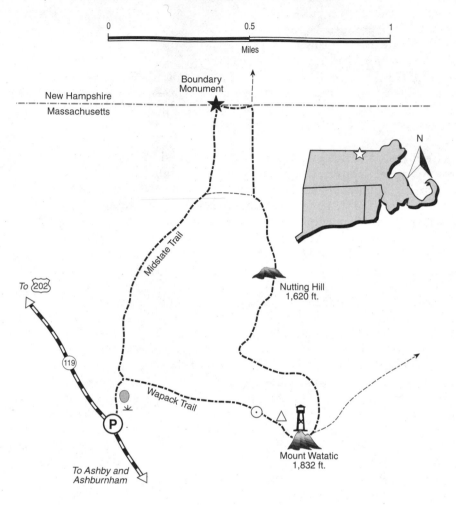

MOUNT WATATIC LOOP

0   0.5   1

Miles

Boundary
Monument

New Hampshire
Massachusetts

Midstate Trail

To 202

Nutting Hill
1,620 ft.

119

Wapack Trail

P

N

To Ashby and
Ashburnham

Mount Watatic
1,832 ft.

ruins of an old ski resort, still following the yellow triangles.

Descend through hemlock-spruce woods, first paralleling and then cross-ing over a stone wall. At 1.8 miles, top Nutting Hill (elevation 1,620 feet). The rock outcrops afford a fine over-the-shoulder look at Mount Watatic, with its ridgeline of spired conifers and Wachusett Mountain in the back-drop.

At 2 miles, the road grade forks. Go right, touring a scenic woods lane lined by big-diameter pine and deciduous trees, pockets of sarsaparilla, and a stone wall. Come to a signed junction at 2.4 miles: North (straight ahead) lies New Hampshire; left leads to the Midstate Trail and the return.

Mount Watatic summit, Wapack Trail, MA.

This short connecting trail travels alongside a stone wall dividing Massachusetts and New Hampshire. Look for granite survey markers dating to the 1800s and one denoting the northern terminus of the **Midstate Trail** (2.5 miles). To return to the MA 119 trailhead, turn left on the Midstate Trail, a 92-mile trail slicing south through Massachusetts to the Rhode Island border.

Follow a fairly level route through a young deciduous woods, graduate to spruce, and recommence crossing rock walls. At 2.9 miles, meet a dirt road and follow it right. The route now shows a steady, moderate descent, deeply eroded in places. Short bypass trails skirt the worst of the wear and tear. The enfolding woods variously blend spruce, pine, and hemlock with the familiar northern hardwoods. Close the loop at 3.5 miles. Reach the trailhead, 3.7 miles.

16 NORTHFIELD MOUNTAIN RECREATION AREA

OVERVIEW

At this 1,500-acre playground, 25 miles of interlocking foot and carriage-width trails offer a variety of hiking and cross-country ski tours. Power lines and a reservoir overlook hint at the site's host, Northeast Utilities; the generating facility lies 700 feet underground. May through October, a bus tour runs to the summit, offering hikers the option of downhill travel only.

General description: Two loops travel the west flank of Northfield Mountain, topping the peak and exploring its ledges. Within the web of trails, find numerous other tour possibilities.
General location: 2 miles north of Millers Falls, Massachusetts.
Special attractions: Conifer-deciduous forest, granite-gneiss ledges, mountain and sheep laurel, vistas, fall foliage.
Length: Summit Loop, 5.8 miles round-trip; Rose Ledge Loop, 3.1 miles round-trip.
Elevation: The Summit Loop shows an 800-foot elevation change; it advances via long, steep ups and downs, topping Northfield Mountain at 1,100 feet. Rose Ledge Loop shows about a 400-foot elevation change, with some sharp pitches.
Difficulty: Summit Loop, strenuous; Rose Ledge Loop, moderate.
Maps: Northfield Mountain trail map (available at site).
Special requirements: Colored diamond markers, trail signs, and numbered intersections help hikers negotiate the web of avenues; carry a map to sort out the options. For hikers interested in taking the bus tour to the summit, phone in advance to check whether they will be running.

Season and hours: Year-round, spring through fall for hiking. Visitor Center: 9 a.m. to 5 p.m., Wednesday through Sunday.

For information: Northeast Utilities, Northfield Mountain Recreation and Environmental Center.

Finding the trailhead: From the junction of Massachusetts 2 and Massachusetts 63 in the village of Millers Falls, go north on MA 63 for 1.9 miles and turn right (east) for Northfield Mountain Recreation and Environmental Center. Start trails at the mapboard behind the visitor center.

The hikes: A 1-mile 15-station **Nature Trail** marked by blue diamonds and interpretive plaques travels the foot of the mountain behind the visitor center. As the two selected trails each overlap the nature trail, hikers also tour the nature trail.

The **Summit Loop** pursues several of the named carriage-width trails through the recreation area's core to claim the Northfield Mountain summit. Start by following **10th Mountain Trail** south (right) along the foot of the mountain, pass a wildlife pond, and continue on 10th Mountain Trail as it curves left up the slope. The trail's broad swath parts a mature pine plantation interspersed by birch and maple.

Curve past the switching station, cross the **Rose Ledge Trail**, and at 0.25 mile, turn left on the **Hemlock Hill Trail**, briefly passing under utility lines. Sumac, wildflowers, and bramble crowd the corridor. Amid hemlock-deciduous woods, again cross the Rose Ledge Trail for a moderate ascent.

Keep to the Hemlock Hill Trail. Platy outcrops and fractured boulders, fern, sarsaparilla, and club moss accent the forest floor. At junction 8 (0.6 mile), continue forward for a clockwise loop, soon finding a picnic site and the "Chocolate Pot" (a warming hut open during ski season). **Rock Oak Ramble** on the right marks the return. At 0.85 mile, a spur to the left leads to a chemical toilet.

With the ascent, oaks and chestnuts join the mix. Soon after, the Hemlock Hill Trail tops out and then dips to cross Reservoir Road at a crosswalk. A hemlock-framed descent follows. At the 1.5-mile fork, turn right on **Ecstasy Ramble**, continuing the descent to **Tooleybush Turnpike** at 1.7 miles.

Again turn right finding a steep incline, including a tight bend dubbed "the Chute" by cross-country skiers. With the climb transition back to woods of birch, beech, oak, and aspen; overhanging branches afford partial shade.

At 2.5 miles, again cross Reservoir Road; sweetfern and mountain laurel decorate the trail's shoulder as more maples appear in the mix. Find junction 32 at 3.4 miles. Turn left for the summit and reservoir overlook, reaching the spur to the viewing platform on the opposite side of the paved summit turnaround. Views pan sterile Northfield Mountain Reservoir, its dam and intake, and sentinel mountains Hermit and Crag. To the north rise Haystack and Stratton mountains and Mount Snow.

Resume the loop at 3.8 miles, turning left at junction 32, once again on **10th Mountain Trail**. Sheep laurel abounds here and along the summit

NORTHFIELD MOUNTAIN RECREATION AREA

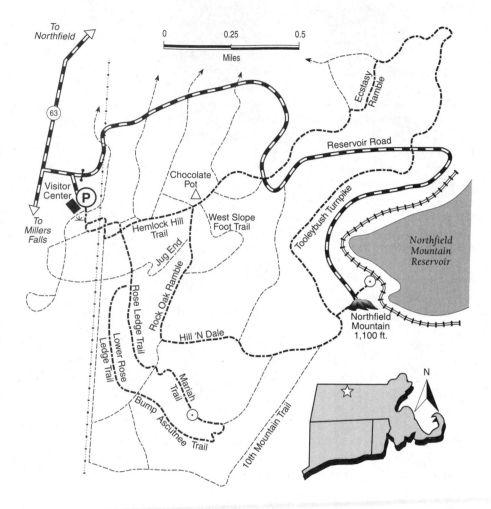

spur. At 4 miles, follow **Hill 'N Dale**, a grassy lane snaking downhill to the right, for a scenic stroll; keep to this trail for the loop. At 4.3 miles, it bears right for a rollercoaster descent.

Reach junction 16 at 4.7 miles, turn right, and follow **Rock Oak Ramble** for a meandering downhill tour amid mixed woods. The descent sharpens past the **West Slope Foot Trail**. Pass **Jug End**, bearing right to close the loop just beyond the Chocolate Pot (5.2 miles). Retrace Hemlock Hill and 10th Mountain trails, returning to the visitor center, 5.8 miles.

For **Rose Ledge Loop** (a foot trail), again follow **10th Mountain Trail**

Rose Ledges, Northfield Mountain Recreation Area, MA.

south along the base of the mountain, but continue straight where it curves left up the hill. Find the marked turn for Rose Ledge on the left and ascend amid a dark pine woods, with birch, maple, and oak. Roots riddle the bed; in places, the path becomes ill-defined.

At 0.25 mile, cross 10th Mountain Trail to tour an attractive woods, avoiding the open utility corridor. Before long, the ledge trail turns right; the nature trail continues straight.

Cross **Hemlock Hill** and **Jug End trails** for a rolling trek, contouring the slope. Mountain laurel, chestnut, and witch hazel contribute to the midstory. Reinforced steps and footbridges ease travel. At 0.6 mile, reach the loop junction; continue straight for a clockwise tour, still ascending.

Dogwoods make a rare appearance amid the low-stature woods. Top the first outcrop ledge at 0.9 mile. Trees at the foot of the slope steal or filter views; keep back from the edge. Rock tripe lichen adorns the rock, and mountain laurel crowns the ledge, recommending a tour in early summer.

At 0.95 mile, hikers may shorten the loop, descending to the right. For the full 3.1-mile tour, follow the **Rose Ledge/Mariah Trail** for a steady, moderate ascent; spurs regularly top the ledge. Most views applaud the immediate area rims, cliffs, and forest; at 1.25 miles claim a southwestern perspective spanning the Connecticut River Valley to the Berkshires.

At junction 33 (1.4 miles), the **Bump Ascutnee Trail** sharply descends to the right; follow it for the loop. This portion of the tour offers side views and a neck-craning appreciation of the 50- to 80-foot vertical cliffs, with their subtle streaking and picturesque fracturing. At 1.5 miles, view a ledge composed of tilted slabs, before reaching the bottom of a cliff favored by rock climbers. Descend and round to the right.

At 1.8 miles, a 100-foot spur to the right presents a bold look at the main cliff, a feature of stark beauty. Broken rock at its base hints at how the cliff has changed over time. Cliffs continue to edge the tour, now more boxy in feature.

Cross **Rock Oak Ramble** at 2 miles, now following the **Lower Rose Ledge Trail**. After a steep pitch, skirt below the low cliffs to travel the wooded edge of a utility-corridor meadow. Birch, maple, and white pine shape the tour. At 2.3 miles, tag a lower-tiered ledge for a western perspective overlooking the corridor. Return to woods, close the loop at 2.5 miles, and retrace the first 0.6 mile to the trailhead.

17 MOUNT TOBY STATE RESERVATION

OVERVIEW

This reservation enfolds an ancient peak (elevation 1,269 feet), rising above the Connecticut River Valley. Outcrops of a coarse conglomerate called "puddingstone," steep ravines, rich forested hollows, marshy bottoms, and dry ridges make the mountain a botanical treasure trove. Naturalists can discover 42 varieties of fern, as well as prized orchids. The described loop travels to the top of Mount Toby reaching an observation tower—a trek that has inspired area visitors since the 1800s.

General description: Traveling part of the Robert Frost Trail and Summit Road (a restricted road closed to vehicles), this loop explores rich woods and obtains a summit panorama sweeping a 50-mile radius. Spurs visit a cabin ruin, side mountain, and Cranberry Pond.

General location: 10 miles north of Amherst, Massachusetts.

Special attractions: Summit panoramas, rich forest, cool brook drainage, pond view, opportunity for solitude, fall foliage.

Length: 5.5-mile loop, including spurs.

Elevation: Find a 750-foot elevation change.

Difficulty: Moderate.

Maps: *Mt. Toby Trail Map* by New England Cartographics, P.O. Box 9369, North Amherst, MA 01059 (available for purchase in area outdoor stores or by writing to the company directly).

Special requirements: The reservation is a learning laboratory. Tread lightly and do not disturb vegetation. Note several trails branching from the loop lead to or pass through private property; carry a map and heed posted notices.

Season and hours: Spring through fall; daylight hours.

For information: University of Massachusetts - Amherst, Department of Forestry and Wildlife Management.

Finding the trailhead: From the junction of Massachusetts 63 and Massachusetts 47 (4.5 miles south of Millers Falls), go south on MA 47 for 1 mile and turn left (east) on Reservation Road. Find the gated trailhead on the right in 0.5 mile, with parking in another 50 feet next to a small headquarters building.

From the MA 47 - MA 116 junction in Sunderland, go north on MA 47 for 3.8 mile and turn right on Reservation Road.

The hike: For a counterclockwise tour, round the gate and take an immediate right on the orange-blazed **Robert Frost Trail** (RF). Find an ascending woods lane, alternately touring amid conifer-hardwood forest and pine plantation. Poison ivy, bramble, sarsaparilla, striped maple, and mountain laurel lend visual interest. Daring squirrels leap through the canopy, while deer flee to safety.

MOUNT TOBY STATE RESERVATION

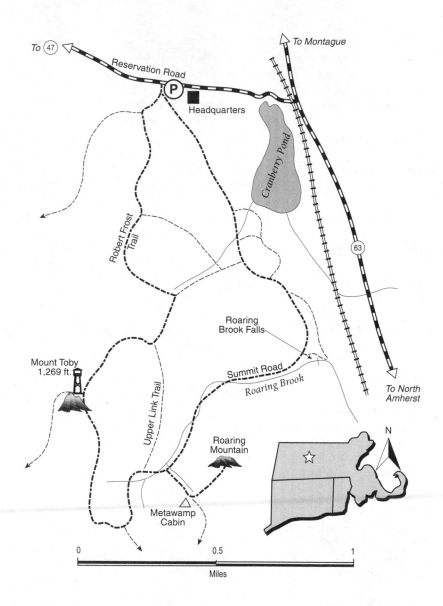

To 47

Reservation Road

P

Headquarters

To Montague

Cranberry Pond

63

Robert Frost Trail

Roaring Brook Falls

Summit Road

Roaring Brook

Mount Toby
1,269 ft.

Upper Link Trail

To North Amherst

Roaring Mountain

Metawamp Cabin

N

0   0.5   1

Miles

At 0.4 mile, the RF (now a footpath) heads left, while a blue-blazed trail continues forward. In another 0.25 mile, the RF turns right, passing amid a mature hemlock stand and below a lichen-painted outcrop rise.

Upon meeting a woods road at 1 mile, turn right to travel a steep shrub corridor, following telephone lines skyward to Mount Toby. Despite the congestion of fern, bramble, laurel, goldenrod, aster, small maples, and birch, the path remains clear. Summer heat can create a sauna effect.

At the trail fork at 1.2 miles, keep to the right for the RF; the red-blazed **Upper Link Trail** continues straight ahead. Be alert at this junction as the red and orange markers can easily be confused. With a steep charge, the RF claims the tree-rimmed, grassy summit (1.5 miles), to find a fence-enclosed 9-story lookout tower. The public may ascend the tower when gates are open; mount at your own risk. Enjoy a 360-degree view with Mount Monadnock in New Hampshire, Mount Ascutney in Vermont, and the Massachusetts landscape with Mount Greylock, the Berkshires, and the Connecticut River valley and peaks.

Remain on the RF, now pursuing **Summit Road** east from the lookout tower, slowly descending along the ridge. Oak, maple, hickory, birch, and hemlock frame the dirt road. Where the descent quickens, encounter cobbles. At 2.25 miles, go left for RF/Summit Road; to the right lies the yellow-blazed **Robert Frost Bypass**.

Along a headwater fork of Roaring Brook, enjoy a serene dark hemlock woods. Within this reservation, find some of the finest eastern hemlock in all of Southern New England.

Deciduous forest, Mount Toby State Reservation, MA.

On the left at 2.5 miles, the **Upper Link Trail** offers an alternative return, looping back to the 1.2-mile junction to retrace the initial 1.2 miles of the RF. For the full 5.5-mile tour, continue descending the woods road, reaching the first detour in 0.1 mile. Here the Summit Road and RF part company. Head right on the RF to add a visit to Metawamp Cabin and Roaring Mountain. For the loop alone, continue forward.

The RF, now a footpath, parallels Roaring Brook upstream reaching the cabin ruin and the white-blazed side trail to Roaring Mountain at 2.8 miles. Be careful near the ruins, as glass, nails, and splintered wood all contribute to the cabin character; a rock fireplace and sturdy door remain in place.

From Metawamp Cabin, cross the brook and charge steeply uphill for 0.1 mile, reaching the broad summit plateau of Roaring Mountain. Absent of vistas, the summit does offer a scenic reflective retreat. Oak, maple, mountain laurel, and huckleberry cloak the summit; a cairn marks the high point.

Return to Summit Road (3.3 miles) and resume the descent, paralleling and crisscrossing Roaring Brook. Hemlocks shade one side of the drainage; deciduous trees the other. An occasional white blaze marks the tour. At 4 miles, the canyon opens up, cobbles disappear, and an easy-to-miss spur plunges to the right reaching a view of Roaring Brook Falls.

Again some of the puddingstone outcrop borders the tour, while telephone poles rise amid the framing woods. At 4.8 miles, find the second detour, a 0.1-mile spur descending right to Cranberry Pond, a good-sized, tree-rimmed pond with vegetated and open glassy waters. MA 63 travels along one side. Return to Summit Road and follow it right, returning to the trailhead gate, 5.5 miles.

18 BROOKS WOODLAND PRESERVE

OVERVIEW

At this remote 464-acre woodland preserve of The Trustees of Reservations, the Swift River Tract offers hikers peaceful strolling amid mixed woods; along river, brook, and pond; and past cultural sites. Ample opportunity exists for nature study, wildlife watching, and solitude. Interlocking woods roads and trails pass freely among the adjoining lands of The Trustees, Harvard Forest, and Massachusetts Audubon.

General description: Three short hikes explore this preserve, traveling along pond, river, and brook, with the brook hike ending at the Indian grinding stones.
General location: 2 miles southeast of Petersham Center, Massachusetts.
Special attractions: Swift River, Moccasin Brook, and Connor's Pond; Indian grinding stones; stone walls and foundations dating back to the early 1800s;

fall foliage; deer, fox, beaver, porcupine, and a host of birds.

Length: Connor's Pond Hike, 1.75 miles round-trip; Swift River Hike, 3 miles round-trip; Grinding Stones Hike, 2 miles round-trip.

Elevation: Connor's Pond Hike, 50-foot elevation change; Swift River Hike, 250-foot elevation change; Grinding Stones Hike, 100-foot elevation change.

Difficulty: All easy to moderate.

Maps: Brooks Woodland Preserve, North Common Meadow, Swift River Reservation map. Purchase a copy from The Trustees of Reservations, Central Regional Office, prior to touring.

Special requirements: Obey the posted rules of the respective land owners; no facilities. Find numbered junctions keyed to the preserve map. The Brooks Woodland foot trails show colored trail markings, the woods roads do not.

Season and hours: Spring through fall, dawn to dusk.

For information: The Trustees of Reservations, Central Regional Office.

Finding the trailhead: From Petersham Center, go 1.8 miles south on Massachusetts 32 and turn left (northeast) on Quaker Drive. From Barre, go 5.6 miles north on MA 32/MA 122 and turn right for Quaker Drive. Go 0.2 mile, finding unsigned parking for a handful of vehicles on either side of Quaker Drive west of the Swift River bridge.

The hikes: The **Connor's Pond Hike** combines a counterclockwise woodland loop with a side trip along the east shore of Connor's Pond. Cross the Swift River bridge, turn right at junction 65, and skirt the cable to follow a scenic woods road downstream. From the bridge, admire small fish wriggling in the clear water of the brook-sized river. Pines shade the corridor.

At 0.15 mile (junction 70), a yellow-marked foot trail veers right for a crescent-shaped detour, staying along the Swift River, following it downstream to the marshy inlet of Connor's Pond. The main trail traverses a low ridge of pines, overlooking a wet-meadow bottom on the left. The paths reunite at junction 71. Resume the counterclockwise tour amid a pine-hemlock woods, before dipping to the snag-riddled meadow bottom and rolling away. Beautiful ferns dress the floor.

At junction 67 (0.4 mile), turn right to visit the east shore of Connor's Pond; bear left for the loop alone. For the pond detour, again bear right at junction 68, descending amid beech, birch, maple, hornbeam, hophornbeam, black cherry, and witch hazel. Cross a scenic bridge over Rutland Brook and round a gate, entering a Massachusetts Audubon property.

Continue south on a wide grassy lane, cross a placed boulder at a drainage, and bear right at the fork to skirt the pond's edge. Initial views find a vegetated cove with lily pads and arrowhead. In fall, goldenrod and aster claim the meadow bank. By 0.7 mile, overlook the dark open water, low rounded western hills, and stunning reflections. Abandoned beaver lodges and an island contribute to the view.

Where the trail meets the entrance road to the Audubon sanctuary (0.95 mile), turn back, retracing the tour to junction 67 (1.5 miles). Complete the

BROOKS WOODLAND PRESERVE

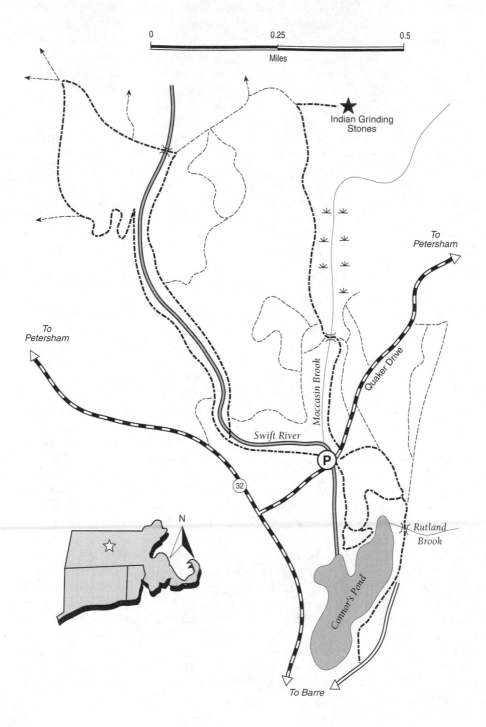

0   0.25   0.5

Miles

★ Indian Grinding Stones

To Petersham

To Petersham

Moccasin Brook

Quaker Drive

Swift River

32

P

N

Rutland Brook

Connor's Pond

To Barre

loop, touring amid similar woods. Turn left at junction 64 to return to Quaker Drive and the river (1.75 miles).

From the parking turnout at the northwest corner of Swift River bridge, round a metal gate, entering Harvard Research Forest for the **Swift River Hike**. Where the road curves right to parallel Swift River upstream, hike a more rustic country lane, softened by grass, littered with pine needles, and shaded by conifer-deciduous woods. Although the woods road and river at times drift apart, enjoy frequent looks at this sparkling brook-sized tannin-colored waterway. Fountains of fern, hobblebush, club moss, and sarsaparilla contribute to the tour.

As secondary trails branch away, keep to the main woods road. At 0.8 mile, the river broadens forming a scenic pool, reflecting its treed shore. In another 0.1 mile, bear left at a river ford, the path upstream quickly deteriorates.

The woods road now switchbacks away from Swift River, touring a mostly deciduous woods interrupted by small groves of spruce, tamarack, hemlock, and pine. At the 1.25-mile fork, turn right, hiking a long grassy straightaway enfolded by rich fern shoulders, a dark stone wall, and high-canopy woods.

At the 1.6-mile intersection, wooden gates bar the routes straight ahead and to the right, while an open woods road journeys left. For the loop, round the gate to the right descending back toward the Swift River and Brooks Woodland Preserve, again finding stone walls and a rich woodsy charm. Look for a good-sized American chestnut tree, a rarity these days; chipmunks scold from nooks in the wall.

With a drainage crossing, travel a sunken grade between two low ridges resplendent in summer green. At junction 35, continue straight ahead to cross a wooden bridge over the Swift River. At the immediate T-junction (junction 45), turn right for the downstream return. Again find a strollable woods road, hemlock and towering pine, and soothing river views.

At 2.15 miles, the spur from 0.9-mile river ford arrives on the right; continue downstream drawing away from the river's edge. At junction 46, bear right, remaining along the river plain for a tranquil woodland tour. Where the woods road forks at 2.75 miles, veer right for a rock-hopping crossing or fording of the Swift River. Close the loop at 2.8 miles, turn left, and retrace the first 0.2 mile to the trailhead.

When waters are especially high, backtrack the tour or go left on the woods road at 2.75 mile, bearing right at all subsequent junctions to return to Quaker Drive east of the bridge at junction 53.

For the **Grinding Stones Hike**, cross the Swift River bridge and continue northeast on Quaker Drive for 100 feet. There look for a foot trail entering the dark hemlock woods on the left side of the road; an orange trail marker and a posted notice of The Trustees of Reservations signal the start.

Hike upstream along Moccasin Brook, a stream the size of Swift River. Pines, maple, oak, black cherry, and birch fill out the forest; beautiful ferns spread at their feet. Roots and an occasional mossy rock ripple the trailbed.

Cross over a couple of stone walls, reaching a woods road. Turn left, pass the plaque honoring John Fiske, and cross the footbridge over Moccasin Brook. Continue straight ahead, bypassing junction 49, to skirt the large open marsh of upper Moccasin Brook, glimpsed beyond the pines. At 0.4 mile, a blue trail heads left; proceed forward on the woods road for a rolling tour, skirting the marsh.

Step through a passage in a rock wall, reaching the 0.65-mile junction (absent a marker, but number 48 on the map); bear right. A mild to moderate ascent follows, with more deciduous trees interweaving the forest.

At the next rock wall (0.95 mile), find a signed junction for Indian Grinding Stones and turn right. In 100 yards, prior to reaching the next stone wall, locate some large frost-fractured boulders and stones revealing mortar depressions and trenches. Here the Nipmuck Indians ground acorns and maize with a stone pestle, pushing the finished meal out the troughs into their baskets. While the worn stone clues are subtle, the discovery provides an interesting peek into the cultural past. Return as you came.

19 WACHUSETT MOUNTAIN STATE RESERVATION

OVERVIEW

This 2,100-acre state reservation protects Massachusetts's tallest mountain east of the Berkshires. The site features hardwood-conifer forest, rock ledges and outcrops, summit panoramas stretching from Boston to Mount Greylock, winter downhill skiing, and some 20 miles of hiking trail, including 4 miles of the long-distance Midstate Trail that cuts south to north through the state's middle.

General description: Two day hikes present the mountain offering: one rounds the eastern base of Wachusett Mountain to Echo Lake; the other scales the north flank and descends via the west flank, visiting Balance Rock and the summit.

General location: 4 miles north of Princeton, Massachusetts.

Special attractions: Summit panorama; mixed woods; spring and summer wildflower, azalea, and mountain laurel blooms; fall hawk migration; autumn foliage.

Length: Bicentennial-Echo Lake Hike, 2.5 miles round-trip; Balance Rock-Summit Hike, 4 miles round-trip.

Elevation: Bicentennial-Echo Lake Hike, 150-foot elevation change; Balance Rock-Summit Hike, 1,000-foot elevation change.

Difficulty: Bicentennial-Echo Lake Hike, moderate; Balance Rock-Summit Hike, strenuous.

WACHUSETT MOUNTAIN STATE RESERVATION

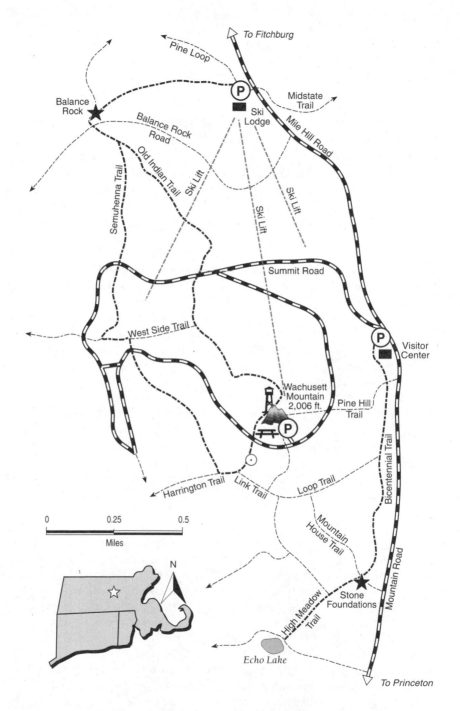

To Fitchburg

Pine Loop

Midstate Trail

Balance Rock

Ski Lodge

Balance Rock Road

Mile Hill Road

Semuhenna Trail

Old Indian Trail

Ski Lift

Ski Lift

Ski Lift

Summit Road

West Side Trail

Visitor Center

Wachusett Mountain 2,006 ft.

Pine Hill Trail

Bicentennial Trail

Harrington Trail

Link Trail

Loop Trail

Mountain House Trail

Mountain Road

0   0.25   0.5
Miles

N

Stone Foundations

High Meadow Trail

Echo Lake

To Princeton

Maps: State forest map.

Special requirements: No overnight camping or fires. Keep dogs leashed. Visitor Center parking can fill September-October when fall hawk migrations and colorful autumn foliage swell visitorship.

Season and hours: Spring through fall for hiking, daylight hours. Visitor Center: 9 a.m. to 4 p.m.

For information: Wachusett Mountain State Reservation.

Finding the trailhead: From Massachusetts 2, west of Fitchburg, take exit 25 and go south on MA 140 for 2.1 miles. There turn right per the sign, following Mile Hill Road. In 0.5 mile, bear right on Bolton Road, and take an immediate left to enter the ski area parking lot and reach the trailhead for the Balance Rock-Summit Hike. For the Bicentennial-Echo Lake Hike, continue south on Mile Hill Road/Mountain Road, for another 1.2 miles and turn right for Headquarters/Visitor Center parking and to find the trailhead.

The hikes: For the **Bicentennial-Echo Lake Hike** start on the west side of the headquarters parking lot at a sign for the **Bicentennial Trail**; blue blazes mark the tour. Cross the footbridge and turn south, contouring the rocky eastern base of Wachusett mountain above Mountain Road. Expect to do some high stepping. Wildflowers and a diverse canopy endorse the tour.

At 0.1 mile, **Pine Hill Trail** arrives on the left, briefly shares the trailbed, and then strikes uphill to the right. At 0.25 mile, descend left; the **Loop Trail** claims the center and right forks. Oak, maple, birch, ash, hornbeam, hophornbeam, hickory, and hemlock variously render shade. Mountain laurel lends a showy accent in early summer. Pass through a gap in a rock wall (0.5 mile), descending away from the rockiness.

Next cross the **Mountain House Trail** at 0.75 mile and continue contouring south. Old stone foundations punctuate the slope below the Bicentennial Trail, as a few old-growth oaks and maples frame the path. Owl, woodpecker, and songbirds may animate the treetops. Beyond the next stone wall, ascend.

At 1 mile, the Bicentennial Trail ends at its junction with the **High Meadow Trail**. To visit Echo Lake, go left on the High Meadow Trail, finding views of Little Wachusett Mountain as the trail passes amid a sumac-scrub clearing and a grove of spindly birch. Re-enter woods, cross another rock wall, and descend to Echo Lake, with shoreline picnic tables and a rock fireplace (1.25 miles). Ash, birch, oak, and maple rim the shallow, artificial pond dammed at its east end. Return as you came to the trailhead (2.5 miles) or devise a loop to the summit, utilizing the cross trails.

For the **Balance Rock-Summit Hike**, start at the ski area parking lot; find the trail at the base of the mountain opposite aisle post 5. Look for the yellow triangle of the **Midstate Trail** on a light post next to the path.

Angle into the woods to the right of the light post, meeting a wood-chip road in 50 feet. To the right is **Pine Loop**; go left toward Balance Rock Road. Ascend slowly touring amid conifer-hardwood forest, reaching an unsigned fork at 0.3 mile. Bear right, staying on the Midstate Trail, passing through a breach in a rock wall to win an audience with Balance Rock (0.4 mile). Here prominently located in a woods opening, a boxy boulder pedestal balances an oversized, tilted round boulder.

Resume the hike heading uphill, still following the yellow triangles; a few species tags identify trees. At 0.5 mile, cross dirt Balance Rock Road, now ascending via **Old Indian Trail**. Historically, Wachusett Mountain was a key gathering site for the Nipmuck Indians; "Wachusett" means "by the Great Hill." A deer or porcupine may precede you on the trail.

Ascend and contour fairly steeply amid pine-oak habitat, crossing a rock wall, reaching the loop junction at 0.7 mile. **The Semuhenna Trail** heads right; continue forward on Old Indian Trail for a clockwise summit loop. Contour the slope, crossing meadowy ski runs. Downhill views find Wachusett Lake. Follow the painted footprints across Summit Road at 1 mile and begin a steep rocky ascent, switchbacking amid platy outcrop ledges and bypassing the **West Side Trail** on the right.

At 1.5 miles, traverse the summit ridge, touring amid low-stature forest. Pass behind the chair-lift terminal and beside a war memorial, coming out at the broad open summit (1.8 miles), attainable by road, with outward radiating trails and vistas. Strolling the summit (elevation 2,006 feet), piece together a full 360-degree view, with Mount Monadnock and the Wapack Range, the Berkshires, the Taconics, Worcester, and Boston.

On a corner of the fence enclosing the summit lookout tower, find a sign for the **Harrington Trail**. Follow it west off the summit to complete the loop. Cross over a road linking picnic sites and angle left across an open outcrop, finding a rugged, rocky descent, sometimes requiring the use of hands. Watch for blazes; oaks clad the upper mountain reaches.

Cross Summit Road and find a difficult step over the 6-foot-tall stone wall. When wet or blanketed by leaves, the hillside rocks require even greater attention. At 1.9 miles, a spur left offers a limited view south toward the towers of Worcester Highland. As the woods grow more mixed, stay the Harrington Trail, bypassing the **Link Trail** on the left. Just ahead, find the **Semuhenna Trail** for the loop; go right.

The Semuhenna Trail offers a more relaxing stroll, enwrapping the slope. The woods feature hemlock, maple, birch, and beech. At 2.6 miles, cross Summit Road; finding picnic sites on either side. Now stay left, following the **West Side/Semuhenna trails**. At a drainage, veer right with the Semuhenna Trail; the West Side Trail continues forward. Once again pursue the yellow markers of the Midstate Trail.

Cross Summit Road, angling right. Descend amid hemlock-deciduous woods and pine plantation, crossing rock walls to close the loop at 3.3 miles. Go left, backtracking the Old Indian and Midstate trails to the ski area, 4 miles.

OVERVIEW

This sanctuary of the Massachusetts Audubon Society presents hikers a varied canvas to explore, with upland meadows, field, mixed woods, pasture, a red maple swamp (now a beaver wetland), and a 1,300-foot monadnock (an erosion-resistant hill). Visitors discover an ancient maple, summit vistas, wildlife ponds, glacial erratics, and tranquil strolling. The fall hawk migration (September-October) and the turning of the red maple leaves prove exciting seasonal draws; a variety of flora and fauna engages naturalists year-round.

General description: Two short loops (one to a summit, the other through pastures) explore the area, with sightseeing options along the way. A third hike links the sanctuary and its neighbor to the north, Wachusett Mountain.
General location: 15 miles northwest of Worcester, Massachusetts.
Special attractions: Bird and wildlife watching, mature forest, fall foliage, spring and summer wildflowers, access to the Midstate Trail and Wachusett Mountain.
Length: Brown Hill Loop, 2.4 miles round-trip; Pasture Loop, 2.4 miles round-trip. Mountain Trail, 4 miles one-way to Wachusett Mountain summit.
Elevation: Brown Hill Loop, 300-foot elevation change; Pasture Loop, 50-foot elevation change; Mountain Trail, 1,000-foot elevation change.
Difficulty: Brown Hill Loop, moderate; Pasture Loop, easy; Mountain Trail, moderate to strenuous.
Maps: Sanctuary brochure.
Special requirements: Per-person access fee or Massachusetts Audubon membership; obey posted rules. Trails are for foot travel only—no bikes, no skis. Leave pets at home. Find the characteristic Audubon blazing, with blue heading away from the trailhead, yellow returning. Numbered posts keyed to the map identify the site's trail intersections and attractions.
Season and hours: Year-round, Tuesday through Sunday and most holidays that fall on Monday. Closed Thanksgiving, Christmas, and New Year's days. Trails: dawn to dusk; office: 9:30 a.m. to 3:30 p.m., Tuesday through Saturday.
For information: Wachusett Meadow Wildlife Sanctuary.
Finding the trailhead: From the town common at Princeton, go west on Massachusetts 62 for 0.6 mile and turn right on Goodnow Road, a rough paved road. Go 1 mile, turning left for trail parking.

The hikes: The sanctuary's **Brown Hill Loop** encircles the site's monadnock feature, allowing easy outward searches to the property's side attractions, with the **Summit Trail** tagging the top. From the parking area, cross Goodnow Road, passing through a breach in the stone wall to the right of

WACHUSETT MEADOW WILDLIFE SANCTUARY

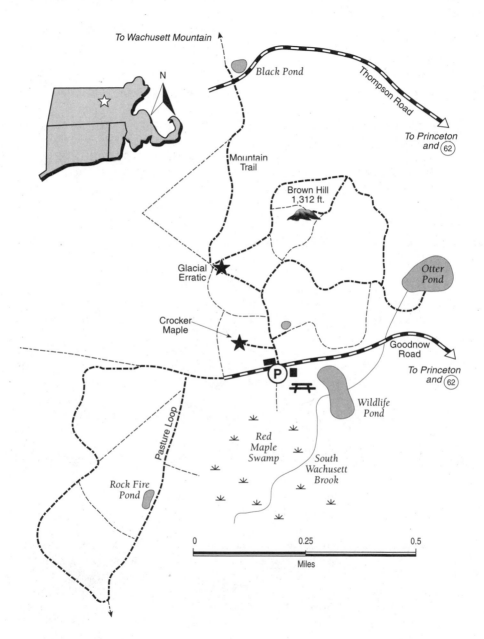

To Wachusett Mountain

Black Pond

Thompson Road

To Princeton and (62)

N

Mountain Trail

Brown Hill 1,312 ft.

Glacial Erratic

Otter Pond

Crocker Maple

Goodnow Road

To Princeton and (62)

P

Wildlife Pond

Pasture Loop

Red Maple Swamp

South Wachusett Brook

Rock Fire Pond

0   0.25   0.5

Miles

the large white colonial house. There follow a mowed path ascending north through a former pasture.

At post 2, detour left to visit Crocker maple, a 250-year-old monarch believed to be one of the largest sugar maples in the United States. It presides at the western edge of the pasture above a moist drainage. Stout, with a lopped top and missing a major arm, this relic captivates onlookers. Conchs cling to the gnarled 6-foot-diameter trunk. Beware of poison ivy near the maple; a bench offers comfortable viewing.

Return to post 2 and continue north through the hayfield. At 0.2 mile, post 4 suggests a 50-foot detour to the right, reaching a small wildlife pond with cattails and tadpoles. Again resume the Brown Hill tour, going straight at posts 6 and 8; junction 8 marks the loop. Now travel a transition meadow with goldenrod, bushes, and small trees.

At post 10, turn right, contouring the foot of Brown Hill for a counterclockwise tour. Pine, oak, hickory, maple, and birch dress the slope, with clearings of blueberry and juniper. At 0.75 mile (post 12), bear left continuing the loop. In another 150 feet, find post 14. Here a side trip to the right leads to Otter Pond.

This side trip passes through young deciduous woods and transition meadow, reaching a research area for studying the rare fringed gentian, a wildflower. Edge a hayfield to overlook Otter Pond from its small dam. Bayberry, juniper, dogwood, oak, and maple rim the vegetated water, while Little Wachusett Mountain rises in the distance. Return to post 14 at 0.9 mile, and continue the loop, ascending steadily, advancing via walkway of stones.

At 1.2 miles, reach post 22, site of one of three summit ascents, and turn left. Follow a stone wall, passing a scenic multi-trunked pine, coming out on the shrub-clad hilltop at post 18. Continue 100 feet to the right to claim the topmost point at post S/1, elevation 1,312 feet. Views sweep 360-degrees, with Wachusett and Little Wachusett mountains, New Hampshire's Mount Monadnock, the Worcester Highlands, and the sanctuary's own red maple swamp, now beaver wetland. In fall the hawk migration funnels south between Wachusett and Little Wachusett mountains, making Brown Hill an ideal spot to stage a skywatch.

Descend, resuming the counterclockwise loop at post 22, rounding amid picturesque pines and a fern understory. Pass post 16, and at junction 26, turn right to conclude the hilltop loop via the **Glacial Boulder Trail**. This trail visits a room-sized erratic surfed to this site on the last glacier some 15,000 years ago. Frost has since fractured the boulder into big chunks. Now follow the stone wall away from the boulder, edging a transition field to close the loop at post 8 (2.1 miles). Descend, ending the hike at 2.4 miles.

For the **Pasture Loop**, hike west from the parking area on Goodnow Road, now a scenic lane defined by stone walls and 200-year-old oak, beech, and ash trees. Round the gate at 0.15 mile, and continue west, passing the northbound **Midstate Trail**, a long-distance trail stretching across Massachusetts from Rhode Island to the New Hampshire border. Turn left at post

Family hike, Waschusett Meadow Wildlife Sanctuary, MA.

3 for the Pasture Loop and southbound Midstate Trail.

A tour of the external loop traverses five pastures isolated by stone walls and forest buffers. In different stages of succession, each pasture boasts a signature flora and fauna. Travel mowed track, woods lane, and foot trail. Continue straight at junctions 5 and 7 and bear left at post 11. The path heading left at post 7 accesses the edge of the swamp/beaver pond.

Find both groomed and unruly meadow pastures. Those left wild show stands of waist-high grasses, bramble, milkweed, and goldenrod, with seed pods adding interest in the fall. At 0.6 mile, between pastures three and four, find Rock Fire Pond, a charming dark-water pool with lily pads and a reflecting rock. Aspen, birch, and maple frame the pool, gentian dot its banks, and whirligig beetles enliven the surface. Warblers lend a cheerful note.

Areas of pine, black cherry, and tall fern add to a tour. After leaving the upland meadow of pasture five, bear right at post 15 for the loop; the Midstate Trail continues south to the left. Travel a richly wooded slope, passing a large quartz boulder on the right at 1.1 miles. The white rock offers a stunning contrast to the dark pine trunks and vibrant ferns.

At post 13, continue left; the spur from post 11 arrives on the right. Enjoy a relaxing woods hike amid hemlock, oak, and beech, with areas of low-growing mountain laurel. A few disturbed openings record the injury and healing from the tornado of 1989. At post 9, either fork returns to Goodnow Road; stay left for the outer circuit. A high-canopy deciduous woods escorts hikers onto the grassy retired lane of Goodnow Road at 2.05 miles. Turn right to end the tour at 2.4 miles.

The **Mountain Trail/Midstate Trail North** may be reached by heading north at post 17 or left at post 6. It continues north through the sanctuary's remote western woods, a rich mixed-deciduous habitat, twice meeting the **West Border Trail** to exit at Thompson Road (a minimally used, rutted dirt road). Across the road lies tree-enclosed Black Pond (1 mile), a dark mirror of water with a soothing aqua hue. Aquatic vegetation or autumn leaves at times claim the pool.

Northbound, the tour continues out of the sanctuary and across public lands to top Wachusett Mountain at 4 miles; be alert for the Midstate Trail blazings as the route utilizes sections of woods roads weaving its way to the peak. Ask for a Wachusett Mountain State Reservation map at the sanctuary office.

General description: This paved, abandoned stretch of the Boston and Maine (B and M) Railroad serves up a scenic travel corridor to hikers, cyclists, skaters, joggers, wheelchair users, and cross-country skiers. The route tours rural, residential, and light industry/commercial areas.

General location: In Northampton, Hadley, and Amherst, Massachusetts.

Special attractions: Wildlife watching, nature study, mixed deciduous woods, swamps, fields, wildflowers, fall foliage.

Length: 8.5 miles one-way.

Elevation: The rail trail is virtually flat.

Difficulty: Easy.

Maps: Guide to the Norwottuck Rail Trail (free copies available at area bicycling and outdoor stores).

Special requirements: Keep to the right, keep dogs restrained on a short leash, and keep to the rail corridor, respecting the neighboring private properties. Rangers patrol regularly.

Season and hours: Year-round, generally spring through fall for hiking, 5 a.m. to 10 p.m.

For information: Norwottuck Rail Trail.

Finding the trailhead: Find the western terminus at Elwell State Park on Damon Road west of Massachusetts 9 in Northampton. Find the eastern terminus on Station Road in South Amherst. Along the south side of Mountain Farms Mall in Hadley, find a central access with parking.

The hike: Start a west-to-east tour, at Elwell State Park. Cross the scenic 0.25-mile-long trestle bridge spanning a side arm of the Connecticut River, 60-acre Elwell Island, and the main flow of the river. Silver maple, elm, sumac, cottonwood, walnut, locust, and wild grape thrive along river and trail.

The bridge enchants with its diagonal-plank walk, rusting steel trestles, and overlacing greenery. Downstream views admire the Calvin Coolidge Bridge; Coolidge was a native son and regular passenger on the B and M Railroad. Upstream views hold rural appeal.

The 7-foot-wide paved lane offers comfortable travel; recycled glass used in the pavement glints in the sun. The tour parallels MA 9, drifting farther from the highway as it journeys east. Mileposts (numbered east-to-west, backtrack for this tour) and road crossings mark off distance. Find crossings well-marked for both motorists and rail-trail users.

Fields, nurseries, cropland, and even a pumpkin patch sweep away left. Autumn tours prove especially enjoyable with the rural backdrop, a dusting of colored leaves, and the noisy chaos of flocking blackbirds. At just under 1.5 miles, pass through historic Hadley Commons, a grassy wayside with tables, waste baskets, and a seasonal drinking fountain; in the past, town

NORWOTTUCK RAIL TRAIL

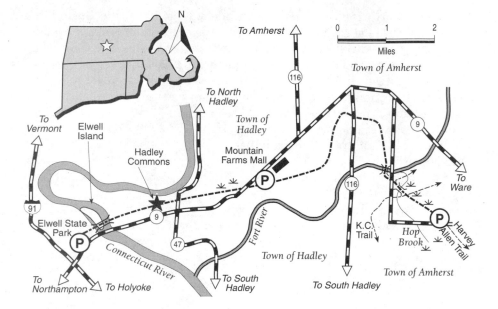

citizens grazed their animals here.

Look for stone pillars bearing the letter "W"; these cued engineers to sound the whistle. On the eastern half of the tour (in Amherst), the path crosses over two granite tunnels dating back to the 1880s. These rail underpasses allowed cows to move from pasture to pasture without crossing the tracks.

Intermittent breaks in the overlacing canopy and bordering trees open up the corridor. The long straightaways prove aesthetically pleasing. A beautiful maple swamp graces the tour approaching the Spruce Hill Road tunnel (2.75 miles). Ahead, travel a sunken grade with a junk yard occupying the rise to the right. An abundance of fern and overlacing trees quickly dismiss the intrusion.

At 3 miles, pass through the MA 9 tunnel, putting the highway and settlement to the left; the rural terrain to the right. Beware of poison ivy along the shoulder. At 3.2 miles, hike past a drive-in eatery that makes the most of having the rail trail for a neighbor by welcoming and serving travelers and posting trail distances. Find benches and tables at the southwest and southeast corners of Mountain Farms Mall (3.75 miles). A dairy farm sprawls to the right. Dairy farming was once a major enterprise in the area.

After 4.25 miles, enjoy an isolated passage amid undeveloped fields and woods. Cross-field views find Mounts Toby and Sugarloaf, rising to the north.

Connecticut River bridge, Norwottuck Rail Trail

Southern vantages present the Holyoke Range. Maple, oak, and elm still frame the trail. Chances for wildlife sightings increase, with skunk, deer, woodpecker, and squirrel. A ranger mentioned a lone moose as a past visitor.

At 5 miles, pass between a golf course and deep woods. The trail alternately travels levee or sunken grades. By 6.25 miles, begin skirting the grounds of Amherst College, with its sporting fields, tennis courts, and posted spruce plantations. Wetlands and conservation lands next neighbor the trail, holding new discovery, including beaver, heron, painted turtle, and frog. Turkey vultures assemble on a popular roosting snag.

At 7 miles, cross the bridge over Fort River, and at 7.25 miles, pass **Fort River Loop**, a hiker-only path descending to the left. Cattail bogs and riparian woodland next frame the rail trail. Gaps in the border afford looks north and south.

Cross the bridge over Hop Brook (7.5 miles) and soon after, pass segments of the **K.C. Trail**, another foot trail. Hornbeam commonly grows along the swamps. At 8.5 miles, end at Station Road, with parking for about 20 vehicles. Across the road, the **Harvey Allen Trail** offers an opportunity to extend the rail-trail tour, now on an earthen bed.

22 MOUNT TOM STATE RESERVATION - DINOSAUR FOOTPRINTS RESERVATION

OVERVIEW

At these neighboring Central Massachusetts sites, discover perhaps the finest vista-ridge tour for the three-state area and walk where dinosaurs roamed. The long-distance Metacomet-Monadnock Trail slices south to north through Mount Tom State Reservation, offering two short skyline tours, with heart-quickening cliffs and restful Connecticut Valley views.

Dinosaur Footprints Reservation, a property of The Trustees of Reservations, offers a short trail system, visiting sedimentary outcrops that contain the tracks of 3-toed dinosaurs. Footprints dating back 200 million years and access to the Connecticut River win over guests at this tiny, but special site.

General description: Three short hikes present the appeal of these two reservations.
General location: West bank of the Connecticut River at Northampton.
Special attractions: Vistas, Triassic-period dinosaur footprints, floral fossils, Eyrie House ruins, Connecticut River access, mixed forests, mountain laurel, fall foliage.
Length: Metacomet-Monadnock (M-M) Trail South, 4.5 miles round-trip; M-M Trail North, 2.8 miles round-trip; Dinosaur Footprints Trail 0.25-mile round-trip.
Elevation: M-M Trail South, 650-foot elevation change; M-M Trail North, 300-foot elevation change; Dinosaur Footprints Trail, minimal elevation change.
Difficulty: M-M Trail South, strenuous; M-M Trail North, moderate; Dinosaur Footprints Trail, easy.
Maps: Mount Tom State Reservation map.
Special requirements: Fee admission to Mount Tom. Tread softly and respectfully. Obey the respective rules for the two sites.
Season and hours: Spring through fall for hiking. Mount Tom: 8 a.m. to 6 p.m. Dinosaur Footprints Reservation: dawn to dusk.
For information: Mount Tom State Reservation; The Trustees of Reservations, Western Regional Office.
Finding the trailhead: From Interstate 91, take exit 18 and go south on U.S. Highway 5. In 3.2 miles, find the Smiths Ferry Road entrance to Mount Tom State Reservation on the right. Continue south on U.S. 5 for another 1.7 miles to find the paved turnout for Dinosaur Footprints Reservation on the left.

The hikes: Start the Metacomet-Monadnock hikes near the Trailside Museum off Smiths Ferry Road (1.6 miles west off U.S. 5, 0.1 mile east of its junction with Christopher Clark Road). Find parking opposite the museum.

For the **M-M Trail South**, follow the white diamond-and-paint blazed earthen lane heading south amid mature hemlocks, west of the Trailside Museum. In 200 feet, catch a glimpse of the rustic museum off to the left. Birch, mountain laurel, witch hazel, and chestnut interweave the forest. Maple and mixed oaks claim the upper canopy. Enjoy a pleasant stroll, following the faint blazes.

At 0.25 mile, find a storage yard to the right; the **Quarry Trail**, following the woods road as it veers left; and the foot trail of the M-M straight ahead. A sign on the M-M indicates "Mount Tom 2 miles." Ascend via a steep root-and rock-bound trail; stone steps and switchbacks advance the ridge assault.

Top the ridgeline (0.4 mile) and continue south, hugging the west rim. A spur soon leads to an impressive rock jut for a grand western perspective of Easthampton, the rural and wooded Connecticut River Valley, and the Berkshires vanishing to the horizon. Continue south for a rolling ridge tour, pocketing better and better views. Ragged breaks and weathered niches create foot- and handholds for mounting the rimrock.

At 0.6 mile, tag Whiting Peak (1,014 feet). Low stature oak, hickory, and pine clothe the summit ridge. At 0.85 mile, the **D.O.C. Trail** heads left; keep to the M-M. The fragmented cliff of Whiting and the stirring profile of Mount Tom hold one spellbound. Autumn paints an especially pretty landscape.

Before long, pursue the narrow ledge of the vertically fragmented cliff of Mount Tom Ridge. The sheer rock plummets 300 feet to a jagged scree skirt and the treed slope tapering to the valley floor. This is not a tour for the timid or foolish.

Where a secondary trail rounds inland at 1.3 miles, continue forward following the white paint blazes for some rock climbing. If you opt to follow the secondary trail, quickly bear right to return to the blazed hike at the scree base of an upper-tiered ledge.

Keep to the west side of the ridge, overlooking pull-apart walls, fractured towers, and pinnacles. Vultures sail the thermals. The brief departures into the woods only amplify the excitement of this otherwise vista-packed tour. At 1.5 miles, overlook a tower station, soon spying the beacon and radio towers atop Mount Tom (elevation 1,202 feet). By 2 miles add over-the-shoulder looks at Amherst, the University of Massachusetts (UMASS), and Summit House crowning the Holyoke Range.

Round the tower facility of Mount Tom, but beware of the hazardous concrete walkway. At the south side of the towers (2.25 miles), enjoy looks at Hartford, Connecticut and the distinct traprock ridges marching south. Where the M-M starts its descent for Massachusetts 141, turn around.

Locate the **M-M Trail North** at the edge of a picnic area opposite the Trailside Museum. Pass north through a boulder barricade, following a paved lane, to take an immediate left uphill. Again white diamonds and blazes indicate the foot trail. Traverse a low ridge, cloaked in hemlock and birch,

MOUNT TOM STATE RESERVATION—DINOSAUR FOOTPRINTS RESERVATION

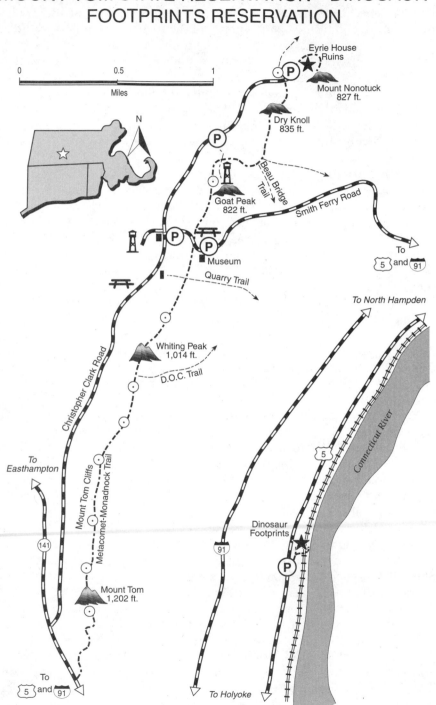

Eyrie House Ruins

Mount Nonotuck
827 ft.

Dry Knoll
835 ft.

Beau Bridge Trail

Goat Peak
822 ft.

Smith Ferry Road

To
5 and 91

Museum

Quarry Trail

To North Hampden

Whiting Peak
1,014 ft.

D.O.C. Trail

Christopher Clark Road

Connecticut River

To
Easthampton

Mount Tom Cliffs

Metacomet-Monadnock Trail

5

141

Dinosaur
Footprints

91

Mount Tom
1,202 ft.

To
5 and 91

To Holyoke

0   0.5   1
Miles

N

with an abrupt western cliff but no views.

Oak, maple, and mountain laurel soon alternate with the hemlocks. .
0.15 mile, veer right for a steep ascent. Where the trail angles left, the grade
calms. Top out at a clearing, finding a 180-degree view, and then detour
right to top Goat Peak.

Descend, cross a woods road, and climb trail and stairs to Goat Peak
(elevation 822 feet). Atop the peak, a 3-story platform unfolds a 360-degree
view, with Mount Tom, the Connecticut River, Holyoke, and the Holyoke
Range. From this tower, bird watchers conduct an annual hawk count.

Return to the clearing at 0.45 mile and resume the M-M north, rounding
the nose of the ridge, passing amid a scenic grove of mountain laurel. Next,
descend, crossing over the same woods road to round the north flank of
Goat Peak.

At 0.75 mile, the blue **Beau Bridge Trail** heads right; keep to the M-M
Trail, passing an easy-to-miss red-blazed trail in 50 feet. Ascend amid oak,
maple, birch, and witch hazel, finding moderate to steep grades, before
again following the ridge. Small ledge features punctuate the woods.

From Dry Knoll at 1.1 miles, overlook an oxbow on the Connecticut River,
UMASS, and Mounts Sugarloaf and Toby. A descent follows, coming out on
Christopher Clark Road (1.25 miles). The M-M continues north, but turn
right to reach Mount Nonotuck Vista Parking and the trail to Eyrie House
Ruins.

To view the ruins, hike from the end of the paved road, contouring uphill
amid deciduous woods. Soon the site's rock walls rise above the trail. At 1.4

Mount Tom view, Mount Tom State Reservation, MA.

yrie House, built into the slope. Find walls 3 feet thick, arched
d collapsed windows; within the central wall, a doorway frames
iew. Return as you came.

aur Footprints Trail descends from U.S. 5, quickly forking.
The boardwalk straight ahead leads to a large canted sedimentary outcrop
just below the highway. The soft rock shows pockmarks from weathering
and footprints left eons ago by a society of 3-toed dinosaurs. While cutting
the highway, workers discovered this important record of the past.

The right fork descends crossing the railroad track to reach the Connecticut River shore, where keen eyes may discover more, though fainter, dinosaur tracks. The outcrop along shore also bears fossil casts of plants and tree
limbs and the ripples from an ancient shallow lake. Spend some time scru-
tinizing the rock and admiring the water.

To more easily identify the dinosaur tracks, envision a 3-toed foot by
grouping your fingers in that arrangement. Now hold your hand above the
depressions. The outcrops hold dozens of prints, coming in three sizes. The
largest belonged to the *Eubrontes giganteus* (a carnivore 20 feet long). The
medium-sized ones record the *Anchisauripus sillimani*, the small prints
Grallator cuneatus. Find some of the best prints in the highway cut, within
10 feet of the boardwalk. Return as you came.

23 METACOMET-MONADNOCK TRAIL, THE HOLYOKE RANGE

General description: This fragment of the long-distance Metacomet-
Monadnock (M-M) Trail offers a rolling ridge tour, with both challenging
and comfortable stretches. It tags bald summits, rocky knobs, and outcrops
for vistas and passes Horse Caves, an interesting area of overhangs and rock
jumbles.

General location: 5 miles north of South Hadley, Massachusetts.

Special attractions: Vistas, varied woods, Summit House, Notch Visitor
Center, fall foliage. Flight path for the spring-fall hawk migration passes
over the western extent of the range.

Length: 9.5 miles one-way.

Elevation: Find a 721-foot elevation change; reach the high point atop Mount
Norwottuck (1,106 feet), the low at the hike's eastern terminus on Harris
Mountain Road (385 feet).

Difficulty: Strenuous.

Maps: Holyoke Range/Skinner State Parks trail map.

Special requirements: Expect areas of steep pitches and rises, with poor
traction; carry plenty of water; and no camping. As the M-M and some of
the cross trails and woods roads do pass through isolated private parcels,

keep to the official trails, respecting private ownership and heeding notices.
Season and hours: Spring through fall for hiking. Gates close 7 p.m. Summit House: 11 a.m. to 5 p.m. weekends and holidays.

For information: Skinner State Park.

Finding the trailhead: From the junction of Massachusetts 116 and Massachusetts 47 in South Hadley, go north on MA 47 for 3.4 miles and turn right on Mountain Road. Go 0.4 mile more and bear right to enter Skinner State Park. Reach Summit House parking in another 1.6 miles (park road open early May to November).

For Notch Visitor Center (a central access point), follow MA 116 northeast from the MA 47-MA 116 junction in South Hadley. To find the hike's eastern terminus, continue north on MA 116 past the Visitor Center and turn east on Bay Street and then south on Harris Mountain Road. The trail is on the right.

The hike: This segment of the M-M travels the bumpy 9 mile ridge of the Holyoke Range. Start the hike at the Summit House, atop Mount Holyoke (elevation 942 feet), for an eastbound tour.

Climb the steps and round the Summit House veranda for a superb panoramic view, with clear days adding looks at Mount Monadnock in New Hampshire, Mount Snow in Vermont. Closer to home, admire the Connecticut River Valley and Mounts Tom and Toby. Round to the east side of the veranda, descend the steps, and follow the white blazes east across the picnic area.

In 0.1 mile, the trail drops steeply from the crest, passing through an oak-maple complex, reaching Taylor's Notch (0.3 mile). Cross the road and remain on the white-blazed M-M, ascending steeply. Beware, the loose basaltic rock can steal footing. Top out at an open outcrop (0.6 mile) for a 180-degree view north.

The well-marked trail now molds to the rolling line of the narrow ridge, without edit or censure. Expect some steep, precarious pitches, and enjoy pockets of mountain laurels amid the deciduous woods. One by one, top the bumps dubbed "The Seven Sisters." Songbirds and both red and gray squirrels offer companionship. At 1.5 miles, find a trail register and another overlook of the valley tapestry.

At an open flat at 2 miles, the M-M curves right; ribbons mark a second trail to the left. The M-M now travels a carriage-width trail, rounding the north face below the crest. Pass amid hemlock and birch, before angling back to travel the dry ridgetop. At 2.9 miles, claim Mount Hitchcock, finding a tumbled beacon of reclining red iron and concrete foundations. The **Hitchcock Trail** descends away right; keep to the M-M.

Descend to tour a stand of magnificent mature hemlock only to ascend sharply from their rich shade. The path now parallels a pair of red pipes. Cross over them, skirt a fenced enclosure, and top Bare Mountain (3.8 miles). Find looks north to the University of Massachusetts (UMASS) and south to Springfield, with the Holyoke Range stretching east. A long rocky descent

METACOMET-MONADNOCK TRAIL, HOLYOKE RANGE

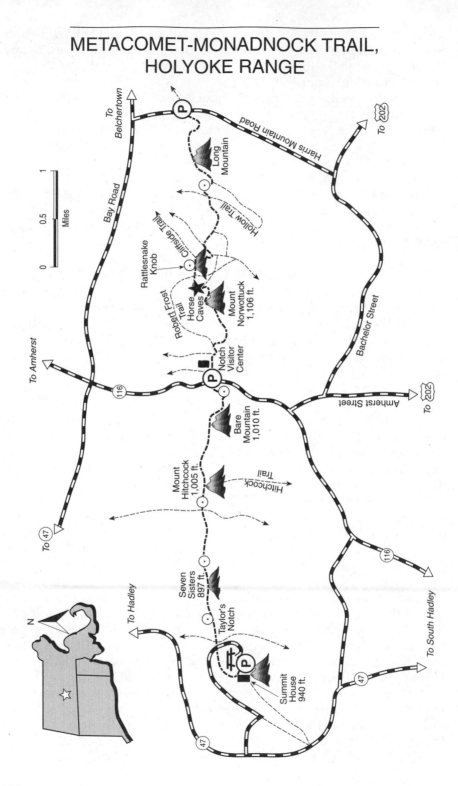

To Belchertown

To 202

Harris Mountain Road

Bay Road

Long Mountain

1
0.5
0
Miles

Hollow Trail

Rattlesnake Knob

Cliffside Trail

Robert Frost Trail

Horse Caves

Mount Norwottuck 1,106 ft.

To Amherst

116

Notch Visitor Center

P

Bachelor Street

Amherst Street

To 202

Bare Mountain 1,010 ft.

Mount Hitchcock 1,005 ft.

Hitchcock Trail

To 47

Seven Sisters 897 ft.

116

Taylor's Notch

To Hadley

N

Summit House 940 ft.

P

47

To South Hadley

47

Summit House, Skinner State Park, MA.

with shallow switchbacks, followed by an'easier stretch amid the big trees of the lower slope leads to MA 116 and Notch Visitor Center across the highway (4.7 miles).

Pass through the visitor center parking lot, following the white-blazed M-M along a cabled-off route at the south end of the lot. Skirt the visitor center building to resume the tour east, passing through a maze of well-marked trails. While near the visitor center and Trap Rock Quarry, be alert for several quick direction changes on the M-M.

The orange-blazed **Robert Frost (RF) Trail** shares the initial distance. Where the shared trail curves left to cross a gravel turnaround beneath utility lines, look for the hike to settle into its ridge-pursuing course. Ascend to a fork: the Robert Frost continues straight, while the M-M bears right on a root-bound tote road, switchbacking uphill.

Follow woods road and foot trail, drawing into the drier forest mix of the upper ridge, reaching the crest (5.5 miles). The interval between paint blazes expands, but the tracked path remains reasonably apparent. At 6 miles, top the rocky summit of Mount Norwottuck, the highest point in the Holyoke Range. Low oaks rim the site filtering looks; best views stretch north.

Follow faint blazes along the outcrop to the next lower tier, and keep right (south). Avoid taking the steep secondary trail down the north flank. The M-M briefly tops the ledge of Horse Caves for a 180-degree eastern perspective, spotlighting Rattlesnake Knob and Long Mountain.

Descend south and east, rounding to the rock jumble and overhangs of Horse Caves for another difficult descent, easing over the rocks. Horse Caves

(5.7 miles) traces its name to revolutionary times. It was here, according to local history, that Daniel Shays sheltered his horses for Shays' Rebellion.

An easier segment of trail leads away from the caves; follow the white blazes. Before long, meet up with the orange-blazed **Robert Frost Trail**, sharing the remainder of the tour east. Regularly blazed, the RF clarifies travel.

Bypass a trail heading left at 6.25 miles to take the 100-foot vista detour in another 0.2 mile. It follows the ridge of Rattlesnake Knob, ending with a bold look at Long Mountain and a grand window to autumn color. Resume the hike, descending east on the M-M/RF. Where the trail bottoms out, find hemlock and beech. Ahead, bear right along a woods road; the **Cliffside Trail** descends left to Bay Road in 0.8 mile. Find junction signs angled for the westbound traveler.

In another 0.1 mile, turn left, still following a woods road, and then stay right as a second trail descends to Bay Road. At 7.25 miles, top a hill with an elevation marker and register. Roll along the ridge and descend to cross **Hollow Trail** (8 miles). As the trail next ascends, an outcrop to the left offers views of Mount Norwottuck.

Top Long Mountain (elevation 906 feet) at 8.6 miles. Next comes a treacherously steep, boot-skidding descent, crying for a switchback. A tame, relaxing tour follows, passing through hemlock-hardwood forest with mountain laurel. Arrive at Harris Mountain Road, with its limited trailhead parking, 9.5 miles. Across the road, the M-M continues its journey toward Mount Monadnock in New Hampshire some 76 miles north.

24 QUABBIN PARK

OVERVIEW

In the Swift River Valley, a 120,000-acre open space protects Quabbin Reservoir, a 39-square-mile man-made lake providing drinking water for the Boston metropolitan area. In the 1930s, the raised waters claimed four towns. Stone walls, cellars, wells, fruit trees, and roads to nowhere hint at the valley's past. At the lake's south end, Quabbin Park engages hikers with foot trails and abandoned roads. The undisturbed open space hosts a variety of wildlife, with likely sightings of deer, bald eagle, turkey, loon, fox, and beaver.

General description: Three short hikes provide a peek at the park's offering. Travel mixed woods, top the summit tower, pass cultural remains, and explore the shores of Quabbin Reservoir, Swift River, and Pepper's Mill Pond.
General location: 5 miles west of Ware, Massachusetts.

Special attractions: Tower vistas, fishing, cultural sites, bald eagles (5 nesting pairs, with 18 remaining year-round), spring wildflowers, fall foliage, fall hawk migration.

Length: Summit Tower-Reservoir Loop, 3.3-mile loop; Swift River Hike, 1.5 miles round-trip; Pepper's Mill Pond Loop, 1-mile loop.

Elevation: Summit Tower-Reservoir Loop, 500-foot elevation change; Swift River Hike, less than a 50-foot elevation change; Pepper's Mill Pond Loop, virtually flat.

Difficulty: Summit Tower-Reservoir Loop, easy to moderate; the other two hikes, both easy.

Maps: Park map, available at visitor center.

Special requirements: The park is a watershed for Boston's drinking water. Dispose of refuse only at the provided receptacles. No smoking, swimming, wading, horses, dogs, camping, or fires.

Season and hours: Year-round, daylight hours only; spring through fall for hiking. Visitor center: 8:30 a.m. to 4:30 p.m. weekdays; 9 a.m. to 5 p.m. weekends.

For information: Metropolitan District Commission, Quabbin Park Visitor Center.

Finding the trailhead: From the junction of Massachusetts 32 and Massachusetts 9 in Ware, go west on MA 9 for 4.2 miles, finding the east entrance to Quabbin Park and the trailhead to Pepper's Mill Pond on the north side of the highway. Continue west on MA 9 another 1.3 miles to reach the middle entrance, heading north into the park for Winsor Dam, the visitor center, and the other two trailheads. Find the west entrance north off MA 9, 1.6 miles farther west.

The hikes: For the **Summit Tower-Reservoir Loop**, start at Enfield Lookout, the summit parking lot, or Hank's Place Picnic Area and travel counterclockwise.

From Enfield Lookout, a popular eagle-watching turnout, locate trail post 23 for the start of hike, 100 feet south of the turnout on the opposite side of the road. Round the gate and hike uphill on an attractive grassy woods road, touring amid white pine, maple, oak, birch, and ash. Huckleberry, fern, and low rock ledges compose the forest floor.

At the T-junction at 0.1 mile, go left remaining on woods road, soon entering a grassy clearing with a wooden shed along its southern edge. Traverse the clearing, and at the far side of the building (0.25 mile), turn right. Faint yellow blazes now point hikers into a stand of spruce for foot-trail travel.

Pass a few abandoned fruit trees to ascend amid a fern-laced forest of tall hardwoods, replaced, in turn, by the low-stature trees and huckleberry bushes of the upper slope. Filtered lighting, the song of the wind, and a swirl of autumn leaves may contribute to a tour. By 0.9 mile, pass amid a stand of "teen-aged" trees, skirting a meadow swath to the hiker's left. Come out at the summit parking area, near a picnic table and post absent its number (post 26 on the map).

QUABBIN PARK

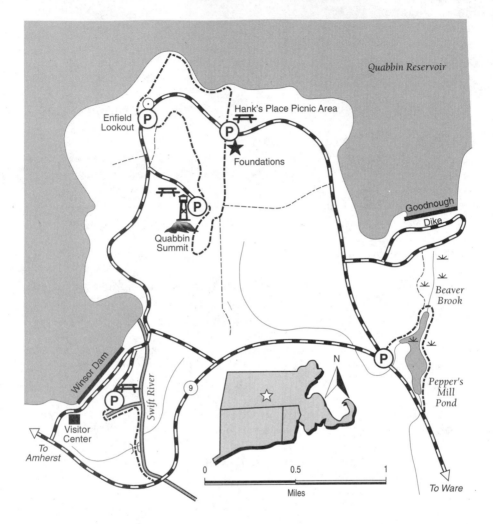

The loop resumes 100 feet to the left, near the end of the rockwork curb of the summit drive; again look for the faint yellow blazes. But first, cross the summit flat to ascend the paved walk to Quabbin Tower (elevation 1,026 feet).

Stairs spiral to the window-enclosed tower loft for views of Quabbin Reservoir, some of its sixty islands, Belchertown, the Berkshires rolling west, and the hilly, wooded Swift River Valley. During the height of hawk migration, some 400 birds a day migrate over the reservoir and past the tower.

Resume the counterclockwise loop at 1.2 miles, skirting the other side of the meadow swath, passing amid oaks. The foot trail descends via lazy sidewinding curves. At 1.6 miles, enter a pine plantation. At 1.7 miles, meet Webster Road (a retired dirt road), and follow it left. A post marks the turn, but it is difficult to spy when hiking the trail in reverse.

Ahead, big sugar and silver maples, ash, and beech trees line the country lane, as do remnant stone walls. To the right pass a deer-study enclosure and later a scenic rock border and stone foundation. At post 24 (2.25 miles), cross the park road to follow a northbound paved and gravel lane, skirting the west side of the open lawn of Hank's Place Picnic Area.

Round another gate, passing between thickety hedgerows with fields to either side. Upon reaching the reservoir at 2.5 miles, turn left to round the cove. Travel either rocky beach or the deciduous-wooded bank. An unmarked footpath parts the woods and overlooks shore; pines slip into the mix.

At 2.85 miles, find a sunken grade ascending left (south) to Enfield Lookout. Follow the maple-lined corridor uphill, pass another deer-study enclosure, and round the meadow slope below the vista, before charging uphill to the park road. Arrive opposite post 23 and turn left for Enfield Lookout (3.3 miles).

At the north end of Winsor Dam, take the side road descending to the base of the dam to reach a picnic area, Winsor Power Station, and the start for the **Swift River Hike**. Park at the picnic area, and hike down the paved authorized-vehicle road to Winsor Power Station. In 100 yards, round the fenced enclosure to follow the foot trail heading downstream along the west shore.

Water emerges in a fury from the power-station spillway. Mature planted pines clad the steep canyon slope, while riprap shapes an unnatural channel, splashed by the remarkably clear waters. Dogwood, bramble, goldenrod, aster, and black-eyed Susan crowd the trail. By 0.2 mile, follow a woods road traversing a broad river bench, with a 10-foot drop to the water. A second path travels the opposite shore.

At 0.3 mile, where the trail curves south, waters from Winsor Dam and the power station merge. Downstream flows a broad, beautiful clear-green river with a natural shore. The lines of the fly-fishermen dance as the river offers catch-and-release sport. Spurs branch to the river for better viewing or access. The woods grow more mixed, offering full shade past a powerline corridor. Grassy points and gentle bends add to the river's charm.

At 0.65 mile, find a low grassy point from which to watch the fish swim. A side brook merges on the right. Downstream, cross a footbridge over this brook; signs caution "use at your own risk." Next, ascend some 25 feet above the river, where mountain laurel adds to the midstory and river overlooks engage. At 0.75 mile, reach a gate near the MA 9 bridge and turn around.

For **Pepper's Mill Pond Loop**, find the trailhead on the east entrance road, north of MA 9 prior to the stone entrance pillars. Post 40 marks the start of a clockwise tour.

Round a gate and proceed east along a grassy woods lane. The hike parallels a drainage, passing amid planted pines and a shrubby understory. In 100 feet, a 2-track angles left; continue forward following the inlet drainage downstream to the pond. Ash, maple, hickory, and chestnut vary the woods, with oaks claiming the upper canopy; beware of poison ivy.

As a foot trail rounds the west shore, lily pads and aquatic grasses decorate the shallows, turtles sun on logs, and fish ripple the water. At 0.2 mile, a grassy point suggests a pause. Vultures make circular passes over the pond, while kingfishers noisily announce their presence. Stranded bobbers rest amid the lily pads.

The path while unmarked is well-trampled, but expect to step over some logs. Sheep laurel colors the banks. Find the remains of an abandoned beaver lodge, gnawed stumps, and collapsed dens. Despite its proximity, MA 9 only minimally intrudes.

At 0.3 mile, pass beneath a utility line and continue upstream along a beaver pond outlet. Before long, find a cable stretched between the shores and cross the stream atop some stones. The height of the cable allows only taller hikers to use it to steady their crossing. With the beaver dam breached, a snag-meadow marsh has replaced the upstream pond.

Now round the east shore of Pepper's Mill Pond, passing back under the power line. A beaver dam has raised the water of an adjacent bog, creating a second pond, briefly reducing the trail to an isthmus. The water-lily bloom or the flush of autumn particularly recommends a tour. Side trails branch to points overlooking Pepper's Mill Pond.

By 0.7 mile, skirt the open water of the outlet cove, crossing the dam and spillway bridge at 0.8 mile. Ascend from the spillway to MA 9 and follow its shoulder west paralleling the inlet drainage back upstream to the trailhead (1 mile).

25 PURGATORY CHASM STATE RESERVATION

OVERVIEW

In its 187 wooded acres, this south-central Massachusetts state reservation cradles a picturesque 0.25-mile-long gorge of jumbled rock enclosed by cliffs. The walls, both sheer and jagged, measure from 20 to 70 feet high. A second chasm on the property, Little Purgatory Chasm, captures the drama in miniature and spotlights a scenic grotto and cascade.

General description: Two tours explore most of the reservation's trails and walkable woods roads. One travels the belly and rim of Purgatory Chasm. The other travels the wooded outskirts, with a side trip to Little Purgatory Chasm.
General location: 10 miles southeast of Auburn, Massachusetts.
Special attractions: An intriguing fissure amid solid rock, mixed forests, varied understory, fall foliage.

Length: Chasm Loop Trail, 0.5-mile loop; Charley's Loop-Little Purgatory Hike, 2.6 miles round-trip.
Elevation: Trails show less than 100 feet of elevation change.
Difficulty: Chasm Loop Trail, moderate. Charley's Loop-Little Purgatory Hike, easy.
Maps: State reservation map.
Special requirements: Wear boots; beware of slippery rock. No food or beverages allowed in the chasm. Do not climb chasm walls without a permit. Apply for permits at the park, and bring personal climbing gear.
Season and hours: Spring through fall, daylight hours.
For information: Purgatory Chasm State Reservation.
Finding the trailhead: From the junction of U.S. Highway 20 and Massachusetts 146 in North Millbury (south of Worcester), follow MA 146 south for 7.1 miles and turn right (west) on Purgatory Road. Reach trailhead parking on the left in another 1.3 miles.

The hikes: For the **Chasm Loop Trail**, start near the picnic shelter and mapboard. A sign points to the chasm, and blue markers lead the way. Pass into the gorge, negotiating the prescribed route over and between the massive boulders and slabs that litter the chasm floor.

The initial walls rise some 20 feet, with ferns invading the seams and fissures. Lichen and mineral stains accent the cliffs, while hemlock and deciduous trees fringe the rim. Amid the rocks, look for etched inscriptions dating to the early 1900s.

The imposing rock shows hues of red, orange, gray, bronze, black, and purple, especially striking when wet. Fissures reveal how the rubble was created; massive overhangs lend drama. After 0.1 mile, dirt trail segments intersperse the boulder scrambles, as hikers descend into the chasm's lower bowl. Here find 70-foot-high sheer walls, with named features. Locate the vertical plummet of "Lover's Leap" and the triangular jut of "The Pulpit," both on the right.

As the walls grade lower near the end of the chasm, find "The Coffin" on the right. Aptly named, this feature holds a coffin-shaped rock in the dark recess of a natural mausoleum. A canted slab for a grave marker completes the image. In the drainage at the chasm's mouth grow iris, fern, and grasses.

Stay the blue loop, swinging left for the return. Skirt the chasm amid a white pine-huckleberry complex, before reaching the rim at "Fat Man's Misery" (0.4 mile). Smooth sides shape this widened fissure, measuring 15 feet deep, 30 feet long, but only 18 inches wide. From atop the outcrop, peer into Purgatory Chasm, gaining new perspective. Where the trail next visits the rim find the boxy opening of "The Corn Crib." Close the tour at the picnic area (0.5 mile).

For the **Charley's Loop-Little Purgatory Hike**, follow the paved lane between the picnic shelter and the stone restroom hut, reaching the cabled-off woods road of **Charley's Loop**; yellow blazes point the way.

Pass amid picnic sites to tour the periphery woods, well removed from

PURGATORY CHASM STATE RESERVATION

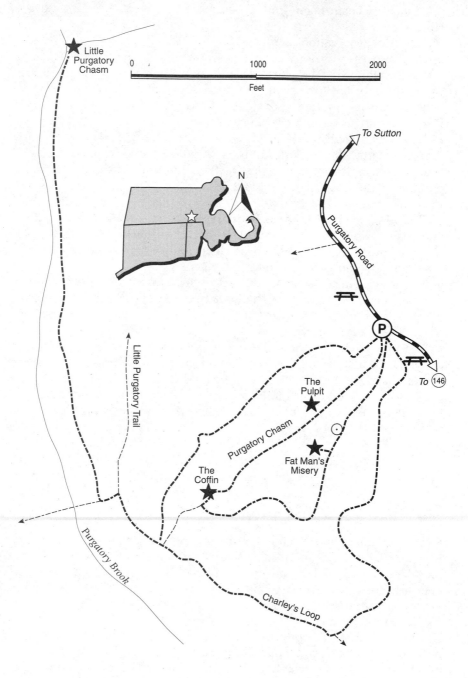

Little Purgatory Chasm

0   1000   2000
Feet

To Sutton

N

Purgatory Road

P

To 146

Little Purgatory Trail

The Pulpit

Purgatory Chasm

Fat Man's Misery

The Coffin

Purgatory Brook

Charley's Loop

Purgatory Chasm, Purgatory Chasm State Reservation, MA.

Purgatory Chasm. Enjoy an attractive lane and comfortable slow descent, touring amid hemlock, hardwood, and pine. Huckleberry, mayflower, twisted stalk, sarsaparilla, and fern contribute to the understory flora. Large boulders offer trailside seating.

At 0.5 mile, turn right, now following yellow and blue markers along a narrow woods road, as it parts a varied woods. Ignore the unmarked side trails and blazes without trails. At 0.8 mile, reach a multiple junction where a hard right on an old woods road enters Purgatory Chasm near The Coffin, the yellow-and-blue blazed Charley's Loop continues on a footpath angling uphill along the chasm's west rim, and the main woods road proceeds straight for Little Purgatory chasm and trail.

Before completing the loop, detour forward on the woods road to visit Little Purgatory Chasm. In less than 0.1 mile find a junction; the main road ahead is **Little Purgatory Trail**. Turn left on the smaller woods road for the **Little Purgatory Hike**. In 50 feet, turn right on an unmarked grassy lane entering woods. Before long, a footpath replaces the vegetated lane, paralleling Purgatory Brook upstream.

Step around and between the rocks of shore, coming to a grotto cupped by 10-foot-high solid rock. There find a small cascade at the confluence of Little Purgatory and Purgatory brooks. Climbing the slope to follow Little Purgatory Brook upstream, gain an overlook of this smaller chasm, before the trail ends in 200 feet.

Future plans call for a return trail. Meanwhile, backtrack downstream, returning to the 0.8-mile junction at 2.3 miles. Follow the yellow-and-blue marked foot trail uphill to the left to complete the clockwise tour of Charley's Loop.

Tour a rock studded forest of beech, maple, white pine, and black and chestnut oaks, adding hemlock as the trail progresses. At 2.5 miles, overlook Purgatory Chasm. Top a rise and descend to the picnic area, arriving amid massive outcrops and boulders.

An alternative return travels the woods road of **Little Purgatory Trail** north to the woods road of **Old Purgatory Trail**. Turn right on Old Purgatory Trail and again on Purgatory Road to return to the picnic area and trailhead for a 3-mile hike; consult the park map.

26 BLACKSTONE RIVER AND CANAL HERITAGE STATE PARK

OVERVIEW

Part of a greater National Heritage Corridor, this 1,000-acre state park celebrates the Industrial Age. Within its borders, find nearly 6 miles of the twisting Blackstone River and some of the best-preserved sections of the 45-mile historic canal that linked Providence, Rhode Island and Worcester, Massachusetts. The Blackstone River both powered manufacturing and transported the raw material and finished product of the region's 18th- and 19th-century mills. Its counterpart canal operated from 1828 to 1848, when it was superseded by railroads.

General description: Two hikes explore the park, traveling multiple-use trails: The Towpath Hike tours a scenic, mostly natural corridor through the old industrial beltway. King Philip's Trail travels the wooded hillside above Rice City Pond, ending at a prominent rock overlook.
General location: East of Massachusetts 122 in Uxbridge and Northbridge.
Special attractions: Historic locks, dams, bridge abutments, and foundation; scenic woods and wetland; vistas; wildlife.
Length: Towpath Hike, 4 miles one-way; King Philip's Trail, 2.6 miles round-trip.
Elevation: Towpath Hike, 50-foot elevation change; King Philip's Trail, 150-foot elevation change.
Difficulty: Both, easy.
Maps: State park map.
Special requirements: Come prepared; mosquitoes can be villainous.
Season and hours: Year-round, spring through fall for hiking. Daylight hours.
For information: Blackstone River and Canal Heritage State Park.
Finding the trailhead: From the MA 122 - MA 16 junction in Uxbridge, go east on MA 16 for 0.5 mile and turn left on Cross Street to find parking for southern terminus of the towpath behind Stanley Woolen Mill.

For King Philip's Trail and the park headquarters, go 1.2 mile north on MA 122 from its junction with MA 16 and turn right on Hartford Avenue. Find parking on the left in 1.3 miles. Reach Plummer's Landing, the northern terminus for the Towpath Hike, on Church Street, east off MA 122, 2.4 miles north of Hartford Avenue.

The hikes: The **Towpath Hike** links the following named park trails: Blackstone Canal and Towpath, Goat Hill Trail, and Plummer's Trail. Northbound, start behind the Stanley Woolen Mill. Built in the early 1850s, this mill processed raw wool into finished dye cloth and supplied American

BLACKSTONE RIVER AND CANAL
HERITAGE STATE PARK

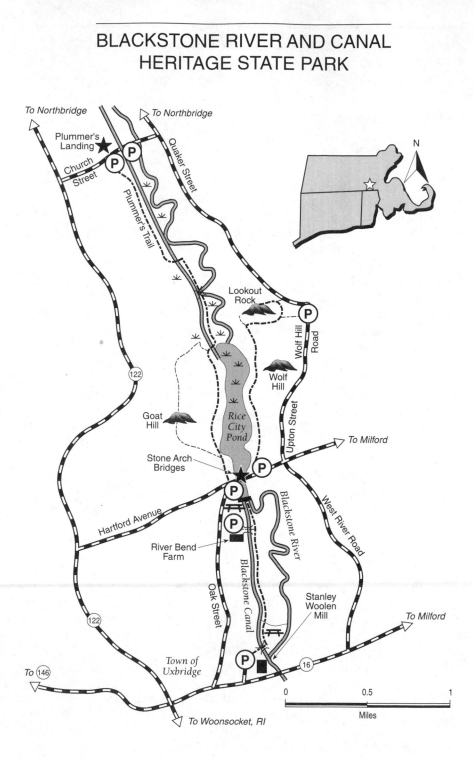

To Northbridge

To Northbridge

Plummer's Landing

Church Street

Plummer's Trail

Quaker Street

122

Lookout Rock

Wolf Hill Road

Wolf Hill

Goat Hill

Rice City Pond

Stone Arch Bridges

Upton Street

To Milford

Hartford Avenue

River Bend Farm

Blackstone River

West River Road

Blackstone Canal

Oak Street

Stanley Woolen Mill

To Milford

122

Town of Uxbridge

To (146)

To Woonsocket, RI

16

N

0   0.5   1
Miles

troops with vital blanket and overcoat fabric.

Hike north on **Blackstone Canal and Towpath**, crossing a footbridge. The levee initially shows an open herbaceous bank, with aspen, oaks, maple, birch, sumac, and elm growing to the sides. Travel the east bank of the dark canal water, passing picnic sites on the right.

At 0.2 mile, cross a bridge at a 1917 spillway, where released waters slip over bedrock speeding to the flowing river. Woods and marsh woodlands now claim the right-hand side of the levee, lending shade and charm to the corridor. Watch for historic rock constructions along the canal.

The channel broadens near the bridge to River Bend Farm on the west shore (1 mile). The scenic red barn, serenely reflected in the canal waters, holds the park visitor center. Turtles, polliwogs, fish, and heron may detain hikers.

At 1.2 miles, reach the dike at Gatehouse Lock, with the Blackstone River flowing to the right and a fine reflection of Stone Arch Bridge to the north. Cross the dike and ascend through a picnic area to Hartford Avenue.

Next, cross the road and pass north through an open field, finding a kiosk and sign for a multiple-use trail. Here follow **Goat Hill Trail** to the right of the kiosk, traveling an earthen lane rounding the base of Goat Hill. Hardwoods mostly screen out any eastern looks at Rice City Pond, now mainly a marsh. Builders created the pond in the 1800s for flood control and a low-water reserve. For this tour, forgo trails ascending left that top Goat Hill; keep to the waterway.

At 1.5 miles, pass below a balanced split-rock, finding an open view of Rice City Pond. The trail now rolls and narrows, encountering rock walls. Pass through a breach in one of the walls, coming to a junction at 2.1 miles. Descend right for Goat Hill Lock and the next canal segment. The stone-lined channel of the lock frames a scenic look south at Rice City Pond.

Cross the canal on cross-laid logs and resume north on **Plummer's Trail**. The levee passes between a wooded bottomland and canal wetland. At 2.5 miles, glimpse the braided glimmer of the Blackstone River as it flows closer to the towpath. An opening where the trail crosses a woods road that accesses the river adds looks at an island and the wooded ridge of Lookout Rock. A few azalea adorn the corridor. At 2.7 miles, footbridges span a breach between canal and river.

At the junction post and bench seat at 2.9 miles, turn left, crossing a filled-in portion of the canal to again hike north along the west shore. Pass between field and woods, skirting a big sycamore at 3.4 miles. Soon after, glimpse a breach mingling river flow with canal water. At the junction at 3.75 miles, go forward for Plummer's Landing; the path to the right leads to a canoe access and picnic area. On the north side of Church Street, excavated foundations recall the store and commercial hub opened by Israel Plummer in 1837.

For **King Philip's Trail**, start at the parking lot west of the headquarters and hike north on a cable-closed gravel lane. Edge a grassy area below the tree and rock slope of Wolf Hill, passing a couple of picnic tables. Oaks,

*River Bend Farm Visitor Center, Blackstone River and Canal Heritage
State Park, MA.*

aspen, and planted pine cover the slope, but the trail remains open.

At 0.2 mile, briefly enter a mature pine plantation. The wetland of Rice City Pond claims the foot of the slope, with skunk cabbage, cattails, loosestrife, and sweet pepperbush. Find the foot trail thin and canted. At 0.4 mile, traverse a gravel flat; a few blue markers point the way. Spurs branch left toward the pond. A screech announces the passing of a hawk overhead.

The trail mildly rolls, keeping some 20 feet above the wetland pond. Stay left, passing an abandoned trail uphill to the right. Dip to cross a drainage (1 mile), again touring a pine flat. At 1.1 miles, reach another junction. The worn dirt trail to the left leads to the base of Lookout Rock with its overhangs and myriad of scrambles to the top. Follow the woods road ascending right between plantation and outcrop for a more tempered approach to the summit.

In 0.1 mile, veer left; the woods road ahead meets Quaker Street. At 1.25 miles, top a rise, finding a second link to this neighborhood street. Here a short spur to the left tops an outcrop for looks at Goat Hill, Rice City Pond, and Stone Arch Bridge.

Resume the rolling hike toward Lookout Rock, soon following either trail or woods road arcing left. Mount the rock at 1.4 miles for a grand area overview. Enjoy the meandering glint of the Blackstone River as it parts the wetland meadow of Rice City Pond; Wolf and Goat hills, shaping the basin; and soaring vultures. Return as you came.

27 LAUGHING BROOK WILDLIFE SANCTUARY

OVERVIEW

Threaded by Laughing Brook and the Scantic River, this 354-acre sanctuary of the Massachusetts Audubon Society engages with woodland, field, riparian, and wetland habitats. On the grounds find an animal rehabilitation center and natural enclosures housing the treated animals that can no longer survive in the wild. The sanctuary also protects the home of Thornton W. Burgess, a children's author who drew from this natural setting for his animal tales. The storyteller's home, a National Historic Place, dates back to 1780.

General description: Four short nature trails examine the sanctuary offering.
General location: In Hampden, Massachusetts.
Special attractions: Bird and wildlife watching; brook, pond, and river; wildflowers; fall foliage.
Length: Big River Loop, 1.2 miles round-trip; Glacial Trail, 2.5 miles round-trip; Circle of the Seasons, 1.15 miles round-trip; Oak Forest Loop (with

wildlife enclosures), 0.25-mile loop.

Elevation: Big River and Oak Forest loops, less than a 40-foot elevation change; Glacial Trail, 200-foot elevation change; Circle of the Seasons, 100-foot elevation change.

Difficulty: All easy.

Maps: Sanctuary trail map; Circle of the Seasons brochure.

Special requirements: Per-person admission fee or Massachusetts Audubon Society membership; obey posted rules. Find the characteristic Audubon blazing, with blue heading away from the trailhead, yellow returning. Numbered posts keyed to the map identify trail intersections.

Season and hours: Year-round, Tuesday through Sunday. Grounds: dawn to dusk; visitor center: 10 a.m. to 5 p.m.

For information: Laughing Brook Education Center and Wildlife Sanctuary.

Finding the trailhead: From the junction of Massachusetts 220 and Massachusetts 83 in East Longmeadow, go south on MA 83 toward Hampden, Massachusetts and Somers Connecticut. In 1.5 miles turn left on Hampden Road, go 2.6 miles, and turn right on Somers Road per the sign for Laughing Brook. Go 0.2 mile and turn left on Main Street. In 2 miles, turn left off Main Street to enter the sanctuary's parking lot. Start all trails behind the education center at the fee and map station.

The hikes: For **Big River Loop**, take the foot trail heading left at junction 1 and in 100 feet, turn left at post 3, hiking downstream alongside Laughing Brook. The brook babbles scenic, dark, and clear amid a shady corridor of maple, oak, hornbeam, elm, and witch hazel.

Cross the footbridge, round behind the Rehabilitation Center, and bear left at post 11, passing the Storyteller's House to cross Main Street at a crosswalk. At the edge of a meadow, bear left on a footpath entering a tanglewood of elm, maple, and grapevine, still pursuing the brook downstream. At 0.25 mile, a spur breaks to the stream as the tour bears right.

At post 13, cross the bridge over the Scantic River; the **Meadow Path** straight ahead holds the return. The Scantic, a designated scenic river, is the "Big River" mentioned in the stories of Thornton Burgess. Post 14 marks the start of the actual river loop; go left for a clockwise tour.

White and red pines dominate the skyline, oak and maple the lower story. Round uphill near a stone wall passing amid pine rows. At post 17, a 0.1-mile spur to the left leads to a river overlook; right continues the loop. The spur crosses a footbridge and rolls along a deciduous-clad slope, ending at a gentle bend of the 18-foot-wide river.

Resume the clockwise loop at post 17, coming upon a junction in 100 yards. To the left find a boardwalk suitable for low-water travel; use the right fork at times of high water. The left fork travels a wetland woods, ending amid a spruce plantation back along the Scantic River. The high-water spur skirts the plantation, rejoining the tour at post 15.

Cross back over the Scantic River (0.8 mile) and retrace your steps to the Education Center, or follow the **Meadow Path** downstream along the river

LAUGHING BROOK WILDLIFE SANCTUARY

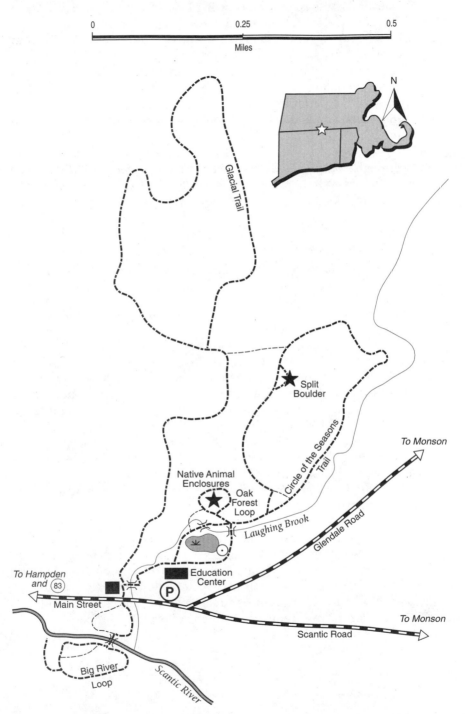

and across the meadow to return to the crosswalk (1 mile), return to the center 1.2 miles.

For the next hike, retrace the start of Big River Loop to junction post 11 (0.15 mile) and turn right, ascending the west ridge above Laughing Brook for the **Glacial Trail**. Spruce and maple clothe the slope. At 0.25 mile, bear left; the ridge widens to a plateau with oak, pine, and hickory filling out the woods. Enjoy a relaxing woods meander, bearing left at posts 18 (0.6 mile) and 19 (the loop junction). Alternately tour amid pine and mixed woods on this rolling tour; in autumn find a pleasant leaf shuffle.

By 1 mile, ascend amid a dark hemlock woods, keeping a sharp eye out for the blue blazes. In places, mountain or sheep laurel, club moss, and huckleberry adorn the woods, and a few aspen enliven the canopy. Step over and through stone walls. Grouse, deer, fox, chickadee, and toad may be spied. At 1.3 miles, yellow markers indicate the half-way point; now look for a few exceptionally big trees. Close the loop at post 19 and return to the trailhead (2.5 miles).

The **Circle of the Seasons** follows the service road heading right from post 1. In 100 feet a gazebo overlooks a small wildlife pond, with willows amid its thickly wooded rim and catfish and minnows in the dark water. Another 50 feet farther find a second gazebo, this one to the right.

Cross the bridge over Laughing Brook and pass post 2 (**Oak Forest Walk**); continuing the Circle. Find the brochure keyed to the discovery of the particular season: hawk and butterfly migrations in fall, snow fleas in winter, wildflowers in spring, and cicadas in summer.

Pine-deciduous woods shade the tour where it parallels Laughing Brook upstream. Post 7 marks the loop (0.15 mile); bear left for a clockwise tour and mild ascent. Hemlocks bring a richer shade. At post 9, again bear left as the route straight ahead cuts the loop. At 0.35 mile, a fork to the right offers a 100-foot side trip to a 9-foot-high cleanly split boulder.

Proceed forward at post 10, passing amid pines; soon, yellow replaces blue as the guiding color. Along a sturdy rock wall, find a 3-foot-diameter pine and an equisized oak, monarchs of the woods. Next, overlook an S-bend of Laughing Brook and bear left at post 8 to bring the loop to a close at post 7 (1 mile). Return to the trailhead (1.15 miles).

The **Oak Forest Walk** heads left at post 2 off the Circle of the Seasons. This tour travels boardwalks and tops attractive tiered platforms for sanctuary overlooks; gates to the wildlife exhibits close at 4 p.m. Among the rehabilitated animals housed at the sanctuary, find a turkey vulture, with its wild kin circling free overhead; bobcat; coyote; wild turkey; deer; and porcupine. Panels provide information about each of the animals. Conclude the circuit via the **Pond Trail**, returning to the trailhead (0.25 mile).

EASTERN MASSACHUSETTS TRAILS

This region features the foothills and flatter reaches of the state, including the white sand beaches and wildlife lands of the northern coast and the inspired landscapes of Cape Cod peninsula. Even near the cosmopolitan center of Boston, prized open spaces offer solitude, natural discovery, and adventure. Lowland woods, meadows, ponds, swamps, rocky hilltops, the sleepy Charles River, pristine dunes, and coastal and bay shores vary travel. Arrive with the Pilgrims, and walk with Thoreau.

28 PARKER RIVER NATIONAL WILDLIFE REFUGE

OVERVIEW

This 4,662-acre national wildlife refuge occupies the southern two-thirds of Plum Island, a classic Atlantic barrier island. Drumlins (low hills left behind by the last retreating glacier) gave rise to the island, collecting ocean-deposited sand and silt, that later fused into a single land mass. The refuge encompasses a dune-beach complex, tidal flat, freshwater marsh, stunted pines, and cranberry bogs.

Piping plovers, which nearly vanished in the 1800s, nest at the seaward toe of the dunes. Because beach-goers inadvertently threaten the bird's success, the refuge closes its beach to the public during the crucial summer nesting season. In 1995, twenty-one piping plover pairs occupied the refuge shore.

General description: Short nature trails explore the various habitats and offer refuge overlooks. When open, the beach offers 6.5 miles of uninterrupted strolling.
General location: South of Newburyport, Massachusetts.
Special attractions: Nesting piping plover and migrating shorebirds and waterfowl; summer-flocking swallows; plum and cranberry picking (from the Tuesday after Labor Day through October 31); clamming; surf fishing; observation platforms and blinds.
Length: Hellcat Swamp Nature Trail, 1-mile loop, with option to extend; Pines Trail, 0.4 mile round-trip; Beach Hike, 6.5 miles one-way.
Elevation: Hikes are flat or show minimal elevation change.
Difficulty: All easy.
Maps: Refuge map.
Special requirements: Entrance fee; when parking lots fill, the refuge closes its gates. Visitors may pick 1 quart of plums and/or cranberries per person

per day. Otherwise, there is no collecting of natural objects, and no collecting of beach-stranded fishing gear. Leave pets at home, keep off the dunes, and carry insect repellent. Green-headed flies and mosquitoes can be annoying even on the beach.

Season and hours: Year-round, sunrise to sunset. Beach closed April 1 through mid- to late-August (Beach segments unclaimed for nests are gradually opened to the public starting July 1.)

For information: Parker River National Wildlife Refuge.

Finding the trailhead: In Newburyport, go north on U.S. Highway 1/ Massachusetts 1A and bear right on Water Street, prior to the Merrimack Bridge. Follow Water Street south, turning left (east) on Sunset/Plum Island Turnpike to enter the refuge on the right. From the entrance station, drive south through the refuge, finding Beach Parking Area 1 in 0.1 mile, Hellcat Swamp Nature Trail in 3.6 miles, the Pines Trail in 4.4 miles, and Parking Area 7 in 6.4 miles. Enter Sandy Point State Reservation south of Parking Area 7. Respect the posted slow speeds, and park only in designated sites.

The hikes: For **Hellcat Swamp Trail**, round the gate following the wide lane north from parking area 4. Pass through a corridor of honeysuckle, wild rose, wild plum, bayberry, Virginia creeper, poison ivy, and poison sumac. Watch your step as a multi-level boardwalk advances the tour.

In 100 yards, the trail forks. The right fork crosses the refuge road for a 0.3-mile boardwalk tour of the dunes (subject to summer closures for nesting birds). Proceed forward for an elevated-boardwalk tour of the freshwater marsh. At 0.1 mile, find **Marsh Loop**, and go left for a clockwise tour.

Loosestrife, sensitive fern, grasses, and cattails grow amid the marsh. Drumlins and treed islands break the flatness of the wetland terrain. Swallows flock over the marsh, while a hawk hunts low to the rushes. At 0.4 miles, a spur heads left to an observation blind.

A wetland woods ushers hikers to the open-air, 3-sided blind. Peering through the viewing slots, locate deer, hawks, gulls, geese, ducks, and other wildlife. Resume the clockwise tour at 0.7 mile, remaining amid wetland trees and shrubs. Close the loop at 0.9 mile, and retrace the initial 0.1 mile to the trailhead.

To extend the tour, hike west from parking area 4 on gravel lane and footpath, reaching a dike beyond the restrooms. Travel atop the dike to a 3-flight observation tower. The platform overlooks the channeled waters of the freshwater marsh and Broad Sound estuary. Watch for geese, gulls, shorebirds, and raptors, with snowy egrets in August. When ready, return to the parking area (0.25 mile).

Just north of parking area 5, the **Pines Trail** journeys west through a stand of runty pitch pine and thick shrub. The site proves a favorite with wintering owls. A loose-sand path explores the habitat. Beach plum and bayberry contribute to the congestion of shrubs. At 0.1 mile find a loop junction; stay left as the path to the right becomes severely pinched and overgrown with poison ivy. End the hike at the wooden barricade at 0.2

PARKER RIVER NATIONAL WILDLIFE REFUGE

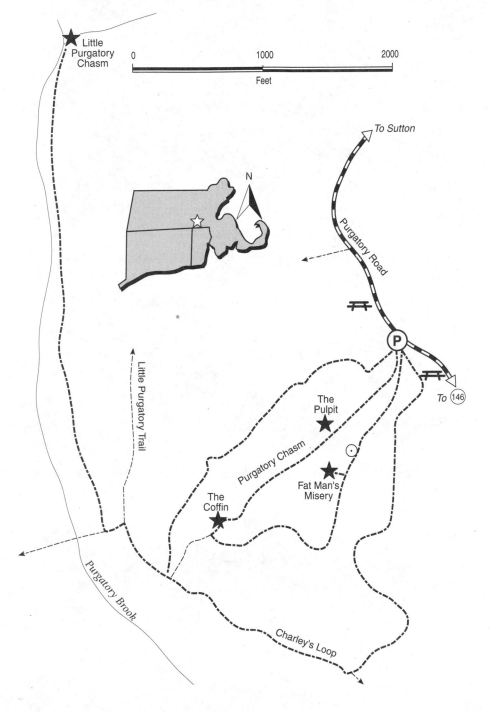

Tidepool rocks, Parker River National Wildlife Refuge, MA.

mile, enjoying a marsh look. Return as you came to the trailhead.

The **Beach Hike** travels 6.5 miles between parking areas 1 broad crystalline-sand beach spreads between the tideline and the ᵕ dunes. On a north-south journey, the natural beach of the refuge quickly replaces the civilized beach of town. A noticeable cant marks the lower beach as the waves break close to shore. When churned by Atlantic storms, find a dazzling show of fury.

Farther south, the tide-washed beach loses its cant for easier strolling, and the waves flatten for a calmer aspect. Boardwalks accessing the parking areas, a breakwater, and Emerson Rocks mark off distance. For the length of the tour, dunes back the beach. Dune grass, false heather, wild rose, and beach plum stabilize the shifting sands. You may be tempted to explore more deeply, but respect this delicate area by traveling only along the board-walk accesses.

Seaweed, buoys, lobster pots, clam shells, and drift logs capture the beach-combers attention, while the rocky tidepools at the south end of the tour draw the curious to their knees. Discoveries include barnacles, seastars, crabs, and snails. In January and February, harbor seals sun on the main beach. Hikers may extend the tour south via the adjoining Sandy Point State Reservation, rounding to a treed point.

29 CRANE MEMORIAL BEACH RESERVATION

OVERVIEW

Once the summer retreat of Chicago industrialist Richard T. Crane, this property of The Trustees of Reservations unites Castle Neck, a white-sand barrier beach backed by spectacular rolling dunes, and Castle Hill, a mansion estate overlooking the natural oceanscape. The Agawam Indians first occupied this area, harvesting fish and shellfish. In 1633, John Winthrop established the first organized settlement here.

General description: Hikes explore Castle Neck, traveling ocean and bay shore and rolling across dunes. Mileage markers and numbered stakes aid hikers.
General location: About 4.5 miles southeast of Ipswich, Massachusetts.
Special attractions: Nesting piping plover and least terns; areas of wild and bathing beach; dunes; salt marsh; stunted forest; cranberry bogs; ocean, bay, and Castle Hill views.
Length: Crane Beach-Essex Bay Hike, 6 miles round-trip; Dunes Loop, 4.1 miles round-trip, with opportunities to shorten.
Elevation: Crane Beach-Essex Bay Hike, 30-foot elevation change; Dunes Loop, 70-foot elevation change.

Birdwatching, Crane Memorial Beach Reservation, MA.

CRANE MEMORIAL BEACH RESERVATION

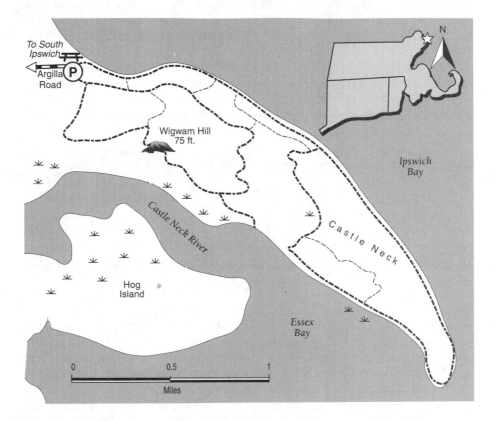

Difficulty: Both, moderate (due to loose sands).

Maps: The Crane Properties map.

Special requirements: Separate admission fees for Crane Beach (Castle Neck) and the Castle Hill site; phone before visiting Castle Hill. No dune play. Although hikers may roam the dunes, keep to the prescribed trails to preserve this special landscape. Rangers regularly patrol the area to police inappropriate behavior. Respect nesting closures, granting the endangered birds a wide safety margin. Beware of poison ivy and Lyme Disease-carrying ticks. Carry water.

Season and hours: Year-round, 8 a.m. to sunset.

For information: The Trustees of Reservations, Northeast Regional Office.

Finding the trailhead: From the junction of Massachusetts 1A and Massachusetts 133 at the South Ipswich village green, go east on Argilla Road for 4.2 miles to enter Crane Beach.

The hikes: For the **Crane Beach-Essex Bay Hike**, cross to the beach on the boardwalk behind the information and first-aid station and turn right (southeast). Dune grass and beach pea anchor the shifting sands, while a broad bathing beach spans the width of the parking area. Most people linger within reach of the bathhouse, leaving hikers a long open-beach invitation.

Low tides unveil an expansive braided beach, stretching well into Ipswich Bay. The cut-off shallow pools and channels isolate bars and islands of rippled sand for an eye-pleasing mosaic. The compressed sands offer easy strolling. High tides present an even-width strand of blinding white sand meeting the brilliant blue ocean. Waves break mildly to shore.

Above the high-tide line, encounter beach closures (April through August), protecting the nests of the piping plover and least tern. Confine strolling to the tide-washed sands.

For the first 0.5 mile, a flat grassy plain grading to dune hills backs the beach. Beyond the 0.5-mile mark, find dune banks abutting the beach, with swallows nesting in the more stable seams. Looks south applaud Cape Ann, over-the-shoulder looks "The Great House" atop Castle Hill.

Drying seaweed and uprooted dune grass scatter the upper edge of the beach. Beginning at 0.9 mile, color-coded trails pass between beach and dunes. Keep to these narrow aisles and pass swiftly to avoid a scolding from the nesting tern colonies.

A gull dropping a clam from 50 feet high, terns bathing in a standing pool, or a piping plover darting across the sand may add to a journey. The dunes variously reveal grass-capped mounds, bald swayback ridges, and turrets of compacted sand. The yellow trail emerging from the dunes at 1.5 miles marks the return from Essex Bay.

Keep to the ocean beach. Near the end of Castle Neck (2.65 miles), the dunes flatten out. Round the broad beach curvature, now overlooking where Castle Neck River meets the mouth of Essex Bay. Gray numbered stakes point the way. Hog Island, a wildlife refuge owned by The Trustees, commands the views, as the bayshore sands easily displace underfoot for a sometimes strenuous workout.

Bypass the first yellow-marked trail entering the dunes at post 10 and continue rounding the pinched bay shore overlooking a tidal marsh with pickleweed and cordgrass. Beach pea dresses the dune. Look for heron and egret amid the marsh. Beyond the marsh, the beach opens up, with low dunes building between the gray stakes and the bay.

At 3.75 miles, turn right on the yellow trail, mounting the dunes for a rolling tour back to the beach. At 3.9 miles, where the yellow spur arrives from post 10, bear left. Low undulations, steep sandy ascents, and beach-bay glimpses highlight the tour. Pockets of aspen, black cherry, beach plum, bayberry, and poison ivy claim the swales; false heather, with its fleeting yellow bloom, mats the slopes. At 4.25 miles, skirt a natural cranberry bog.

At 4.4 miles, where the blue trail continues the journey through the dunes, follow the yellow trail out of the dunes and onto the beach. Turn left on the beach at 4.5 miles, and hike back to the parking area (6 miles).

The **Dunes Loop** leaves the southern end of Crane Beach Parking Area next to a large sign posting the reservation rules. This open tour ties the green and red trails into a counterclockwise loop (backtracking the numbered posts).

Pass through a tree-shaded corridor and turn right at 0.1 mile, following a 4-foot-wide sandy track, edging the forested dunes. False heather spreads between trail and woods.

At 0.6 mile, approach a segment of wooden fence, briefly passing amid an open stand of pitch pine, wild plum, red oak, and birch. In places, shifting sands engulf the lower branches of the pines, and winds cause the aspens to tremble. An open dune follows. Bear right on the red trail (0.8 mile) for the 4-mile loop; the green trail heads left for a shorter tour.

Round a bowl and top Wigwam Hill (elevation 75 feet), for an overlook of Castle Neck, Essex Bay, Hog Island, and the ocean. With a steep descent, find afternoon shade amid some red maple and cherry trees, but beware of poison ivy. More forest and shrub thickets follow as the trail ascends and rolls to the next bay view, overlooking a salt-marsh plain.

Dip bayside finding a junction at 1.5 miles. To the right a 0.7-mile round-trip detour tags the bay shore at the marsh; high tides steal much of the tidal flat. Solitude and fine views of the bay and Hog Island recommend the detour.

Now, resume the counterclockwise loop through Castle Neck Dunes, enjoying a tapestry of open sand, forest, shrub pockets, and beach grass. Deer, red fox, harriers, and the yellow-rumped warblers of fall may grace a tour. In winter, snowy owls have been known to take refuge amid the protected dunes.

At 2.6 miles (post 14), continue straight ahead, still backtracking the red numbers; the red-marked spur to the right accesses the yellow and blue trails and ultimately the beach. The trail next rolls topping a series of dune rises for ocean overlooks. At 3.25 miles, again continue straight as another spur breaks toward the beach.

Green-colored posts now point the way as the trail traverses and rolls up the sides of open sand bowls. At the 3.5-mile fork, bear right, and at 3.7 miles, bypass yet another spur to the beach. Respect closures to protect the nesting birds and the integrity of the dunes themselves, as the loop draws closer to the parking area and recreational beach. Close the loop at 4 miles, reach the parking area, 4.1 miles.

OVERVIEW

A joint-agency open space at the town intersect of Boxford, Andover, and Middleton, Massachusetts offers tranquil woods strolling, wetland ponds, and a historic farmsite. The Bald Hill Reservation encompasses 867-acre Boxford State Forest, the 390-acre J.C. Phillips Wildlife Sanctuary, and nearly 370 acres of the Essex County Greenbelt Association. The site boasts a varied flora, both familiar and rare. Cobbles host hepatica, bloodroot, and columbine; bogs feature rose pogonia and swamp azalea; and the woods seclude yellow wood sorrel, violet, and lady slipper.

General description: Within the reservation's interlocking trail system, multiple round-trip and loop hike options exist; the selected loop unveils the typical discovery. Carry a map to plot travel and negotiate the numbered trail junctions.

General location: 2 miles southwest of Boxford.

Special attractions: Mixed forest, wetland, ponds, historic farmsite, wildflowers, wildlife, fall foliage.

Length: 7.7 miles round-trip, with spur to Bald Hill.

Elevation: Find a 100-foot elevation change.

Difficulty: Easy to moderate.

Maps: Bald Hill Reservation map (generally available at trailhead); Boxford State Forest map.

Special requirements: No hiking off the trail in the wildlife sanctuary between April 1 and July 1. Overnight camping is by special permit only. Look for metal posts or wooden number tags on nearby trees to identify junctions.

Season and hours: Spring through fall; area closes 30 minutes after sunset.

For information: Boxford State Forest; Essex County Greenbelt Association.

Finding the trailhead: From Interstate 95, take exit 52 and follow Topsfield Road west to Boxford (1.2 miles). From the town triangle in Boxford, go west on Main Street for 0.3 mile and turn left (south) on Middleton Road. Find marked parking for Bald Hill Reservation on the right in 1.6 miles. Be alert as the small parking lot adequate for 3 to 5 vehicles is set in from the road amid woods and a neighboring residence.

The hike: Follow the gated dirt fire lane of Bald Hill Road west into J.C. Phillips Wildlife Sanctuary, passing amid hemlock interspersed with oak, pine, and birch; skunk cabbage dots a drainage to the left. Cross a small dam to a shallow pond and marsh, coming to junction 17 at 0.25 mile.

Stay Bald Hill Road as it traverses the reservation east to west. Beyond post 16, find the shrubby outer limits of Crooked Pond, a popular birding site. A 20-foot detour left at 0.4 mile (post 15) provides the only open look at

Club moss, Bald Hill Reservation, MA.

BALD HILL RESERVATION

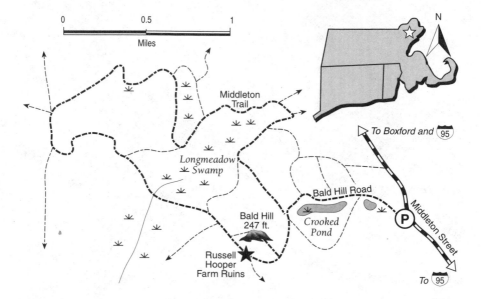

the scenic dark oval, with lily pads and still-water reflections, backed by stately hemlock. Beware of the log fragments' tendency to shift and settle beneath one's weight. Enjoy a marvelous harmony of bird cheeps and frog ribbits.

Later, white pines replace the hemlock, and snags rise near the pond. At an inlet crossing, look for turtles. Remain on Bald Hill Road, bypassing post 14 and bearing left at post 13 (the loop junction). Gently ascend to leave the wildlife sanctuary at post 12 (1.1 miles). Here a 0.2-mile detour to the right tops Bald Hill, a 247-foot drumlin (glacial hill). The grassy summit rimmed by trees is a pleasant retreat but lacks views.

Resume the clockwise loop from post 12 at 1.5 miles; white blazes occasionally mark the tour. Where the trail parallels a rock wall dividing grassy plots (beyond post 11), look for the stone fireplace, chimney, and flooring recalling the old Russell Hooper farmhouse (1.8 miles); sumac and rhododendron grow near the site.

Hike behind the sign identifying the farm to observe the foundation and floor of the old barn (1784 to 1946). From the farmstead, locate the continuation of Bald Hill Road at junction post 10 downhill to the left.

Stay Bald Hill Road, counting down the numbers to post 6 (3.7 miles), for a pleasant rolling woods stroll. More snags pierce the woodland of pine, oak, and maple. At 2.5 miles, cross a dark-spilling brook, its bank sprinkled with wildflowers. At 2.9 miles, skirt a marshy woods. Before long, round past a pair of unsightly rusted-out wrecks, reaching post 6.

Here turn right on a secondary woods road, leaving Bald Hill Road; a rock wall parallels this secondary route. At post 6A (4.1 miles), take a sharp right, resuming the rolling meander, skirting seasonal ponds.

At junction 30 (4.8 miles), opt for either fork; each travels the wooded outskirts of a marsh to meet at post 18. For this description, continue straight (bear right), touring the regimented pine plot of Willis Woods, before turning left at post 31 to reach 18. (Note: For this area, the numbers seen in the field and those on the agency maps may not correspond completely. The numbers cited represent the actual numbers seen along the trail.)

At junction 18, bear right on the woods road of **Middleton Trail** (a left for hikers who chose to go left at junction 30). Shagbark hickory now adds to the woodland. Ahead, skirt the northern extent of Longmeadow Swamp, turn right on a foot trail at post 19, and keep right at posts 20 and 21.

At an unmarked junction at 6.4 miles, stay left on the same path/woods road. At junction 26, bear left to close the loop at post 13 (7 miles). Backtrack Bald Hill Road through the wildlife sanctuary, reaching the trailhead at 7.7 miles.

31 BREAKHEART RESERVATION

OVERVIEW

At this Metropolitan District Commission (MDC) property, outcroppings and rocky topped hills, freshwater lakes, mixed woods, and an interlocking network of trails engage hikers. Long ago, this site drew Native Americans, offering food, shelter, and stone for tools. Colonial settlers worked the land as farms, and at the turn of the century, a private hunting and fishing reserve occupied what is now Breakheart. Lore traces the name to the 1860s, when lonely, brokenhearted Civil War soldiers trained at this then far-off site.

General description: Two short hikes, one traveling along lakes, the other along ridges, present the area offering.
General location: 5 miles northwest of Saugus, Massachusetts.
Special attractions: Boston skyline, Central Massachusetts, and New Hampshire vistas; spring-summer flowering shrubs and flora; fall foliage; fishing; wildlife watching.
Length: Lakes-Eagle Rock Hike, 3 miles round-trip (2.2 miles when summer parking is available at Silver Lake); Ridge Trail-Hemlock Road Loop, 2.7-mile loop.
Elevation: For each, find less than 200 feet of elevation change.
Difficulty: Both, moderate.

Maps: Reservation map.

Special requirements: Keep dogs leashed. Swim only at the designated beach at Pearce Lake.

Season and hours: Year-round, dawn to dusk for walk-in traffic; vehicle access in summer only.

For information: Breakheart Reservation.

Finding the trailhead: From Interstate 95, take exit 44 for U.S. Highway 1 South/Massachusetts 129 West and go south on U.S. 1 for 2.5 miles. Take the Lynn Fells Parkway exit, go 0.3 mile, and turn right on Forest Road. In another 0.3 mile, find year-round parking at the headquarters and summer access to the site's 2-mile one-way Pine Tops Road. Start trails from the headquarters parking lot year-round. In summer, hikers may choose to start the Lakes-Eagle Rock Hike from Silver Lake.

The hikes: For the **Lakes-Eagle Rock Hike**, hike Pine Tops Road counter to traffic, starting left (west) of the headquarters. In 0.4 mile, reach Silver Lake parking; look for a signed blue-blazed trail heading left, north of the parking area entrance. The **Breakheart Hill Trail** leaves the opposite side of Pine Tops Road.

Hike counterclockwise along the wooded north shore of Silver Lake. Initially, find the trail wide with a wood-chip surface, passing amid oaks, sassafras, pine, highbush blueberry, and sweet pepperbush. Rock outcrops open the shoreline allowing access and viewing of this Q-shaped lake, with its tree-and-rock shore and scenic island.

The trail then narrows, and hemlocks appear where it curves left. Unmarked side trails and a grassy road branch off the lake circuit; keep to the shoreline. On the west shore prior to a small dam and spillway bridge, turn right at a green post to descend a wide improved trail to Pearce Lake. Find attractive stonework, small pools, a flume, and a bench; the structures harken back to the private hunting and fishing reserve and the Civilian Conservation Corps camp. Jewelweed, goldenrod, cattail, and joe-pyeweed adorn the small wetland.

Next ascend the steps, cross the bridge, and descend to Pearce Lake shore, or access its shore via an underpass. Turn left for a clockwise tour of this large, claw-shaped water; blue blazes continue to guide hikers. Travel is on a thin, rolling footpath. At 0.3 mile, an outcrop slopes 20 feet to the water. Again enjoy a picturesque rock-and-woods shore and treed islands; reflections, tints of fall, heron, and osprey heighten the beauty.

Along the west shore, pass below scenic cliff outcrops. Upon crossing a footbridge spanning the neck of a small cove, continue straight to resume the shoreline trek; other blue routes branch left. Cross-lake views find the designated swimming area.

At 0.95 mile, a wooden post indicates Eagle Rock to the left; for the lakes tour alone continue straight. A side trip to Eagle Rock follows blue-paint blazes up the outcropping, topping the high point for a 360-degree panorama. Admire Pearce Lake, Castle Hill, the wooded reservation, Boston's

BREAKHEART RESERVATION

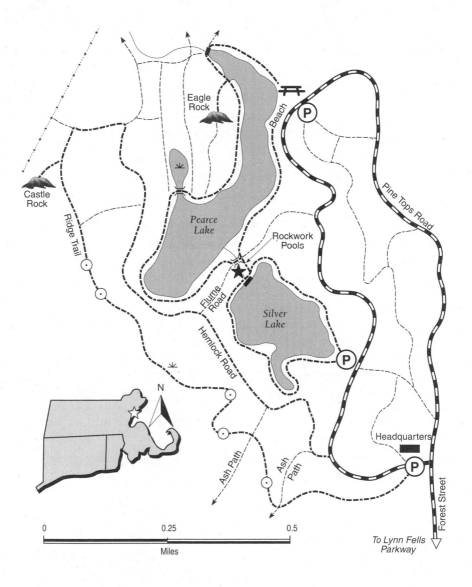

Eagle Rock

Castle Rock

Ridge Trail

Pearce Lake

Rockwork Pools

Beach

Flume Road

Hemlock Road

Silver Lake

Pine Tops Road

Headquarters

Ash Path

Ash Path

Forest Street

To Lynn Fells Parkway

N

0   0.25   0.5

Miles

city skyline, and the surrounding towers, silos, and steeples. Graffiti alone mars the aloof point. Return to Pearce Lake (1.15 miles) and turn left.

Cross the spillway, round the developed beach, and resume the wooded shoreline hike, enjoying cross-lake views of Eagle Rock. At 1.65 miles, parallel a small flume upstream to the underpass and return to Silver Lake. Back at Silver Lake, turn right crossing the dam and spillway. Dogwoods, aspen, sheep laurel, and sweet pepperbush accent the tour. Round the outcrop-narrowed bay arm to conclude the loop at the picnic area 2.2 miles.

For the **Ridge Trail-Hemlock Road Loop**, hike Pine Tops Road west from the headquarters (counter to traffic) and turn left near the start to follow the white-blazed **Ridge Trail**. Pass amid oaks, hophornbeam, maple, hazelnut, fern, and berry bushes for a rolling tour; oaks soon win dominance.

At 0.3 mile, cross **Ash Path** and top an outcrop for views of the Boston skyline, ocean harbors, and woods. Bearberry and circular lichen mottle the ridge outcrop. Descend and again cross Ash Path for the full 2.7-mile tour; turn right on Ash Path to shorten the loop. Ascend and traverse a ridge of low-stature oaks, with open outcrops broadening the previous view.

Next descend, traversing a red maple swamp via boardwalk, only to return to the rocky ridge (0.8 mile). At 1.05 miles, the **Ridge Link Trail** heads right, offering another opportunity to shorten the loop; continue straight ahead.

Ascending to the rocky crest at 1.2 miles, curve right with the white blazes; avoid taking the wide, unmarked trail to the left. At 1.25 miles find a junction post. To the left, faint yellow blazes mark an old road leading to the top Castle Rock and a sweeping overlook. The powerline corridor below the rocky outpost both opens and intrudes on the view.

Resume the loop at 1.35 miles, passing between Castle Rock and another outcrop rise. Descend to a T-junction with a dirt road (**Spruce Path**) and turn right, still pursuing the white blazes. At 1.6 miles, meet and turn right on **Hemlock Road** (a closed paved route, now a pedestrian way) for a pleasant, rolling tree-framed return.

At 1.9 miles, Ridge Link Trail merges on the right as hikers glimpse Pearce Lake. Hemlocks now alternate with the high-canopy hardwoods. At 2.25 miles, Ash Path arrives on the right. Glimpse Silver Lake and pass Ash Path a second time, meeting Pine Tops Road at 2.5 miles. Turn right to close the loop and return to the trailhead at 2.7 miles.

32 WALDEN POND STATE RESERVATION

OVERVIEW

Walden Pond State Reservation and the surrounding town conservation lands protect a growing open space around Walden Pond, where Henry David Thoreau built his one-room cabin and pursued his experiment in simplicity, living and working in nature's society. While the experiment lasted but two years (1845 to 1847), his commitment to wilderness and a philosophy of "nature for nature's sake" outlasted his lifetime, spawning the contemporary conservation movement.

At the cabin site, find a simple mound of hand-placed stones honoring his vision. Daily, visitors make a pilgrimage to the site, adding their own stones and pebbles to this growing primitive memorial. In 1965, Walden Pond won National Historic Landmark distinction.

General description: An easy tour travels the perimeter of Walden Pond and visits the Thoreau cabin site and memorial.
General location: 1.5 miles south of Concord, Massachusetts.
Special attractions: 61-acre Walden Pond, Thoreau cabin site and replica cabin, diverse woods, fall foliage, swimming, fishing, interlocking side trails, bookstore/visitor center.
Length: 1.8-mile loop, including cabin detour.
Elevation: The Pond Path shows a 30-foot elevation change.
Difficulty: Easy.

At Thoreau cabin site, Walden Pond State Reservation, MA.

WALDEN POND STATE RESERVATION

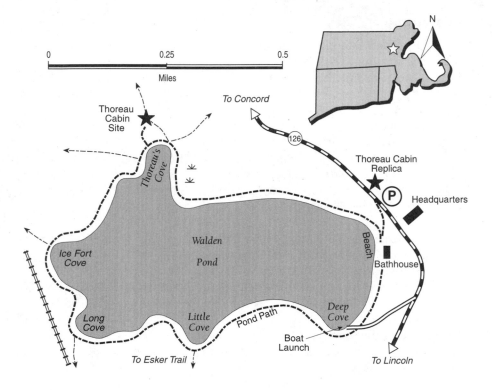

Maps: State reservation map.

Special requirements: Fee area. Note, in summers, parking lots may fill on weekends, and cars parked along the highway will be towed. Keep to trails and designated sites for sitting. No fires, no pets. Carry a map to explore the other area trails; purchase maps or books for the conservation lands at the visitor center. Off-season and daybreak visits better capture the serenity and reverence of the site.

Season and hours: Year-round, 5 a.m. to sunset.

For information: Walden Pond State Reservation.

Finding the trailhead: From Interstate 95/Massachusetts 128, take exit 29B and go west on MA 2 for 4.6 miles. Turn south on MA 126 and go 0.4 mile, finding the entrance on the left. Park and take the crosswalk over MA 126 to Walden Pond.

The hike: Begin a clockwise tour of the **Pond Path** at the bathhouse. For a visit to the cabin site alone, bear right (counterclockwise) for the shortest approach. The spring-fed, clear-water jewel of Walden Pond proves an engaging host.

Clockwise, follow the 4-foot-wide trail, rounding some 20 to 30 feet above shore. The path tours a scenic second-growth woods of white pine, hemlock, birch, oak, maple, and chestnut, with sweet pepperbush, huckleberry, and sweetfern.

In the morning, find nature's society. The mirror-still water reflects the leaf and evergreen shore, bird songs fill the air, and a mist often rises from the pond's surface. A solitary canoe or a family of ducks parting the water completes the image of serenity. Midday May through September, expect a more uproarious greeting as human society descends on the lake.

Round past the undeveloped boat launch at Deep Cove (0.1 mile). At Little Cove (0.45 miles), an unmarked side trail branches left toward the **Esker Trail**. The Pond Path continues contouring the slope above Walden Pond, offering no access until 0.6 mile. The clarity of the water reveals bass, sunfish, and perhaps a passing turtle.

The trail now rounds above Long and Ice Fort coves, touring below an active rail line. Keep toward the pond. At 0.95 mile, stone steps descend to a deep drop-off. Soon after, a couple more designated spurs lead to the water's edge.

Beyond a tiny cattail marsh, at the curve of Thoreau Cove, take the trail to the left at 1.25 miles to reach the cabin site (a sign indicates the turn for counterclockwise travelers). Locate the site and memorial 200 feet up slope.

At this solitary place, find the cabin plot, chimney and woodsite, an enduring quote, and the simple stone memorial. The place exudes an aura of reverence, where visitors speak in whispers. On the slope above the cabin, Thoreau had planted some 400 white pines, felled by hurricane in 1938. Stumps now hint at Thoreau's woods.

Resume the loop, soon rounding above the developed swimming beach. Return to the bathhouse, 1.8 miles. Returning to the parking lot, find a replica of the one-room cabin and a statue of Henry David Thoreau.

33 BROADMOOR WILDLIFE SANCTUARY

OVERVIEW

At this 600-acre sanctuary of the Massachusetts Audubon Society, a fine network of nature trails explores pond, marsh, red maple swamp, field, forest, and the Charles River shore. Within each microenvironment, find signature plant and wildlife discoveries. Seasonal variations enrich the tours.

General description: Three short hikes applaud the site's diversity and tranquillity. Visit pond, marsh, and river; explore a red maple swamp; and top a glacial-deposit hill.
General location: In South Natick and Sherborn, Massachusetts.
Special attractions: Spring, summer, and fall flowering annuals, shrubs, and aquatics; mixed forests; wildlife sightings.
Length: Mill Pond/Marsh-Charles River Hike, 3 miles round-trip; Blueberry Swamp Hike, 2.4 miles round-trip; Indian Brook-Glacial Hill Hike, 3 miles round-trip.
Elevation: All show less than 60 feet of elevation change.
Difficulty: Easy.
Maps: Sanctuary trail map.
Special requirements: Per-person admission fee or Massachusetts Audubon Society membership. Maps for loan or purchase; find intersections numbered,

Interpretive talk, Broadmoor Wildlife Sanctuary, MA.

keyed to the map. Blue blazes travel away from the visitor center; yellow ones return to the center. No dogs, bikes, or picnicking.

Season and hours: Year-round, Tuesday through Sunday and holidays that fall on Monday, but generally spring through fall for hiking. Trails: dawn to dusk. Visitor Center 9 a.m. to 5 p.m. weekdays; 10 a.m. to 5 p.m. weekends and holidays.

For information: Broadmoor Wildlife Sanctuary.

Finding the trailhead: From the center of South Natick, go 1.7 miles west on Massachusetts 16 and turn left (south) to enter the sanctuary. From MA 16 - MA 27 junction at Sherborn, go 1.5 miles east on MA 16 and turn right. Start hikes at the visitor center, descending the gravel lane south into the sanctuary.

The hikes: The **Mill Pond/Marsh-Charles River Hike** tags the numbered junction posts from 1 to 11 in sequence.

Descend from the visitor center, hiking the gravel lane framed by pine, oak, and maple. Poison ivy flourishes, climbing the tree trunks. Keep to the lane until the bridge crossing. Along the marsh, birch and beech join the ranks. Sweet pepperbush, cinnamon fern, and mayflower adorn the tour.

Split-level Broadmoor Bridge has a viewing deck for admiring the marsh of Indian Brook. Areas of open water, pond lilies, arrow arum, duckweed, cattail, and a dense expanse of the pervasive purple loosestrife contribute to an engaging tapestry. Mink, muskrat, frog, heron, and dragonfly cause fingers to point. Departing the bridge, find a scenic tree-shaded outcrop, with azalea scenting the early-summer air.

At post 3 (0.3 mile), continue straight; wood chips and pine needles soften the trail as it rolls along the marsh shore. Dense berry bushes and low maple steal marsh views. Again continue forward at post 4 crossing another bridge. Geese frequent the open water and sometimes the rock outcrops amid the woods. White pond lilies decorate the water in mid-July.

To the sides of the trail at posts 5 and 6, find the sites of a 1700s sawmill and a gristmill; a pair of grinding stones mark where the gristmill stood. Continue straight ahead at each of the junctions. Go left at post 7, and bear right at post 8 to travel a tree-shaded lane, edge a field overlooking the pond, and pass beneath some nice shade maples.

Continue straight at post 9, passing a monument noting the Stillman family's generosity. Soon after, parallel a rock wall to the South Street crossing at post 10.

At 0.95 mile, post 11 marks the loop junction; go left for a clockwise tour amid a complex of pine, oak, and huckleberry. This rolling semi-shaded tour leads to the Charles River (1.5 miles). Enjoy a few open overlooks as the trail continues along the wide, sleepy canoe water. Duckweed colors the edge, while the screech of an osprey draws eyes skyward. Sweet pepperbush, azalea, and tupelo hug the shore.

At 1.9 miles, draw away from the river to bring the loop to a close at post 11 at 2.05 miles. Return as you came, reaching the visitor center at 3 miles.

BROADMOOR WILDLIFE SANCTUARY

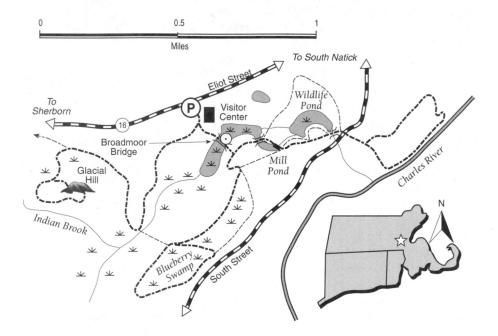

For the **Blueberry Swamp Hike**, retrace the start of the first tour crossing over the main bridge, but turn right at junction post 3 (0.3 mile). Pass through a pine-maple woods with poison ivy, huckleberry, and fern. Wood chips soften the wide trail.

At post 12 (0.4 mile), find a 3-way junction and turn right. At 0.8 mile, reach post 14 and **Blueberry Swamp Loop**. The paths to the left and straight ahead shape the loop; the right fork leads to **Indian Brook and Glacial Hill trails**.

Go left for a clockwise tour of the swamp, traveling a mixed hardwood corridor with sweet pepperbush. Squirrels leap through the treetops. By 0.9 mile, round the red maple swamp; the ground often dries by summer. Highbush blueberry contributes to the vegetation, as does a fickle showing of skunk cabbage. At post 13 bear right, continuing the swamp circuit; **Quacking Frog Trail** heads left.

At 1.15 miles, bear left easing gently up slope away from the swamp. Soon after, bear right as an unmarked trail arrives on the left. At the 1.3-mile junction, near the boundary, keep right; to the left lies a gate. A boardwalk now crosses the swamp for closer looks at the swamp habitat and snags. Travel mixed forest to close the loop at post 14 (1.6 miles), return to the visitor center at 2.4 miles.

For the **Indian Brook-Glacial Hill Hike**, descend the gravel lane turning right at post 2, prior to reaching the bridge. Cross a service road and skirt a field touring on an exposed mowed track. Aspen, oak, maple, and a dense shrub border of honeysuckle, wild grape, sumac, and Virginia creeper add to the tour. Looks left find the maple-lined drainage of Indian Brook. Oak woods then embrace the journey to post 15 and a T-junction (0.65 mile).

Go right for Glacial Hill, ascending a grassy woods road; the incline soon flattens. Oak, hickory, pine, and maple compose the woods, while glimpses over the left shoulder spotlight a snag-filled wetland of Indian Brook. Beaver-raised waters claimed the trees. At 1.2 miles, find an unmarked T-junction and turn left, still traveling a woods road, now rounding a red maple swamp with highbush blueberry.

Post 16 marks the loop; go left for clockwise tour of the donut-shaped glacial-deposit hill. Ascend an oak-maple flank, top the hill at 1.4 miles, and encircle the depression; leafy branches screen out views. With a dip to the center, find vernal pools giving rise to cinnamon ferns and other greenery. The trail then returns to the rim, with yellow blazes guiding the way. Descend, finding overlooks of the swamp, before closing the loop at 1.75 miles. Return to the trailhead at 3 miles.

34 BLUE HILLS RESERVATION

OVERVIEW

At this 7,000-acre open space south of Boston proper, some 125 miles of interlocking trail offer hikers a plethora of tour options. The skyline hills prove natural destinations and centerpieces for loop travel. The selected three hikes hint at the discovery and challenge found at this superb urban wild—a Metropolitan District Commission (MDC) property.

General description: Three day hikes of varying length and difficulty explore key features of the Blue Hills chain.
General location: 10 miles south of downtown Boston.
Special attractions: Vistas, observation towers, historic weather station, diverse forest, rock features, wildlife sightings, fall foliage.
Length: Great Blue Hill-Skyline Loop, 4.5 miles round-trip; Tucker Hill Loop, 2.9 miles round-trip; Chickatawbut Tower Loop, 0.8 mile round-trip.
Elevation: Great Blue Hill-Skyline Loop, 360-foot elevation change; the other two hikes, each show a 140-foot elevation change.
Difficulty: Great Blue Hill-Skyline Loop, strenuous; Tucker Hill Loop, easy; Chickatawbut Tower Loop, moderate.
Maps: Reservation map; purchase at Trailside Museum or from the map

BLUE HILLS RESERVATION

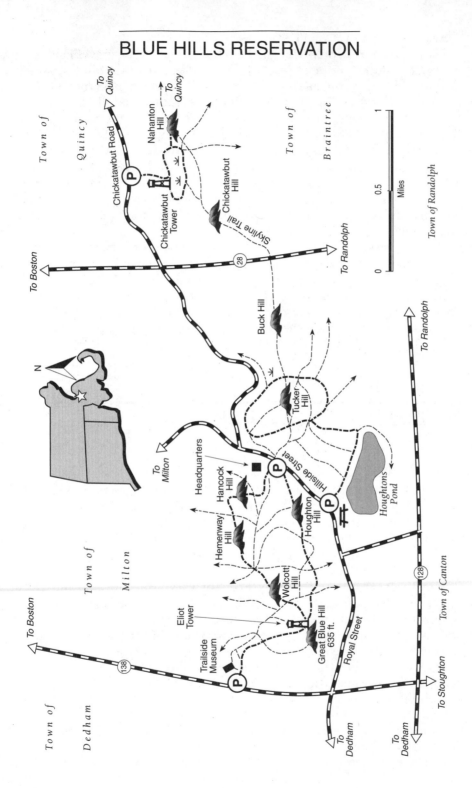

dispenser on the front porch of the headquarters.

Special requirements: Admission fee to Trailside Museum; keep pets on leash. Carry a map to sort out the numbered trail intersections and unnamed trails and to track the progress of the color-blazed trails.

Season and hours: Year-round, spring through fall for hiking. Trails: dawn to 8 p.m.; Trailside Museum: 10 a.m. to 5 p.m. Wednesday through Sunday.

For information: Blue Hills Trailside Museum or Blue Hills Reservation Headquarters.

Finding the trailhead: From Massachusetts 128, take exit 2 and go north on MA 138 for about a mile, finding the signed entrance to the Trailside Museum on the right. For Houghtons Pond parking (Tucker Hill Loop), again proceed north from exit 2 on MA 138, but turn right (east) on Royal Street, and continue 1.2 miles to the entry gate.

For the headquarters and Chickatawbut Tower Loop, continue east on Royal Street, which becomes Hillside Street as it bears north. Look for the headquarters on the left in another 0.25 mile, next to the State Police Offices. For Chickatawbut Tower, continue 0.5 mile past the headquarters, turn right on Chickatawbut Road, and stay on it for about 2 miles, crossing MA 28. Find the trail heading south opposite the turnout for Chickatawbut Overlook.

The hikes: For the **Great Blue Hill-Skyline Loop** start at the Trailside Museum parking lot, south of the museum. Follow the red-dot trail mounting the stairs up the west flank of Great Blue Hill for Eliot Tower and the weather observatory. Great Blue Hill, elevation 635 feet, is the highest point on the Atlantic Coast south of Maine. Mixed deciduous and evergreen clad the slope.

At 0.1 mile, top a granitic outcrop amid small birch, and find seasonal looks at the ski area to the south. Cross over Summit Road (an alternative approach to the peak), ascending amid outcrops and pines. At 0.5 mile, the trail swings right; keep a sharp eye out for blazes.

At a concrete post, turn left to reach the Observation Tower in 100 feet. The attractive stone tower has an open deck, covered breezeway, fireplace, and spiral staircase to its top. Long, rectangular open-air windows offer views in all four directions. Admire the wooded open space, Boston city skyline, Houghtons and Ponkapoag ponds, the castle-like top of the weather observatory, and the bumpy Blue Hills skyline.

Continue rounding Eliot Tower in a clockwise direction. Pass the red **Coon Hollow Trail**, which returns to the museum. Near a stone walkway/ bridge erected in 1904, in honor of landscape architect and key preservationist, Charles Eliot, find the **North Skyline Trail** descending at post 1063. Cross the bridge to reach the **South Skyline Trail** at post 1066, and follow it off the hill for a counterclockwise tour of the **Skyline Loop**. Blue rectangular blazes mark the Skyline Trail.

Find a sharp descent, rocky and wooded. Deer, red fox, or grouse may divert the eye, as may looks east and south across the reservation. At 1 mile, a dirt road arrives on the left; a detour along it leads to a small pond and a

Nahanton Hill view, Blue Hills Reservation, MA.

Wolcott Hill loop. Continue straight following a spring runoff downhill. At 1.3 miles, squeeze through a jumble of big granite boulders. Oak and beech shade the tour as the trail flattens.

Cross a dirt road at 1.5 miles and bypass junction 1123, crossing a log over a small drainage; skunk cabbage dots the woodland. The South Skyline now rolls, crossing over **Houghton Path** to mount Houghton Hill. Top Houghton Hill, a round-topped bump with glacier-planed rock, at 1.8 miles. Branches restrict views, blueberries offer sweet summer tastes.

At junction 1152, bear right following a rocky road uphill, and at junction 1156, again bear right for a steep, rocky downhill pitch to Hillside Road and the State Police Offices (2 miles). For the loop, hike north along the shoulder of Hillside Road, going past the Mounted Police Stables to pick up the **North Skyline Trail** near the Reservation Headquarters; again look for the blue rectangular blazes.

The North Skyline Trail reveals a similar rugged persona, touring pine-oak woods and rocky slopes. It bears north for a steep ascent of Hancock Hill. Although burned in 1987, the succession of young trees already has claimed some of the view. Looks pan seaward and north to Boston.

With an abrupt down and up, top Hemenway Hill for southern views and an admiration of the wooded terrain. Now descend steeply, cross the dirt road of **Wolcott Path**, and begin a rolling, rocky woods ascent of Wolcott Hill. A summit rock outcrop with lone-standing pine provides a fine vantage for viewing Eliot Tower and Great Blue Hill. With another rocky pitch and climb, the North Skyline Trail reaches Eliot Tower (3.7 miles). Bear right to return as you came, or hike **Coon Hollow Trail** downhill to the Trailside Museum (4.4 miles).

For a long-distance **Skyline Hike** (9 miles one-way), instead of taking the Skyline Loop, cross Hillside Road at 2 miles to pick up the Skyline Trail, as it proceeds east across the reservation. It continues much as it did, touring full woods and topping rocky hills. Pitch pine and scrub oak claim the dry hilltops, and the dips and climbs become less sharp. End near St. Moritz Ponds in Quincy.

For **Tucker Hill Loop**, park at Houghtons Pond and hike toward the beach, bearing left (east) to round the pond. Travel a yellow/green-blazed dirt lane, passing behind the bathhouse (0.1 mile). At 0.3 mile, the green **Tucker Hill Trail** continues forward (east), no longer paralleling shore. The surface briefly changes to pavement, as hikers tour a mixed woods interspersed by dogwood. Reach the loop junction at 0.6 mile and go left.

A few spruce enter the mix as the loop crosses over the **Skyline Trail**. American beech suffer the inevitable carving of initials, and Canada mayflowers adorn the woods floor. At 1.25 miles, curve right paralleling above Chickatawbut Road. At 1.4 miles, tour slightly higher up the flank of Tucker Hill. Where the trail follows a narrow wooded lane at 1.5 miles, find the slope of Tucker Hill more pronounced, with big granite boulders at its base.

Ascend steadily, touring a dark hollow woven by some beautiful big trees. At 1.7 miles, cross the Skyline Trail as it descends from Tucker Hill and proceeds east. Soon after, cross the **Massachuseuck Trail**. Then at 1.9 miles, bear right amid a scenic grove of white pines to close the loop at 2.3 miles. Retrace the paved and dirt roads past Houghtons Pond to reach the trailhead at 2.9 miles.

For **Chickatawbut Tower Loop**, ascend the stairs heading south opposite the turnout for Chickatawbut Overlook; yellow dots mark the tour. Reach a stone picnic shelter with the stone observation tower set back from it, at 0.1 mile. When open, the 50-foot tower overlooks the treetops for a fine area panorama. When the tower is closed, take the Nahanton Hill detour for a view.

Go left at the tower for a clockwise loop, but watch closely for the faint yellow blazes as the popularity of the area has introduced a lot of pretenders to the trail. After a short descent, the loop curves right. Here detour left, ascending the rock stairs to the summit of Nahanton Hill (0.3 mile). The summit's low, rounded northern outcrops offer a grand view of Boston, its harbor and harbor islands, and a distant New Hampshire peak rising above the haze.

Return to the loop at 0.4 mile, and resume the clockwise tour, going right at junctions. Pass between a couple of granite knobs and skirt a wetland woods, before closing the loop at the tower at 0.7 mile. Descend to the trailhead at 0.8 mile.

35 PONKAPOAG POND TRAIL

General description: This trail encircles a large pond south of the Blue Hills chain and offers a close-up look at a bog.

General location: Blue Hills Metropolitan District Commission Reservation, 10 miles south of Boston, Massachusetts.

Special attractions: Scenic open-water pond and enfolding bog, rare Atlantic white cedars, bog boardwalk, spring and summer wildflowers, carnivorous plants, wildlife.

Length: 4 miles round-trip.

Elevation: Find an 80-foot elevation change.

Difficulty: Easy to moderate.

Maps: Blue Hills Reservation map; purchase at the Trailside Museum (1 mile north of Massachusetts 128 at exit 2) or from the headquarters at 695 Hillside Street (take exit 3 off MA 128 and go north for Houghtons Pond; find the headquarters west off Hillside Street, 0.25 mile north of Houghtons Pond).

Special requirements: Keep pets leashed. Carry insect repellent, and be respectful of the sensitive bog habitat.

Season and hours: Year-round, generally spring through fall for hiking. Dawn to 8 p.m.

For information: Blue Hills Trailside Museum or Blue Hills Reservation Headquarters.

Ponkapoag Boardwalk, Blue Hills Reservation, MA.

PONKAPOAG POND TRAIL

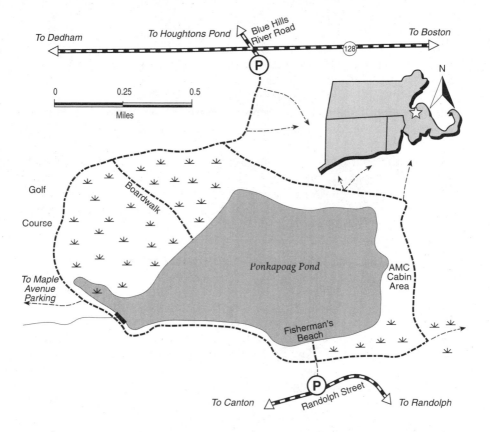

Finding the trailhead: Locate the trail on the south side of MA 128 at exit 3. Start at the gated road heading south off the exit ramp at Blue Hills River Road. Find parking for 4 vehicles; do not block gate. Alternatively, park at the west or south lots at Houghtons Pond (north of MA 128), and hike south on Blue Hills River Road to the trailhead.

The hike: For this green-dot tour, hike south uphill on the closed dirt road, passing amid pine-oak woods with some big trees. Canada mayflower dresses the floor in early spring. At 0.25 mile, reach the loop junction (intersection 5241), and bear right for a counterclockwise tour.

Soon tag the loop high point, isolated by woods, and descend to lake level. At junction 5176 near a YMCA camp, a detour left leads to the cedar bog; the path straight ahead continues the loop.

For the detour, pass through a small open area and bear left to reach a stone marker and signboard for the bog trail (0.6 mile). Lots of blue butterflies flit about in early May. Built originally in 1947, the **Ponkapoag Board-walk** traverses a National Environmental Study Area—a unique spongy land-scape, in between a solid and a liquid. Sphagnum moss, carnivorous plants, Atlantic white cedar, leatherleaf, cranberry, and highbush blueberry con-tribute to the bog anatomy. Blue-flag iris and sheep laurel add floral accents.

Chained end-to-end, the 15-inch-wide planks offer a narrow walkway across the bog. Beneath the planks, spy the original corduroy boardwalk. Walk gingerly and limit one hiker per plank, as the walkway gives with the liquid-land; sometimes the coffee-steeped water laps over the edge. In a few areas, find paired planks for convenient passing. Amid the open sphagnum bog, geese rear their young; sunlight glints off the open-water channels. At the end of the boardwalk, find the first open view of Ponkapoag Pond.

Retrace the boardwalk and resume the pond tour at 1 mile, bearing left. Soon round a gate to travel the woodland buffer to Ponkapoag Golf Course; the bog commands views to the left. Flickers, blue jays, robins, mourning doves, Canada geese, and red-winged blackbirds enliven the tour. At 1.6 miles, round a second gate, leaving behind the golf course to find the Maple Avenue entry on the right.

The woods-and-bog tour continues with occasional gaps in the vegetation affording open looks at Ponkapoag Pond. Cross a small spillway framed by birch, and travel the woods below a residential area. Violet, trout-lily, jack-in-the-pulpit, marsh marigold, and buttercup sprinkle springtime color.

At 2.3 miles, find the Randolph Street access and a spur to Fisherman's Beach, a 100-foot-long beach, offering a view of Great Blue Hill. The pond circuit continues now following a dirt road through a more varied wood-land.

At 2.8 miles, curve left, continuing to round the pond. At 3 miles skirt the overnight cabins of the Appalachian Mountain Club (AMC), available by reservation only. Descend away from the cabins, pass through the AMC parking lot, and follow the orange and green blazes west, again on foot trail.

Cross a small brook at 3.4 miles and stay with the green blazes, continu-ing west along a rise to close the loop at 3.75 miles. Return to the trailhead at 4 miles.

36 BORDERLAND STATE PARK

OVERVIEW

Managed from the start for wildlife and nature appreciation, the 1906 estate of botanist Oakes Ames and his artist wife Blanche offers present-day travelers a fine natural arena to explore. Within its 1,772 acres, find ponds, a cedar swamp, field, woods, and rocky hills, as well as a superb system of short trails, suggesting a variety of tours.

General description: Two hikes incorporate many of the trails, applauding the area's varied habitats and overall relaxation. One features the ponds, the other the wooded rocky hills.
General location: 5 miles south of Sharon, Massachusetts.
Special attractions: Stone mansion; old quarry; scenic ponds; spring flowering trees, shrubs, and wildflowers; Atlantic white cedar swamp; wildlife watching; fishing; fall foliage.
Length: Leach Ponds Loop, 4-mile loop (3.5 miles for the shorter loop); Northern Trails Hike, 7.4 miles round-trip.
Elevation: Leach Ponds Loop, 30-foot elevation change; Northern Trails Hike, 100-foot elevation change.
Difficulty: Leach Ponds Loop, easy. Northern Trails Hike, moderate.
Maps: State park map.
Special requirements: Fee area. Mansion shown via guided tour.
Season and hours: Year-round, 8 a.m. to sunset.
For information: Borderland State Park.
Finding the trailhead: From Interstate 495, take exit 10 and go east on Massachusetts 123 for 3.4 miles. There turn left on Poquanticut Avenue, following signs for the park. Go 1.3 miles and turn left on Massapoag Avenue to reach the entrance on the right in another 2 miles. Start Leach Ponds Hike at the lower parking lot near the mansion or at the visitor center parking lot (follow signs for pond and lodge); start the Northern Trails Hike at the visitor center.

The hikes: Starting the **Leach Ponds Loop** at the lower parking lot, hike the wide surfaced path past a small information station to cross the groomed lawn stretching before the 1910 English-style stone mansion, an ivy-clad square fortress, with rooftop bell. The site's formal landscaping shows a circular hedge with fountains.

At the T-junction (0.1 mile), a right leads to the mansion; go left for Leach Pond. A second junction quickly follows. Here a left leads to the visitor center and **West Side Trail**; a right leads to the pond, lodge, and all other trails. Go right.

Tour a closed gravel road amid hardwood forest, going left at the fork. Either prong reaches the single-room stone lodge that overlooks picturesque

BORDERLAND STATE PARK

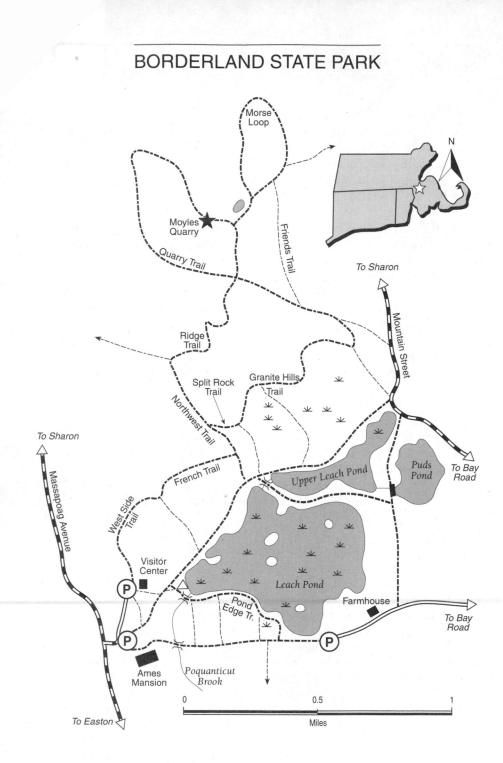

Morse Loop

Moyles Quarry

Quarry Trail

Friends Trail

N

To Sharon

Mountain Street

Ridge Trail

Split Rock Trail

Granite Hills Trail

Northwest Trail

French Trail

Upper Leach Pond

Puds Pond

To Bay Road

To Sharon

Massapoag Avenue

West Side Trail

Visitor Center

P

Leach Pond

Farmhouse

To Bay Road

Pond Edge Tr.

P

P

Ames Mansion

Poquanticut Brook

To Easton

| 0 | 0.5 | 1 |

Miles

Leach Pond at 0.25 mile. Swallows roost in the eaves of the building. White pine, birch, and red maple shade the shore of sizable Leach Pond, while white pond lilies accent a mosaic of red and green pads atop the shallow water. Frog, heron, and sunfish animate the stage. For the loop, go left on the carriage road, returning via the **Pond Edge Trail** to the right.

The carriage road extends a relaxing tour, with spurs to pondside benches. Many of the named trails branch left from this key travel artery. Pass a small side pond, touring a branch-overlaced corridor, with accents of dogwood; glacial erratics scatter the woods. Along the shore azalea, sweet pepperbush, sheep laurel, and highbush blueberry spread floral cheer. Created in 1825, Leach Pond allowed then-owner, Colonel Leach, to manipulate the water level in the cedar swamp downstream on Poquanticut Brook.

Past the junction with the **Northwest Trail**, find a pond loop option (1 mile). The path to the right travels the beltway between Leach Pond and Upper Leach Pond for a 3.5-mile tour, while the carriage road straight ahead travels the perimeter of both ponds for the full 4-mile tour. Both offer looks at Upper Leach Pond. Go forward for the longer tour.

Upper Leach Pond, the smaller of the two, shows more open water with an attractive rim of birch. Pass the left-bound spurs to **Granite Hills Trail**, still enjoying a mixed forest and occasional pond glimpses. Where the carriage road meets Mountain Street (a public road) at 1.7 miles, turn right. The hike then resumes on the right in 200 feet.

Follow a grassy 2-track south amid woods, skirting Puds Pond to the east. Keep to the doubletrack. A small dam extends the first (and last) open view of Puds Pond, showing minimal aquatic vegetation, with a private residence across the way; no swimming. At 2.25 miles, the spur from the shorter loop arrives on the right to share the remainder of the tour.

Continue south edging a field decorated in daisy and clover to meet a dirt park road (accessed off Bay Road), near the park's white farmhouse. Turn right; mature sugar maples now usher hikers to a gate (2.8 miles) for the return leg of the hike. Round the gate to once more admire Leach Pond.

At 3 miles, locate **Pond Edge Trail** to the right. It offers a pleasing 0.75-mile shoreline stroll back to the lodge. The carriage road offers an easier stroll and thus faster return to the mansion area (4 miles). Both returns offer glimpses of the Atlantic white cedar swamp and Poquanticut Brook. Side trails branch between the two return trails.

For the **Northern Trails Hike**, the second hike, start at the west side of the visitor center, following the marked **West Side Trail**. Beyond the small manicured lawn, travel a carriage-width path through beech-oak woods with sassafras, witch hazel, and huckleberry. At 0.2 mile bear right, keeping to the West Side Trail. Maples crowd the moister pockets as plank boardwalks span the wet reaches.

At 0.5 mile, go left on the **French Trail** to explore the northern park. This rock-studded foot trail passes amid multi-ton boulders. Ahead, a spur tops an outcrop, while the French Trail rounds the rock's base. Sun penetrates the woods. Generally the trails go unblazed, but a few markers guide hikers amid the outcrop areas. At 0.9 mile, go left on the cartpath of the **Northwest Trail**, passing beneath a fuller umbrella of leaves.

Pass **Split Rock Trail** on the right (the loop's return) and a nearly hidden pond on the left. At 1.5 miles, turn right on the **Ridge Trail**, an undulating footpath weaving amid low-growing oaks and open rocks. Upon topping the ridge, encounter a few false paths worn into place by mountain bikers; most digressions are brief, soon merging with the prescribed trail.

At 2.2 miles, reach a multiple junction: The left and middle forks shape the **Quarry Trail** loop; the right fork continues the Ridge Trail. Go left for a clockwise tour of the Quarry Trail, traveling a scenic narrow footpath through rich mixed woods, with a moister understory. Keep right at junctions. At 3.1 miles, reach Moyles Quarry on the right. A sign marks the tree-filled gap that provided stone for a viaduct on the Boston and Providence Railroad in the early 1800s. At a map post at 3.2 miles, turn left for **Morse Loop**.

Pass through a gap in a rock wall and skirt a small pond on the left, coming to the loop junction. Clockwise, walk amid young pines, full oaks, and a hemlock grove. Keep to the main trail as side spurs branch to area streets or dead-end. At 3.9 miles, continue straight, and in another 200 feet bear right, forgoing the **Friends Trail**. Upon closing the loop, turn left, return to the Quarry Trail, and again go left.

Where hikers return to the Ridge Trail (4.4 miles), resume left. At 5 miles, pass the southern end of the Friends Trail, arc around a room-sized boulder, and turn right to reach the **Granite Hills Trail** at its upper loop. Go right, touring mixed woods and outcroppings, passing the junction for the upper and lower Granite Hills loops. Soon after a pair of footbridge crossings, turn right on **Split-Rock Trail** (6 miles).

Skirt a split boulder cracked like an egg and the trail's acclaimed Split Rock, incorporated into a rock wall. The fissure of the latter measures several feet wide. Follow the rock wall to close the loop at **Northwest Trail** (6.3 miles). Go left, backtracking the Northwest, French and West Side Trails to the visitor center (7.4 miles).

37 CARATUNK WILDLIFE REFUGE

OVERVIEW

This 200-acre refuge of the Audubon Society of Rhode Island actually lies in Massachusetts. The tranquil property provides a wildlife oasis amid a growing residential area. Field, woodland, and transitioning shrub habitat vary travel. Grouse, oriole, kingbird, bluebird, cardinal, meadowlark, various flycatchers and warblers, and the site's signature woodcock engage bird watcher and casual naturalist.

General description: Three short color-coded nature strolls explore the refuge.
General location: In Seekonk, Massachusetts.
Special attractions: Bird and wildlife watching; mixed woods; wildflower fields; carnivorous plants; pond, bog, and brook.
Length: Red Trail, 0.5-mile loop; Yellow Trail, 1.6 miles round-trip; Blue Trail, 3 miles round-trip including side spurs.
Elevation: Trails show a modest elevation change.
Difficulty: Red Trail, easy; the other two, easy to moderate.
Maps: Refuge trail map.
Special requirements: Per-person admission fee or membership in the Audubon Society of Rhode Island; obey posted rules. No pets. Beware of poison ivy.
Season and hours: Year-round, spring through fall for hiking. Trails: dawn to dusk; visitor center/office: 10 a.m. to 4 p.m. daily, except Fridays and Mondays.
For information: Caratunk Wildlife Refuge.
Finding the trailhead: At the Massachusetts-Rhode Island border, take exit 1 off Interstate 195 and go north on Massachusetts 114A/Rhode Island 114 for 3 miles. At the intersection of RI 114 (Pawtucket Avenue) and Newman Avenue in East Providence, go right on Newman Avenue/MA 152 for 2.2 miles. Turn right on Brown Avenue at the sign for Ledgemont Country Club. In 0.7 mile, turn right to enter the refuge.

The hikes: All trails start behind the visitor center barn. Follow the mowed track beyond the butterfly garden across an open field to pass between a pair of cedar snags at the field's far end. Queen Anne's lace, black-eyed Susan, clover, grasses, and poison ivy grow amid the field. Occupants of the refuge's many birdhouses, resident rabbits, and woodchucks may suggest raising the binoculars.

At 0.1 mile, reach the tour junction. The yellow and blue trails follow the mowed track to the left, while the red trail pursues the one heading right. All routes are well-blazed.

For a clockwise tour of the **Red Trail**, go right, touring a shrub corridor and young forest alongside a beautiful high stone wall masked by Virginia creeper, poison ivy, wild grape, and honeysuckle. Next curve into a fuller, maple-rich woods.

The red tour requires three brook-crossings; find footbridges for each. Skunk cabbage, sweet pepperbush, and fern dress the drainages. After the second bridge enter an open flat of big pines and travel a wetland levee to the third crossing. Emerge at an open field and bear left, keeping both the field and the visitor center barn to your right. Return to the center near the owl enclosure and kiosk, at 0.5 mile.

For the **Yellow Trail**, a rockier tour, go left at 0.1 mile, following the dual-blazed yellow and blue route, passing along a vine entangled stone wall. At 0.2 mile, turn right; the blue trail continues straight ahead. Travel a dense shrub corridor interspersed with a few big willows to enter a tight woods composed of small maples. At the 3-way junction (0.3 mile), the central and right fork shape the yellow loop, while a spur heads left to the blue trail.

Continue straight for a clockwise tour, passing through a shrubby complex of oak and hickory, briefly merging with the blue trail. In a few feet, a white spur branches to the woodcock platform; stay straight for the yellow loop, now touring fuller woods. Where the white spur returns, turn right to travel downstream along Coles Brook, its current at times barely detectable. Gradually, the trail draws closer to the brook.

At 0.7 mile, a connector to the blue trail crosses a footbridge; stay straight for the yellow tour, coming to a junction near some eye-catching boulders. Stay left for the outer loop. At 0.9 mile, find Monument Rock, a large wedge-shaped slab braced against a tree, and turn right.

Sweet pepperbush perfumes the air in spring, witch hazel in fall. Continue forward at the next trail intersection to reach a T-junction (1.1 miles). Turn right. Soon after, a cutoff trail merges on the right. Briefly, a steamy meadow-and-shrub transition area interrupts the woods. Close the loop at 1.3 miles, return to the barn at 1.6 miles.

The **Blue Trail** shares the first 0.2-mile of the yellow trail description. It then continues straight, edging the wildflower field. At 0.25 mile, where the blue trail enters the shrub corridor to the right, opt instead to proceed forward on the white trail rounding Muskrat Pond. Where the mowed track forks in a few feet, bear right, traveling an open cathedral-like aisle enfolded by sumac, wild grape, and honeysuckle. Snare rare glimpses of the pond to the right.

At 0.4 mile, reach a dock for an open view of Muskrat Pond and the resident ducks, fish, bullfrogs, and perhaps a mink. The sundew, a carnivorous plant, finds suitable growing conditions near the pond. Round the pond and overlook a cattail edge, before meeting and following the blue trail left.

Soon after the yellow trail merges on the right, find a second white trail; this one leads to the woodcock viewing platform. Follow it left off the blue trail, touring an aspen-shrub habitat to reach the wooden platform over-

CARATUNK WILDLIFE REFUGE

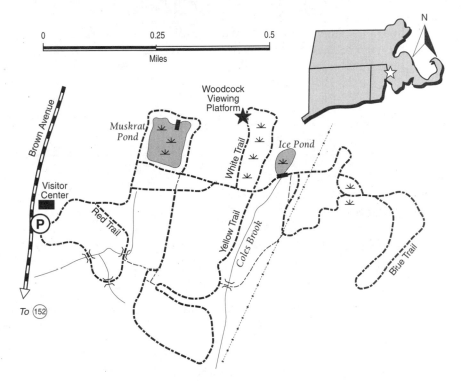

looking a low shrubby hill. Look for swallows, woodchuck, grouse, and woodcock. From the platform, swing right touring a wetland woods and shrub-transition habitat, returning to the blue trail at 1 mile, just as the blue and yellow trails part company. Go left.

Cross a small dam on the Ice Pond drainage, avoiding a blue cutoff spur on the right to continue the blue tour. Next find a moderate ascent through exposed habitat. Cross under the utility wires and over a 2-track (the loop junction), drawing deep into a hardwood forest, following a rock wall.

At 1.35 miles, go left to explore the remoter reaches of the refuge. Here boardwalk segments skirt a bog. Sphagnum moss, azalea, sweet pepperbush, highbush blueberry, beech, birch, and red maple weave a rich fabric.

Keep left to reach the **Hemlock Loop** at 1.5 miles; this meandering circuit explores a mature hemlock grove sandwiched between hardwood stands. Close the Hemlock Loop, and at 2 miles, either go right, retracing your steps to the core blue loop, or turn left continuing to skirt the bog, touring a wetland forest via boardwalk and trail. With either choice, bear left upon meeting the blue thoroughfare.

Travel hardwood forest and again enter the utility corridor, going right on a 2-track. At 2.5 miles, close the loop where the foot trail first crossed the utility corridor. Turn left aiming for a gap in the shrubs to return to the visitor center.

For the return, keep to the blue trail, forgoing all side-trips. A gap in the tree border offers a farewell look at Muskrat Pond. Reach the barn at 3 miles.

38 CAPE COD CANAL

OVERVIEW

The building of this canal eliminated 135 miles of open-ocean navigation around the isthmus of Cape Cod, and in doing so opened up a fine recreation corridor for bicycle rides, family strolls, exercise walks, fishing, and nature study. Scenic paved lanes travel both banks of the canal, with nearby hiker trails visiting a Native American council grounds, a World War II fortification, and the canal's past.

Miles Standish first proposed the canal in 1623. In 1772, George Washington ordered a construction survey, but not until 1918 did Cape Cod Canal become a reality.

General description: Parallel bike-and-pedestrian ways travel the canal's north and south shores much of the way between Cape Cod Bay and Buzzards Bay. On the north shore, find Bournedale Interpretive Trail and Sagamore Hill Trail, two short trails that introduce the area history.
General location: At the neck of Cape Cod, Massachusetts.
Special attractions: Fishing, bird watching, historical sites, spring flowers, azalea, multiple accesses (some with comfort stations).
Length: Northern Bike-and-Pedestrian Way, 7 miles one-way; Southern Bike-and-Pedestrian Way, 6.5 miles one-way; Bournedale Interpretive Trail, 0.8-mile loop; Sagamore Hill Trail, 0.7-mile round-trip.
Elevation: Bike-and-Pedestrian Ways, flat; Bournedale Interpretive Trail, 20-foot elevation change; Sagamore Hill Trail, 50-foot elevation change.
Difficulty: All easy.
Maps: Cape Cod Canal Recreational Guide.
Special requirements: Scusset Beach State Reservation at the east end of the northern pathway and the site of the Sagamore Hill Trail charges a seasonal entrance fee. Be mindful of poison ivy and beware of slippery canal riprap. Keep pets leashed.
Season and hours: Year-round, recreation areas: 9 a.m. to dusk; Field Office: 9 a.m. to 4 p.m. weekdays.

CAPE COD CANAL

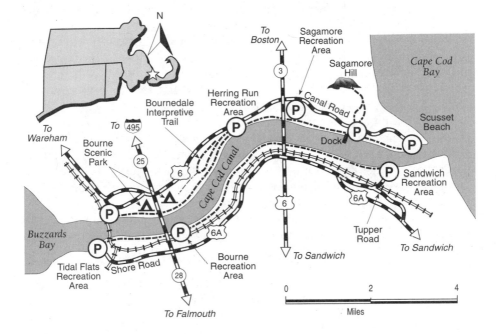

For information: U.S. Army Corps of Engineers, Cape Cod Canal Field Office.

Finding the trailhead: In the Bourne-Sagamore area, find the canal bounded by U.S. Highway 6/Canal Road to the north, U.S. Highway 6A/Sandwich Road to the south.

From east to west, access the Northern Bike-and-Pedestrian Way at Scusset Beach State Reservation, at Sagamore and Herring Run recreation areas, and at Buzzards Bay below Railroad Bridge. Locate the field office at Buzzards Bay off Academy Drive. Find the Bournedale Interpretive Trail heading west from Herring Run Recreation Area; the Sagamore Hill Trail heads north within Scusset Beach State Reservation.

From east to west, reach the Southern Bike-and-Pedestrian Way at Sandwich Marina, Bourne, and Tidal Flats recreation areas.

The hikes: The **Northern and Southern Bike-and-Pedestrian Ways** extend similar linear tours overlooking the long straightaways and gentle curvature of Cape Cod Canal. The eastern extreme of the southern pathway has a strong industrial flavor with a power plant, tanks, and the close proximity of a parallel rail line. The elongated campground at Bourne Scenic Park abuts a half-mile stretch of the northern bikeway.

For the most part though, wooded buffers and an abrupt slope isolate the canal trails from the residential and town areas. Find the northern pathway more open, for continuous canal and cross-canal views. An intermittent thick tree-and-shrub border along the southern pathway affords more shade. The enfolding terrain gradually rises east to west.

Three attractive bridges span the corridor contributing to views and serving as benchmarks: from east to west find Sagamore Bridge, Bourne Bridge, and the vertical-lift rail bridge. Find the channel lights numbered. To track progress, multiply the number on the light by 100 feet to determine the distance from/to the canal's east entrance.

Steep riprap banks dip to the tide-influenced canal water; saltwater fisherman often occupy the rocks. Seaweed and algae color the submerged rocks, while mussels, barnacles, snails, and starfish cling to the water-lapped jumble. Gulls, herons, and cormorants pass along the canal, as yellow warblers and jays pulse between the hillside shrubs. Find benches for reflecting, feeling the breeze, and admiring the amiable canal host.

On the canal's north shore, find **Bournedale Interpretive Trail** at the west end of Herring Run Recreation Area (located west of Sagamore Bridge off U.S. 6). Descend the stairway and turn right. Just beyond a thin drainage, locate the sign for the self-guided loop.

Ascend the steps and bear west, traveling a foot trail contouring the wooded slope between the bikeway and MA 6. Pine, oak, red cedar, cherry, sumac, azalea, milkweed, greenbrier, and sweetfern cloak the slope and enrich the tour. At 0.2 mile, reach the loop.

Bear left, enjoying frequent canal views before returning to the woods and shrubs. Overlook the bikeway, the canal, and the boats moving through the channel. Plaques describe the canal's reconstruction in 1937 and the original digging from 1911 to 1914.

At 0.4 mile, find a 3-way junction. Here the loop swings right, returning along a higher contour; the **Bournedale Hill Trail** continues west along the wooded slope, reaching a gate at Bourne Scenic Park in another mile. Stairs descend to the bikeway for an alternative loop return. Keep to the interpretive trail loop.

Oak, pine, maple, and beech shield the trail from the roadway as more interpretive plaques mark the tour. One identifies a glacial erratic (a boulder surfed here on a sheet of ice, thousands of years ago). Return to the trailhead, 0.8 mile.

East of the small rotary at the entrance to Scusset Beach State Reservation, look for the unmarked **Sagamore Hill Trail**, as it heads north at a gate opposite the parking lot for the fishing pier and a bait and snack shop. Park at the lot and cross the park road for the trail.

Round the gate, following the mowed fire lane north. Signs explain the cultural significance of the site as an Indian Council Ground and World War II artillery encampment. A congestion of shrubs and small trees frame the corridor; plaques identify fox grape, greenbrier, and tupelo.

At 0.25 mile, an overgrown path to the right offers an uneventful, wooded return for a loop. Proceed forward across a clearing, which records the encampment site of the 241st Coastal Artillery Battery C. Now keep to the main groomed trail as it bears left and up the hill to find a ready room and a Panama gun mount. Recessed in the slope, the ready room has a steel arched entry. If you duck inside, beware of the downward hanging bolts.

From here, stairs ascend to the bald summit of Sagamore Hill (0.35 mile), where the Wampanoag and other local tribes came together for discussion. Views pan east to Cape Cod Bay; interpretive panels mark the summit. Return as you came.

39 WELLFLEET BAY WILDLIFE SANCTUARY

OVERVIEW

On the forearm of Cape Cod, this 1,000-acre sanctuary of the Massachusetts Audubon Society (MAS) occupies a prized location on Wellfleet Bay and Harbor. In 1928, the land supported the private Austin Ornithological Research Station. Today, the sanctuary owes much of its diversification to Dr. Austin's efforts to sculpt the land and promote vegetation that would attract birds. Saltmarsh, spring-fed waters, upland pine-oak woods, field, and edge communities compose the sanctuary's vital jigsaw puzzle.

General description: Interlocking loops explore the property, with three hikes incorporating much of the trail system.
General location: Cape Cod at South Wellfleet.
Special attractions: Bird watching, an observation blind, a saltmarsh boardwalk, spring flowering shrubs.
Length: Silver Spring Trail, 0.6-mile loop; Goose Pond-Try Island Hike, 2 miles round-trip; Bay View-Fresh Brook Hike, 1.6 miles round-trip.
Elevation: Trails show a maximum 30-foot elevation change.
Difficulty: All, easy.
Maps: Sanctuary map. Purchase guide for Goose Pond Trail at the nature center.
Special requirements: Per-person admission fee or MAS membership. Obey posted rules; no pets. Beware of poison ivy. As high tides can claim the boardwalk and access to Try Island (note the name), heed tides and allow sufficient time for travel to and from the sites.
Season and hours: Year-round. Trails: 8 a.m. to dusk, daily. Nature Center: 8:30 a.m. to 5 p.m., Tuesday through Sunday (daily, Memorial Day through Columbus Day).
For information: Wellfleet Bay Wildlife Sanctuary.
Finding the trailhead: In South Wellfleet, just north of the Eastham town line, turn west off U.S. Highway 6, entering the wildlife sanctuary. Look for

WELLFLEET BAY WILDLIFE SANCTUARY

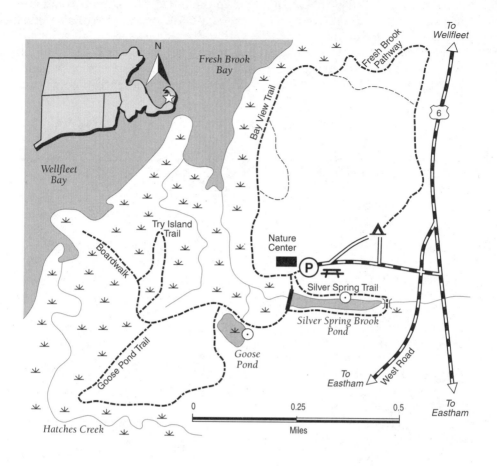

the blue and white MAS sign.

The hikes: All trails start near the nature center.

The **Silver Spring Trail** encircles Silver Spring Brook where a small dam broadens the channel. Head south away from the nature center on a wood-shavings path, bearing left; a sign indicates "Silver Spring."

Pitch pine and deciduous shrubs line the path leading to a bench over-looking the dark, silty pool on Silver Spring Brook. Red-winged blackbirds enliven the air. Red maple, highbush blueberry, sheep laurel, sweet pepperbush, and winterberry grow along the pond. Painted turtles rest on the logs, and pond lilies decorate the surface in summer.

Circle the pond in a clockwise direction. A small dock provides up and downstream views. In places thick splotches of algae claim the water's edge.

Reach the south shore via a footbridge for a tour along the low pine-clad ridge. Pine needles soften the trail, while a woodpecker telegraphs his location.

At 0.5 mile, meet and bear right on the **Goose Pond Trail**, crossing over the earthen dam. A cattail marsh and salt meadow capture the spill water; looks span to the bay. At post G/3, where the **Bay View Trail** heads left, proceed ahead on the Goose Pond/Silver Spring Trail, reaching the center, 0.6 mile.

The **Goose Pond-Try Island Hike** explores the southern sanctuary. Hike south on the wood-shavings path, bearing right at the information board. Be alert as the numbered attractions occur in rapid-fire succession. Pass the **Bay View Trail** on the right, cross the earthen dam to Silver Spring Brook, and keep south, avoiding the **Silver Spring Trail** on the left.

A broad pine-needled trail continues the tour. As it swings right, overlook Goose Pond to the left, the matted marsh meadow of Silver Spring Brook to the right. Phragmites (plumed reeds) and cattails edge and protrude into the water. Look for a secluded birding blind on the pond's left shore.

Cross the outlet via boardwalk, reaching a vista seat. At 0.25 mile, go right (counterclockwise) to pursue the numbers in sequence. An observation deck adds views of wooded Try Island and the bay. Travel a transition habitat, reaching the open estuary and a junction at 0.4 mile; amid the red cedars to the left find Marsh Cabin.

When tides allow, turn right to add tours of **Try Island Trail** and the **boardwalk**; bear left for the Goose Pond Trail alone. Opting for the island-boardwalk detour, find the first access to Try Island Trail on the right just past the junction; locate the second approach on the right at the start of the boardwalk. Bypass both to hike the boardwalk.

Fish riffle the channels, while birds and deer leave tracks in the soft earth. The boardwalk allows for close scrutiny of the estuary and its workings. Fiddler crabs poke out from holes or threaten one another with their single oversized claw. The walk ends at a small, quartz-sand barrier beach; sun-dried mussel, snail, and clam shells strew the sands. Gulls and shorebirds often occupy the area. Beware of sinking sands closer to the water.

Return along the boardwalk and take the first left to add the **Try Island Trail**. On the loose-sand rise, find mats of lichen, stunted red cedar, beach plum, oak, and pignut hickory. Benches offer area overlooks. Exit the woods, cross a salt meadow, and resume the Goose Pond Trail at 1.2 miles.

Bear right, edging the marsh, discovering sea lavender and glassworts; beach homes across the way steal from the site's wildness. The trail then curves to travel a low wooded rise. At 1.6 miles turn left; here the sandy trail parts a patch of bearberry, drawing into an open area. Woods again claim the tour as it approaches Goose Pond. Close the loop at 1.75 miles, retracing the first 0.25 mile to the trailhead.

The **Bay View-Fresh Brook Hike** explores the northern extent of the property. Go south on **Goose Pond Trail** and turn right (north) for the **Bay View Trail** at post G/3. Edge the saltwater marsh touring below a low pine

Goose Pond, Wellfleet Bay Sanctuary, MA.

rise. Bearberry pushes through the grassy forest mat. Expans
recommend touring.

At 0.2 mile veer into the woodland, now composed of
trees and beach plum, coming to a junction. From April
active osprey nest may close the right fork; both forks re
In 200 feet, the left fork reaches a gap that allows a peek at the
The trees of the rise stand no more than 10 to 15 feet tall.

More marsh views follow, as the trail totters from saltmarsh edge to pine
upland. Upon crossing a corner of the marsh (0.5 mile), reach benches and
a junction. Bear left for a clockwise tour of **Fresh Brook Pathway**; either
way completes the **Bay View Loop**.

On a clockwise tour of the pathway, travel a pine-oak upland at the north-
ern perimeter; benches overlook the textured marsh drainage of Fresh Brook.
Mosses turn the sides of the rolling trail green, as taller oaks frame the path.
As a side trail heads left, bear right for the loop.

At 0.9 mile, turn right to complete the **Fresh Brook Loop** at 1.1 miles,
and return as you came to the nature center (1.6 miles). Or follow the Bay
View Trail left, paralleling U.S. 6 south, passing through woods and the
site's tent campground to reach the nature center at 1.4 miles.

40 CAPE COD NATIONAL SEASHORE, BEACH HIKE

General description: Between the narrow spit of Coast Guard Beach in
Eastham and Race Point Beach in Provincetown, to the north, the national
seashore unfurls an unrivaled 25-mile-long invitation to discovery. Pass
through monitored areas for swimming, wading, and sunbathing and little-
traveled natural areas for reverie.
General location: Cape Cod, Massachusetts.
Special attractions: Nesting piping plover and terns; clean crystalline sands;
multiple access points, some with restrooms and water; wildlife sightings;
beachcombing (no collecting).
Length: 25 miles one-way.
Elevation: The hike is flat.
Difficulty: Easy to strenuous, depending on length.
Maps: *Cape Cod National Seashore Official Map and Guide.*
Special requirements: Fee area(s). Keep off the abutting sandbank and
dunes; cross only at designated sites. Between April 15 and November 15,
expect to encounter some oversand vehicles between High Head and Race
Point. All oversand drivers must secure a permit. Respect private property
and closed areas protecting nesting sites and sensitive dunes. Carry water.
Season and hours: Year-round, 6 a.m. to sunset.
For information: Cape Cod National Seashore, Park Headquarters.

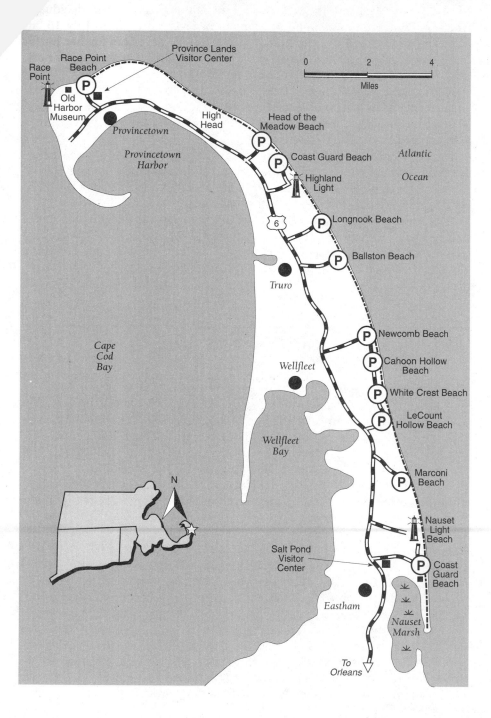

Race Point

Race Point Beach

Province Lands Visitor Center

Old Harbor Museum

Provincetown

Provincetown Harbor

High Head

Head of the Meadow Beach

Coast Guard Beach

Highland Light

Atlantic

Ocean

6

Longnook Beach

Ballston Beach

Truro

Cape Cod Bay

Newcomb Beach

Cahoon Hollow Beach

White Crest Beach

Wellfleet

LeCount Hollow Beach

Wellfleet Bay

Marconi Beach

N

Nauset Light Beach

Salt Pond Visitor Center

Coast Guard Beach

Eastham

Nauset Marsh

To Orleans

0   2   4
Miles

Finding the trailhead: On Cape Cod, go north from Eastham on U.S. Highway 6 East; multiple marked turns access the national seashore east off the highway. Find Salt Pond Visitor Center off U.S. 6 in Eastham; there pick up a map to plot travel.

The hike: Traveling the forearm and raised fist of Cape Cod peninsula, a south-to-north stroll of the national seashore begins at Coast Guard Beach (1.8 miles east of Salt Pond). Start below the retired Nauset Coast Guard Station, a charming, weathered white building with green shutters and red roof.

Glacial activity formed the cape. Find its southern beaches backed by a low, continuous sandbank or bluff, replaced by wind-sculpted dunes north of Head of the Meadow. Throughout, a light-colored sand sweeps to the ocean. An occasional thunder clap of surf peppers the otherwise constant ocean roar.

A thin fingerlike spit stretches south 2 miles, separating the tidal flat of Nauset Marsh from the ocean. From this spit, overlook the longer spit of Nauset Beach isolated to the south. Cross-marsh looks find Fort Hill. In 1927, author/naturalist Henry Beston built a cottage on the sands overlooking this estuary and led a solitary life for 1 year; find his Cape Cod impressions recorded in *The Outermost House*.

Northward from Coast Guard Beach, find an uninterrupted avenue of glistening sand. In about a mile, pass below Nauset Light, a maritime beacon with its upper third painted red, set back amid low pines. The breeze

Nauset Coast Guard Station, Cape Cod National Seashore, MA.

whips white spray from the crest of the long waves breaking near shore. Patches of pebbles with bits of white shell alter the look of the beach; farther north, cobbles strew the shore. Both tide and season may influence discovery.

Due to riptides and an unpredictable ocean floor, rangers encourage hikers to confine their wading to protected beaches at Coast Guard, Nauset Light, Marconi, Head of the Meadow, and Race Point. Lobster pots, buoys, skate eggcases, and clam shells divert the eyes, as do feeding terns, harbor seals, and raucous gulls. At 3.25 miles, find the stairway access to Marconi Beach. Sands drift over the lower steps, while wild roses top the 30-foot bluff. Farther north lies Marconi Station, where the first trans-Atlantic cablegram was sent.

LeCount Hollow Town Beach (5.25 miles) and White Crest Town Beach (6 miles) mark off distance; for each, a steep sandy slope serves as access. In places, the slope to the water becomes more pronounced. Grasses now claim the slip face at the foot of the cliff. Find the town beach facilities more primitive and seasonal in availability; some offer no sanitary facilities at all. Despite the bluffs grading higher, rooftops sometimes peek over their tops.

The town beaches of Cahoon Hollow (7 miles), Newcomb Hollow (8.5 miles), and Ballston (11 miles) sound off one's progress. At Ballston Beach, snow fences line the bluff, ushering hikers to the sanctioned access gap. Round a wetland to reach its parking area; loose sand taxes the legs. More homes top the headland.

Reach Longnook Beach at 12.5 miles; a broad U-shaped gap in the bluff signals its access. The bluffs now measure 70 feet high, and loose sand hints at the dune character farther north; beware of these sliding, unstable cliffs. A flat, narrow strand welcomes carefree strolling as a long remote beach stretches north.

At 14 miles, find the next landmarks, radar station domes and the stained white-brick tower of Highland Light, the first lighthouse on Cape Cod, built 1798 and replaced in 1857. It rises 183 feet above sea level and remains active. Reach Coast Guard Town Beach in about a mile.

At Head of the Meadow (15.5 miles), find the start of the 10-foot-high dunes, with the beach curvature accounting for a slightly different wave action. A seaward cant again meets the ocean, seabirds bob in the water, and horseshoe and spider crabs wash to shore. At times, the sand takes on a pink hue.

At High Head (17 miles), passing ducks may hint at a marsh and Pilgrim Lake cradled amid the dunes. This is the start of the oversand vehicle area. It extends north some 6 miles to the tip of Race Point.

Looks west across the dune find the profile of a stone tower, Pilgrim Monument in Provincetown. Inland from Race Point Beach, find Province Lands Visitor Center and **Old Harbor Museum Boardwalk**, an interpretive trail relating facts about shipwrecks and the early lifesavers, and about some possible marine mammal sightings. The northern beach shows a coarser-grained sand that easily displaces beneath the foot. Facing mostly north, the beach receives less punishment from the Atlantic, offering milder waters for the frolic of youngsters. End at the visitor center or at the tip of Race Point.

41 CAPE COD NATIONAL SEASHORE, NORTHERN NATURE TRAILS

OVERVIEW

The national seashore extends a varied collection of nature trails that examine the cultural and natural history and early commerce of the area. Explore cranberry bog, cedar swamp, and migrating dunes and visit the site of a spring where Pilgrims first tasted the sweet water of the New World.

General description: Ten short nature trails (five in Eastham) disperse Cape Cod National Seashore; find the featured trails north of Eastham at Wellfleet, Truro, and Provincetown.
General location: Cape Cod, Massachusetts.
Special attractions: Historical sites; a rare Atlantic white cedar swamp; estuarine, pond, and seashore vistas; spring flowering annuals and shrubs; fall foliage; bird watching.
Length: Featured hikes range between 0.5 and 1.25 miles in length.
Elevation: Find less than a 100-foot elevation change.
Difficulty: All, easy to moderate.
Maps: National seashore map; pick up interpretive brochures at the park visitor centers or trailheads.
Special requirements: Fee area. No pets. Carry insect repellent and beware of poison ivy. Hikers may purchase a plant identification guide at the visitor center; it identifies plants seen at numbered sites along the park trails.
Season and hours: Year-round; 6 a.m. to sunset.
For information: Cape Cod National Seashore, Park Headquarters.
Finding the trailhead: Locate trailheads east off U.S. Highway 6 in Wellfleet, Truro, and Provincetown; brown signs mark the turns. First, find Salt Pond Visitor Center east off U.S. 6 in Eastham; there pick up a map to plot travel.

The hikes: The *Wellfleet Area* boasts an award-winning nature trail, the 1.25-mile **Atlantic White Cedar Swamp Trail**. Turn east off U.S. 6 for Marconi Station and proceed 1 mile to the station parking lot.

This premier trail invites a slow appreciative turn. Hike west off the parking lot loop, finding the loop junction for the trail in 50 feet. Go left for a clockwise tour passing through dwarf woods, mature pines, and black oaks to cross a single-lane dirt road, reaching the cedar swamp (0.5 mile).

A scenic boardwalk meanders through the picturesque dense cedar stand, where a wonderful aura of mystery clings to the site on gray, foggy days. Mossy mounds add to the texture. Historically the trees measured 4 feet in diameter, but those fell to harvest long ago. Turnout benches suggest a leisurely admiration.

Reach the boardwalk's loop junction at 0.6 mile; go left. The forest opens up, losing the intermingling deciduous trees and shrubs. Knotted cedars, intriguing branchworks, and moss-and-lichen-reclaimed stumps add to the tour. Beware, the boardwalk can be slippery when wet.

At 0.7 mile, the right fork completes the boardwalk loop for a backtracking return to the parking lot. Go left for a loop return to the trailhead, following the "Old Wireless Road," the 1903 route to Marconi Station.

From the oak and sheep laurel outskirts of the swamp, ascend steadily via the sandy road, rediscovering the same woods habitats encountered on the descent; midway find a bench. The hike ends at 1.25 miles.

Three nature trails begin in the *Truro Area*: **Pamet Cranberry Bog, Small's Swamp, and Pilgrim Spring trails**.

For the **Cranberry Bog Trail**, turn east on North Pamet Road in Truro, go 1.5 miles, and park in the small lot below the Environmental Education Center. Cross North Pamet Road to start this 0.5-mile trail, passing amid pine and beach plum, with a bearberry understory. The trail rolls, with reinforced steps advancing the tour. At 0.1 mile look for the long arm of a pine that bowed to the ground, re-rooted, and again shot skyward. Soon after, overlook the bog and descend to round it.

A boardwalk passes amid highbush blueberry and various other shrubs and grasses, reaching this sometimes-soggy remnant of a cranberry bog. Bogs of American cranberry naturally thrive in kettle depressions amid the dunes; in the 1800s, such bogs were cultivated into a commercial enterprise. Berries typically ripen in September-October. Reach the abandoned Bog House at the end of the boardwalk and return as you came.

For **Small's Swamp and Pilgrim Spring trails**, go east at the sign for Pilgrim Heights and proceed to the interpretive center at the end of the road. The shelter overlooks the site toured by Small's Swamp Trail.

For the 0.75-mile **Small's Swamp Trail**, pass through the shelter, descending log-braced steps to the loop junction (0.1 mile). Stay left alongside a rustic rail fence, passing amid pitch pine and black oak; grass, bearberry, and fern patch the floor. A dense woodland thicket claims the flat. At 0.25 mile, a boardwalk skirts a wetland area. Ascend amid a shower of white spring blooms, reaching a vista with interpretive signs.

Below stretches Salt Meadow, a saltgrass meadow threaded by a dark-water channel isolated from the ocean by dunes. This site marks the demarcation between the glacial headland and the wind-formed Provincetown Hook. Offshore in 1778, the wreck of the *Somerset*, a British man-of-war, allowed the colonists to capture the British sailors. From the second interpretive sign, the trail curves back into pitch pine woods to close the loop and return to the trailhead (0.75 mile).

CAPE COD NATIONAL SEASHORE
NORTHERN NATURE TRAILS

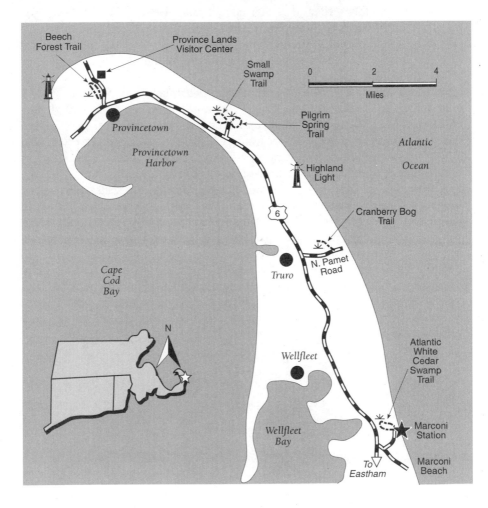

The 0.7-mile **Pilgrim Spring Trail** begins to the right of the shelter, entering a stand of 25-foot-tall pines; needles soften the path. At 0.2 mile, draw into the open, coming to a vista with interpretive panels. The view overlooks Salt Meadow; archaeological finds date Native American presence to this site 2,000 years ago.

Descend a set of steps and travel a passage through woods and scrub thicket to reach the small monument denoting the Pilgrim discovery of the freshwater spring on November 16, 1620. Led by Miles Standish, the first Pilgrims followed the tracks of Indian and deer to locate this water. Near the site, find a table and the paved bike path.

Resume the clockwise loop ascending back toward the parking area. Cross a pine-clad hilltop, traverse the picnic area, and round past a seasonal restroom, returning to the interpretive shelter.

Near *Provincetown*, reach the last nature trail, **Beech Forest Trail**, 0.5 mile north off U.S. 6 on Race Point Road. This figure-8 trail unites a 0.75-mile pond loop and 0.25-mile beech forest loop. The tour skirts Beech Forest Pond, a wildlife pond pinched at the middle by marsh grass; pond lilies decorate the dark stillness.

From the marked trailhead, pass through a mixed woodland on a log-lined loose-sand path. Canada mayflower and flowering trees and shrubs recommend a spring tour. Small birds animate the treetops; geese and meadowlark sound from nearby. Before long, the trail rolls along a tree-reclaimed dune. Dense vegetation denies pond views.

At 0.3 mile, bear right to add **Beech Forest Loop**. The signature tree abounds as the trail travels a "canyon" passage amid dune rises; most of the beech trees have escaped the degradation of initial-carvers. A boardwalk segment advances the trail. At 0.4 mile, begin the rolling return, ascending and descending log-braced steps, traversing the wooded dunes. Sassafras, oak, and pine intermingle with beech.

At 0.55 mile, again meet **Pond Loop** and bear right for an outer tour of the figure-8, mildly descending to round Beech Forest Pond. Where the trail again ascends, find a pond overlook. Pitch pines create a more open border for stealing pond glimpses; shrubby islands mark this glacial kettle pool. Pass the restroom to end hike at 1 mile.

42 CAPE COD NATIONAL SEASHORE, EASTHAM AREA NATURE TRAILS

OVERVIEW

The national seashore boasts a superb assembly of short nature trails that introduce both the cultural and natural history of the area. Journey to the past, visiting sites that harken back to the Native Americans, the Pilgrims' arrival, colonial settlement, and maritime history. Explore kettle ponds, marsh, red maple swamp, and coastal forest.

General description: Ten short nature trails disperse the length of Cape Cod National Seashore. Five lie within easy reach of Eastham/Salt Pond Visitor Center; locate the others to the north at Wellfleet, Truro, and Provincetown.
General location: Cape Cod, Massachusetts.
Special attractions: Historical sites; marsh, pond, and coastal vistas; spring flowering shrubs; bird watching.
Length: Featured hikes range between 0.2 and 2 miles in length.
Elevation: Find less than a 100-foot elevation change.
Difficulty: All, easy to moderate.
Maps: National seashore map; pick up interpretive brochures at the park visitor center or at the trailheads.
Special requirements: Fee area. No pets. Carry insect repellent and beware of poison ivy. Hikers may purchase a plant identification guide at the visitor center; it describes the vegetation seen at the numbered posts along park trails.
Season and hours: Year-round; 6 a.m. to sunset.
For information: Cape Cod National Seashore, Park Headquarters.
Finding the trailhead: Locate trailheads east off U.S. Highway 6 in Eastham; brown signs mark the turns. Also find Salt Pond Visitor Center in Eastham; there pick up a seashore map.

The hikes: At the southernmost trail site, the **Red Maple Swamp and Fort Hill Nature Trails** interlock, suggesting a single 2-mile tour. Reach the common trailhead by way of Governor Prence Road. Find parking on the left in 0.3 mile, east past the historic Penniman House.

From the northeast corner of the parking lot, edge field and woods, with cross-field looks at the coast. At 0.1 mile, the swamp and Fort Hill trails go their separate ways; go left, touring the wishbone-shaped **Red Maple Swamp Trail** first. Pass through a corridor of eastern red cedar and bear left.

Log-braced earthen stairs descend to the flat of the red maple swamp, where a curving boardwalk continues the tour. Mosses clump at the feet of shrubs, and a thick mat of algae and decaying leaves caps the standing water.

At 0.25 mile, the left fork allows hikers to shorten the swamp loop; stay right for the full tour. Catbrier and raspberry entangle the trail's sides; soggier reaches can be especially buggy. Woodpecker, robin, chickadee, and blue jay may divert attention, as another scenic boardwalk continues the tour. Netted chain fern and snags contribute to the woods.

At 0.5 mile, the cutoff arrives on the left; again bear right. Interpretive plaques identify highbush blueberry, fox grape, winterberry, and sweet pepperbush. Just ahead, a left leads to Hemenway Landing, a small boat launch on the estuary; go right for Skiff and Fort hills. Find broken shell and paved surfaces, as the trail rounds a seasonally-open restroom.

At 0.7 mile, three benches overlook Nauset Marsh, with its low-tide mosaic of open water and salt meadow grass. The paved trail then returns to a red cedar corridor, coming out at Skiff Hill (0.75 mile). Here find a covered open-sided interpretive kiosk and a relocated 20-ton boulder. Distinctive grooves record where Nauset Indians sharpened their implements on the abrasive metamorphic rock.

Now follow the **Fort Hill Trail** as it heads seaward near the kiosk. By 0.8 mile, traverse a low bluff, edging a rolling field partitioned by rock walls. Continue to enjoy overlooks of Nauset Marsh. Rabbits and bobwhites favor the field. At a large stone at 1.1 miles, enjoy a final view of the marsh as it opens to the sea. Pass and ascend through field topping Fort Hill at a parking area (1.2 miles) for an admiring look at the rock, field, and woods terrain.

Pass through a gap in the fence, descending through field and amid black locust trees to encircle the Penniman House, a picturesque 2-story Second French Empire mansion topped by a cupola. Swallows dart from the open basement. A whalebone archway hints at how Penniman made his fortune at sea. Orange lichens mottle the bone. End at the parking area at 2 miles.

Start both the **Buttonbush and Nauset Marsh trails** at Salt Pond Visitor Center.

The 0.2-mile **Buttonbush Trail** serves blind and low-vision visitors with guide ropes, touch cues for signaling steps, and large-type and Braille interpretive plaques.

Below the parking area, head east from the amphitheater, bearing left for a clockwise loop. This circuit travels to a boardwalk overlooking Buttonbush Pond, a kettle pond about 2 feet deep left behind by receding glaciers some 18,000 years ago. Winterberry, wild rose, and grape adorn the area. In spring, cream floral balls top the 3-foot-tall buttonbush, aiding in its identification. Midway, pass the **Nauset Marsh Trail**. Pass amid beach plum and bayberry closing the loop.

Reach the 1.2-mile **Nauset Marsh Trail** east of the visitor center and to the right of the amphitheater. Descend toward the open shore of Salt Pond. On Sundays, a kayaker or clammer may capture attention. Road noise from U.S. 6 intrudes.

This classic freshwater kettle pond became brackish when breached by

CAPE COD NATIONAL SEASHORE, EASTHAM AREA NATURE TRAILS

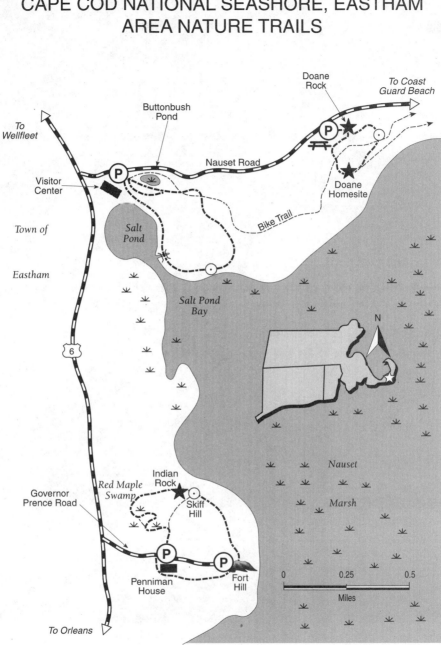

Doane Rock

To Coast Guard Beach

Buttonbush Pond

To Wellfleet

Nauset Road

Visitor Center

Doane Homesite

Town of

Salt Pond

Eastham

Bike Trail

6

Salt Pond Bay

N

Nauset

Red Maple Swamp

Indian Rock

Marsh

Governor Prence Road

Skiff Hill

Penniman House

Fort Hill

0   0.25   0.5

Miles

To Orleans

Fern, Red Maple Swamp Nature Trail, Cape Cod National Seashore, MA.

tide. Saltgrass, seaside lavender, and cordgrass accent its shore, while beach plum and oak claim the slope rising above the wide hiking lane. Keep to shore, reaching the outlet and tidal channel; cross a footbridge; and tour the dike. Do not stray from the trail as private property lies to the right.

Enter woodland, crossing over a 2-track, following signs to the right. Stairs ascend to an overlook bench at 0.6 mile; low tides reveal a scenic mudflat. A gull feeding on crabs, and clammers with their rakes and buckets, hint at the food-rich habitat. The circuit continues through open cedar, coming to a junction: to the right, find Doane Memorial; the path straight ahead continues the loop.

A more mixed woods frames the open aisle of the foot trail. Round a small wetland with lilies and buttonbush before the trail again rolls uphill. Twice cross the bike path, meeting the **Buttonbush Trail** at 1.1 miles. Go left with the traffic flow to end at the amphitheater.

Go 0.9 mile east from Salt Pond Visitor Center to reach the 0.5-mile **Doane Loop Trail**, a wheelchair-accessible route.

Start from the first parking area, following the wide paved path away from the designated wheelchair-accessible parking space. Doane Rock lies to the left; the loop to the right. Detour left a short distance to view the largest glacial erratic deposited in the park. Glaciers carried Doane Rock to this site an estimated 12,000 years ago. Some 18 feet of its height points skyward, while another 12 feet remain locked in the ground. The boulder spans 45 feet.

The loop bypasses the restroom and crosses the park road at a crosswalk to travel a mixed pine-oak woods. Cross a second road and a paved bike trail to reach a sign for Doane Memorial at 0.2 mile. View the homesite of Deacon Doane across the roadway. A foundation and stone marker commemorate the settlement of Nauset/Eastham by seven Pilgrim families who broke from the Plymouth majority, coming here in 1644.

Bypass a trail branching to the beach, following Doane Loop as it bends left. Cross back over the bike trail, finding a spur to vista bench. Sights include the Nauset Coast Guard Station, the marsh, and ocean. Return to the picnic area at the second parking lot and return to the start.

43 SOUTH CAPE BEACH STATE PARK

OVERVIEW

A relative newcomer to the Massachusetts Forests and Parks system and part of the Waquoit Bay National Estuarine Research Reserve (NERR), this 401-acre park has all the earmarks of an up-and-coming star. The Department of Environmental Management (DEM) has slated improvements for facilities, trails, and roads, but even as the park struggles through infancy, hikers find enjoyable discovery. Crystalline sand beaches; vital ponds and wetlands; nesting piping plover, tern, and osprey; and an off-season wilderness solitude, all recommend a foot tour.

General description: An inland nature trail and pair of beach hikes explore the park offering.
General location: Southwest corner of Cape Cod, Massachusetts.
Special attractions: Coastal and bay beaches; estuarine and freshwater ponds; marsh, coastal shrub, and woods habitats; bird watching; surf fishing; beachcombing (no collecting).
Length: Great Flat Pond Trail, 1-mile loop (plans call for re-design and expansion of this trail). Dead Neck Beach-Waquoit Bay Hike, 3.7 miles round-trip; Eastward Beach Hike 1.6 miles round-trip.
Elevation: All are flat.
Difficulty: Great Flat Pond Trail and Eastward Beach Hike, both easy; Dead Neck Beach-Waquoit Bay Hike, moderate.
Maps: South Cape Beach map (generally available in a map box at the start of the Great Flat Pond Trail).
Special requirements: Vehicle admission fee in summer; no dogs. Respect nesting sites, granting birds a wide margin of safety. Note, future plans call for a developed trail along Sage Lot Pond.
Season and hours: Year-round, daylight hours.
For information: South Cape Beach State Park; Waquoit Bay NERR.
Finding the trailhead: From the Mashpee Rotary on Massachusetts 28, take Great Neck Road south. In 2.6 miles where Main Road curves right, continue forward on Great Oak Road, following signs for the park. In another 2 miles, turn left on the unpaved entrance road. Within a mile, find a paved road heading left; it leads to the state park's parking lot and beach boardwalk. The dirt road continues, ending at a town beach parking area.

The hikes: All hikes start from the state park parking area.
Find the circuit of the **Great Flat Pond Trail** north of the parking area. Pass through forest of pitch pine and oak and follow a narrow sandy footpath amid waist- to chest-deep shrubbery, skirting a vast salt-marsh meadow and pond—Great Flat Pond. Huckleberry, highbush blueberry, azalea, sheep laurel, bracken fern, and greenbrier compose much of the floral congestion.

SOUTH CAPE BEACH STATE PARK

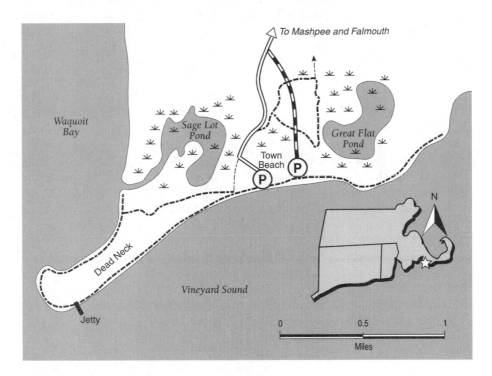

The loop twice crosses the paved park road. Amid the woods, beware of poison ivy, and look for pockets of lady slipper.

Obstructed side trails branching toward Great Flat Pond indicate the sites for future boardwalks and marsh overlooks. Meanwhile, keep to the primary loop, traveling foot trail, berm, and boardwalk. Where the loop does allow for open views, admire the head-tall grasses of Great Flat Pond. Be careful on the plank boardwalks when wet or frosty conditions exist.

For the **Dead Neck Beach-Waquoit Bay Hike** and **Eastward Beach Hike**, start at the state park's beach boardwalk. Hikers who choose to start at the town beach 0.1 mile west, need to adjust the mileages accordingly.

Turn west (right) upon reaching the south-facing beach for the **Dead Neck Beach-Waquoit Bay Hike**; views pan Vineyard Sound to Martha's Vineyard. Travel loose, light-colored crystalline sands, passing below low dunes trimmed in wild rose, dune grass, and poison ivy. The strand measures some 40-feet wide, depending on tide. A filament of dark seaweed often records the tideline.

Lifeguard perches mark Town Beach, where anglers cast their lines in the off-season. Terns, cormorants, and shorebirds commonly divert attention. At 0.4 mile, a beach-access trail leads to Sage Lot Pond; keep to the beach.

Off-season visits promise wonderfully wild walks, with discoveries of crab claws and carapaces, snails, and slipper shells, as well as a rainbow spectrum of seaweed: tubular, leafy, or stringy. At 0.6 mile, a spur accesses a closed dirt track linking Sage Lot Pond with the jetty area to the west. Sinking beach sands work the calf muscles.

Before long, skirt the fragile nesting sites of the piping plovers, staying well below the mesh enclosures. If tides prohibit doing that, turn back. The well-being of the plover supersedes any rights or wishes of the hiker. At 1.5 miles, reach a rock jetty capped by flat rocks, walkable when storm and seas allow.

The beach tour continues now rounding Waquoit Bay, offering admiring looks at Washburn Island, the beautiful bay curvature, and Waquoit Bay National Estuarine Reserve on the far shore. Find small estuarine pools and a finer, compressed sand for easier strolling; moonshells, clams, and scallops dot the white sand. Sign posts rise amid the flat to the right, and dunes swell to 6 feet tall.

At 2.5 miles, prior to reaching the estuarine grasses and open-water mouth of Sage Lot Pond, find a path heading inland to a jeep road, for a loop return. But first detour along the bay 0.1 mile farther to view the pond's outlet. Discoveries may include weathered snags and posts providing roosts for seabirds; a fishing boat marooned in the mud; and swans, ducks, and cormorants sharing the sheltered water.

South Cape Beach, South Cape Beach State Park, MA.

Return to the 2.5-mile junction and hike inland, following the jeep trail as it curves left to appreciate Sage Lot Pond; to the right leads back to the coastal shore (avoid taking during nesting season). The jeep track offers grand overlooks of Sage Lot Pond. Red and white shore roses, daisies, and beach pea sprinkle seasonal color, as a reclaimed flattened dune stretches right. At 3.2 miles, take the foot trail to the right, return to the beach, and turn left (east) to complete the tour at the boardwalk (3.7 miles).

For the **Eastward Beach Hike** turn left (east) upon reaching the south-facing beach. Again find areas of the leg-taxing, sparkling sands, but with 5- to 6-foot-tall dunes backing this part of the strand. At 0.15 mile, a gap in the dunes offers a peek at Great Flat Pond, its open water, and marsh shore.

At a broad sandy point at 0.3 mile, pebbles crunch beneath the shoe. Before long, snowfences collect and hold the sand, as the tour passes below a golf course. Keep to the beach. Here a second point of land (the ending for the tour) comes into view. Reach the tour's cobbly end point at 0.8 mile.

As residences now rise above the beach to the east, turn back here. Views west find Woods Hole, Elizabeth Islands, and Martha's Vineyard.

WESTERN CONNECTICUT TRAILS

The Connecticut River forms a natural divide, slicing Connecticut into east-west halves. West of the river, find the rugged, steep and hilly terrain of Litchfield Hills and the traprock ridges rising from the Connecticut River Valley. A flatter coastal plain meets Long Island Sound to the south.

Typically, southern hardwoods with hemlock groves and pine plantations shade travel. Red maple swamps splash intense red splendor on the autumn landscape, while mountain laurel grows with abandon. Tulip poplar is showy both in bloom and size. Stone walls, charcoal sites, and Native American and colonial history spice travel. Hike forest, hilltop, rocky ledge, brook, pond, swamp, and a Housatonic River reservoir. Roam a giant's anatomy and hide with the exiled British judges who ordered the execution of Charles I.

44 PEOPLES STATE FOREST

OVERVIEW

This 3,000-acre forest, purchased by public subscription in the 1920s, stretches east from the West Branch Farmington River in northwest Connecticut. It contains a diverse forest with stately trees, one of the best overlooks in the state, and Barkhamsted Lighthouse, an historic Indian settlement. Touring the forest, find a splendid system of interlocking trails; the described loop incorporates several of them.

General description: This rolling day-hike loop passes amid relaxing woods and showers of mountain laurel, snaring a pair of prized overlooks and passing historic sites.
General location: 5 miles north of New Hartford, Connecticut.
Special attractions: Historic Indian cemetery, cellar holes, diverse woods, vistas, bird watching, fall foliage.
Length: 6.1 miles round-trip.
Elevation: The loop shows a 550-foot elevation change.
Difficulty: Moderate.
Maps: State forest brochure (generally available at site).
Special requirements: Fee charged weekends, Memorial Day weekend through Columbus Day weekend. Pets must be leashed. Find the trails color-coded; look for blazes of the actual color or with a colored dot on a blue background.
Season and hours: Year-round, spring through fall for hiking. Open 8 a.m.

PEOPLES STATE FOREST

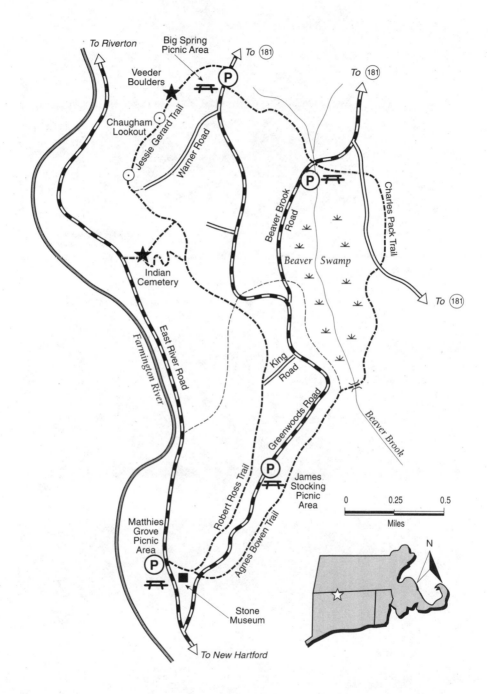

To Riverton

Big Spring Picnic Area

To (181)

Veeder Boulders

P

Chaugham Lookout

Jessie Gerard Trail

Warner Road

To (181)

P

Beaver Brook Road

Charles Pack Trail

Indian Cemetery

Beaver Swamp

To (181)

Farmington River

East River Road

King Road

Beaver Brook

Greenwoods Road

0   0.25   0.5

Miles

P

Robert Ross Trail

James Stocking Picnic Area

Matthies Grove Picnic Area

P

Agnes Bowen Trail

N

Stone Museum

To New Hartford

Viewpoint, Peoples State Forest, CT.

to sunset. Stone Museum: Sunday afternoons, Memorial Day through Columbus Day, with Saturday hours added July and August.

For information: Peoples State Forest.

Finding the trailhead: From New Hartford, go west on U.S. Highway 44 for 1.4 miles, and turn north on Connecticut 181. In 1 mile, turn right to cross the Farmington River. Exiting the bridge, turn left on East River Road. Pass Greenwoods Road on the right in 0.8 mile; it travels north through the heart of the forest, accessing trails and recreation areas. In another 0.2 mile, turn left off East River Road for Matthies Grove Recreation Area and trailhead parking.

The hike: This loop travels the **Robert Ross, Jessie Gerard, Charles Pack, and Agnes Bowen trails**, all named for benefactors of Peoples State Forest. From the information board and map box at Matthies Grove Recreation Area, cross East River Road and hike east on the blue-blazed **Robert Ross Trail**, passing between a pair of posts.

Ascend along the soft bed of an old road grade, touring amid white pine-deciduous woods. At 0.1 mile, find Stone Museum, a small, seasonally open natural history museum. Skirt it, veering left across a gravel parking area to resume the tour.

Pass amid some head-tilting big trees and bear left at the 0.2-mile junction with **Agnes Bowen Trail** (the loop's return). Foot trail now continues the tour, ascending amid mixed forest with mountain laurel, maple-leaf viburnum, fern, and sarsaparilla; a few tulip poplars grace the woods.

The blue trail tops out at 0.6 mile; now descend a picturesque laurel corridor. Pass the occasional rock sporting a squirrel's acorn harvest. At 0.8 mile, bear right, following a woods road to the Kings Road turnaround; there angle left into forest. Where the trail forks, bear right, staying the blue blazes for a similar rolling tour through relaxing woods.

At 1.3 miles, angle uphill, crossing the Agnes Bowen Trail. Now, a defined slope drops away west to the Farmington River. The terrain grows rockier, as the tour passes below an outcrop crest with rounded cliffs and sharp-edged breaks.

Descend steeply for a short distance, meeting the southern branch of the yellow **Jessie Gerard Trail** (1.65 miles). It descends left, reaching Barkhamsted Lighthouse (the site of Chaugham's cabin); an Indian settlement cemetery, with primitive head and foot stones; and ultimately, East River Road (0.25 mile). Chaugham, a Native American, married the rebellious daughter of an American colonist. At night the light from his cabin shown like a beacon, alerting stagecoach travelers that New Hartford rested but 5 miles off.

For the loop, follow a shared-segment of the Robert Ross/Jessie Gerard Trail uphill to the right. At 1.8 miles, meet the northern branch of the Jessie Gerard Trail, which descends 299 stone steps toward Chaugham's cabin; bear left (south) where it forks to view the cellar hole and graves. For the loop, continue climbing. In autumn, skeins of honking geese pass south over the Farmington River.

At 2 miles, the blue trail heads right to Warner Road. For the loop, stay the yellow **Jessie Gerard Trail** for a treacherously steep ascent over stone steps and canted outcrops, reaching the first of two overlooks at 2.1 miles. It offers a mostly wild view south out the Farmington Valley. When dressed in fall foliage, the landscape inspires. Top the ridge and hike north through forest to claim Chaugham Lookout (2.4 miles), for a northwestern perspective that overlooks the rural charm of Riverton.

The loop resumes north, still following yellow blazes for a slow descent amid hemlocks. Pass the bookend multi-ton Veeder Boulders, 2.5 miles. The descent quickens. Soon, bear right on a woods road to reach Greenwoods Road, the main forest artery. Turn right and resume the hike, following the yellow **Charles Pack Trail** (2.9 miles), as it heads left just beyond Big Spring Recreation Area.

Pass the rock-rimmed circular pool of Big Spring and descend along Beaver Brook, touring rich hemlock-hardwood forest. Despite a rocky forest floor, the trail remains relatively rock-free. Cross a side brook on hewn logs to reach little-used Beaver Brook Road. Go left, cross the brook on the road bridge, and turn right, following blazes through Beaver Brook Recreation Area, a small, rustic picnic site.

Ascend through similar forest upon a less defined path, now relying on blazes. At 3.65 miles, cross Pack Grove Road, a dirt woods road, to contour the hemlock slope above it. Proceed over a scenic rock wall and descend to cross Pack Grove Road a second time. Big hemlocks continue to embellish the tour; find more rock walls and foundations. At the fork at 4.65 miles, bear right and descend to cross a footbridge over Beaver Brook.

As the trail ascends, it skirts Beaver Swamp, betrayed only by a change of lighting in the forest. At 4.8 miles, leave the Charles Pack Trail and follow the orange **Agnes Bowen Trail** left to close the loop.

Enjoy a scenic rolling stroll, once again amid greater concentrations of mountain laurel. Skirt the edge of James Stocking Recreation Area to descend a rocky root-bound foot trail along a drainage. Tulip trees inspire. At 5.8 miles, cross the drainage via stones to cross Greenwoods Road. Close the loop at the 0.2-mile junction (5.9 miles) and backtrack the blue Robert Ross Trail to Matthies Grove parking.

45 SHARON AUDUBON CENTER

OVERVIEW

In Northwest Connecticut, this 684-acre wildlife sanctuary of the National Audubon Society offers 11 miles of foot trail that meander past brook, pond and bog, across wooded ridge, and through unkempt fields dotted with wildflowers. The Lucy Harvey Multiple-use Interpretive Area near the museum offers an easy 0.3-mile trail explaining the area's natural and cultural history.

General description: Two hikes stitch together several named trails, exploring the east and west halves of the sanctuary. The east hike visits two ponds and tours woods and field. The west hike remains primarily in woods, basked in solitude.
General location: 3 miles south of Sharon, Connecticut.
Special attractions: Bird and wildlife watching, ponds, gardens, historic sites, spring maple sugaring, fall foliage.
Length: East Loop, 2.5 miles round-trip, including a side trip on the Woodchuck Trail; West Loop, 1.7 miles round-trip.
Elevation: East Loop, less than a 100-foot elevation change; West Loop, 250-foot elevation change.
Difficulty: Both, moderate.

Fern frond, Sharon Audubon Center, CT.

Maps: Sanctuary map (available at the trailhead mapboard or center office); borrow a brochure for Lucy Harvey walk at the office.

Special requirements: Per-person admission fee or National Audubon Society membership; obey posted rules. No pets.

Season and hours: Year-round, spring through fall for hiking. Trails: dawn to dusk; Office: 9 a.m. to 5 p.m. Monday through Saturday and 1 p.m. to 5 p.m. Sunday.

For information: Sharon Audubon Center.

Finding the trailhead: From the junction of Connecticut 4, Connecticut 41, and Connecticut 343 at the southern outskirts of Sharon, go east on CT 4 for 2.2 miles and turn right (south) to enter the sanctuary. From the CT 4 - U.S. Highway 7 junction in Cornwall Bridge, go west on CT 4 for 5.2 miles to reach the sanctuary entrance.

The hikes: Loop hikers encounter multiple junctions. As not all of the junctions have signs, carry a map. The West Loop receives less traffic; when leaves obscure trails in autumn, be especially alert for the few markers and any natural clues to the trail. Both hikes start from the mapboard at the south end of the parking lot.

For the **East Loop** pass behind the mapboard and turn left, following the **Lucy Harvey Multiple-Use Area Trail** upstream along a ditch and Herrick Brook. The ditch and Ford Pond (just ahead) supplied water to Handlin Mill, a saw and cider mill that formerly stood behind what is now the center office. Maple, sumac, witch hazel, and wild grape edge the corridor.

In 100 yards, reach the grassy cart path of **Bog Meadow Road** (the old town road) and turn right, leaving the Lucy Harvey tour. Cross a small bridge, pass the rustic Ice House, and veer left on a foot trail ascending the earthen levee along Ford Pond. This large pond shows a filmy surface and vegetated shallows, enfolded by grasses, shrubs, and woods. When autumn paints the brim and calls forth skeins of honking southbound geese, the setting becomes electric.

At the pond's southwest corner, find the loop junction: to the left travels the **Fern Trail**; ahead lies the **Hendrickson Bog Meadow Trail**. Follow the Fern Trail left as it hugs the south shore of Ford Pond. Hemlock groves and stands of maple, ash, and birch claim the shore, with at least six species of fern at their feet. A tulip tree drops showers of blooms in spring and its unique leaves in fall. Encounter some rock and roots.

Keep to shore, avoiding a connecting spur to the Hendrickson Bog Meadow Trail. Beaver-girdled and fallen trees open the tour. Soon after, overlook the cattail reaches of the upper pond. Oaks fill out the canopy. As the trail draws away from Ford Pond, reach a junction (0.4 mile). This time, go left on the **Hendrickson Bog Meadow Trail** to continue clockwise on the East Loop; the Fern Trail continues straight ahead.

Cross a boardwalk and tour a marsh-woods habitat with maple, ash, and birch. At 0.5 mile, go left to add a tour of the **Woodchuck Trail**; go right for the loop alone.

SHARON AUDUBON CENTER

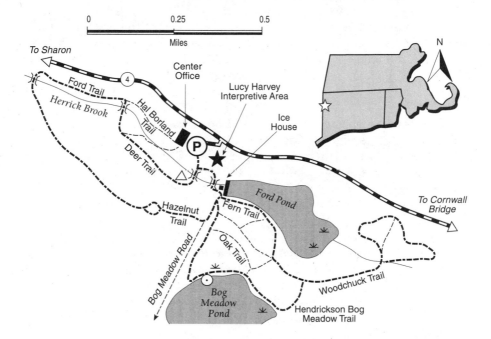

For this "see-the-sanctuary" tour, go left traveling a grassy path through multi-story forest, paralleling some deep drainage cuts. At 0.75 mile, reach the loop junction for the Woodchuck Trail. Clockwise, travel a faint road grade amid younger forest and bear left, finding some scenic old maples. Begin passing through a couple of meadows or fields. Goldenrod, aster, Queen Anne's lace, and milkweed sprinkle the sites in fall.

At 1.1 mile, meet a 2-track, follow it right for 30 feet, and then turn left, entering a third field. Grouse may sound in the distance; birdhouses mark the field. Ascend steadily to reach the fifth field near the boundary; enjoy a northwest view, looking down the field and through a notch.

Bear right and descend. At 1.4 miles, bear left, entering woods to close the Woodchuck Loop in 100 yards. Go left, returning to the junction with **Hendrickson Bog Meadow Trail** (1.7 miles); there turn left for the East Loop.

Pass through shady forest and round the base of a rocky slope, arriving at the grassy bank of Bog Meadow Pond, another big open pond with a shrub shore, backed by snags and forest. Geese sometimes stop over. Along the boardwalk, find highbush blueberry, bog grass, buttonbush, and loosestrife.

At 1.9 miles, a boardwalk spur heads left for 100 feet, reaching a platform at the edge of the pond for a farewell look. Resume the hike, re-entering woods now isolated from the pond. At the next junction, continue forward; the path to the right accesses the **Oak and Fern trails**.

Soon, the Hendrickson Bog Meadow Trail curves right beneath pines to travel a small field enlivened by crickets; bear right at the upcoming fork. Return to woods, staying on the Bog Meadow Trail, passing the Oak Trail on the right. On the left, **Bog Meadow Road** parallels the route. After a mild ascent to a field find a slow descent through mixed woods. Exit a hemlock grove to close the loop at the **Fern Trail** (2.4 miles); return to the trailhead 2.5 miles.

For the second sanctuary tour, **West Loop**, pass behind the mapboard, bear right, and descend to cross Herrick Brook on a footbridge. Next round behind the Explorer's Hut and turn right on the **Deer Trail**, contouring the slope downstream. Maple, birch, oak, and hemlock clothe the slope; mossy boulders pierce the forest duff. Where the trail grows obscure, maintain a contour line slightly higher than the hut. A few remaining interpretive numbers offer clues to the trail.

By 0.1 mile, an old road grade clarifies travel as the trail contours and mildly descends, paralleling Herrick Brook downstream. At 0.25 mile, the Deer Trail ends at the blue **Hal Borland Trail**. Bear left on the Borland Trail, remaining on the road grade for a sharp descent. Cross a footbridge over the scenic 10-foot-wide brook and bear right, ascending to a junction in 50 feet. The Borland Trail continues right, while the **Ford Trail** heads left, advancing the West Loop.

The Ford Trail passes amid hemlocks, touring the wooded slope below CT 4; roadway sounds provide hikers with another bearing. Deer commonly add to a tour. Travel a rolling contour paralleling Herrick Brook downstream to the next footbridge at 0.65 mile. After crossing, head upstream 50 feet to locate an arrow pointing out a steep ascent alongside a stone wall.

As the trail angles left, settle into a comfortable rolling tour along the upper slope. Striped maple, witch hazel, and hazelnut form the midstory. At 1.2 miles, find the **Hazelnut Trail** junction; either way continues the tour. To the right follow a faint road grade masked by leaves with a few huckleberry and oak reclaiming the bed. At 1.35 miles, the forks merge; continue forward, still following a road grade.

Descend, skirting a stone-reinforced flat where bundled limbs and a cairn with an open flue may be spied. Chipmunk and mouse likewise investigate the scene. Just ahead reach the sunken grade of **Bog Meadow Road** and follow it left downhill to Ford Pond. Pass below the levee and Ice House and turn left to return to the center (1.7 miles).

OVERVIEW

Centerpiece to this Connecticut state park, 88-acre Burr Pond dazzles travelers with its clear waters; in the 1850s the watery impoundment powered early industry, including the world's first condensed milk factory. The encircling trail travels the pond's richly wooded rim interrupted by a small wetland. It visits quiet coves, a peninsula, and rock cave. A second trail originates in the park, the Muir Trail; it offers a wooded journey south through Paugnut State Forest to Sunny Brook State Park (2.5 miles northwest of Torrington).

General description: The Pond Loop may be toured alone or joined with the Muir Trail for a longer day hike.
General location: 5 miles north of Torrington, Connecticut.
Special attractions: Attractive pond, diverse forest, mountain laurel and wildflowers, memorials, wildlife, fall foliage.
Length: Pond Loop, 3.2-mile loop; Pond Loop-Muir Trail Hike, 8.1 miles round-trip.
Elevation: Pond Loop, less than 100 feet in elevation change; Pond Loop-Muir Trail Hike, about 400 feet in elevation change.
Difficulty: Pond Loop, easy; Pond Loop-Muir Trail Hike, moderate.

Burr Pond, Burr Pond State Park, CT.

Maps: State park map; Torrington and West Torrington 7.5-minute USGS quads; John Muir Trail/Paugnut State Forest map from the *Connecticut Walk Book*.

Special requirements: Fee area.

Season and hours: Year-round, spring through fall for hiking. Open 8 a.m. to sunset. Off-season visits focus on nature.

For information: Burr Pond State Park.

Finding the trailhead: From Connecticut 8, take exit 46 for Burrville, head west on Pinewoods Road for 0.5 mile, and turn left. In 1 mile, turn right on Burr Mountain Road for the park. Find the entrance on the left in 0.5 mile. Start the hikes from the beach area.

The hikes: At the developed swimming beach, bear right for a counter-clockwise tour of **Pond Loop**, finding the trail as it enters the woods beyond the paddle boat/canoe rentals. Briefly tour the lower edge of a picnic area, enjoying beautiful still-water reflections of both the treed rim and a scattering of shoreline boulders. Hemlock, birch, maple, beech, pine, witch hazel, and showy mountain laurel shape an attractive passage. Noteworthy big trees slow hikers' strides.

Where the trail gets pinched by Burr Mountain Road, find ash and basswood shadowing the wetland shrubs and jewelweed drainages. Pass through the boat-launch parking area to resume the woods stroll. Vulture, ducks, grouse, owl, and kingfisher may suggest one raise the binoculars. At 0.6 mile, find a rock seat at the water's edge; nearby grow wild grape, dogwood, and arrowhead.

Before long, pass through a boggy area; boardwalks and footbridges advance the trail. On the right at 1 mile, find a memorial on a room-sized boulder; it honors an area forester (1886 to 1945). A former beaver pond now stretches right, while mountain laurel dresses the pond's edge.

Pass under a utility line, contouring the slope farther above the pond. At 1.65 miles, an unlabeled blue trail heads right, accessing the Muir Trail; forgo this spur, keeping to the Pond Loop. Upon descent, look left to find Big Rock Cave, a skyward-tilted boulder with a blackened overhang.

Again pass through a shrubby utility corridor, reaching a peninsula spur at 2 miles. Follow the spur left through laurel and hemlock, reaching the outcrop nose of the peninsula for pond viewing and lazing in the sun. Resume the counterclockwise Pond Loop at 2.3 miles, rounding amid hemlock and birch.

At 2.5 mile, reach the labeled **Muir Trail**, heading right. For the 3.2-mile Pond Loop alone, continue rounding shore, returning to the picnic area via the footbridge below the dam. For the longer **Pond Loop-Muir Trail Hike**, go right.

Ascend through similar forest, weaving amid the rocks, soon passing a scenic split boulder. Chestnut, maple, and oak join the ranks as the hike turns right on an old woods road. At 2.75 miles, cross the width of a utility corridor, gaining looks out the cut notch, and in another 0.1 mile, turn left

BURR POND STATE PARK

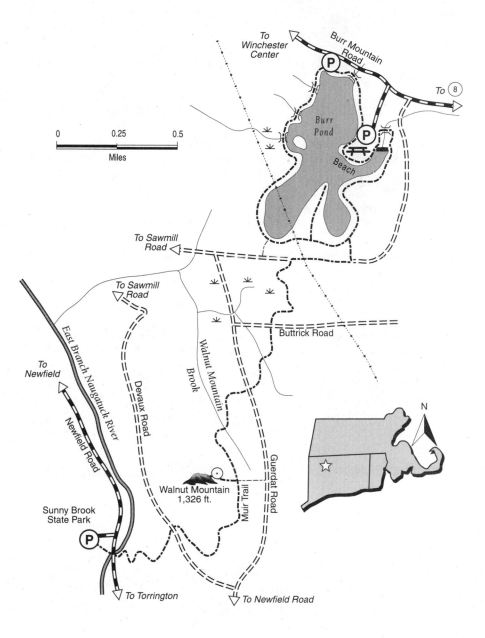

To Winchester Center

Burr Mountain Road

To 8

Burr Pond

Beach

0   0.25   0.5
Miles

To Sawmill Road

To Sawmill Road

Buttrick Road

East Branch Naugatuck River

To Newfield

Newfield Road

Devaux Road

Walnut Mountain Brook

Guerdat Road

Muir Trail

Walnut Mountain 1,326 ft.

Sunny Brook State Park

N

To Torrington

To Newfield Road

to again follow foot trail. Pines now intersperse the hardwoods, with many of the pines revealing multiple trunks.

Descend, bearing left to skirt a meadow and snag area, likely a reclaimed beaver pond given the girdled trees in the area. The added light from the clearing brings a burst of laurel. At 3.4 miles, cross Buttrick Road, a dirt forest road, and angle left, touring an open pine forest of evenly spaced tall straight trees. The trail contours, passes amid a scenic stand of beech, and crosses pallets spanning a muddy stretch.

At 3.65 miles, find back-to-back crossings of a woods road and Guerdat Road; the trail remains well-blazed. Next ascend from the upper drainage of Walnut Mountain Brook, and bear left on a road grade (3.8 miles). At the junction at 3.95 miles, a right turn leads to Walnut Mountain, a left turn leads to Guerdat Road, and the path ahead completes the Muir Trail.

Detour right, ascending a winding cobbled road. On a rock at 4.1 miles, a faint red arrow points out a tree-framed view overlooking the crowns of the immediate hardwood forest toward the next rise. A tree-ringed grassy circle marks the top (elevation 1,390 feet). Return to the Muir Trail at 4.35 miles, and turn right (south).

Round along the ridge of Walnut Mountain, traversing an outcrop; cairns help point the way. Next, descend sharply, touring amid the boulder and rock slabs of the lower slope to cross Devaux Road. Beyond a beech grove and wet area, turn right, descending beside the cobbly East Branch Naugatuck River.

Past a memorial to the area trail builder, ascend the rocky embankment of Newfield Road, cross the road bridge, and descend left through forest to the parking lot of Sunny Brook State Park, a primitive park (5.15 miles). Backtrack to the Burr Pond and the loop trail, 7.4 miles.

Go right to conclude the counterclockwise tour, exploring the bay arm where the dam is located. At the dam and spillway (7.85 miles), continue forward along the outlet, bearing left on a woods road. Cross a footbridge and turn left, following the outlet upstream past the dam, to return to the picnic area at a gate behind the restroom building (8.1 miles).

General description: This segment of the long-distance Metacomet Trail tours the rolling ridge of Talcott Mountain, topping rock outcrops and visiting Heublein Tower for vistas.

General location: 3 miles west of Bloomfield, Connecticut.

Special attractions: Heublein Tower, diverse woods, vistas, mountain laurel, wildflowers, fall foliage, hawk migration.

Length: 9.75 miles one-way.

Elevation: Find a 650-foot elevation change.

Difficulty: Moderate to strenuous.

Maps: Talcott Mountain State Park map; Avon 7.5-minute USGS quad; The Metropolitan District Talcott Mountain Reservoir Area map (purchase from the Metropolitan District Commission (MDC) administration building, located north off Farmington Road/Connecticut 4 at the Farmington-West Hartford town line).

Special requirements: No food, drink, or pets in Heublein Tower. Keep pets leashed while hiking. Obey respective rules for MDC and state park lands.

Season and hours: Spring through fall, 8 a.m. to sunset. Heublein Tower: 10 a.m. to 5 p.m. Thursday through Sunday, mid-April through August, and daily Labor Day through October. As staffing may alter tower hours; phone the parks office for current information.

Cliff edge, Talcott Mountain State Park, CT.

Penwood and Talcott Mountain state parks.

Finding the trailhead: With multiple access points, the Metacomet allows for various length round-trips and for shuttle hikes as well. Find the southern terminus at MDC's Hartford Reservoir 6; turn north off U.S. Highway 44, 2.2 miles east of CT 10. Central to the tour, find entry roads to Penwood and Talcott Mountain state parks diagonal to one another off CT 185, 3 miles west of Bloomfield.

For undeveloped Wilcox Park to the north, go 1.1 miles northwest on CT 185 from Penwood State Park and turn right on Terrys Plain Road. Go 2.7 miles and turn right on Wintonbury Road, following it 0.3 mile to the dead-end. Round the barricade to find the blazes of the Metacomet Trail in 20 feet.

Shuttle hikers should refrain from using Mountain Road (reached south off CT 315 just west of the CT 315 - CT 189 junction), as it is narrow with minimal road shoulder. For hikers who do use it, avoid blocking driveways or clogging the turnaround.

The hike: The Talcott Mountain leg of the Metacomet Trail passes through MDC land, Talcott Mountain and Penwood state parks, and the open space of Wilcox Park. Northbound, start along the gated woods road, touring the west shore of Hartford Reservoir 6. Avoid the 2-track bearing right toward the dam.

Look for the blue-blazed **Metacomet Trail** as it arrives on the left. Stay the reservoir road, touring an uncommon diversity of trees, including mixed oaks, spruce, pine, maple, hemlock, beech, birch, dogwood, basswood, hickory, ash, and tulip poplar. The glare from the reservoir filters through the thick mesh of hemlock, adding to the serenity of the tour. Where secondary trails branch left, keep to the dirt road. Cross over a pair of drainages with scenic stonework bridge rails at 1.1 and 1.2 miles. Near the end of the reservoir (1.45 miles), angle left uphill, following the blue blazes.

Low boulders riddle the forest floor, as the woods remain diverse and soothing. Enjoy a meandering tour of mild gradient, coming to a T-junction with a second woods road at 1.95 miles. Go left and take a quick right ascending via foot trail. Next cross a woods road to ascend a shrubby power-and-gas line corridor. From the corridor, bear left on woods road, still plodding uphill, still touring beautiful woods. A massive chestnut oak rises to the left at 2.35 miles.

Angle right across a paved lane to travel the Talcott Mountain ridge. Round a radio tower, and travel the rock outcrop of the western rim. Below a picnic pavilion, overlook the abrupt western slope toward Simsbury. Oak, laurel, and cedar favor the rim; look below for a breakaway pinnacle.

Reach the 165-foot-tall Heublein Tower at 2.7 miles. When open, its Observation Room provides a panoramic view spanning an estimated 1,200 square miles. Locate Mount Monadnock in New Hampshire and the blue sliver of Long Island Sound. Historic displays and re-created rooms also suggest a look. In fall, enjoy the foliage and hawk migration.

METACOMET TRAIL, TALCOTT MOUNTAIN

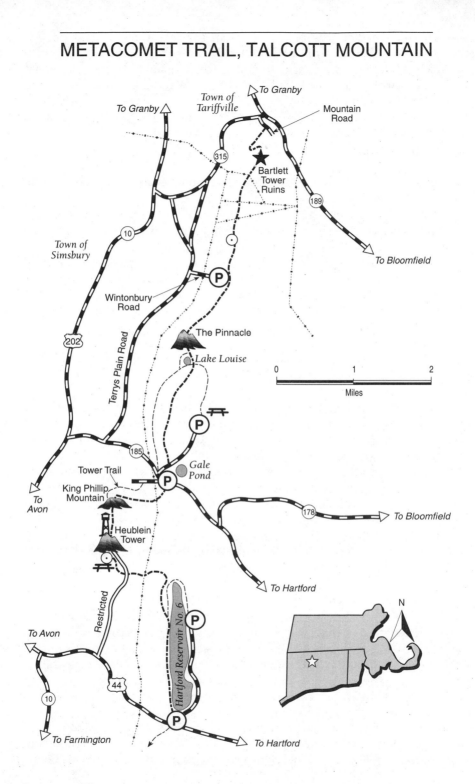

To Granby

Town of Tariffville

To Granby

Mountain Road

315

Bartlett Tower Ruins

189

To Bloomfield

Town of Simsbury

10

P

Wintonbury Road

Terrys Plain Road

202

The Pinnacle

Lake Louise

0   1   2

Miles

P

185

P

Tower Trail

Gale Pond

King Phillip Mountain

To Avon

Heublein Tower

178

To Bloomfield

To Hartford

Restricted

To Avon

Hartford Reservoir No. 6

P

10

44

P

N

To Farmington

To Hartford

Northbound, round west below Heublein Tower, enter a hemlock pocket, and turn left on **Tower Trail**, a woods road descending toward the entrance of Talcott Mountain State Park. In 100 yards, the blue-blazed Metacomet Trail turns right (north) to travel King Phillip Mountain; the Tower Trail travels the west rim below the mountain.

The Metacomet now rolls from laurel corridor to outcrop knoll, until 3.4 miles, where it descends an old road grade amid tall forest. In 0.25 mile, turn right on a footpath, and stay attentive as quick directional changes follow.

Angle right across a utility corridor, reaching a woods road heading toward some residences. At the road, take a quick left, briefly edging the shrubby utility corridor before veering right through hemlock-birch woods. Cross (or wade) a brook, and cross CT 185 to enter Penwood State Park (4.25 miles).

Hike north through the lower parking area and up the park road, skirting Gale Pond (no access). At 4.45 miles, turn left off the park road, ascending a wooded slope returning to the rolling ridge of Talcott Mountain. Find 2.5-foot-diameter hemlocks, prior to a ridge sag. In the sag, avoid the spur heading left.

Where the trail rises out of the sag, a brief detour left reaches a high point for a seasonal glimpse at the Farmington Valley. Resume the Metacomet Trail as it descends north, traveling along a wide earthen lane. At its junction with a red-blazed trail (5.4 miles), go left.

Coming off a small rise, veer right through tight young hemlock and bear left, ascending amid laurel to top an outcrop and follow the ridge north. Pass a stone pedestal 50 feet off the trail and descend to the park road at Lake Louise (6.2 miles), finding a dock and tables.

Bear right to round the shrubby east bank of the lake, touring a marshy maple woodland. Pass below a retained scree slope, coming to a junction at 6.35 miles. A left continues the lake basin tour; the Metacomet heads straight only to turn uphill to the right in 50 feet.

Follow foot trail and a steep stone stairway, top the ridge at a picnic flat, and bear left, still ascending. Next tag The Pinnacle for views west at Simsbury, the Farmington River Valley, and the hazy ridges disappearing west. To the south locate Heublein Tower. At the concrete foundations of an old lookout tower, a white-blazed trail heads right; stay north.

At 6.65 miles, bypass an alternate red-dot trail that descends left. The ridge tour continues amid woods, rounding and topping rocky knolls and dipping through sags, but gaining no views. Often near the rocky knolls, well-tracked side paths pass the more challenging blazed route. At 7.35 miles, begin the steep descent; look for a switchback and watch footing. Reach the closed dirt road in Wilcox Park east of the barrier on Wintonbury Road (7.5 miles). Shuttle hikers may end here.

The Metacomet however continues north. Skirt a private residence and ascend a cedar-deciduous slope to a birch flat. With a rolling ascent, claim an open outcrop (8 miles); it overlooks a utility corridor at the woods below

and the Farmington Valley beyond. A vibrant burst of autumn f[ ]
one forgive the intrusion of the power lines.

At 8.25 miles, pass through the first of three utility corrid[ ]
blazes join the blue ones. Descend east from the crest, come[ ]
road, and turn left, staying the blue blazes; the yellow tour heads right on
the woods road. Next, pass through a dark hemlock grove, descend the
width of another utility corridor, and cross a red-blazed woods road. Draw
back west atop the ridge, finding some grand big trees, snags, and split
trunks. At 9.1 miles, cross the final utility corridor with looks east and west
out its clearing.

Again roll between knoll features, passing from foot trail to carriage road
at 9.45 miles. Descend 250 feet, finding the Bartlett Tower ruins on the
right. The 40-foot-tall red-brick chimney and stone fireplace recall a recreational development and signal a turnaround for round-trip travelers. Seasonally, swallows pepper the skies.

Northbound travelers, descend the carriage road, turning right on a foot
trail at 9.6 miles. Pass through mixed woods coming out on Mountain Road
9.75 miles, the northernmost point for this description.

48 MACEDONIA BROOK STATE PARK

OVERVIEW

Originating with a gift of land from the White Memorial Foundation of
Litchfield, Connecticut, this 2,300-acre Connecticut state park nudges the
New York state border. Split in half by the clear-skipping waters of Macedonia
Brook, the park offers exciting ridgeline tours, vistas, peaceful woods, and
stonework from the past. During the Revolutionary War, some 100 Scatacook
Indian volunteers manned signal fires atop these and other area ridges of
the Housatonic Valley.

General description: A demanding loop travels the east and west ridges
framing the Macedonia Brook drainage.
General location: 4 miles northwest of Kent, Connecticut.
Special attractions: Vistas, ridge and valley forests, spring wildflowers,
mountain laurel, wildlife, fall foliage.
Length: Ridge Loop, 6.8-mile loop.
Elevation: Find a 700-foot elevation change.
Difficulty: Ridge Loop, strenuous. Find the East Ridge Hike, moderate; the
West Ridge Hike, rigorous.
Maps: State park brochure.
Special requirements: Fee for campground only; keep pets leashed. Note,
a brief difficult rock descent and climb on the west ridge may be unsuitable

ʃ children and novice hikers. Use hands, and beware of difficult footing and the likelihood of scrapes.

Season and hours: Year-round, spring through fall for hiking. Open 8 a.m. to sunset.

For information: Macedonia Brook State Park.

Finding the trailhead: From the junction of U.S. Highway 7 and Connecticut 341 in Kent, go west on CT 341 for 1.7 miles and turn right following the sign for Macedonia Brook State Park. Go 0.8 mile, reaching the park at the junction of Macedonia Brook and Fuller Mountain roads. Follow Macedonia Brook Road into the park, reaching the trailhead at the bridge in 0.5 mile, the headquarters in 0.9 mile, and the campground in 1.3 miles.

The hike: Start the **Ridge Loop** where the park road crosses over Macedonia Brook, 0.4 mile south of the headquarters; park at the small picnic area at the northwest corner of the bridge. For a counterclockwise tour, follow the blue-blazed trail as it heads east from the south side of the bridge, making a steady assault on the east ridge. Travel a mixed-age, multi-story forest with a wildflower-sprinkled floor, soon viewing the rocky crest.

By 0.2 mile, trace the ridgetop north, still ascending. This ridge offers the milder tour, exploring a peaceful wooded top. The west ridge entices with vistas and mountain laurel, but has a complicated rock passage.

Mixed oaks favor the ridgetop. Enjoy the companionship of deer, gray squirrel, chipmunk, woodpecker, scarlet tanager, and passing geese. At times, veils of fog rise from the valley drainages. A yellow-blazed trail descends left to the park core; stay the blue-blazed trail. Stone walls now intersect the path, while birch, maple, and hickory mix with the oaks. The Ridge Loop next crosses over the green-blazed trail that links the campground (left) with Fuller Mountain Road (right).

At 1.5 miles, descend sharply, but watch your footing, especially when the path is masked by leaves or rain-soaked. A scenic fern floor awaits at the bottom. Contour the east slope, coming out on a woods road. Follow it left for a spell, descending above a headwater of Macedonia Brook. At 2 miles, turn right on a footpath to cross the rocky brook. False hellebore, skunk cabbage, and moss accent the watery ribbon.

Ascend and gently roll, now touring along the western base of the east ridge, finding a congested, leafy woods. At 2.4 miles, meet Keeler Road (a dirt road), cross the road bridge, and enter the woods on the other side of Macedonia Brook. Or, detour south on Keeler Road to reach a water pump and pit toilet before continuing the loop.

Follow the marked trail between brook and rock wall before turning left to pass through a gap in the wall. Yellow violet and jack-in-the-pulpit grow near the brook. Big trees complement the tour, offering little clue that in 1848, the demand for charcoal fuel had virtually denuded these slopes. Ahead find a sharp descent marked by steep short pitches and a riddling of rocks. Hemlocks cloak the moister slope.

MACEDONIA BROOK STATE PARK

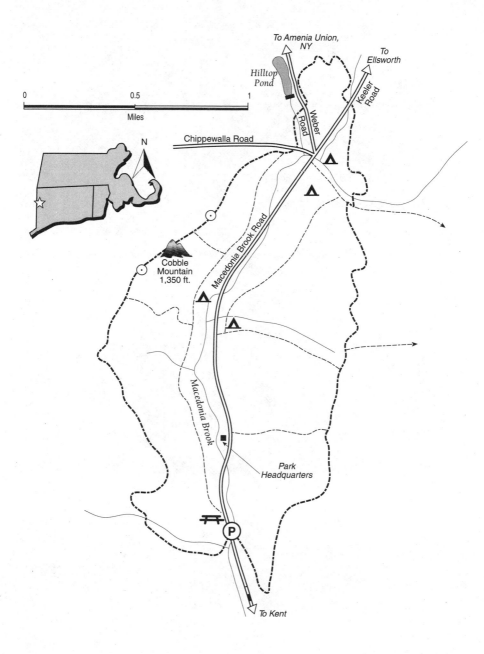

To Amenia Union, NY

To Ellsworth

Hilltop Pond

Weber Road

Keeler Road

Chippewalla Road

Macedonia Brook Road

Cobble Mountain 1,350 ft.

Macedonia Brook

Park Headquarters

To Kent

0   0.5   1

Miles

N

Jack-in-the-Pulpit, Macedonia Brook State Park, CT.

At 3 miles, the right fork leads to a view of Hilltop Pond, a private dammed water with a pretty birch shore. The Ridge Loop bears left, paralleling the wooded slope just above Weber Road. At 3.25 miles, cross Weber Road to follow a gated, grassy woods road back into the park; a garter snake may slither by. At 3.7 miles, cross dirt Chippewalla Road, keeping to the same woods road. In 200 feet, hike the foot trail heading right for a sashaying woods climb.

Patches of mountain laurel herald the ridgetop. At 4.2 miles, travel a rounded bald outcrop amid low oaks, glimpsing neighboring ridges. Descend south along the west ridge, finding an open view atop a steep, slanted rock face. Here admire the Macedonia Brook drainage with its evergreen treetops piercing the leafy canopy and gain looks at Cobble and Chase mountains. Be careful descending as footholds are few and the rock surface is boot-polished.

At 4.4 miles, reach a thin drainage where the green trail descends left to the campground. Ahead find a treacherous ascent, tracing a thin, canted ledge along a small chasm, followed by a challenging rock scramble. While the ascent is difficult, downhill hikers protested even more loudly; some scooting downhill on their backsides. This route formerly tested the mettle of the Appalachian Trail trekker, until trail designers re-routed the national scenic trail.

Top the ridge at 4.6 miles, touring the lichen-mottled outcrop of Cobble Mountain for western views. At 4.75 miles find the most expansive view, overlooking a broad New York valley, the cliff-sided ridge below, and the distant Catskills and Taconics. Vultures soar the thermals.

Next descend coming to a junction with the white trail. It continues the steep descent left for the campground, while the blue Ridge Loop bears right for a rolling, contouring tour amid mountain laurel and rich hardwood forest; enjoy a taller, fuller forest than that on the rocky crest. At 6 miles, the descent accelerates; bear left just before a side drainage, still touring amid rich woods. Twice cross the side brook via stones to end at the small picnic area, 6.8 miles.

OVERVIEW

Snuggled in the Berkshire foothills of Northwest Connecticut, this 4,000-acre private reserve offers the public some 35 miles of trail and woods road to explore. Devoted to conservation, education, research, and suitable recreation within a natural arena, the Foundation has set aside 600 acres as "Natural Area", allowing the lands and habitats to change and prosper free from intervention. Ten acres of old-growth forest, a premier boardwalk, Bantam Lake and River, mixed woods, marsh, and ponds further endorse the area.

General description: Three short hikes present the diversity, visiting lake shore, swamp, and hilltop.
General location: In Litchfield and Morris, Connecticut.
Special attractions: Boardwalks and observation platforms, bird and wildlife sightings, spring and summer wildflowers, old-growth trees, fall foliage, museum/nature center.
Length: Lake Trail, 1 mile round-trip; Little Pond Boardwalk Hike, 3.2 miles round-trip; Apple Hill Trail, 3.2 miles round-trip.
Elevation: Lake Trail, 20-foot elevation change; Little Pond Boardwalk Hike, virtually flat; Apple Hill Trail, 200-foot elevation change.
Difficulty: Lake Trail and Little Pond Boardwalk Hike, both easy; Apple Hill Trail, moderate.
Maps: Foundation guide map (purchase at museum).
Special requirements: Admission fee for museum, trails free. Obey posted rules. Purchase a map to learn blazing scheme and sort out trail options. Expect some soggy reaches.
Season and hours: Year-round, generally spring through fall for hiking. Trails: dawn to dusk. Museum: 9 a.m. to 5 p.m. Monday through Saturday and noon to 5 p.m. Sunday (May through October); 8:30 a.m. to 4:30 p.m. Monday through Saturday and 9 a.m. to 4 p.m. Sunday (November through April).
For information: White Memorial Conservation Center.
Finding the trailhead: From the Connecticut 63 - U.S. Highway 202 junction in Litchfield, go southwest on U.S. 202 for 2.1 miles and turn left on Bissell Road, followed by a right on Whitehall Road to reach White Memorial Conservation Center in 0.5 mile. There begin the Lake Trail and Little Pond Boardwalk Hike.

For Apple Hill Trail, continue east on Bissell Road from its intersection with Whitehall Road for 0.6 mile, and turn right on Whites Woods/Alain White Road. In 1.6 miles, turn right on East Shore Road. Find the gated north trail terminus on the left in 0.7 mile; reach a southern terminus in another 0.9 mile. Park roadside, and do not block gates.

WHITE MEMORIAL FOUNDATION

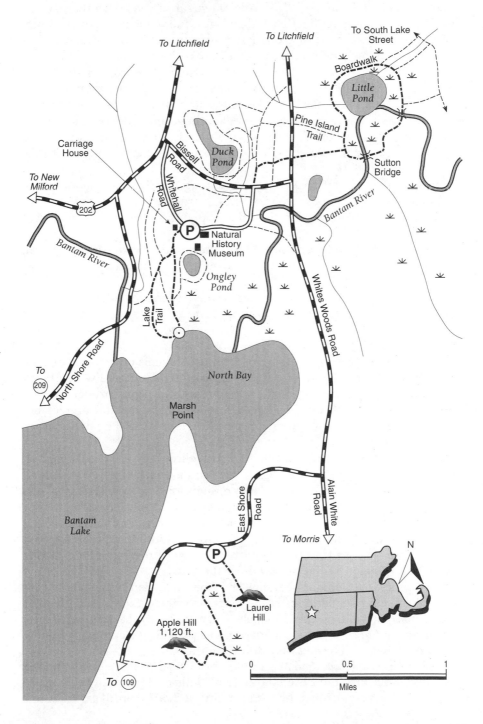

To Litchfield

To Litchfield

To South Lake Street

Boardwalk

Little Pond

Pine Island Trail

Carriage House

Bissell Road

Whitehall Road

Duck Pond

Sutton Bridge

To New Milford

202

Bantam River

Bantam River

P

Natural History Museum

Ongley Pond

Whites Woods Road

Lake Trail

North Shore Road

To 209

North Bay

Marsh Point

Bantam Lake

East Shore Road

Alain White Road

To Morris

P

Laurel Hill

Apple Hill 1,120 ft.

To 109

N

0   0.5   1

Miles

The hikes: For the yellow-blazed **Lake Trail**, start below the Carriage House in the Conservation Center area, following a dirt road along the back side of a stone wall and bear right. Ancient sugar maple adorn the start. At 0.1 mile, reach the loop junction and go right, following a woods road. Impressive gnarled oak and tamarack now contribute to the tour. Stay with the yellow blazes, where side trails branch or cross the route.

Descend to a marsh woodland, and at 0.3 mile, go left on a narrow foot trail, touring fuller forest. Roots snake across the path, while poison ivy scales the tree trunks. Cross a duckweed-coated channel, gaining glimpses of Bantam Lake. At 0.7 mile, find concrete pilings and a boardwalk leading to a lake observation tower. Overlook the marshy edge of North Bay with Marsh Point across the water. Gold finch, swallows, ducks, and swans may add to the scene.

Continue the counterclockwise tour, staying briefly along shore before bearing left through marshy woods. Parallel a rock wall and pass through a break in an intersecting wall to close the loop and return to the trailhead at 1 mile.

For the **Little Pond Boardwalk Hike**, start on the **Self-guiding Nature Trail** (brochure sold at museum), following the unsurfaced road heading east just north of the museum.

At 0.25 mile, turn left, traveling an attractive marsh meadow, with slow, glassy Bantam River flowing along the opposite side. Where the nature trail turns left, continue forward, crossing Bissell Road at 0.5 mile. A few old-growth trees punctuate the tour.

A pine-hemlock forest next houses the tour; travel is on a scenic needle-strewn lane. At 0.6 mile, reach the **Little Pond Trail**, blazed with a black square within a white square, and follow the trail right through choked forest. Cross Whites Woods Road at 0.75 mile, tour a mixed evergreen-deciduous woods, and bear left, rounding an open field. After the route changes to foot trail, find the loop junction (1 mile).

Go right for a counterclockwise tour, traveling the site's acclaimed elevated boardwalk, passing through woods and a dense stand of 8-foot-tall phragmites (plumed reeds). Cross Bantam River via Sutton Bridge. Lily pads top the margins of the glassy stream; canoeists part the waters.

Standing water, tufted marsh grass, and cattails bring a rich texture to the marsh. In places, shrubs shape a tight, humid corridor. Again cross Bantam River and pass a side trail branching right, toward the boundary. Maple, pine, skunk cabbage, and fern now dress the tour.

At 1.4 miles, overlook a horseshoe river bend shaded by grand old willows. Ahead, enjoy open looks at the marsh-bordered Little Pond. Keep to the pond circuit, as a side trail branches right to South Lake Street. Lilies, arrowhead, cattail, bog grass, and dark pools provide exceptional viewing. Geese, swallows, and beaver may draw attention.

Depart the boardwalk, and at 2.1 miles, prior to closing the loop, find the red triangles marking the **Pine Island Trail**. This trail travels a deep woods to encircle Duck Pond, aided by the **Mattatuck Trail**. For hikers seeking a longer tour, Duck Pond offers a logical extension; consult your map. For Little Pond alone, continue forward closing the loop at 2.2 miles, turn right, and retrace the hike to the museum, 3.2 miles.

On a north to south tour, the blue-blazed **Apple Hill Trail** ascends a grassy woods road, passing amid tall thin trees weaving a full canopy. In 0.1 mile, veer left as indicated by an arrow; here mountain laurel foreshadows the ascent of Laurel Hill. Upon skirting a gnarled split-branched oak, a foot trail replaces the old road. Leaves and fallen birch nearly hide a collapsed rock wall lining the tour.

Descend, touring some soggy reaches; generally enough stones and roots allow hopscotch travel. Skunk cabbage, wood anemone, purple violet, starflower, and jack-in-the-pulpit shout in springtime, and the forest becomes more mixed, both in variety and in age. At 0.6 mile, a narrow boardwalk passes through a bog with highbush blueberry, hellebore, tufted grasses, duckweed, and moss. Laurel showers the exit. Chickadee, pileated woodpecker, scarlet tanager, and warblers delight travelers.

At 1 mile, pass a small circular dark-water pond, with a larger marshy water beyond the trees to the left. Noisy ducks and geese betray its location. At 1.1 mile, find a junction; here a 0.2-mile round-trip detour left adds a view of the snag-riddled marsh. A right resumes the hike to Apple Hill.

En route to the hill, pass a marshy patch and an oak old-timer. The climb briefly intensifies, before reaching the brushy top. Follow the grassy swath, bearing right at the junction; the trail branch heading left leads to the southern trailhead. Reach the one-story summit Observation Tower at 1.5 miles (1.7 miles with wetland detour). Vistas pan Bantam Lake, the rolling forested hills, and area farms. Return as you came.

50 SESSIONS WOODS WILDLIFE MANAGEMENT AREA

OVERVIEW

In its 455 acres, the Wildlife Management Area (WMA) demonstrates various land management and wildlife enhancement practices, explained by two self-guiding loops. Explore mixed woods and small meadow clearings; brook, marsh, and vernal pond; laurel thicket; and a backyard wildlife habitat. Sightings of deer, fox, beaver, wild turkey, cardinal, heron, and pileated woodpecker may add to a tour; carry binoculars.

General description: Two short loops explore the WMA.
General location: In Burlington, Connecticut.
Special attractions: Bird and wildlife watching, marsh/beaver pond,

observation tower, waterfall, diverse woods, spring-flowering shrubs.

Length: Beaver Pond Trail, 2.6-mile loop, with an additional 0.7 mile of side spurs; Deer Sign Trail, 0.6-mile loop.

Elevation: Beaver Pond Trail, 140-foot elevation change; Deer Sign Trail, 40-foot elevation change.

Difficulty: Both, easy.

Maps: WMA map; generally available at trailhead register.

Special requirements: Keep pets leashed. No collecting and no feeding of wildlife. Beware of ticks and poison ivy.

Season and hours: Year-round, but generally spring through fall for hiking. Sunrise to sunset.

For information: Sessions Woods Wildlife Management Area.

Finding the trailhead: From the junction of Connecticut 4 and Connecticut 69 in Burlington, go south on CT 69 for 3.3 miles and turn right to enter Sessions Woods WMA.

The hikes: Both of these trails welcome "Sunday" strolling, with seasonal discoveries bringing hikers to their knees or tilting their heads skyward. Gravel or cinder-surfaced service roads host travel.

Look for the start of the **Beaver Pond Trail** on the right-hand side of the entrance road as you turn into the parking lot. This counterclockwise, mildly rolling tour travels rich hardwood forest of maple, oak, hickory, black cherry, and birch, with a varied shrub understory consisting of brambles, brier, sassafras, and chestnut. Near the start, the blue **Tunxis Trail** arrives on the

Beaver Pond Trail, Sessions Woods Wildlife Management Area, CT.

SESSIONS WOODS WILDLIFE MANAGEMENT AREA

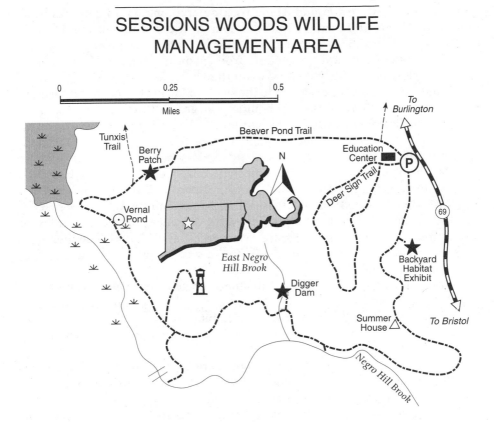

right and briefly shares the tour. Interpretive signs introduce vegetation and explain management practices.

In clear-cut openings, wildflowers abound. Amid the forest and wooded swamps, mountain laurel, sheep laurel, azalea, and pond lilies up the ante. Benches on the tour suggest one pause. In stillness, the wildlife often comes to you.

At 0.5 mile, find the first of the side spurs branching left to a berry patch. The Tunxis Trail departs to the right soon afterward.

Next, pass some big pines, arriving at the beaver pond and marsh (0.75 mile). This vast snag-filled pond particularly captivates when capped with pink and white pond lilies, when reflecting its autumn-tinted rim, or when a family of deer drinks at its edge. Managers artificially manipulate the water level using pipes. By drawing the water down, they prod the beaver back into action, raising the pond level. Check to see if the osprey nesting platform has any occupants.

Beyond the main pond, a quick spur left leads to a vernal pond and its observation platform, rimmed by mountain laurel. Salamander and frog may be spied. More wetland, some rock outcropping, and hemlocks now mark the loop. At 1.1 miles find the spur to the 25-foot-tall observation tower (elevation 756 feet). The crow's nest of the 3-story tower puts hikers above the trees for views stretching from Avon to Meriden. Resume the hike in 0.25 mile, quickly coming upon the waterfall spur.

This 0.25-mile detour descends to the right, following footpath and earthen stairs, reaching the waterfall on bouldery Negro Hill Brook. The drainage shows massive boulders and slabs, with the falls spilling in rivulets through rock crevices. Following heavy rains, a more lively falls surges over and through the rock.

Resume the counterclockwise loop at 1.6 miles. Side trails branch to Digger Dam (a fish enhancement weir) and to Negro Hill Brook. The trail remains mainly wooded with occasional meadow openings. At 2.4 miles, keep to the service road, touring a scenic pocket of white pine. At 2.7 miles, a spur heads left to Summer House, a covered pavilion with benches and vistas of the ridges to the south. Soon after, a second spur to the left leads to the outdoor classroom.

At 3 miles, turn right to explore the fenced backyard habitat, with identified plantings and a frog pond. Butterflies, dragonflies, and songbirds animate the enclosure. From the backyard habitat, return to the service road. Close the loop, rounding a maintenance building, to exit at the parking lot (3.3 miles).

Find the trailhead for the **Deer Sign Trail** to the left of the Education Center. Round the gate and follow the service road to the right for a counterclockwise tour. The circuit passes through forest and meadow. Look for a bat shelter that can support 300 bats, nesting boxes and platforms, and brush piles for wildlife shelter. A few large boulders punctuate the tour. Along the trail, interpretive plaques explain how the management of each microcosm promotes wildlife. Midway, a bench suggests a more reflective appreciation. Close the loop at 0.6 mile.

51 RAGGED MOUNTAIN PRESERVE TRAIL

General description: Within this 563-acre open space acqu
the Land and Water Conservation Fund, a demanding loop journeys through
restful mixed woods and traverses a stirring cliff rim.
General location: In Berlin, Connecticut.
Special attractions: Vistas, an exciting tiered and broken ridge, mixed woods,
wildlife sightings, fall foliage.
Length: 6.1-mile loop.
Elevation: Travel from a trailhead elevation of 230 feet to a summit elevation
of 761 feet atop Ragged Mountain.
Difficulty: Strenuous.
Maps: Meriden and New Britain 7.5-minute USGS quads.
Special requirements: Use caution along the rim. Boots recommended to
protect ankles. Be especially careful following rain, frost, or heavy dew.
Avoid during times of snow and ice.
Season and hours: Year-round, as weather allows.
For information: Conservation Commission, Berlin Town Hall.
Finding the trailhead: At the junction of Connecticut 372 and Connecticut
71A in Berlin, go south on CT 71A for 1.2 miles and turn right (west) onto
West Lane. Go 0.6 mile, reaching the trailhead where West Lane ends at
Wigwam Road. Find roadside parking for up to a dozen vehicles. Or, arriving
from the Berlin junction of CT 71 and CT 71A, go 1.1 miles north on CT 71A

Ragged Ridge, Ragged Mountain Preserve, CT.

.urn left on West Lane proceeding to the trailhead.

The hike: At the trailhead, a boulder plaque commemorates the acquisition of Ragged Mountain Memorial Preserve. Enter the conservation land and follow the blue blazes with the red dots, bearing left. A narrow woods road hosts the tour, ascending amid hemlock, oak, maple, beech, and birch. Huckleberry and only a handful of other understory species pierce the leaf duff.

At 0.3 mile, go right on a footpath for a slow gradual ascent. Poison ivy caps the rocks and wraps trees, spiraling skyward. The trail grows more rocky and rolling. Blazes appear at regular intervals, clueing travelers to subtle direction changes.

By 0.5 mile, begin traversing amid outcrops and along the rim. As the low cliffs grade higher, gaps in the woods afford southeastern glimpses. Where the cliffs plummet some 100-feet, views pan Hart Ponds and the wooded terrain; swans ply the water. Rain cloud, fog, or excessive humidity bring an uneasy aura of mystery.

Wild rose, blueberry, strawberry, and meadow grass accent the dark-rock realm. The trail mostly hugs the edge with brief woods lapses. Red eft, toad, slug, turtle, and spotted salamander may entertain the curious. But be on guard; the area is known to have copperheads.

Mounting the next rim level, look for a pull-apart section of cliff isolated from the main wall by a deep fissure. Views continue to pan Hart Ponds, adding looks at the Hanging Hills of Meriden. Some Indian pipe and prince's pine lend floral accent. Where the trail dips, enjoy a fuller maple woods; low oaks dress the open rock.

Soon after a fissure serves up a southwestern view and a chance to admire the vertical-cliff profile, reach the **Metacomet Trail** (1.7 miles). Here bear right on the Metacomet for the loop, now following blue blazes and touring the summit of Ragged Mountain. Find more spurs of climb, some requiring hand assists, with better views trending west.

By 2 miles, rock climbers shout instructions from the cliffs below, and a steep climber's trail with wire-mesh steps descends to the left. More hemlocks shade the tour. Where the trail splits take either fork, as they soon merge. To the right, pass through woods, emerging atop an outcrop at 2.4 miles. Keep to the blue-blazed route.

A short detour left from the trail at 3 miles reaches the rim rising directly over Wesel Reservoir for a dizzying look over the cliff. One early summer, a spotted turtle had, strangely enough, chosen this forbidding site for laying her eggs. Grant all wildlife a wide margin.

At the junction at 3.1 miles, depart the blue Metacomet Trail and leave the ridge, once again following the blue blazes with the red dots and once again following woods road. In the next few tenths, look for the trail to take a couple of turns, all well blazed. Hemlock, hickory, oak, and maple weave a relaxing tour.

At 4 miles, turn right off the woods road, taking a footpath through a

RAGGED MOUNTAIN PRESERVE TRAIL

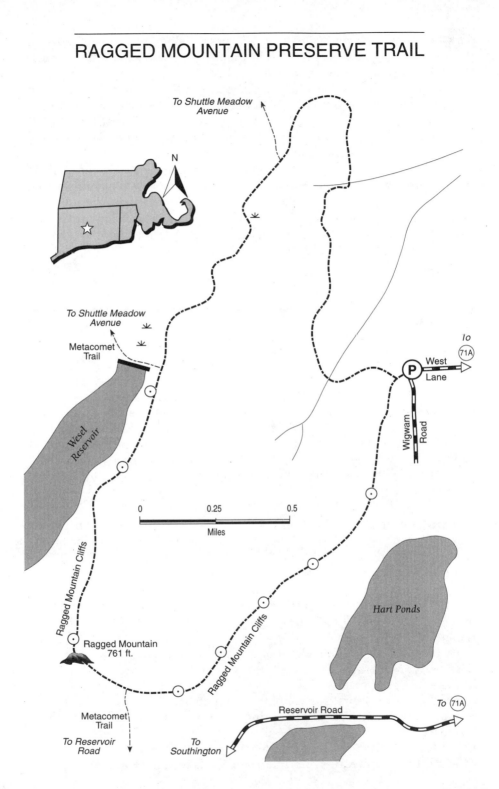

To Shuttle Meadow Avenue

To Shuttle Meadow Avenue

Metacomet Trail

Wesel Reservoir

Ragged Mountain Cliffs

Ragged Mountain 761 ft.

Ragged Mountain Cliffs

Metacomet Trail

To Reservoir Road

Hart Ponds

P West Lane

Io 71A

Wigwam Road

0   0.25   0.5
Miles

Reservoir Road

To Southington

To 71A

dark hemlock-oak stand. The hike now passes along the wooded edge of Panther Swamp and rolls over low hilly bumps. The woods grow more mixed. Stay the blue blazes with the red dot.

The spur heading left at 4.4 miles leads to Shuttle Meadow Avenue; keep right, returning to woods road. Both the spur and the main trail have the same blazing scheme. Descend steadily, remaining amid woods, and skirting a privately owned grassy flat. American basswood and birch join the mix, with bigger diameter trees enhancing the scene.

At 5.1 miles, turn right, following a foot trail, ascending a rocky slope near an often dry drainage, with a seasonal falls. Traverse a manmade rock wall before topping out at 5.3 miles. After a brief descent, contour the wooded slope and again descend. At 5.8 miles, turn right on a woods road, still following blazes. Close the loop at 6 miles, and turn left, reaching the trailhead on West Lane at Wigwam Road at 6.1 miles.

52 SOUTHFORD FALLS STATE PARK

OVERVIEW

At this charming 120-acre Connecticut state park, find scenic picnic lawns with big shade trees, Papermill Pond, a cascading falls tumbling through a small gorge, the sparkling tannin-colored waters of Eight Mile Brook, and a covered bridge. While short, the trail system visits each of these features and travels a wooded hillside reaching a low tower, now mostly enclosed by trees. Historically, the racing falls powered various mills, including an early match factory.

General description: With easy-to-moderate grades, this loop travels downstream along Eight Mile Brook, ascends the hill rising east of the brook, and returns along Papermill Pond.
General location: 4 miles southeast of Southbury, Connecticut.
Special attractions: Pond, falls, and brook; hemlock-hardwood forest; covered bridge; millstones, a steam-engine foundation, and remnant sluice pipe; mountain laurel; fall foliage.
Length: 1.5-mile loop.
Elevation: Find a 300-foot elevation change.
Difficulty: Moderate.
Maps: State park map.
Special requirements: No camping; keep pets leashed.
Season and hours: Year-round, spring through fall for hiking. Open 8 a.m. to sunset.
For information: Southford Falls State Park.
Finding the trailhead: From Interstate 84, take exit 16 and go south on

Connecticut 188, passing through Southford to reach the park on the left in 2.9 miles.

The hike: From the parking area at Papermill Pond, hike the wide gravel lane heading south along the west shore to reach the falls and the core of the park. Papermill Pond reflects its wooded shore; the wake from a muskrat may distort the watery image. In 200 feet, reach the upper bridge above the dam and falls, marking the loop junction. Forgo crossing, continuing south (downstream) along the west shore, maneuvering over the open rock outcrop to view Southford Falls.

Natural outcrop and scenic stonework shape the racing multi-directional cascades of Southford Falls. The longest drop of the 12-foot-high falls measures 6 feet. Find a beautiful juxtaposition of black rock and tiered white streamers. From the falls, Eight Mile Brook slips through a narrow rocky gorge, dropping in stages, exciting eye and ear.

Downstream at the covered bridge (0.15 mile) find a more sedate, gently riffling brook. Red with white trim, Burr Arch Bridge (built 1972) replicates a circa 1804 design. Nearby locate the stones and other evidence of the site's milling heritage. Pass through the bridge.

On the east shore, turn left for the falls loop alone, gaining new perspectives on it and the gorge, before crossing the upper bridge at 0.3 mile. For the longer loop to the tower, turn right following the east shore of Eight Mile Brook downstream; red blazes mark the tour.

Enjoy a rich woods of maple, birch, aspen, tulip, elm, and hemlock. At

Southford Falls, Southford Falls State Park, CT.

SOUTHFORD FALLS STATE PARK

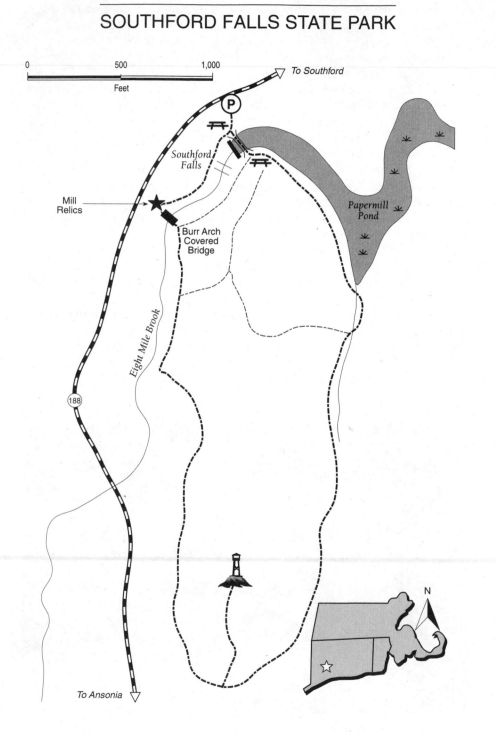

0   500   1,000
Feet

To Southford

Southford Falls

Mill Relics

Burr Arch Covered Bridge

Eight Mile Brook

188

Papermill Pond

N

To Ansonia

0.25 mile (junction 3), bypass a spur on the left, offering yet another option. Where a small boardwalk traverses a moist bottomland, find t. tannin-tinted waters of Eight Mile Brook within easy striking distance. Just beyond the walk, look for the red-blazed trail to head left uphill, leaving behind the brook (0.4 mile).

Laurel, witch-hazel, beech, and tall oak clothe the west-facing slope. Round behind an outcrop knoll for a contouring ascent; below hear the drone of CT 188. Find a few hazelnut and maple-leaf viburnum. With another uphill pulse, top a small outcrop overlooking the wooded slope. Now round left, coming to the tower junction at 0.75 mile; a sign points out the turn for clockwise travelers. Go left for the tower, right to continue the loop.

For the tower spur, ascend left amid oak and laurel, reaching the two-story platform (0.85 mile). Trees enfold three sides, but hikers earn a south-western glimpse of a neighboring ridge and a rural scene, pretty in autumn flush. A secondary trail crosses the summit and descends the east slope amid a laurel thicket. Backtrack to the loop junction, and turn left.

Travel the upper reaches of the eastern slope, passing amid oaks and tall mountain laurel. Where the trail tours below an outcrop crest, maples fill out the forest, while mountain laurel wanes from the mix. Soon pass through a hilltop depression where outcrops sweep up both sides of the bowl. Here tulip poplar and aspen add their signature leaves.

Veer right up the side of the bowl, again passing amid mountain laurel, coming to a plank walk and junction at 1.3 miles. To the left lies Eight Mile Brook for an alternative return. Bear right to complete the loop near the pond.

Reach the marshy end of Papermill Pond in 200 feet. Scenic boulders mark the far shore, while greenbrier, highbush blueberry, and sweet pepperbush crowd the immediate bank. Traverse the open lawn, passing between a shelter and the pond shore to close the loop at the upper bridge (1.5 miles). From the bridge, look for pickerel amid the aquatic vegetation; often a heron stalks the shallows for shimmery minnows.

Occupying the east shore of Lake Zoar, a long lake impoundment on the Housatonic River, this 605-acre Connecticut state park offers lake, brook, woods, and crest discovery. The name, legend says, refers to the price colonists paid the Pootaluck Indians for hunting and fishing rights in this area: a brass kettle. In 1919, the raised lake waters swallowed the site of the historic Indian village, erasing all record of this farming people, who operated a sophisticated drum communication system that could relay a message 200 miles in just 2 hours.

General description: Three day-hikes of varying difficulty incorporate the area's nature and hiking trails, presenting the park's natural merit. Each offers lake overviews, but only the Pomperaug-Oxford Loop accesses Lake Zoar.

General location: 5 miles south of Southbury, Connecticut.

Special attractions: Lake Zoar overlooks and access, small waterfall, picturesque Kettletown Brook, rich hemlock-hardwood forests, flowering dogwood and mountain laurel, fall foliage.

Length: William Miller Trail, 0.5-mile round-trip to vistas (1.75-mile loop); Pomperaug-Crest Loop, 3.7 miles round-trip; Pomperaug-Oxford Loop, 6.5 miles round-trip.

Elevation: William Miller Trail, 100-foot elevation change. For both the Pomperaug-Crest Loop and the Pomperaug-Oxford Loop, find a 450-foot elevation change.

Difficulty: William Miller Trail, easy. Pomperaug-Crest Loop, moderate. Pomperaug-Oxford Loop, strenuous.

Maps: State park map.

Special requirements: The state park and Jackson Cove Recreation Area to the south, both charge seasonal vehicle fees. Hikers must keep pets leashed; no trail camping, no fires.

Season and hours: Year-round, spring through fall for hiking. Open 8 a.m. to sunset.

For information: Kettletown State Park.

Finding the trailhead: From Interstate 84, take exit 15 and head south on Kettletown Road, following signs for the park. In 3.5 miles, turn right on George's Hill Road to find the entrance on the left in 0.8 mile. Start all hikes from the day-use areas.

To access the Pomperaug Trail at Jackson Cove Recreation Area, forgo taking the right-hand turn onto George's Hill Road at 3.5 miles; instead, continue south another 1.3 miles on Maple Tree Hill Road, and then proceed forward on Jackson Cove Road for 0.2 mile.

KETTLETOWN STATE PARK

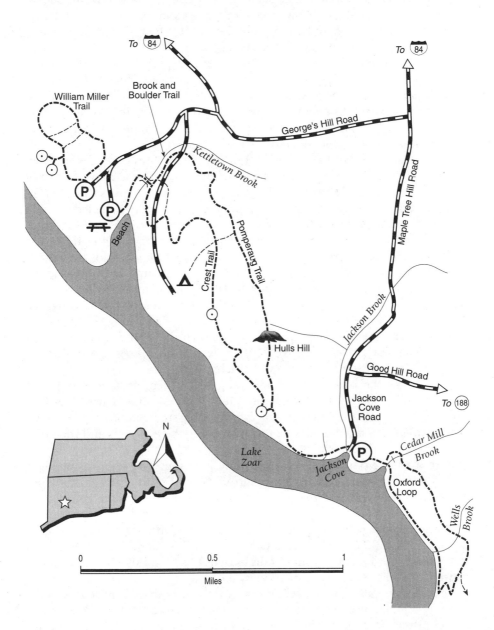

William Miller Trail

Brook and Boulder Trail

To 84

To 84

George's Hill Road

Kettletown Brook

Pomperaug Trail

Crest Trail

Maple Tree Hill Road

Beach

Hulls Hill

Jackson Brook

Good Hill Road

Jackson Cove Road

To 188

Cedar Mill Brook

Oxford Loop

Lake Zoar

Jackson Cove

Wells Brook

N

0   0.5   1
Miles

The hikes: For the **William Miller Trail**, take the park road toward the Youth Group Camp to find this blue-blazed trail (a barricaded woods road) heading north to the right of a kiosk; look for it where the road forms a loop. Ascend amid hemlock, oak, birch, hickory, dogwood, beech, and tulip poplar, bearing left at the trail's loop junction in 100 feet. Seasonally, leaves soften the appearance of the woods road.

Above the trail to the left, admire the outcrop crest of a small hill. Before long, a spur marked by an orange dot on a blue blaze journeys left to top the hill. Where the vista spur branches at 0.2 mile, either fork leads to a view. The left vista overlooks a more natural lake setting, featuring the steep tree-mantled drainage. The vantage to the right has a wilder cliff aspect and overlooks a more developed shore.

Return as you came (0.5 mile), or opt for the 1.75-mile clockwise loop. Find the loop well-blazed, touring time-healed woods road and foot trail through diverse woods. Stay left, forgoing two cut-across spurs that shorten the loop. Be attentive to blazes. Jay, deer, and grouse may be spied.

For better parking, start the **Pomperaug-Crest Loop** below the bathhouse at the beach, hiking the paved and gravel-surfaced lane following Kettletown Brook upstream. Come to a footbridge and a sign for the nature trails at 0.1 mile. Cross the bridge and turn left (upstream), backtracking the numbers of the **Brook and Boulder Nature Trail** from B6 to B1.

Enjoy a meandering tour amid the boulders overlooking the rushing cascades of Kettletown Brook; hemlocks contribute a soothing darkness. At post B1, bear left, following blue blazes to reach the **Pomperaug Trail** on the opposite side of the park road (0.3 mile); a sign marks the trail. Find nearby parking for only a couple of vehicles.

Now follow the blue-blazed Pomperaug Trail, encountering a couple of quick direction changes before settling into a steady line of travel. A foot trail leads through the hemlock-birch forest, passing remnant rock walls. The ascent grades from moderate to steep before the trail tops and traverses a low ridge (0.8 mile).

With a rolling descent reach the 1-mile junction. The spur to the right (blazed with a white dot on blue background) leads to the campground and **Crest Trail**, allowing hikers to shorten the tour. Stay left for the Pomperaug Trail.

The Pomperaug Trail dips to a moist bottom with sweet pepperbush, then ascends amid oak and birch. Outcrops and boulders riddle the woods. At 1.4 miles, find a rush of mountain laurel. At 1.65 miles, top the outcrop summit of Hulls Hill for a framed view east.

Next descend along the sparkling mica-rich outcrop and through woods, reaching a junction and locator map at 1.9 miles. Here the blue Pomperaug Trail continues straight for Jackson Cove Recreation Area and **Oxford Loop**. To complete the **Pomperaug-Crest Loop**, bear right on the **Crest Trail** marked by a white dot on blue background.

The Crest Trail mounts a low rocky knoll for a limited seasonal view; it then descends the knoll, circling back on itself, contouring the hemlock slope. With a brief steep climb, top the ridge rising above Lake Zoar (2. miles). At 2.3 miles, a short spur leads to a restricted lake view. Briefly pull away from the rim, returning to the western crest for better views at 2.6 miles. Find a sketchy presence of mountain laurel amid the high-canopy forest.

Descend a hemlock slope, crossing over a stone wall to reach a junction at 3 miles. Here the Pomperaug-campground connector from the 1-mile junction arrives on the right; the campground lies to the left. Proceed forward to return to the nature trails and vehicle. Blue blazes again lead the way.

Ascend the ridge above the campground, passing behind a huge boulder. Now angle downhill, taking a switchback before coming to a set of wooden steps descending left; a foot trail continues right. Either way returns to the trailhead; right returns via the **Brook and Boulder Trail**.

Descend left on the **Upland Nature Trail**, angle left across the park road, and descend more steps, coming out at the viewing platform of the **Hemlock Trail**, returning to the lush hemlock drainage of Kettletown Brook. Glimpse the beach across the way and follow the Hemlock Trail to the brook footbridge, returning to the trailhead at 3.7 miles. With its boardwalk in disrepair and rocks erupting in the trail, the Hemlock Trail no longer serves wheelchair users.

For the **Pomperaug-Oxford Loop**, follow the above trail description to the 1.9-mile junction, but forgo taking the **Crest Trail**. Instead, remain on the blue-blazed **Pomperaug Trail**, finding a steep 0.25-mile descent to the Lake Zoar shore.

At the lake, the trail curves left, following the shoreline south. Dogwood, hemlock, maple, birch, and upper-canopy oaks frame the way. Clearings offer open lake views; beware of poison ivy. Round a small cove and cross a brook on a rickety hewn log to contour the slope some 30 feet above shore. Dogwoods remain bountiful, showy in spring bloom, dashing in autumn red.

A steep pitch leads to the rock-hopping crossing of Jackson Brook and the boat launch of Jackson Cove Recreation Area (2.5 miles). Traverse the gravel parking lot, picking up the trail at the southeast corner. Clinging seeds of the bordering weeds are a nemesis in late summer and fall. Enter the woods, coming to the loop junction at Cedar Mill Brook (2.6 miles).

Here the blue-blazed Pomperaug Trail heads upstream to the left; the white-dot **Oxford Trail** continues forward along shore. Stay along shore for a counterclockwise tour; beautiful maples fill the drainage, while a sycamore rises near the junction. Contour 10 feet above shore, again finding dogwoods in the mix. At 2.95 miles, come to an open flat with rocks extending into the water. Hemlocks next shade travel.

Cross Wells Brook and ascend some log-recessed steps to travel a higher contour. Wells Brooks shows a rocky drainage with pretty cascades. Just beyond, find an old millrace (a flume for washing logs down to the lake/ river for milling). Now climb via switchbacks, reaching the **Pomperaug Trail** at 3.15 miles. Turn left to close Oxford Loop and return to the trailhead.

:, the Pomperaug Trail continues south for another 1.5 miles. ing the Oxford Loop, contour the upper slope amid hemlock, briefly to cross Wells Brook. Where the trail forks at 3.3 miles, ⌐er road/path; the woods become more mixed. Reach the tour's rocky high point at 3.55 miles. Here you may spy garnet crystals and you'll certainly find a seasonal view.

Again descend amid hemlock, with a steep descent along Cedar Mill Brook at 3.75 miles. An 8-foot rock face interrupts the stream, seasonally hosting a racing falls. At 3.9 miles, close Oxford Loop, and backtrack the Pomperaug Trail, returning to its junction with the **Crest Trail** at 4.6 miles, returning to the trailhead, 6.5 miles.

54 SLEEPING GIANT STATE PARK

OVERVIEW

The trails of this state park travel the anatomy of one of south-central Connecticut's most prominent landmarks—Sleeping Giant. Rising 700 feet and sprawling over 2 miles, the Giant serves up grand panoramas. In 1977, the entire trail system won national recreation trail distinction. Color-coded blazes identify the six east-west trails, while red geometric shapes point out the five north-south routes. Together, they suggest multiple loop tours; obtain a brochure from the ranger or from a map box at the information board near the entrance.

General description: The two hiking loops chosen to represent this award-winning trail system travel mixed hardwood forest and picturesque mountain laurel groves, topping rocky outcrops and cliffs for grand overlooks.
General location: 8 miles northeast of New Haven, Connecticut.
Special attractions: Stone observation tower; vistas of Long Island Sound, West Rock Ridge, and the northern traprock ridges; dramatic cliffs and bald outcrops; June-flowering mountain laurel; bird and wildlife watching.
Length: Tower Path-Blue Trail Loop, 3.6-mile loop; White Trail-Violet Trail Loop, 6-mile loop.
Elevation: Each loop shows a 650-foot elevation change.
Difficulty: For the Tower Path-Blue Trail Loop, find the Tower Path, easy; the Blue Trail (part of the Quinnipiac Trail), strenuous. For the White Trail-Violet Trail Loop, find the White Trail strenuous and the Violet Trail, easy.
Maps: State park brochure (usually available at entrance station or at the entrance information kiosk).
Special requirements: Seasonal day-use fee. Expect steep grades, rocky terrain, and sections requiring hand assists.
Season and hours: Spring through fall, 8 a.m. to dusk. Icy conditions make

ledges and cliffs too treacherous for travel.

For information: Sleeping Giant State Park.

Finding the trailhead: From the junction of Connecticut 10, Connecticut 68, and Connecticut 70 in Cheshire, go south on CT 10 for 5.3 miles and turn left (east) on Mount Carmel Avenue. Reach the park entrance on the left in 0.3 mile.

The hike: The **Tower Path-Blue Trail Loop** joins two of the park's most popular—although leagues apart in difficulty—trails; stay the Tower Path for an "easy" round-trip tour.

From the east side of the picnic area parking lot, take the wide, graveled **Tower Path** marked "pedestrians only". Maple, oak, hemlock, birch, beech, and dogwood weave a canopy of texture and full shade, while a vibrant midstory of young trees and mountain laurel engages the eye. Where chestnut oaks claim the canopy more sun penetrates.

At the many junctions, keep to the gravel tower road, switchbacking ever higher for a steady, moderate climb. By 0.8 mile, find tree-filtered looks at the cliff and boulder rubble shaping the Giant's chin. Ahead, a monument honors a leader in preserving the park.

Cross to the other side of the mountain, encountering more boulders. Near its intersection with the **Blue Trail** (1 mile), the road briefly flattens. Cross the Blue Trail a second time to top Mount Carmel (the Giant's left hip) at 1.6 miles, reaching an attractive 4-story stone tower with arched observation windows at each level.

Summit tower, Sleeping Giant State Park, CT.

Ramps ascend the summit tower; vistas applaud the surrounding forest, rounded ridges, and basalt features and sweep the New Haven skyline to Long Island Sound. Backtrack the Tower Path, or return via a rugged descent on the **Blue Trail**.

For the more challenging return west, find the first blaze of the Blue Trail on the southwest corner of the tower; avoid following the blue blazes that head northeast. Travel a rocky terrain, passing through similar woods, with a few azaleas in the mix.

Upon crossing the Tower Path sharply ascend to and then steeply pitch from the Giant's waist, staying the Blue Trail. At 2.2 miles, again cross the Tower Path, for a calmer tour along the north side of the Giant's chest only to charge up the rocky back side of the chin, which elsewhere presents a conspicuous cliff profile.

Where the trail levels, enjoy views. After a steep 20-foot rock descent (requiring hands), a short spur leads to a series of dizzying vertical-cliff overlooks; views pan to the Giant's chest. After 2.6 miles, find a grueling descent through low-stature forest and over canted rock faces, skirting the abandoned quarry.

Now descend from the Giant's head, bottoming out at the quarry. Road noise echoes up the Elbow, as hemlocks fill out the forest. At the base of the hill, follow Mill River downstream, and turn left prior to reaching CT 10. Close the loop at the picnic area, 3.6 miles.

For the second tour, the **White Trail-Violet Trail Loop**, follow the more difficult White Trail first, returning via the calmer violet-blazed route for a counterclockwise tour.

Find the **White Trail** heading north from the picnic area loop, cross a footbridge, and ascend, contouring the slope. Maples, beech, American basswood, oak, and hickory overlace the trail. Pass below a talus slope, soon ascending the rocky base. Overhead loom dramatic reddish-brown cliffs, crags, and overhangs, partially veiled by leaves.

At 0.3 mile, the white trail crosses over the wide **Tower Path** to resume its twisting ascent, advancing via rock stairs and passing showy displays of mountain laurel. Contour below the fissured cliff and breakaway blocks of the Giant's chest before topping the heaving rise at 0.6 mile. Chestnut oaks and shrubs vegetate the rises. Here find an open view of the chin and a ledge overlooking the campus of Quinnipiac College, before descending to contour a wooded slope.

Across the **Orange Trail**, the descent steepens. Ahead, contour the talus base of the right hip (1 mile). Ledges provide toe holds for the scramble to the top of the hip (1.1 miles). Gain more views of the south-central Connecticut neighborhood.

Resume the rigorous workout, migrating down the Giant's anatomy. Cross the **Red Circle Trail** to ascend a rocky slope, topping the right knee (1.75 miles). Again cross the Orange Trail for a rolling tour amid mountain laurel to claim Hezekiah's Knob (2.3 miles); at times, storm clouds enfold the Giant. Descend through woods and laurel and skirt an outcrop of pillow basalt

SLEEPING GIANT STATE PARK

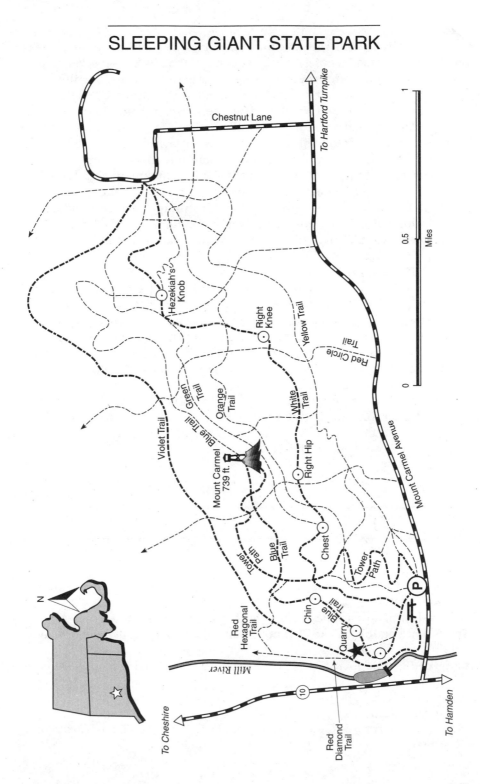

ending the Giant's right foot.

Green and Yellow trails, reaching a kiosk near a limited access
t Lane (2.9 miles). In the vicinity of the kiosk, find seven blazed
ting outward; several suggest alternative returns. For this hike,
pursue the violet blazes, returning along the left side of the Giant.

By contrast, the **Violet Trail** offers a sleepy woods walk. Large oak and
tulip poplar punctuate the forest; the fallen orange-and-green blooms of the
tulip tree may decorate the leaf mat. Encounter low rock walls and logs or
stepping stones at muddy sites. Hemlocks join the mix as hikers approach
the rocky ridge of the Giant's left hand (3.9 miles); mountain laurel showers
this low ridge. With a rocky descent, tour below a similar ridge feature.

At 4.2 miles, cross the **Red Circle Trail**, resuming an easier undulating
tour, contouring amid mature forest and mountain laurel. At 5 miles, hear
the first drone of CT 10; until this time, the tour has been remarkably insu-
lated from intrusion. The laurel show pretty twisted trunks, as hikers cross
the **Red Hexagonal Trail**.

At 5.5 miles, cross the **Red Diamond Trail** near the abandoned quarry,
a red-rock cliff and scar to the left. Find a concrete shell to the right. Descend steeply along a rockwork wall and a second ruin, where an eroding
staircase advances the trail. Arches mark some of the standing walls; poison
ivy and Virginia creeper reclaim the ruins. Follow the gravel lane away
from the ruins to reach a foot trail for a contouring descent above the pond
impoundment on Mill River.

Cross the end of the breached dam and pursue the river downstream.
The **Red Diamond and Blue trails** briefly merge and depart. Now turn
left away from the river to enter the west side of the picnic area near the
dumpsters. Close the loop at 6 miles.

55 ZOAR TRAIL

General description: In Lower Paugussett State Forest, on the west shore
of Lake Zoar, this blue-blazed loop applauds lake and woods, with a side trip
to a waterfall.

General location: 1 mile north of Stevenson, Connecticut.

Special attractions: Lake Zoar access and vistas, waterfall, diverse woods,
wildlife, fall foliage.

Length: 6.5-mile loop (5.1-mile loop, when a seasonal trail closure is in
effect).

Elevation: Find a 500-foot elevation change.

Difficulty: Moderate.

Maps: Southbury 7.5-minute USGS quad; Lake Zoar Area Trails, *Connecticut
Walk Book*.

Special requirements: Respect seasonal trail closure on loop.
Season and hours: Spring through fall, daylight hours.
For information: Paugussett State Forest.
Finding the trailhead: From Interstate 84, take exit 11 and follow the signs to Connecticut 34. Turn east on CT 34, heading toward Stevenson, Derby, and New Haven, for 4.9 miles. There turn left on Great Quarter Road and follow it northeast 1.3 miles to where it ends at a turnaround and parking area. Westbound CT 34 travelers find Great Quarter Road 0.2 mile west of the CT 34 - CT 111 junction in Stevenson; turn right.

The hike: Round the rock barrier, and follow a closed woods road north amid hemlock-hardwood forest; squirrels enliven the canopy. With the exception of side paths branching away to skirt a fallen tree and a badly eroded spot, the woods road guides travelers the first 0.25 mile, touring a wooded flat above the steep wooded slope to Lake Zoar, sparkling beyond the trees. Maple-leaf viburnum, fern, and sassafras decorate the understory.

The grade now becomes path-like ascending the steep lakeside slope. By 0.4 mile, descend toward the water. Tulip poplars rise amid the hemlock and birch. Soon, come within striking distance of shore, gaining cross-lake views of Jackson Cove Recreation Area, and north-south views of this long impoundment of the Housatonic River.

The trail rolls along the slope before following a recessed woods road to the waters edge. The raising of the lake waters created several roads to nowhere. Find a rockier tour ahead, as the trail vacillates from 10 to 100 feet above shore. At 0.9 mile, find a bouldery lake slope, with cross-lake views of the steep, treed eastern ridge and a plunging outcrop. Autumn colors particularly recommend the view.

Remain close to the water, finding a thin sandy beach with stump seating at 1.1 miles. Maple, oak, and ash line shore. From the beach, ascend a woods road, placing a low rise between trail and lake. Cross a drainage and bear left. Before long, glimpse a waterfall below the trail. Where the trail comes to the Prydden Brook crossing, postpone crossing and bear right, following the brook downstream to the falls. Tulip poplar again grow near the brook.

At 1.5 miles reach the falls, a series of cliff and rock jumbles adorned with white streamers and weeping moss. From the falls, the footpath continues to shore. The waterfall proves a satisfying destination for an alternative 3-mile round-trip hike. Return upstream, cross Prydden Brook, and continue uphill on an old road grade.

At 1.75 miles, come to a junction. Travel the footpath to the right from August 16 to March 30. Remain on the woods road April 1 to August 15. The loop's footpath travels a sensitive nesting area, so respect the posted wildlife closure.

When permissible, follow the blue blazes right along a sometimes faint foot trail, traversing a hemlock-hardwood plateau and rounding the slope above shore. Gradually descend, coming to a junction (2.4 miles) just beyond a jut overlooking the lake and a sign for southbound travelers

ZOAR TRAIL

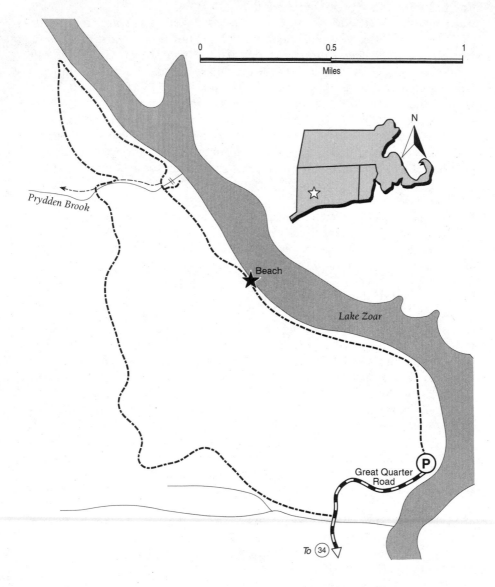

0   0.5   1

Miles

N

Prydden Brook

Beach

Lake Zoar

Great Quarter
Road

P

To 34

indicating "Scenic Trail next 2.4 miles." Here the **Zoar Trail** turns le[ft]
blazes and a small sign indicate the turn. Avoid the path straight ahea[d]
leads to private land.

The trail steeply sidewinds and angles up slope, topping the ridge at 2.7
miles. Tour choked hemlock stand and deciduous woods. At a T-junction
with another path, go left. Round below a rocky knoll, keeping the knoll to
your left, then veer right, descending amid hemlocks to merge with a woods
road (the alternative route from the 1.75-mile junction) at 3.4 miles. The
remainder of the tour is common to both loops. April through mid-August
hikers reach this point by following the woods road uphill for 0.25 mile,
paralleling and overlooking the Prydden Brook drainage.

Turn right on the woods road (continue forward if already on it). Enjoy a
beautiful passage framed by tulip poplar, maple, beech, oak, and birch,
with mountain laurel, sweet pepperbush, and witch-hazel. In about 0.1 mile,
look for the blue-blazed **Zoar Trail** to turn left off the woods road.
The narrow footpath is easy to miss, cued only by a small ribbon and paint
blazes on a tree offset from the road.

Cross the brook via stones and ascend amid laurel and beech. The tour
now rolls from outcrop knoll to outcrop knoll. Deer, woodpecker, and hawk
may add to a tour. Atop the rocks Lake Zoar is but a distant gleam, as this
leg of the journey focuses on the woodland. Rock tripe and green lichen
adorn the rocks, as do flecks of mica, seams of quartz, and garnet nodes.
Stay the blue blazes.

At 4.5 miles (summer hikers subtract 1.4 miles from the recorded distances), start the descent. Laurel continues to decorate the rolling, contouring route. Amid a wooded bottom at 4.9 miles, come to the first of two back-
to-back junctions with a lightly-traveled trail blazed with a blue dot on yellow background; keep to the blue-blazed **Zoar Trail**.

Find one last ascent of a rocky rise before descending via a rock-rein-
forced woods road and leafy footpath; at times muddy pockets riddle the
trail. Traverse a flat outcrop for looks across the immediate forest, and descend, skirting a private property to the right. Exit onto Great Quarter Road
near a "no outlet" sign at 5.9 miles, turn left, and hike 0.6 mile on **Great
Quarter Road** to close the loop at the trailhead.

_____ _____ral Connecticut, this state forest offers hikers a tranquil woodland retreat and access to Pattaconk Reservoir. The forest boasts a fine trail system, well-blazed, with numbered junctions that correspond to the state forest map and posted field mileages. Find incremental and cumulative mileages listed on the back of the state forest map.

General description: The selected two hikes incorporate most of the forest trail system, exploring pond, woods, laurel groves, and low rock ledges. To reach the reservoir, hike north on the Pattaconk Trail.

General location: 5 miles south of Haddam, Connecticut.

Special attractions: Scenic reservoir, mixed hardwood forest, mountain laurel and rare orchids, wildlife, fall foliage.

Length: Circuit Walk, 3.3-mile loop; Pattaconk to Cockaponset-Wildwood Loop, 9.7 miles round-trip.

Elevation: Circuit Walk, 150-foot elevation change; Pattaconk to Cockaponset-Wildwood Loop, 200-foot elevation change.

Difficulty: Circuit Walk, easy. Pattaconk to Cockaponset-Wildwood Loop, moderate.

Maps: State forest map.

Special requirements: Bring water.

Season and hours: Spring through fall for hiking, 8 a.m. to sunset.

For information: Cockaponset State Forest.

Finding the trailhead: From Connecticut 9, take exit 6 and go west on CT 148 for 1.7 miles. There turn right (north) on Cedar Lake Road (east of the CT 148 - CT 145 junction), go 1.6 miles, and turn left at the sign for Pattaconk Lake State Recreation Area. Find large dirt parking lots on either side of the road, prior to reaching the barricade in 0.3 mile.

The hikes: Start both hikes by rounding the barrier and following the blue blazes to the right. Bear right at the fork, coming to a four-way junction at 0.1 mile.

For the **Circuit Walk**, head left (south) on the **Pattaconk Trail**, following the blue blaze with a red dot. Pass through mixed woods, with beech, witch hazel, maple, oak, and mountain laurel, ascending a low ridge with a rocky crest. Amid the rock, find mossy shelves and fern caps, with chestnut oaks favoring the ridgetop.

Descend for a rolling tour, crossing over secondary trails and woods roads. The heart of the woodland reveals oak and beech. At 1.1 miles, start a long, steady descent, cross a drainage, and at 1.45 miles, curve left. To the right lies private property. At the upcoming brook, find two blazed crossing sites; take your choice and turn left upon crossing. Mossy rocks adorn the brook.

234

Cross abandoned Filley Road (a paved road), reaching junction 2 at 1.65 miles. To the right lies CT 148; bear left on the blue **Cockaponset Trail** to complete the Circuit Walk, touring a mature, multistory forest.

Initially, the trail shows a less refined bed, with more roots and rocks. From an impressive beech grove, cross a brook to tour an esker-like low, flat ridge, where tulip poplars find a niche. Deer, grouse, woodpecker, and mouse may surprise travelers.

When the trail begins a long steady climb, it improves in quality. Cross a faint jeep track and a rocky drainage, ascending to the southern parking lot at 3.3 miles.

For the **Pattaconk to Cockaponset-Wildwood Loop**, go right at the 4-way junction at 0.1 mile, hiking north on the **Pattaconk Trail** (blue with a red dot). The wide hiker avenue travels the west shore of Pattaconk Reservoir, a scenic pond displaying an irregular shoreline. Spurs branch to the canted sandy bank. Sweet pepperbush, azalea, and witch-hazel dot the shore. At 0.25 mile, pass a natural stone sofa overlooking the water. Yellow and white pond lilies spangle the shallows.

Ahead, the trail rolls along the wooded rocky slope, briefly drawing away from the pond to cross a sometimes muddy inlet. Pass a split rock, touring a bouldery site to resume north along shore. A congested leafy bank filters views of a lily pad cove. Cross a second rocky inlet atop flat stones, leaving the reservoir (0.8 mile).

Cross rocky Pattaconk Brook at 1 mile. Here the blue **Cockaponset Trail** pinches toward the Pattaconk Trail. Keep right, following the red-dot blazes

Cockaponset Trail, Cockaponset State Forest, CT.

for a relaxing woods stroll; both trails again meet at junction 6 (1.25 miles). This marks the end of the Pattaconk Trail. Continue north on the Cockaponset Trail, touring amid scenic large-diameter trees.

Travel a wooded tier between ledges, reaching little-used Old Country Road (a dirt road at 2 miles). Turn left on the road, finding the blue blazes heading north in 0.15 mile. Reach junction 8. The old woods road to the right is the **Old Forest Trail**; stay the blue Cockaponset footpath, now ascending. The trails again meet at junction 9.

Before long, the Cockaponset Trail overlooks an extensive marsh of phragmites (plumed reeds) and snags. Cross the low rockwork dam, to round the marsh via a snug green aisle of sweet pepperbush, sassafras, oak and jungle-like mountain laurel. A scenic outcrop rise with ledges and overhangs overlooks the trail (2.5 miles).

Honeycombed, folded, and fractured outcrop rises continue to frame the trail. Small clearings hint at the forest management. At 2.75 miles, reach junction 9, continuing north on the Cockaponset Trail. Turn right on Jericho Road at 3 miles. Where the trail reaches Jericho Road, look for a tiny plot of rare orchids staked off to the right; admire but do not touch.

Via the roadway, cross a small drainage, turning left in 100 feet; again find a passage characterized by tight laurel and rock outcroppings. Just ahead reach the loop junction. Stay the blue Cockaponset Trail, returning via the red-dot **Wildwood Trail** on the left.

On the Cockaponset, ascend and round amid outcrops, edging a standing dead forest of pines, where the pole-like trunks rise above the young hardwoods reclaiming the site. Top an outcrop overlooking a wooded draw and pass the footings of an old lookout (3.5 miles). The trail now rolls, snakes, and twists back on itself, passing from outcrop ridge to draw and back. Scenic rock steps advance the trail.

At 4 miles come to Jericho Road a second time, turn left for 50 feet, and pick up the trail on the right. Here tall laurel shapes a forest within a forest. At 4.5 miles, look for a couple of quick direction changes, coming out at the clearing of an old camp.

Cross Jericho Road one last time (4.75 miles), finding the continuation of the blue Cockaponset Trail to the left of a trail marked only by two wooden posts. Slowly descend to junction 14 (5.25 miles). Here the red-dot **Wildwood Trail** continues the loop straight ahead; the Cockaponset Trail bears right (north) to Beaver Meadow Road.

Follow the Wildwood Trail into an inviting hemlock grove and ascend to a woods road. Hike right along the woods road, and take a quick left, returning to a foot trail to reach and travel a ridge where mountain laurel thins. Again tour amid pine snags and striking outcrops to close the loop at 6.65 miles; backtrack to the trailhead 9.7 miles.

COCKAPONSET STATE FOREST

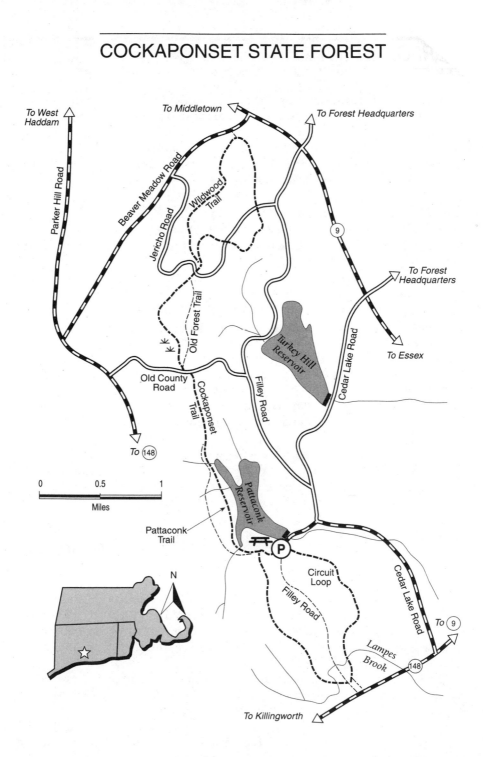

ption: In south-central Connecticut, this hike combines two
ong West Rock Ridge, an elongated traprock mountain with
rust-colored cliffs.

General location: West Rock Ridge State Park, northwest of New Haven.

Special attractions: Historic Judges' Cave, vistas, mid-June to July mountain laurel blooms, evergreen-deciduous woods.

Length: 13.6 miles total, linking two round-trip tours.

Elevation: Find a 400-foot elevation change.

Difficulty: Moderate, with uneven rocky footing.

Maps: Regicides Trail, *Connecticut Walk Book*; New Haven 7.5-minute USGS quad.

Special requirements: Carry water; none available along trail.

Season and hours: Spring through fall, 8 a.m. to dusk. Nature Center: 10 a.m. to 4 p.m. Monday through Friday, closed holidays.

For information: West Rock Ridge State Park.

Finding the trailhead: From the corner of Fitch Street and Whalley Avenue (Connecticut 63) in New Haven, go north on Fitch Street for 0.6 mile and turn left on Wintergreen Avenue; brown signs for West Rock Ridge State Park mark the turn. Keep to Wintergreen Avenue, turning left onto Brookside/ Wintergreen Avenue at 0.9 mile. Find the state park on the left in 0.5 mile; locate West Rock Nature Center and trail parking on the right 0.1 mile farther.

The hike: A divided trail travels the western escarpment rim and crest of West Rock Ridge, touring rock outcrop, mixed woods, and mountain laurel stands, snaring select views along the way. The southern 1.2-mile round-trip visits a page from seventeenth-century English-American history at Judges' Cave.

Reaching the **Regicides Trail** is anything but straight-forward. From the nature center parking lot, cross Wintergreen Avenue and follow the paved foot trail beyond a pair of wooden posts to enter West Rock Ridge State Park.

Traverse its abandoned parking lot to exit at the rock barrier, coming out near the entrance station. There, turn right on Baldwin Parkway (closed due to budget cuts). Where the road forks ahead, bear left and keep a sharp eye out for a wide, unmarked earthen trail ascending the slope to the right (0.1 mile from the station).

Take it for 0.2 mile, passing through a maple-mountain laurel corridor to reach the blue-blazed **Regicides Trail** at Buttress Gap. A left leads to the Judges' Cave in 0.6 mile; a right offers the primary tour.

To the left (southbound), watch for blazes pointing away from the initial trailbed and up the slope in 200 feet. Maple, oak, and hickory frame the way, replaced by an oak-studded top. Rounded outcrops present city views

REGICIDES TRAIL

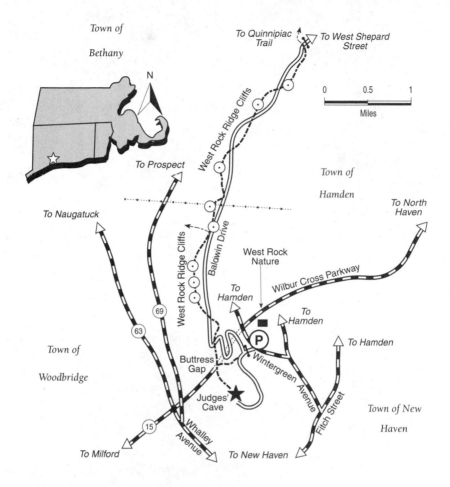

to the west, as the trail journeys over the tunnel for Wilbur Cross Parkway.

At 0.9 mile, blue blazes indicate that the official trail heads right, but the forks rejoin at an oak-shaded picnic site. Here a former road likewise accesses Judges' Cave, a barn-sized boulder-jumble where overlapping rocks create cave-like entries, overhangs, and short passages. On a nearby outcrop, look for meticulously carved names that date to the mid-1800s.

At this spot, American colonists shielded Judges Edward Whalley and William Goffe, two of the three regicides who issued the death warrant for Charles I. With the restoration of Charles II to the British throne, the judges themselves became fugitives. Hiding here, they eluded royal agents for three months before escaping to Massachusetts. When through exploring, return to Buttress Gap (1.6 miles) for the tour north.

Bird nest, West Rock Ridge State Park, CT.

Northbound from the gap, the blue blazes point out a quick, steep, ro
ascent. If you can steel yourself to make the grade, you'll find the rest of th
tour gently rolling, with earthen segments between the rocky stretches.

West Rock Ridge, a volcanic dike eroded free, towers 400 feet above the
valley floor. Atop the western escarpment (1.7 miles) oaks, eastern red cedar, and berry bushes interspersed with outcrop, boulders, and crags shape
the tour. Beware of poison ivy; a roadway drone echoes up slope.

Drifting away from the escarpment and past an airplane beacon, the trail
briefly follows a gravel service road. Stay alert for the blazes which point
out a descent to the right in 200 feet; this turn lacks the traditional double
blaze of the Connecticut Blue Trail system. Maple, hickory, and dogwood
enfold the way.

At 2 miles, cross forsaken Baldwin Parkway (the first of six crossings) and
pass three radio towers, returning to woods. Mountain laurel threads beneath the chestnut, white, and red oaks. A second parkway crossing brings
a return to the western escarpment, with limited looks at marshy Konolds
Pond and cross-valley looks at a wooded ridge. Open views trending north
now occur about every 0.2 mile.

Oak-hemlock stands alternate with mountain laurel groves. Both obscure views, but the smoother trail eases walking. At 4 miles, the red-blazed
North Summit Trail heads left as the Regicides Trail approaches and crosses
a former vista turnout on the parkway.

When next at Baldwin Parkway, follow it left a few hundred feet before
returning to the rim for a partial view of Lake Dawson. Deer, owl, grouse,
and woodpecker are the wild cards. More views follow, as do more parkway
crossings.

The crossing at 5.7 miles puts hikers on the east side of the ridge amid an
oak and rocky meadow habitat. Where the trail slips back west, find a 180-
degree view lauding the bumpy spine of West Rock Ridge. The trail with-
holds an eastern perspective until 6.7 miles, where views pan a field-rimmed
pond, city skyline, and woods.

As the trail curves away west, it tags Baldwin Parkway one last time (at
7.4 miles). For the Regicides tour alone, return to the gap (13.2 miles), and
retrace the initial 0.4 mile to the parking lot. For a less demanding return,
loop back along the tree-shaded and time-softened Baldwin Parkway. The
blue-blazed route continuing north offers either a shuttle option to hikers
who spotted a vehicle at the start of the **Sanford Trail** (consult *Connecticut
Walk Book*), or a long-distance trek on the state's **Quinnipiac Trail**.

In southwestern Connecticut, this 1,720-acre preserve owned by The Nature Conservancy (TNC) contributes to a critical open space measuring nearly 10 square miles. Combined with adjoining town, trust, and water company lands, the reserve provides habitat that encourages wildlife breeding and diversity. The Den boasts some 20 miles of interlocking trails for a variety of tours, exploring woodland, swamp, rock ledges, and ravines. Cultural sites enhance the journey.

General description: A broad-swinging loop travels several of the named trails, touring much of the preserve; side spurs visit granite ledges and a bouldery ravine.

General location: In Weston and Redding, Connecticut.

Special attractions: Rich hardwood forest, historic sites, granite ledges, limited vistas, wildflowers (including 14 species of violet), flowering shrubs, fall foliage, wildlife.

Length: Den Loop, 5-mile loop (7.2 miles with the suggested side trips).

Elevation: Travel from a trailhead elevation of 300 feet to a ledge elevation of 550 feet.

Difficulty: Moderate.

Maps: Preserve map.

Special requirements: Donation suggested; register at the map/information board at the parking lot. No pets, no bikes, no smoking, no picnicking, no fishing, and no swimming. The preserve has its own blazing scheme: red indicates woods road, yellow indicates foot trail, and white indicates a trail that is part of the greater Saugatuck Valley trail system. Find trail junctions numbered in correspondence with the map, aiding navigation and trail selection. Most junction posts display an arrow pointing the way back to the parking lot. The Den offers no amenities.

Season and hours: Year-round, spring through fall for hiking. Sunrise to sunset, with gates locked promptly at sunset.

For information: Devil's Den Preserve.

Finding the trailhead: From Connecticut 15 (the Merritt Parkway), take exit 42 and travel north on CT 57 for 4.8 miles. There turn right (east) on Godfrey Road, go 0.5 mile, and turn left on Pent Road. The route changes to dirt, entering the preserve. With the Den located within 35 miles of New York City, the parking lot can fill on weekends.

The hike: The suggested **Den Loop** begins on the **Laurel Trail**; locate it over your left shoulder as you look at the preserve map-and-information board. A carved sign, post 21, and public phone, all mark its start. Round a

DEVIL'S DEN PRESERVE

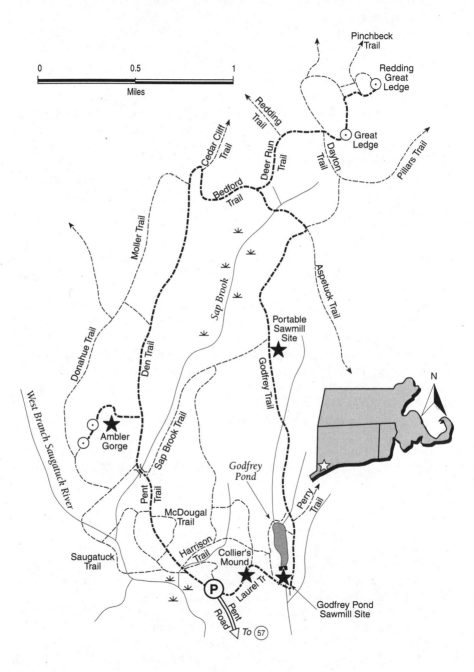

0   0.5   1

Miles

Pinchbeck Trail

Redding Great Ledge

Redding Trail

Great Ledge

Dayton Trail

Pillars Trail

Cedar Cliff Trail

Deer Run Trail

Bedford Trail

Moller Trail

Sap Brook

Aspetuck Trail

Donahue Trail

Den Trail

Portable Sawmill Site

Godfrey Trail

West Branch Saugatuck River

Ambler Gorge

Sap Brook Trail

Godfrey Pond

N

Pent Trail

McDougal Trail

Perry Trail

Saugatuck Trail

Harrison Trail

Collier's Mound

Godfrey Pond Sawmill Site

P

Laurel Tr.

Pent Road

To ⑤⑦

log gate, following the red-and-white blazed wood-shavings lane into the preserve.

Slowly ascend, touring a rich woods of oak, maple, and beech, with witch hazel, mountain laurel, and sweet pepperbush filling out the midstory. A scenic stone wall briefly lines the trail. At 0.2 mile, reach a collier's mound exhibit, a conical stack of wood with interpretive signs. Charcoal burning was a chief Weston industry in the 1800s; more than 40 charcoal burn sites or remnant collier huts riddle the Den.

Pass through a gap in a stone wall at post 22, turn right, and then keep right at an upcoming junction. Stone walls and large boulders accent the woods. Tulip poplar, hickory, and birch contribute to this visually rich tour, bathed in relaxation. At 0.4 mile (post 31), bear left onto the **Godfrey Trail** and then detour left at post 32.

The detour leads to the Godfrey Pond Sawmill Site, with a restored dam and historic ruins dating from the 18th century. Resume the loop, reaching the top of the dam to view the attractive pond, shaped like a painter's palette. Stay with the red and white blazes, rounding the leafy south rim of Godfrey Pond.

At post 34, a spur branches to the pond; bear right for the loop, traveling near the east boundary. Fall litters the lane with a vibrant collage of shape and color. At 0.6 mile (post 35), bear left staying the Godfrey Trail; the **Perry Trail** journeys right. Where a yellow trail branches left, again keep to the Godfrey Trail, enjoying the towering tulip poplars and attractive beech.

At 1.2 miles, pass a split rock on the right, and in another 200 feet, look right for what might be a reclaimed charcoal mound. Sinewy hornbeam and dogwood contribute to the woods. At 1.5 miles, find a rusted steam boiler, tiger engine wheel, smokestack, and flywheel from a portable sawmill that operated here from the late 1800s to the early 1900s. A 30-foot-deep stone-lined well likely supplied water. Rustic interpretive panels blend with the setting.

Stay the red/white Godfrey Trail, passing **Sap Brook Trail** on the left. Soon after, pass through a breach in a rock wall, to find the **Aspetuck Trail**, arriving at an angle on the right (post 64, 2.1 miles). The Aspetuck, together with Perry Trail, offers a shorter loop-return option. Bear left for the full tour, now following the **Bedford Trail**.

In a few feet, the **Godfrey/Pillars Trail** descends right, reaching a stone-pillar entry off CT 53 in 1.1 miles. En route, it tours inviting woods, passes extensive stonework, and affords a glimpse of Saugatuck Reservoir. Keep to the Bedford Trail for the loop, descending and contouring the base of a hill, traveling a marshy site.

At 2.6 miles as the Bedford Trail curves left, be alert for an easy-to-miss, although marked, junction (post 54). Detour right on the yellow-blazed **Deer Run Trail** to reach both Great Ledge and Redding Great Ledge.

With a rolling ascent, in 0.25 mile, cross through a gap in a stone wall, arriving at post 55. Bear right; the **Redding Trail** arrives on the left. After the **Dayton Trail** arrives on the right, round a stone wall at post 56 and

Flywheel, Devil's Den Preserve, CT.

again bear right for the ledges. Travel a sun-drenched woods of oak, maple, and a few hickory, arriving at Great Ledge, a long granite ledge with a 70- to 100-foot cliff. This featured ledge offers both open and tree-framed looks across the Saugatuck Valley woodland and distant flat ridges.

Traverse Great Ledge and descend through woods, passing the marker for Weston-Redding town line. Ahead, the yellow blazes to the left lead to the **Pinchbeck Trail**; continue forward on the white trail for Redding Great Ledge.

At the T-junction (a loop junction), go right to top Redding Great Ledge, finding an open look at Saugatuck Reservoir (3.4 miles) with its treed point and islands. Tall, twisted laurel accent the tour; deer frequent the woods. Backtrack (or complete the white loop and backtrack) to the Bedford Trail at post 54 (4.2 miles); bear right, resuming the counterclockwise tour.

Bypass the yellow **Cedar Cliff Nature Trail** and the **Moller Trail**, both on the right, slowly ascending to a plateau of red and chestnut oaks. With a gradual descent, again find a mix of birch, beech, maple, and tulip poplar, with the **Donahue Trail** heading right at post 49. At 5.2 miles, continue forward as the trail's name changes from Bedford to **Den Trail**.

Round below outcrop ledges and cliffs, coming to the yellow-blazed **Ambler Gorge Trail**. Detour right on this trail, still rounding the outcrop, descending to a bouldery bowl and jumble-rock ravine. Seasonally, a cascade graces the jumble. Books of muscovite (a kind of mica) glisten in the granite.

Cross the hewn log with its chicken-wire wrapping and ascend to two

tagging the second one at 5.9 miles. Although the trail contin-
ir steps and resume the Den Loop back at post 44 (6.2 miles).
erclockwise circuit now descends, passing amid a high-canopy
.. At post 10, bear left crossing a footbridge over Sap Brook. Stay the
red/white blazes, rounding toward the parking lot, now following the **Pent Trail** (The Bedford, Den, and Pent trails are all parts of a single route; only the name changes.) Do not veer from this main woods road.

Ahead, the tour rolls and skirts outcrop hills, with the **McDougal trails**, **Saugatuck Trail**, and **Harrison Trail** all branching off this final leg of the hike. At 7 miles, pass junction post 5, finding a pair of sentinel tulip trees. Soon after, reach an overlook to the right; it presents the marshy drainage of the West Branch Saugatuck River at Saugatuck Refuge. Reach the parking area, 7.2 miles.

EASTERN CONNECTICUT TRAILS

Eastern Connecticut holds a gentler terrain, a landscape of mild undula-tions, glacier-flattened ridges, and picturesque outcrop hills. The region cradles the largest forest in the state and a stretch of undeveloped shore along Long Island Sound. Travel rolling woodlands of southern hardwoods, eastern hemlock, and planted pine; enjoy splendid displays of mountain laurel; explore remote ponds; and tour a rare rhododendron and Atlantic white cedar swamp.

59 BIGELOW HOLLOW STATE PARK

OVERVIEW
Near the Massachusetts border, this Connecticut state park boasts large ponds, deep woods, and tranquillity. The ponds invite tours. Circuits ex-plore Bigelow and Breakneck ponds and visit Mashapaug Pond. Nipmuck State Forest abuts the park, expanding open space and wildlife habitat.

General description: Three pond circuits of varying difficulty introduce this state park, its water, wildlife, and forest.
General location: 20 miles northeast of Vernon, Connecticut.
Special attractions: Picturesque ponds with secluded coves, peninsulas, and shrubby islands; deep hemlock woods; conifer-hardwood forests; mountain laurel; beaver sites; fall foliage.
Length: Bigelow Pond Loop, 1.8-mile loop; Mashapaug Pond View Trail,

5.1-mile loop; Breakneck Pond Loop, 6.4 miles round-trip.

Elevation: Bigelow Pond Loop, 30-foot elevation change; Mashapaug Pond View Trail, 200-foot elevation change; Breakneck Pond Loop, 100-foot elevation change.

Difficulty: Bigelow Pond Loop, easy to moderate; Mashapaug Pond View Trail, moderate; Breakneck Pond Loop, strenuous.

Maps: State park map.

Special requirements: Seasonal fee area. No camping.

Season and hours: Year-round, generally spring through fall for hiking. Open 8 a.m. to sunset.

For information: Bigelow Hollow State Park.

Finding the trailhead: From Interstate 84, take exit 73 for Union, and go east on Connecticut 190 for 2 miles. Turn right (east) on CT 171, go another 1.4 miles, and turn left to enter the park. All trails start from Bigelow Pond Picnic Area at the north end of Bigelow Pond (about 0.75 mile into the park).

The hikes: For **Bigelow Pond Loop** and the **Mashapaug Pond View Trail**, start to the left of the regulations sign, following the blue-and-white blazes through the picnic area. Turn right near the pond's shore, cross a boardwalk over the inlet brook, and reach a trail fork (0.05 mile). Here the Mashapaug Pond View Trail heads uphill to the right; Bigelow Pond Loop follows the yellow blazes left for a counterclockwise tour.

Go left for **Bigelow Pond Loop**, touring a boulder-studded woods, en-

Nature study—Breakneck Pond Trail, Bigelow Hollow State Park, CT.

joying full shade. Pass between a regal hemlock and gargantuan boulder, rounding the west shore of this elongated pond sculpted by small islands and points. Boughs overhang the water, shrubs crowd the shore. Enjoy mountain laurel, sweet pepperbush, and fern, but watch your step on this rocky, root-bound trail.

At 0.75 mile, travel along the guard rail of CT 171 to reach the east shore; the highway bank acts as a dam. Ahead, turn left off a gravel fire lane prior to a gate to resume the foot-trail tour. Hemlock and pine needles offer a cushiony bed, as the east shore trail rounds some 15 feet above shore. Openings provide anglers with pond access.

At 1 mile, veer right, coming to a junction below a wooden gate. Although the yellow loop continues right, take the 0.1-mile spur left, reaching a mushroom-shaped peninsula, with a scenic outcrop, picnic table, and deep drop-off. To the north, the peninsula shapes a shallow bay. Return to the loop, hiking north through the boat launch/picnic area and across a peninsula rise to end at Bigelow Pond Picnic Area 1.8 miles.

At the 0.05-mile junction, beyond the inlet boardwalk, go right ascending the hill for the blue-and-white-blazed **Mashapaug Pond View Trail**. At 0.1 mile, reach the loop junction. Go straight for the Mashapaug Pond parking lot and boat launch, returning via the fork on the left. Be attentive to blazes as the path is new and not yet well-trodden.

Find a rolling ascent amid hemlock, maple, birch, and oak, interrupted by pockets of fern. At 0.7 mile, descend and cross a closed service road before reaching the picnic area shore and turning left. Find a water pump and pit toilets at Mashapaug Pond Picnic Area.

Mashapaug Pond is a vast deep pond with a forested edge and private property bordering much of its shore to the north. The state park trail travels the wild southern extreme. The clear water and gravelly bottom entice swimmers and waders.

At 1.1 miles, a yellow-blazed spur to the right reaches a large peninsula. The spur then forks, leading to picnic tables and small beaches. Oak, white pine, and laurel clad the point. Here, too, gain a better perspective of the pond's size.

Return to the loop (1.25 miles), and turn right, touring a hemlock shore; avoid the yellow trail on the left. Laurel thrives where pines and oaks win a stronghold. At the end of a second peninsula, find two small islands linked by a barely submerged sand spit. Round a long lake arm, staying within woods. At 1.75 miles, continue forward to return to Bigelow Pond; a left returns to Mashapaug Pond's parking and boat launch.

Cross a small inlet, still paralleling the shore north. At 2.4 miles, draw away from Mashapaug Pond for a pleasant hemlock-hardwood forest stroll. At a T-junction, turn left uphill, avoiding the abandoned yellow-blazed trail to the right. At 2.75 miles, stay with the blue-and-white blazes, again forgoing a yellow-blazed trail on the right.

Meander through alternating groves of hemlock and laurel, then enter the more open woods of a select cut. Cross a woods road and top a low pine-

BIGELOW HOLLOW STATE PARK

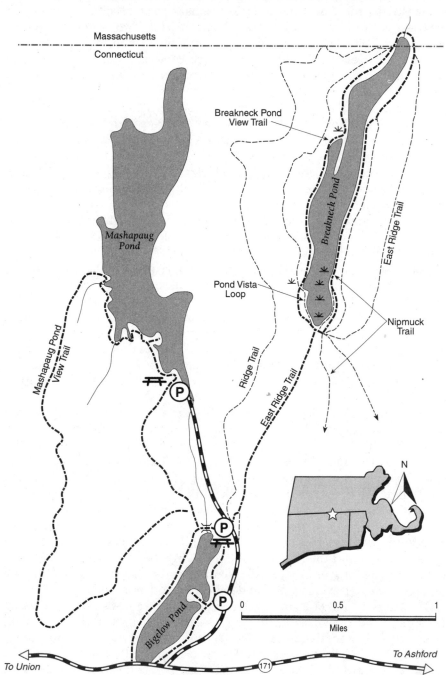

Massachusetts
Connecticut

Breakneck Pond
View Trail

Breakneck Pond

East Ridge Trail

Mashapaug
Pond

Pond Vista
Loop

Nipmuck
Trail

Mashapaug Pond View Trail

Ridge Trail

East Ridge Trail

N

Bigelow Pond

0   0.5   1
Miles

To Union

171

To Ashford

clad hill, finding a three-foot-tall stone wall. Descend and roll through fuller forest, closing the loop at 5 miles. Return to the trailhead 5.1 miles.

For **Breakneck Pond Loop**, cross the park road, reaching a kiosk and mapbox, and follow the white-blazed **East Ridge Trail** right; the **Ridge Trail** (blazed blue with an orange bar) heads left. Upon meeting a closed logging road, bear left (north) for Breakneck Pond, still following the white blazes through a deep hemlock woods intermixed with white pine, oak, and black cherry. At the fork (0.2 mile) stay left.

At 1 mile, bear left to reach the marshy southern end of Breakneck Pond and the loop junction. Here the East Ridge Trail heads right, leading to the blue **Nipmuck Trail**; go left on **Breakneck Pond View Trail** (white dot on blue blaze) for a clockwise loop.

In a few feet, veer right on the orange-blazed **Pond Vista Loop** to travel closer to shore, passing amid mountain laurel, hemlock, and pine, viewing beaver-gnawed trees. After rounding a knoll, find lily pad waters and a scenic bowed-arm pine, followed by an open look seemingly down the length of Breakneck Pond. Rolling wooded ridges enfold the water.

At 1.2 miles, return to Breakneck Pond View Trail, following it right. Beaver-raised waters flooded the logging road, requiring a brief re-route. A few feet ahead, turn right off the rocky logging road, returning to footpath; be alert for this key blaze.

The rugged, undulating footpath of Breakneck Pond View Trail now hugs the shoreline, following it north. Enjoy kingfisher, heron, and woodpecker. Open water and shrubby islands characterize the pond. At 2.1 miles, cross a beaver dam, discovering that what had appeared to be the pond's end was actually an island-pinched channel. The long water stretches north, lapping into Massachusetts.

At 2.7 miles, pass below a cluster of boulders adorned in rock tripe lichen to travel a low ridge clad in hemlock and hardwoods. Toward the lake lies a marsh. Prior to the pond's outlet (3.2 miles), reach a junction. To the left lies the Ridge Trail (blue with orange bar). Stay the Breakneck Pond View Trail, cross the outlet, and bear right on a logging road to continue the shoreline tour, hiking the blue-blazed **Nipmuck Trail**.

Pass the Massachusetts-Connecticut state line monument, where the white-blazed East Ridge Trail angles up slope. Keep to the pond, reaching a scenic point with towering pines overlooking a pond mat of aquatic blooms. At 3.6 miles, bear right off the roadway, still following the blue blazes, rolling but never straying far from shore. Abundant mountain laurel weaves through the forest. Next, traverse a glacial deposit of rocks and boulders.

Cross a picnic flat (4.75 miles), finding rougher trail. A second flat shows buttonbush and highbush blueberry, frogs and whirligig beetles. At 5.1 miles, cross-pond views find a beaver lodge. At the upcoming junction, the orange-blazed trail (right) stays closer to the pond, closing the loop at 5.4 mile. Take the blue-blazed trail and turn right where it meets the white-blazed East Ridge Trail to close the loop, 5.5 miles. Retrace the East Ridge Trail south to the trailhead, 6.4/6.5 miles.

OVERVIEW

Mashamoquet (Mushmugget) Brook, meaning "stream of good fishing", flows west to east across this 1,000-acre northeast Connecticut state park composed of rolling wooded terrain, natural rock features, and picturesque swamp. A pair of interlocking loops explore the rolling woods, while a simple nature trail introduces the swamp habitat. Stone walls web the park hinting at its early settlement; an old grist mill, maintained as a museum, recalls the milling past.

General description: The two selected day hikes capture the relaxation of the woods and the richness of the wetland.
General location: 15 miles northeast of Storrs, Connecticut.
Special attractions: Fishing, bird watching, swamp, mixed woodland, outcrop ledges and natural rock features, spring flora and fall foliage, mountain laurel.
Length: Wolf Den Swamp Nature Trail, 0.5-mile loop; Blue Loop, 4.4 miles round-trip.
Elevation: Wolf Den Swamp Nature Trail, minimal elevation change; Blue Loop, 400-foot elevation change.
Difficulty: Wolf Den Swamp Nature Trail, easy; Blue Loop, moderate.

Hiker bridge, Mashamoquet Brook State Park, CT.

MASHAMOQUET BROOK STATE PARK

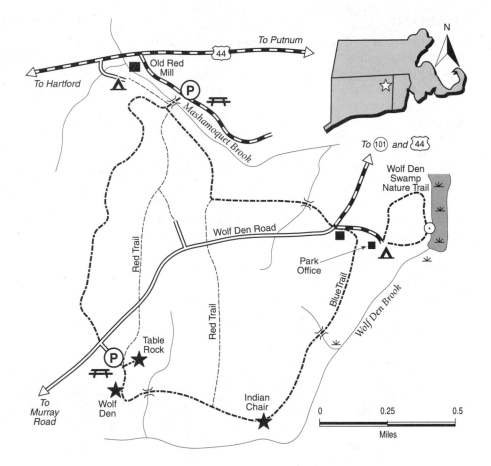

Maps: State park map.

Special requirements: Seasonal fee area, weekends and holidays only. To avoid fee, park at the visitor center for free.

Season and hours: Year-round, generally spring through fall for hiking. Open 8 a.m. to sunset.

For information: Mashamoquet Brook State Park.

Finding the trailhead: At the U.S. Highway 44 - Connecticut 97 junction in Abington, go east on U.S. 44, finding Mashamoquet Brook Campground on the right in 1 mile; the main day-use entrance and the trailhead for Blue Loop on the right in 1.2 miles; and CT 101 in 2 miles. There turn right on CT 101, go a few yards, and turn right on Wolf Den Drive to reach the park office/visitor center, Wolf Den Campground, and nature trail.

The hikes: Find the start of **Wolf Den Swamp Nature Trail** on the east side of the park road opposite the park office. Borrow a photocopy of the nature trail guide from the park office, if one is not available at the trailhead.

This 18-station interpretive trail begins rounding a broad open lawn where a three-story white birdhouse shelters swallows. The trail then tours the shore of the snag-pierced swamp, with skunk cabbage, tufted grasses, arrowhead, cattail, and phragmites (plumed reeds). Geese, red-winged blackbird, woodpeckers, fish, frog, and turtle enliven the swamp; at times insects annoy. Travel the narrow wooded buffer between swamp and lawn, reaching a dock and bench, before drawing away through pine plantation to close the loop at 0.5 mile.

For the **Blue Loop**, start at the picnic area, crossing the footbridge over Mashamoquet Brook, downstream from Old Red Mill. Near the bridge, a diversion rejoins the main brook shaping a long wooded island. Large boulders rim the clear, tannin-colored water.

On the south shore, find a spur heading upstream to Mashamoquet Brook Campground (Campers locate this spur between sites 11 and 12, descending 0.2 mile to the hike's start). To reach the Blue Loop, follow yellow blazes away from the brook to the base of a ridge and angle uphill to the right on a wide rock-studded lane. Soggy patches may mar travel following snowmelt or rain. The woods consist of hemlock, oak, and birch.

Top the ridge, meeting the **Blue Loop** trail at 0.2 mile; go left for a clockwise tour. Sounds of nature now replace the hum of the roadway. Follow a 4-foot-wide earthen lane, coming to a junction with the **Red Trail** in 100 yards. Stay left for the blue tour, traveling a shared section of trail.

Quite a few snapped trees hint at recent harsh weather, and scenic stone walls intersect the trail. Enjoy an overlacing canopy of dancing leaves. In late fall and winter, when the leaves depart, spy nests or perhaps an owl.

At 0.6 mile, the Blue Loop bears left, while the Red Trail continues ahead. Mountain laurel contribute to the tour, as the trail descends steadily to cross a footbridge over a thin tributary of Mashamoquet Brook (1 mile). Find maple, hemlock, and false hellebore here. The relaxation of the woods invites thoughts as well as feet to wander. At 1.1 miles, reach the paved road to the park office and Wolf Den Campground. Turn right; blazes mark the signs.

At 1.2 miles, look for the Blue Loop trail to head uphill to the right reentering woods beyond the park office/information center; **Wolf Den Swamp Nature Trail** begins on the opposite side of the road. A big pine stands at the gateway to the Blue Loop, while a white barn lies uphill to the right.

Pass through a gap in a 3.5-foot-high stone wall, returning to hemlock-oak habitat. In places, the stone wall incorporates the natural outcrop ledge. The trail rolls, topping exposed bedrock, where hikers can admire the woodland and wait for wildlife to come to them. Laurel again interweaves the forest; solitude abounds in the off-season.

The trail grows narrower with rocks studding the path. At 1.7 miles, descend from the main outcrop area to cross a footbridge over a small brook supporting a false hellebore wetland. A spring-drained rocky area follows; jack-in-the-pulpits favor the moist site.

Topping an outcrop at 2.1 miles, look for a yellow arrow pointing to the ledge that holds Indian Chair, a natural rock sofa complete with back and arm rest. The seat offers a squirrel's-eye view of the woodland, with vultures soaring by.

Continue clockwise on the Blue Loop, touring woods with a fuller midstory. The Red Trail again merges, as hikers descend to a drainage boardwalk, where marsh marigolds complement the dark water. Now climb steeply, reaching Wolf Den, 2.5 miles; look for the impression of a former plaque. Here rock ledges shape a boxy opening leading to a crawlspace, 30 feet long. In 1742, Israel Putnum crept into the den, shooting a wolf that had annoyed area farmers.

In another 0.1 mile, reach a three-pronged junction, where a 200-foot spur to the right leads to Table Rock—an elevated 10-foot by 20-foot natural slab. The Red Trail heads straight, and the Blue Loop trail heads left, passing through dense laurel, reaching the rustic Wolf Den State Park Picnic Area (2.7 miles). From here, hike out the graveled access road reaching Wolf Den Drive in 0.1 mile. Look right to locate the Blue Loop trail where it heads north off Wolf Den Drive.

Resume the tour north through similar forest, finding dense laurel where the roadway opening brings added light. Enjoy a mildly descending, relaxing woods stroll. At 3.9 miles, bear right, avoiding the closed path ahead; yellow arrows point out the re-route. Close the Blue Loop at 4.2 miles, and hike the Yellow Trail downhill, ending at the bridge (4.4 miles).

61 JAMES L. GOODWIN STATE FOREST

OVERVIEW

Abutting 13,000-acre Natchaug State Forest, this 2,171-acre forest contributes to a vital open space and wildlife habitat in northeast Connecticut. Hikers find a fine network of blazed trails. Ponds, swamps, rolling hardwood forests, meadows, tree plantations, and an abandoned rail line vary travel.

General description: A broad swinging loop travels foot trail and woods road through forest and plantation, exploring Pine Acres Pond and Swamp and visiting Black Spruce Pond. The loop incorporates part of the long-distance Natchaug Trail.
General location: 10 miles southeast of Storrs, Connecticut.
Special attractions: Goodwin Conservation Center and arboretum; observation blind; bird and wildlife watching; guided nature walks;

rhododendron, laurel, azalea, and pond lily blooms; diverse woods; fall foliage.

Length: Pine Acres Pond Loop, 5.1-mile loop.

Elevation: Find a 200-foot elevation change.

Difficulty: Moderate.

Maps: State forest map.

Special requirements: None.

Season and hours: Year-round, generally spring through fall for hiking. Dawn to dusk.

For information: Goodwin Conservation Center.

Finding the trailhead: From the junction of U.S. Highway 6 and Connecticut 169 in Brooklyn Center, go west on U.S. 6 for 7.3 miles and turn right (north) on Potter Road for the state forest. Find parking on the right in 0.2 mile. Arriving from the west, go 3 miles east on U.S. 6 from its junction with CT 198 in South Chaplin and turn left on Potter Road.

The hike: For **Pine Acres Pond Loop**, go past the information board, hiking toward the boat launch on a gravel access road. In 200 feet, take the yellow-blazed trail to the right, rounding a gate to follow a woods road to the southern end of Pine Acres Lake, a 133-acre lake built in 1933. Planted white pine and Norway spruce, rhododendron, bramble, poison ivy, jewelweed, and red maple frame the corridor. For a brief spell, the trail travels near U.S. 6, separated by a thin row of cedar, spruce, and hemlock.

At 0.2 mile, where the yellow-blazed trail draws away from the pond, follow the mowed swath along shore to cross the dam and spillway footbridges. Enjoy open looks at the dark-water pond, its mats of pond lily, arrowhead, and rimming trees. From the second bridge, follow the white blazes to round the pond's east shore. Travel spruce plantation and hardwood forest, finding sweet pepperbush, azalea, and highbush blueberry along shore; scenic showings of tall fern amid the woods.

Travel a mostly flat, root-bound trail, with spurs branching to shore. At 0.6 mile, a gap in the border offers looks at the snag-pierced pond, a watery "bed of nails." Spy a beaver lodge, geese, ducks, cormorants drying their wings, and likely a heron. Beyond a beech-clad rise recently favored by beaver find an old woods road leading to shore for open views of the pond's lily-pad blanket, treed islands, and cattail swamp to the north; keep to the white-blazed trail, journeying north.

At the 1.2-mile junction, a red blaze at the right points out a shorter return loop option; to the left, a white-blazed spur leads to Governors Island; ahead, the primary trail, also blazed white, continues north. Take the island detour, following an attractive levee edged by small pine and dense herbs and forbs, fragrant in early summer. A loop then explores the island, reaching an observation deck and a second viewpoint, overlooking the surrounding bog. Travel amid pine-oak woods and mountain laurel.

Return to the 1.2-mile junction (1.5 miles) and follow the white blazes north. The thick woods severely limit swamp views. By 1.9 miles, follow a

JAMES L. GOODWIN STATE FOREST

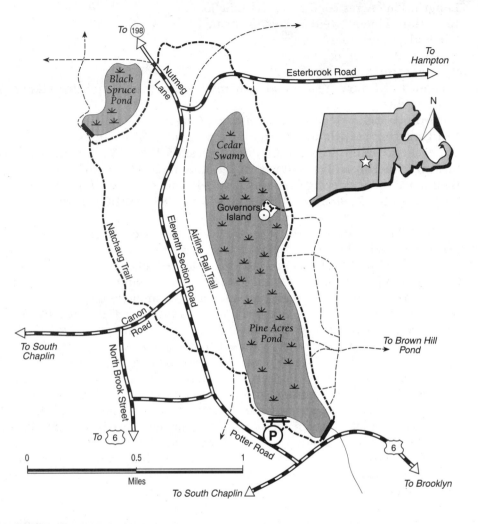

woods road away from Pine Acres Swamp, paralleling a stone wall through a pine plantation. In another 0.1 mile, follow the foot trail left, passing through a breach in the stone wall to reach Esterbrook Road. Hike 100 feet to the right to resume the white trail on the opposite side of the road, now touring a scenic recessed woods road.

At 2.3 miles, veer right into a stand of spruce and then descend sharply left to tour a sunken grade along the abandoned rail line. Before long, angle right, pass over the gravel railroad bed, and resume the tour amid a lovely hardwood forest graced by ferns.

Cross 11th Section Road at 2.75 miles. The white blazes now lead around the east shore of Black Spruce Pond, but a dense shrub border denies views. Find the trail rocky and sometimes muddy. Azalea and both mountain and sheep laurel decorate early-summer tours. Cross a corduroy section and go right on an attractive leaf-littered woods road. Here papery wasp nests may be found by late summer hikers. Glimpse the outline of the pond and its snag-filled waters.

Amid a stand of pines at 3.25 miles, meet the blue-blazed woods road of the **Natchaug Trail** and follow it left (south) for the loop. A 250-foot detour right reaches the earthen dam for an open look at Black Spruce Pond, its beaver lodge, lily pads, and many snags.

Ascend south and bear right on the narrower woods road at the fork. Grasses invade the bed, and ferns dress the shoulder as the Natchaug Trail passes amid hardwood forest and conifer plantation. The blue blazes occur less frequently, so be alert for the direction change that occurs at 3.95 miles.

Here the Natchaug follows a foot trail to the left, passing through a plantation interspersed with maple, birch, and sassafras and crossing rock walls. On paved Canon Road, turn left, resuming the southbound trail beyond a blazed utility pole on the right.

Find a similar tour leading to 11th Section Road. Angle right across 11th Section Road, descending once more through conifer plantation; the unruly bramble grabs hikers. At 4.6 miles, cross the abandoned railroad grade, touring a maple wetland. Boardwalks and corduroys allow hikers to escape the soggiest reaches, as the trail again nears Pine Acres Pond.

As the trail rounds the west shore, multiple spurs branch to views. Pass

White oak, James L. Goodwin State Forest, CT.

an upturned pine, a beaver scent mound, and a beaver lodge prior to reaching the observation blind (5 miles). Beyond the blind, turn right ascending the slope. The trail comes out near the privies below the parking area (5.1 miles).

62 GAY CITY STATE PARK

OVERVIEW

At this 1,569-acre east-central Connecticut state park, explore peaceful woodlands, the Blackledge River, swamps and ponds, and the historic remains of an 18th-century settlement, Gay City. Started by an isolationist religious sect in 1796, Gay City's early success centered around its mill—originally a sawmill, later a woolen and paper mill. The blockades in the War of 1812, the Civil War deaths of the town's young men, and fire, each played a role the demise of Gay City.

General description: Two circuits explore the park's woods, wetlands, and history, traveling both woods road and foot trail.
General location: 5 miles southeast of Manchester, Connecticut.
Special attractions: Historic mill ruins, ditches, cellar holes, cemetery, and stone walls; azalea; hardwood forest; wetlands; wildlife; fall foliage.
Length: Pond Loop, 2.6-mile loop; Outer Loop, 5-mile loop.
Elevation: Each shows about a 100-foot elevation change.
Difficulty: Both, easy.
Maps: State park map.
Special requirements: Fee area; pets on leash.
Season and hours: Year-round, generally spring through fall for hiking. Open 8 a.m. to sunset.
For information: Gay City State Park.
Finding the trailhead: Find the park 3 miles south of Bolton off Connecticut 85. From Interstate 384 (eastbound access only), take exit 5, and go south on CT 85 for 4.5 miles, turning right (west) to enter the park. Also find a marked route to the park starting off U.S. Highway 6; watch for signs to guide you at junctions.

Start both hikes on the blue-blazed Gay City Trail, a westbound gated woods road 0.3 mile into the park. Park in the lots just prior to the trailhead or at a small picnic area just beyond it.

The hikes: Round the gate on the blue-blazed **Gay City Trail**, hiking the dirt road toward the Youth Group Camp, passing amid tall oak, birch, and maple. In 100 feet, where the road forks, the red-blazed **Outer Loop** heads left. Stay right, following the blue blazes past the youth camp and downhill between scenic old-growth maples to reach the white-blazed **Pond Loop**, prior to the Blackledge River bridge (0.2 mile). Turn right (upstream) for the Pond Loop; the Gay City Trail continues across the bridge to reach the **Shenipsit Trail** in 2 miles.

For the Pond Loop, hike upstream along the east bank of the brook-sized Blackledge River. A breached beaver dam has left behind barren muddy banks where a pond once stood. Follow the white blazes along foot trail and woods road, paralleling the river. Soon cross a bridge over the rockwork canal from the old woolen and paper mill. View the stone legacy of the mill at the head of the canal; Virginia creeper and fern poke from the rock crevices. Frogs favor the murky standing pools.

Continue upstream, now passing between the river and a ditch that carried water to the mill. The stairs to the right ascend to the upper beach parking area. Reach Gay City Pond at 0.4 mile and turn left to cross its earthen dam. This small reservoir shows a stark shore, a small treed island, and mats of pond lily. Look for water snake, frog, or mink.

From the dam, follow the old woods road touring above the pond's shore; a secondary path briefly explores shore. Oak, maple, birch, and hemlock shade the way, while colorful fungi protrude from the leaf mat attracting the eye. Enjoy a restful, rolling woods meander.

At the fork at 0.65 miles, bear left, soon merging with the red-blazed **Outer Loop**. Continue north (right), crossing a drainage bridge. Rock walls add to the woods.

Stay right at 0.95 miles, leaving the red-blazed trail and descending on an old woods road likely echoing back to Gay City. Be careful descending as fallen leaves can easily steal footing. Cross a footboard over a tiny drainage, ascending to meet the **Orange Trail** at a T-junction. Turn right; a few azalea now add to the tour.

Red maple, fern, highbush blueberry, and sweet pepperbush herald the Blackledge River crossing at 1.3 miles; plank ramps lead to and from the bridge. Now go left, following a foot trail along Gay City Pond, snaring an overlook of the beaver lodge, island, and beach. At 1.5 miles, stay left for the loop; the right fork leads to the beach.

Pass lower beach parking and a cellar depression, returning to a woods road for a pleasant ramble. Turn right upon meeting the Orange Trail for a second time. Overlook a former beaver pond, now a snag-filled meadow, again enjoying floral shrubs. A woodland tour then leads to the park road; come out opposite an open field. Detour left 200 feet to view the old cemetery, where thin tablets mark graves from the 1800s. Go right (west) to close the loop at 2.6 miles.

For the **Outer Loop**, a popular weekend trail, head left off the **Gay City Trail** in 100 feet, touring amid large maples and a full rich forest with birch, ash, oak, and hickory; ferns dress the floor. Upon meeting a second woods road at 0.3 mile, bear right. Rock walls now contribute to the woodland serenity. A slight descent finds Blackledge River at 1 mile. Sweet pepperbush and azalea adorn the river banks, while branches overlace the water.

GAY CITY STATE PARK

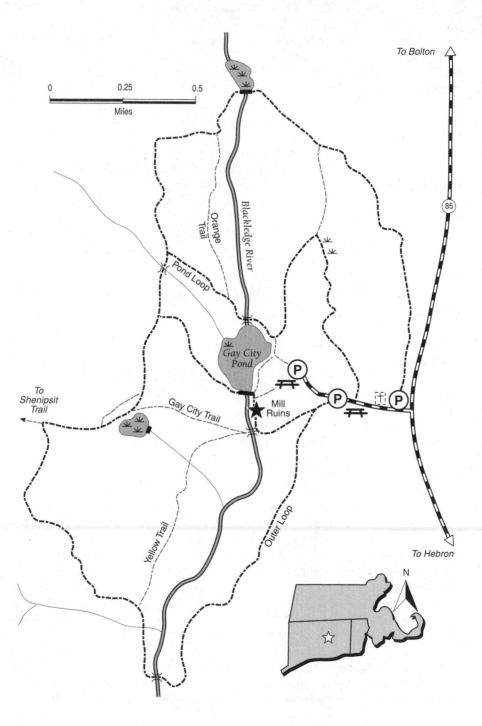

0   0.25   0.5
Miles

To Bolton

85

Blackledge River

Orange Trail

Pond Loop

Gay City Pond

To Shenipsit Trail

Gay City Trail

P

P

P

Mill Ruins

Yellow Trail

Outer Loop

To Hebron

N

Cross the bridge and ascend away from the river, turning lef
foundation where a yellow-blazed connector now heads forwa
miles, a short spur leads to a boulder; follow the red blazes.

Next come to a T-junction with the blue-blazed **Gay City Trail**
bound (going left at the junction), the Gay City Trail reaches the **Shen.**
Trail in 1.3 miles. For the Outer Loop, follow the blue and red blazes to the
right, cross a small drainage, and slowly descend, traveling parallel to a
woods road.

At another small drainage (2.3 miles), bypass an alternate trail marked by
a red "A", which heads left. At 2.4 miles, a short spur heads right reaching a
large lily pond. Look for night heron, swallows, and other birds; frogs abound.
In another 200 feet, the red and blue blazes part; again follow the red-blazed
Outer Loop, going left. Soon the alternate trail rejoins the woodland tour on
the left.

The Outer Loop's red blazes briefly join the white blazes of the **Pond**
Loop. After they separate, watch for the red-blazed trail to descend right on
a wide footpath. Reach the wetland forest of the river drainage and stay left,
merging with the **Orange Trail** for a spell. At 3.6 miles, cross an old rockwork
dam. A beaver dam now blocks the spillway, creating a pond. Look for a
lodge on shore to the left. At 3.8 miles, the Orange Trail leaves on the right.

At 4 miles, depart the woods road, heading right on a foot trail, touring a
wetter forest near CT 85. Here ash joins the mix. Cross the winter parking
lot to reach the park road near the entrance (4.7 miles), and turn right hiking 0.3 mile along the park road to close the loop.

63 PACHAUG STATE FOREST

OVERVIEW

In southeast Connecticut abutting Rhode Island, Pachaug State Forest
represents the largest state-held forest in Connecticut, covering some 30,000
acres. The hikes discussed in this write-up originate from the headquarters
area and incorporate portions of two long-distance trails: the Pachaug and
Nehantic. Discover a rare rhododendron-white cedar swamp, stocked ponds,
a rocky brook, and natural and planted forests.

General description: Three hikes make up this forest sampler. Visit the
rhododendron-white cedar swamp, top a high point for a vista, and explore
along brook and pond, touring foot trail and woods road, hardwood forest
and conifer plantation.
General location: 12 miles northeast of Norwich, Connecticut.
Special attractions: Rhododendron Sanctuary, Atlantic white cedar swamp,
stocked fishing ponds, historic cellar holes and stone walls, wildlife watching,

.l foliage.

Length: Rhododendron Sanctuary Walk, 0.5-mile round-trip. Nehantic Trail to Mount Misery, 1.6 miles round-trip; Phillips Pond Loop, 12.5 miles round-trip (may extend or shorten).

Elevation: Rhododendron Sanctuary Walk, flat; Nehantic Trail to Mount Misery, 170-foot elevation change; Phillips Pond Loop, 280-foot elevation change.

Difficulty: Rhododendron Sanctuary Walk, easy. Nehantic Trail to Mount Misery, moderate. Phillips Pond Loop, strenuous.

Maps: State forest map. Nehantic Trail-Pachaug Trail map, *Connecticut Walk Book*.

Special requirements: High water can make portions of the Rhododendron Sanctuary impassable.

Season and hours: Year-round, generally spring through fall for hiking. Open 8 a.m. to sunset.

For information: Pachaug State Forest.

Finding the trailhead: From Interstate 395, take exit 85 and go east on Connecticut 138 to Voluntown, 5.8 miles. Continue east on CT 138/CT 165 for 0.8 mile and turn north on CT 49. In 0.6 mile, turn left (west) on Headquarters Road to reach the forest attractions. Trailheads radiate from the road fork in 0.7 mile: Locate the Rhododendron Sanctuary and Nehantic Trail to Mount Misery off Cut-off Road to the left. Start Phillips Pond Loop on the right at the CCC Youth Group Camp Area.

The hikes: Find the Rhododendron Sanctuary 0.1 mile west of Headquarters Road on the north side of Cut-off Road, opposite an open field and Mount Misery Campground. A blue **Nehantic Trail** blaze and a sign mark the **Rhododendron Sanctuary Walk**.

On cushiony trail, pass amid hemlock, oak, maple, and pine, bearing right to round an island of trees. Azalea, mountain laurel, sweet pepperbush, highbush blueberry, and red maple announce the swamp.

By 0.1 mile, travel a levee amid the wetland forest, finding cedar, sphagnum moss, bog grass, and a captivating jungle of rhododendron, growing 40 feet tall, sporting 8-inch leaves and, in July, brandishing glorious floral pompoms. Twisting skyward through the cedar-hemlock canopy, the rhododendron shape a brief, but exciting passageway of texture and shape. Corduroys aid passage. The sanctuary walk ends, taking a small loop at 0.2 mile.

From the loop, three sets of hewn logs head west into the cedar swamp, for views of yet another interesting habitat with standing water, stringy cedar trunks, elevated root islands, moss, and fern. Turn around for the sanctuary walk alone. When conditions are sufficiently dry, hikers may continue through the swamp and then left on a woods road, following the **Nehantic Trail to Mount Misery**.

Generally though, Mount Misery hikers should forgo this "swamp connection", and instead hike west along Cut-off Road from the Rhododendron

Sanctuary entrance. In about 0.2 mile, the Nehantic Trail crosses the road; watch for the blue blazes just past a gated woods road on the right. This woods road parts the Atlantic white cedar swamp, offering an alternative viewing access when floods submerge the sanctuary walk.

Turn left (south) off Cut-off Road, following the **Nehantic Trail to Mount Misery**, at 0.2 mile (0.4 mile for swamp-travelers). Tour amid hemlock, pine, oak, and mountain laurel on a well-marked, well-traveled trail. Pockets of fern, some rock studding, and sheep laurel bring visual interest. Soon, turn right on the relocated trail for a switchbacking ascent of the slope; avoid the abandoned erosion-causing trail ahead.

Top a rise and round over an outcrop, encountering oaks, twisted pine, and a more open cathedral, with limited outward looks. Where the trail descends to a drainage, be careful on the loose gravel; snags reach skyward with imploring arms. At 0.6 mile, bear right for another switchbacking ascent.

At 0.8 mile, mount a rock outcrop hosting patches of pitch pine and scrub oak for a 180-degree eastern perspective of glacier-planed ridges and lowland forest, with pines towering above the leafy crowns. Backtrack, or hike the Nehantic Trail over the summit of Mount Misery (elevation 441 feet) and down its slippery outcropped side to Firetower Road (0.9 mile).

For **Phillips Pond Loop**, start at the CCC Area, following the blue-blazed **Nehantic Trail** east up the grassy slope from the stone pillars on Headquarters/Trail Road. Enter the pines, coming to the Nehantic-Pachaug trail junction (0.1 mile). Turn left (north) on the **Pachaug Trail**, also blazed in

Rhododendron Sanctuary, Pachaug State Forest, CT.

blue, to make a broad-swinging loop around Phillips Pond. The Nehantic Trail continues east to Beachdale Pond Picnic Area in 0.75 mile.

Northbound, the Pachaug Trail contours the wooded slope east of Headquarters/Trail Road. Look for deer, raccoon, and woodpecker and be ready for quick direction changes wherever the trail meets woods roads. Drainages can muddy the going.

Near an old ruin, meet a woods road and turn left for a birch-lined passage ending at a boulder barrier. Pass through the barrier and hike left, reaching Trail Road south of Lowden Brook Picnic Area (1.35 miles). Turn right and pass between boulders on the right to resume the Pachaug Trail.

Hike northeast past some picnic tables, touring a rocky footpath amid maple, hickory, ash, beech, pine, hemlock, and birch, following Lowden Brook upstream. Mountain laurel and sweet pepperbush favor the drainage. Lowden Brook shows dark mossy boulders and sparkling cascades. Muddy sites record wildlife visits. Expect a rugged, ankle-torquing trail for this riparian tour, with faint blazes for guides.

Veer upslope from the brook, passing stone walls, before swinging left and finding easier footing. Return brookside at 2.35 miles, cross the brook, and enter a spruce plantation. Next, angle right across Gardiner Road, following a gated woods road toward Phillips Pond; grasses push up through the bed, while ferns shower the shoulder.

Be alert as the trail zigzags through a selection of woods roads. At 2.75 miles, near an impressive stone foundation, the blue-blazed Pachaug Trail turns right, touring a plantation, while a **white-blazed trail** continues forward to Phillips Pond. Stay the Pachaug Trail.

At 3.1 miles, the **Cut-over Trail** (red dot on blue) arrives from Phillips Pond; again keep to the Pachaug Trail, which continues forward for a counterclockwise loop. Blazes now occur at regular intervals.

The tour alternates between hardwood forest and conifer plantation, passing a spring and catch basin on the right at 3.85 miles. Angle right across paved Hell Hollow Road at 3.9 miles, to follow a wide foot trail through a spruce grove. Stone walls now partition the plantations. At the 4.3-mile fork, bear right for the Pachaug Trail, contouring a rocky slope. At a T-junction in 0.1 mile, turn left on the yellow-blazed **Pachaug-Quinebaug crossover trail** for the loop; the Pachaug Trail heads right.

Follow the yellow blazes downhill, turning right in 20 feet to contour an oak and birch hillside, with sassafras, chestnut, and huckleberry weaving an understory. Where the trail traverses a wooded plateau, find a scenic beech grove.

At 5.15 miles, turn left on single-track, dirt Flat Rock Road (closed to vehicles here), following yellow blazes to meet the blue-blazed **Quinebaug Trail** in 0.2 mile. Go left (east) on the Quinebaug Trail to continue the loop, or detour right (north) about 0.5 mile to find Lockes Meadow, a wetland meadow and popular birding site.

East, the Quinebaug Trail starts out on a rocky, exposed roadbed, passing Devils Den, an assemblage of rocks on the left. After 5.7 miles, descend and

PACHAUG STATE FOREST

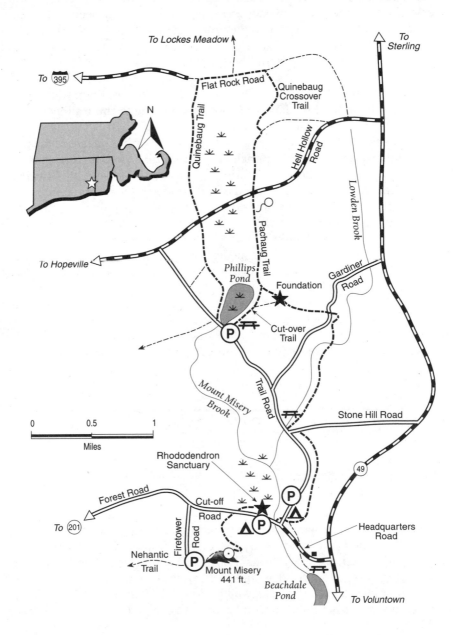

look for the trail to bear left on a narrower woods road, prior to where Flat Rock Road changes to pavement.

Here the rolling tour temporarily regains its country lane charm, with overlacing branches of dogwood, ash, maple, birch, and beech. Beyond a pine plantation, find the trail cobblier, more exposed, and scarred from illegal vehicle use. Next round a gate (7 miles), hike right on Hell Hollow Road for 100 feet, and resume the trail on the left.

Descend amid hardwoods, soon passing a stand of mature white pine on this more inviting stretch of the Quinebaug Trail. Where the trail turns left at 7.5 miles, snipped huckleberry shoots poke through the trailbed. Meander pine plantation and mixed forest, slowly descending. By 8.3 miles, glimpse a red maple swamp, hinting at Phillips Pond. At 8.6 miles, arrive at the pond near the dam, departing the Quinebaug Trail, which now turns right.

Cross the earthen dam and footbridge, viewing picturesque Phillips Pond with its limited open water, vegetated islands, and aquatic plants. Pass through the picnic area and turn left near the information sign, following the **Cutover Trail** (red dot on blue) at 8.7 miles. (Find water pump and privies in the vicinity of Phillips Pond.)

Round the barrier, touring a maple-draped trail, skirting the pond's marshy outskirts. At 8.85 miles, hikers have the option of returning to the Pachaug Trail via the white-blazed trail to the right, shaving 0.3-mile from the total distance, or keeping to the red dot-marked crossover. In each case, upon closing the loop, pursue the Pachaug Trail's blue blazes south to return to the trailhead. Follow the red-dot blazes to reach the Pachaug Trail at 9.4 miles and turn right, retracing the initial 3.1 miles to the CCC Area.

64 DEVIL'S HOPYARD STATE PARK

OVERVIEW

At the heart of this 860-acre Connecticut State Park, find the tumbling streamers and dark-rock escarpment of 60-foot Chapman Falls. (The myth that gives the park its name says the potholes that riddle the foot of the falls cliff were burned into the rock by the Devil's hooves as he hopped about avoiding the water, making this his "hopyard.") Brook-sized Eight Mile River, a charming covered footbridge, and loop trails through mature and varied forest complete the offering. Dogwood, mountain laurel, and azalea herald spring; in autumn, enjoy the contrast of the green eastern hemlock spires and the colorful hardwood crowns.

General description: Chapman Falls Trail and three loops explore much of the parkland: Witch Hazel Loop explores the southwest corner of the park above Muddy Brook; the Vista Trail circles from Eight Mile River to a ridgetop vista and back; and the Loop Trail tours a hillside forest.

General location: 8 miles east of East Haddam, Connecticut.

Special attractions: Waterfall and cascades, attractive river and side brooks, mature hemlock, spring floral showcase, bird and wildlife sightings, fishing, fall foliage.

Length: Chapman Falls Trail, 0.2 mile round-trip; Witch Hazel Trail, 2.2 miles round-trip; Vista Trail, 2.75-mile loop; Loop Trail, 0.8-mile loop.

Elevation: Chapman Falls Trail, 80-foot elevation change; Witch Hazel Trail, 250-foot elevation change; Vista Trail 300-foot elevation change; Loop Trail, 200-foot elevation change.

Difficulty: Chapman Falls Trail, easy; Witch Hazel Trail, moderate; Vista Trail, strenuous; Loop Trail, moderate.

Maps: State park map.

Special requirements: Fee area; keep pets leashed. Boots recommended.

Season and hours: Year-round, spring through fall for hiking. Open 8 a.m. to sunset.

For information: Devil's Hopyard State Park.

Finding the trailhead: From the small village of Millington (6 miles east of East Haddam), go cast on Haywardville Road, following signs for the park. In 0.7 mile, turn right (south) on CT 434 (Hopyard Road). In 0.75 mile, turn left for the falls; go another 0.25 mile south, turning left for the picnic area and loop trailheads.

The hikes: For **Chapman Falls Trail**, cross the road from the parking area and descend the stairs and a short side path angling left to reach a rock outcrop with boulder seating for viewing the 3-tiered 60-foot drop. Here, lacy waters curve around and spill over an escarpment of reddish-hued Scotland schist. Stepped ledges, eroded potholes, and a dark plunge pool contribute to the viewing, as does an enfolding woods of maple, oak, birch, azalea, dogwood, and mountain laurel.

The potholes, eroded cylindrical holes ranging from inches deep to several feet in diameter and depth, are among the finest of their kind in New England. Contrary to the myth, potholes are created by the persistent abrasion of stones caught and swirled by the stream's eddies. Return as you came, 0.2 mile.

For the **Witch Hazel Trail**, park in the first riverside picnic area (the southernmost one), and hike the gated woods road located near the picnic area entrance. Follow the red blazes to reach the yellow-blazed Witch Hazel loop.

Hike downstream along Eight Mile River on a woods road framed by eastern hemlock, towering oak, maple, dogwood, and mountain laurel, with a sprinkling of violet and wild geranium. Across the Muddy Brook footbridge, the lane narrows to trail-width and bears right to cross CT 434. On the west side of CT 434, locate the yellow-blazed loop (0.4 mile), and go straight for a counterclockwise tour.

Hike upstream on a woods road along the hemlock-filled drainage of

Muddy Brook. A few big birch accent the woods. Soon turn left on a footpath, touring closer to the brook to reach Baby Falls, a ledge drop with a pretty 3-foot cascade (0.6 mile). Climb steadily, passing from eastern hemlock to a deciduous forest bursting with fern and dotted by huge boulders. Next enter a passageway of 10-foot-tall mountain laurel, vibrant even when not in bloom.

Top out at a huckleberry flat (1.1 miles) and descend, backtracking through laurel grove, fern-deciduous woods, and hemlock stand. Watch your footing. Close the loop at 1.8 miles, return to the picnic area at 2.2 miles.

For both the orange-blazed **Vista Trail** and blue-blazed **Loop Trail**, start at the covered pedestrian bridge located at the picnic area. The scenic bridge spans Eight Mile Brook, shows rustic wood siding, and sports beam-framed windows for viewing the waterway's rich hemlock drainage and draping deciduous trees.

Cross to the east shore, and go right (downstream) for a counterclockwise tour of the orange-blazed **Vista Trail** and to reach the blue-blazed Loop Trail in 0.1 mile. Tour a wide surfaced trail amid mature hemlock, white pine, and hardwood. Laurel and azalea border the brook-sized river.

Soon after the blue blazes depart to the left, the orange-blazed trail narrows to a footpath, rolling up and over the rocks of the lower slope to reach the river bank at 0.3 mile. Fern and moss complement the tannin-darkened water. Stay along the river for a tricky root-and-rock riddled tour.

Cross a drainage and return to the river where the bank is 8 feet above the water. Veer left here for a steep climb crossing side drainages to gain the ridge. The trail attacks the slope head on and shows erosion damage that could be reduced or eliminated by a properly switchbacked trailbed. At the upper slope, ledge overhangs draw notice.

Round to the top of the ridge, coming to a junction (1 mile): Turn right for the 0.1-mile vista spur; left continues the loop. First go right, descending to the vantage for an open look at the surrounding forested hills, and a pasture and pond below. Mountain laurel frames the view.

Now resume the loop traversing the ridge flat, exploring a leafy woods pierced by hemlock snags. Ferns, grass, Virginia creeper, and wildflowers penetrate the duff. Find a moderate descent, once again hugging the line of the slope and crossing small drainages heralded by mountain laurel and skunk cabbage; the descent now steepens.

Look for deer feeding on colorful fungi. Amid a choked hemlock grove, look for a side path heading right to a grand old oak. Resume the loop, descending amid scenic beech trees and white pines, crossing a rocky drainage at 2.2 miles. At 2.25 miles, a connector descends left across a brook to the blue-blazed **Loop Trail**. Stay the orange blazes.

Tour mixed woods along the laurel and azalea banks of the narrow brook as you follow it downstream. At an unmarked junction (2.5 miles) curve left, heading toward the covered bridge and flume. Side spurs to the right lead to views of a seasonal falls and the shore of a broadened Eight Mile River. An unseen Chapman Falls thunders upstream. Close the loop and

DEVIL'S HOPYARD STATE PARK

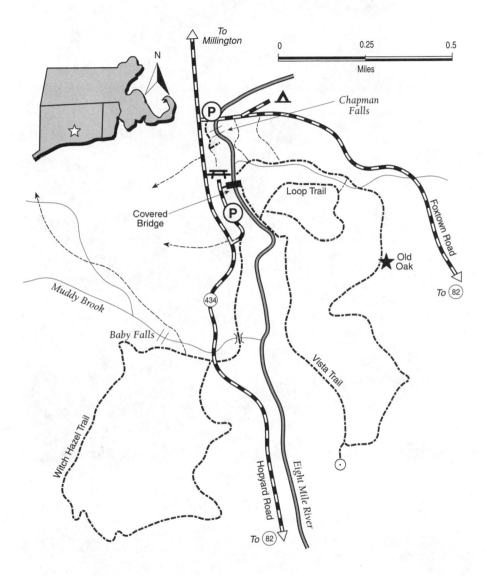

To Millington

0   0.25   0.5
Miles

Chapman Falls

P

Loop Trail

Foxtown Road

To 82

Old Oak

Covered Bridge

P

Muddy Brook

434

Baby Falls

Vista Trail

Witch Hazel Trail

Hopyard Road

Eight Mile River

To 82

Ancient Oak, Devil's Hopyard State Park, CT.

pass through the bridge 2.75 miles.

For the blue-blazed **Loop Trail**, cross through the bridge and turn right, following the blue and orange blazes for 0.1 mile. There turn left, touring an oak and laurel hillside, ascending to a healing fire zone, with its recovering midstory and unscathed big trees. Leave the burn, reaching the loop junction 0.2 mile; go left, passing amid hemlock, dogwood, and maples for an easy, comfortable tour. Bypass the connector to the orange-blazed trail, top out, and then descend, again enjoying laurel. Close the loop and return to the start 0.8 mile.

65 HARTMAN RECREATIONAL PARK

OVERVIEW

At this 302-acre open space find north-south trending ridges separated by wooded valleys and wetlands. Across the property, several stone ruins and miles of stone walls recall a thriving colonial settlement. Interlocking, color-coded trails probe the park and link to the Nehantic State Forest trail system. Foot trails and cart roads from early settlement lead the way.

General description: Two main loops explore much of the park. The orange-blazed Heritage Trail strings past cultural ruins, while the red-blazed Nubble and Ridges Trail rolls from ridge to ridge, tagging interesting cliff and rock features.

General location: Northeast corner of Lyme, Connecticut.

Special attractions: Relaxing hardwood forest; interesting rock features; 17th-, 18th-, and 19th-century stone walls and foundations; intriguing historic cemetery; abundant mountain laurel; fall foliage, bird watching.

Length: Heritage Trail, 3-mile loop; Nubble and Ridges Trail, 3.75-mile loop.

Elevation: Both show a 200-foot elevation change.

Difficulty: Both, moderate.

Maps: Park map, generally available at the open-air schoolroom and picnic area.

Special requirements: No motor vehicles, fires, or collecting. In this color-coded trail system, yellow blazes indicates a connector trail, white blazes a dead-end. Bring water, and beware of poison ivy, which is abundant throughout the park.

Season and hours: Year-round, sunrise to sunset.

For information: Hartman Park Manager.

Finding the trailhead: From the Connecticut 82 - Connecticut 156 junction east of Hadlyme, go south on CT 156 East for 1.7 miles and turn left (east) on Beaver Brook Road in North Lyme. Go east on Beaver Brook Road for 2.6 miles and turn left (north) on Gungy/Grassy Hill Road. Find turnout parking for Hartman Park on the right-hand side of Gungy Road in 1 mile.

The hikes: For the **Heritage Trail**, cross over Park Road (a gated dirt road) to follow an orange-blazed footpath through a young forest of maple, beech, and oak. At 0.1 mile, the green-blazed **Nature Loop** arrives and shares the way. Find sweet pepperbush amid the moister woodland reaches.

Now parallel the silver-blazed Park Road, crossing back over it at 0.2 mile. Keep to the orange blazes, as the pink-blazed **Beaver Pond Loop** heads left. The Heritage Trail itself offers a glimpse of the snag-meadow marsh and beaver pond before crossing a small footbridge at the site of an old sawmill. At 0.3 mile, reach the picnic area/open-air classroom on a flat above the beaver pond and locate a mapboard and box of trail maps.

Cross Park Road and hike uphill, leaving behind the green-marked trail and crossing a yellow-blazed one. Dogwoods lend springtime bloom. At 0.5 mile, a white-blazed spur leads to the well-preserved foundation of an old barn. Shortly after, the orange-blazed trail briefly follows Park Road north. At a cellar hole and rock foundation from the Lee Farmhouse, ascend right through old fields overgrown with cedar and encroached by oaks and maples.

Where another yellow-blazed connector trail heads left, bear right for the "Big Scramble," a switchbacking climb through mountain laurel, topping Chapman Ridge. The trail now journeys north, skirting the various stoneworks of Chapman Farm.

At 0.95 mile, bypass the blue-blazed **Chapman Path** on the left and travel the open shrub thicket of the powerline corridor. A spur to the right tops some rocks for a better vantage looking west out the corridor. Watch for vultures and hawks, before returning to the woods to travel a scenic beech grove.

Descend Chapman Ridge, again finding abundant mountain laurel and passing a stone fireplace, to hike Park Road to the right. Tour amid aspen and tulip poplar, viewing rockwork that records another old farm. Soon after, bear left from the road; look for the circular depression from an old charcoal kiln at the turn.

Pass through a fern-filled glen, rounding below a huge boulder outcrop, and again ascend. At 1.7 miles, the red blazes of the **Nubble and Ridges Trail** briefly join the Heritage Trail on Three Chimneys Ridge. Where the two trails separate, a white-blazed spur leads to a compound of rockworks, including three small fireplaces.

Stay the Heritage Trail, descending past an enormous boulder against which a barn once stood, and bear left briefly following orange and yellow markers. Woody grapevines drape between the trees. Ahead, stay the orange blazes for a rolling ascent of Jumble Ridge (2 miles). Along this stretch, look for a split rock measuring 6.5 feet tall.

At 2.3 miles turn left, where yellow blazes lead right. A white-blazed spur leads to the circular trench of another 19th-century charcoal kiln. More ruins and a second pass through the powerline corridor advance the tour.

Next, pass yellow blazes to the left. To the right, white markers lead to a

HARTMAN RECREATIONAL PARK

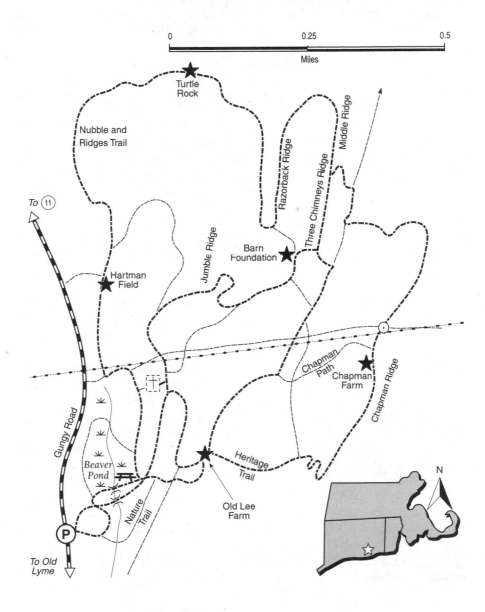

0   0.25   0.5
Miles

Turtle Rock

Nubble and Ridges Trail

Middle Ridge

Razorback Ridge

Three Chimneys Ridge

To (11)

Jumble Ridge

Barn Foundation

Hartman Field

Chapman Path

Chapman Farm

Chapman Ridge

Gungy Road

Beaver Pond

Heritage Trail

Nature Trail

Old Lee Farm

P

To Old Lyme

N

simple ancient cemetery atop a small knoll. Low, lichen-riddled, unetched stones planted in the earth indicate the burial sites. The arrangement of the stones indicates the work of humans rather than nature.

Return to the orange-blazed Heritage Trail and bear right, to complete the counterclockwise tour. At Park Road, go right, passing through the school-room/picnic site, returning to the trailhead (3 miles).

For the red-blazed **Nubble and Ridges Trail**, round the gate off the parking lot and hike north along the silver-blazed Park Road. Cross a stone bridge, where cardinal flowers adorn the drainage, and at 0.25 mile, pass through the picnic area/open-air schoolroom. There, pick up a trail map.

Now find the red blazes of the Nubble and Ridges Trail bearing left, sharing the way with the pink-blazed **Beaver Pond Loop.** View the over-grown pond to the left, while traveling a fully shaded foot trail. At 0.4 mile, bear right, staying with the red blazes. Many ferns dress the woods floor, as a few dogwoods contribute to the overhead canopy. Before long, a white-blazed spur leads to a beaver dam.

At 0.5 mile, bypass a yellow-blazed trail on the right, coming to a T-junction with Powerline Road. Go left passing through the shrubby corridor to follow a dirt path to the right, re-entering mixed hardwood forest; watch for the turns. Rock walls again line portions of the tour.

Enter Hartman Field, overgrown with a few reclaiming red cedar, or fol-low the red markers along its shaded eastern edge. The trails merge where a yellow-blazed connector trail heads left. Resume the forest walk, finding another yellow-blazed connector heading right.

At 1.25 miles, locate the overhang of Cave Cliff above the trail to the left. Other interesting rock features of quartzite, schist, and gneiss now charac-terize the tour, including a broken overhang dubbed "Snout." Find the trail rolling, fully forested, and bursting with beautiful pockets of laurel.

Next travel atop the outcrop of Bald Nubble, a large, open rock slope without views. More named, lichen-etched outcrops engage hikers, before the trail descends through a forested drainage. Now follow an old cart road until the trail makes a U-turn north.

At 1.9 miles, tour the open vista-less ledge of Razorback Ridge. The trail then dips and climbs, reversing direction to top Middle Ridge and follow a rock wall along its crest. Where it travels Three Chimneys Ridge, the or-ange-blazed **Heritage Trail** shares its path; stay the red blazes.

At 2.5 miles, reach Park Road and turn right to complete the tour. Pass under power lines and through forest, returning to the picnic area/school-room flat (3.5 miles), the trailhead (3.75 miles).

66 NAYANTAQUIT TRAIL

General description: This rolling loop passes though a gentle terrain of low ridges and mixed forest, promising solitude and relaxation. A side trip to the deep clear waters of Uncas Pond for a picnic lunch or a quick swim punctuates the tour.

General location: 5 miles southeast of Hadlyme, Connecticut.

Special attractions: Solitude, wildlife sightings, historic stone walls and foundations, pond refreshment, fall foliage.

Length: 5 miles round-trip.

Elevation: Find a 400-foot elevation change, with the low point at Uncas Pond, the high point at Nickerson Hill.

Difficulty: Moderate.

Maps: Hamburg 7.5-minute USGS quad; Nayantaquit Trail map, *Connecticut Walk Book*.

Special requirements: Swimming is at your own risk.

Season and hours: Year-round, depending on snow conditions. Open 8 a.m. to sunset.

For information: Nehantic State Forest.

Finding the trailhead: From the junction of Connecticut 82 and Connecticut 156 (east of Hadlyme, west of North Plain), go south on CT 156 East for 1.7 miles, reaching North Lyme. There turn east on Beaver Brook Road, go 1.9 miles, and turn right (south) on Keeny Road. Reach trailhead parking on the right in 1.3 miles; the final 0.3 mile of travel is on dirt road.

The hike: Named for an Indian tribe that hunted in this part of Nehantic State Forest, this loop wins over travelers with its relaxing familiarity. From the parking area, hike in on the gated dirt road, taking an immediate left, following blue blazes. In the woods, find a trail sign and the number 1, indicating the official start. Along the loop, the numbers 1 through 10 indicate key junctions or features.

Tour a young forest of oak, maple, birch, dogwood, sassafras, shadbush, and hazelnut, with an understory of huckleberry and sarsaparilla. Cross a scenic rock wall and pass a huge boulder on the left, coming to the loop junction (site 2), at 0.2 mile. Go left for a clockwise tour, traveling a thin, mildly inclined path.

Reach a high point (site 3) near the edge of a plateau. Boulders and the occasional stump dot the forest, which, although young, provides a full leafy umbrella. Next, find a sometimes-steep descent, entering a mature oak-hickory complex. As the trail weaves amid the boulder outcrops and later rolls, enjoy the different visuals and mood of the tour. Cross a thin (often dry) brook, pass a regal 4-foot-diameter tulip poplar, and cross a rock wall.

Next top Brown Hill at 0.9 mile, coming to a junction in a small transition meadow. The loop continues to the left; a cutoff trail heads right for a shorter

NAYANTAQUIT TRAIL

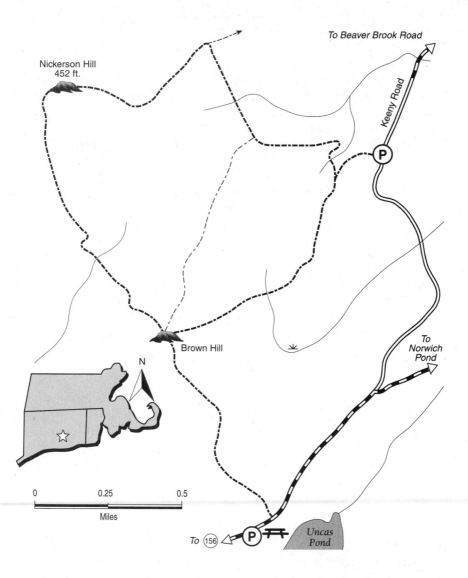

Nickerson Hill
452 ft.

To Beaver Brook Road

Keeny Road

P

Brown Hill

To
Norwich
Pond

N

0   0.25   0.5

Miles

To (156)   P   Uncas
Pond

tour. Along the cutoff, hikers find stone walls and foundations recalling the land's domestic history as pasture and farmland. Keep left for the full loop, quickly reaching site 4, where the spur to Uncas Pond heads left; the loop turns right.

Go left for Uncas Pond, passing quietly, as wild turkey or deer may be spied. Descend off Brown Hill, passing a doghouse-sized rock shelter to travel a tall mixed-deciduous woods. Roll up and over the next outcrop rise, reaching a paved road (site 10), 1.6 miles.

Hike the road to the right and turn left entering Uncas Pond Picnic Area, an attractive site with tables, barbecues, and pit toilets. Touring south along the steep bank of this big pond, find sharply descending footpaths accessing a thin beach shore. At the south end of the picnic area, reach an open rock and sand beach (1.8 miles). Sparkling blue, the deep waters of Uncas Pond suggest a dip. Find the pond's rim mostly wild and forested with a couple of homes visible across the way. A few pond lilies decorate the edge water.

Backtrack to the loop junction (site 4) at 2.6 miles, and resume the clockwise tour (straight upon return). Follow the blazes, making a couple of quick direction changes to travel a tranquil country lane bathed in filtered lighting. Pass alongside a stone wall shaded by a gnarly old oak. Ahead the lane yields to a logging road recently reinstated for harvest use. Bear right, cross a drainage culvert (3 miles), and again turn right at 3.1 miles.

Just ahead, turn left off the woods road, ascending a footpath amid oak, hickory, and beech to top a small hill. In 0.2 mile, cross a stone wall to travel the summit of Nickerson Hill, tagging the hike's high point (elevation 452 feet) at 3.6 miles. Here large round boulders dot a sloping outcrop, which affords only stolen views southeast, as the foreground forest shoots skyward. Nearby stand spiny armed snags, young deciduous trees, and cedars.

At junction 7, a spur to the left reaches a woods road that returns to parking. Bear right for the loop. In the leafy canopy, insects create the sound of high-tension wires. Next find a series of crossings over woods roads, a brook, and a secondary trail. At 4.4 miles, reach junction 8, where the cutoff trail rejoins the tour on the right. Proceed ahead.

With a steady descent, cross the width of a long meadow swath, brimming with wild berry, sumac, herbs, and forbs; keep an eye out for poison ivy. Cross a plank over a small brook to tour a wetter maple woodland and pass through a goldenrod opening to close the loop at site 2. Return to the trailhead at 5 miles.

67 BLUFF POINT STATE PARK AND COASTAL RESERVE

OVERVIEW

This hike tours Connecticut's last vestige of undeveloped coast—an 800-acre wooded peninsula bounded by the Poquonock River and Mumford Cove and extending into Long Island Sound. A sandy spit offers coastal and bay discovery. Designated a coastal reserve, facilities are few and in keeping with the area's character.

General description: This easy multiple-use loop travels closed dirt roads, touring a coastal woodland, sandspit, and bluff.
General location: Eastern outskirts of Groton, Connecticut.
Special attractions: Long Island Sound and bayshore discovery; wildlife sightings of deer, raccoon, and sea, shore, and woodland birds; historic 1700s homesite of Governor Winthrop.
Length: 4.8 miles round-trip.
Elevation: Find a 100-foot elevation change.
Difficulty: Easy.
Maps: State park map (usually available at park).
Special requirements: Bring water; none at park.
Season and hours: Year-round, 8 a.m. to sunset.
For information: Bluff Point State Park and Coastal Reserve.
Finding the trailhead: From Interstate 95, take exit 88, go 1 mile south on Connecticut 117, and turn west on U.S. Highway 1. In 0.3 mile, turn south on Depot Road at the sign for the park. Bear right and pass under the railroad tracks to reach the gravel parking lot, picnic area, and trail in 0.4 mile.

The hike: From the center of the picnic area, hike the gated woods road, paralleling the Poquonock River toward the sea. Swans sometimes ply the bay. Anglers line the riprap shore, while sea kayakers dig their way to Long Island Sound. Across the river sits tiny Trumbull Airport.

The modest-grade trail travels the perimeter of a mixed oak-hickory woods, with sassafras, hawthorn, cherry, and the occasional eastern red cedar. Greenbrier, wild grape, and bramble contribute to the understory tangle. At the 0.1-mile junction, go right for a counterclockwise loop. Short spurs branch to a gravelly Poquonock shore, its width dependent on tide. In spring, look for a pair of osprey atop the offshore nesting platform.

Near an offset barricade of concrete blocks, the trail opens up, skirting a grassy tidal marsh with cattails at one end. In such open areas, native beach plum, beach pea, and red and white shore roses grow. At 0.5 miles, a secondary foot trail travels closer to the bay, rejoining the tour at 0.8 mile.

Meanwhile, the main woods road passes between a bouldery, forested

BLUFF POINT STATE PARK AND COASTAL RESERVE

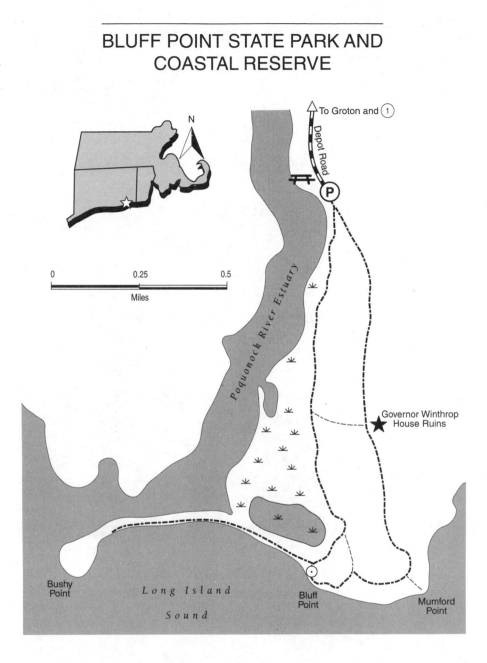

To Groton and ①

Depot Road

P

Poquonoch River Estuary

Governor Winthrop House Ruins

Bushy Point

Long Island

Sound

Bluff Point

Mumford Point

N

0   0.25   0.5
Miles

Poquonock River estuary shore, Bluff Point State Park and Coastal Reserve, CT.

hill and the tight tangle of the bayward woods. A semi-overgrown colonial rock wall lines the road, adding interest and charm. At 0.7 mile, bear right; the road fork to the left offers a cutoff to shorten the loop.

Where the main road and secondary bay route merge (0.8 mile), the tour offers glimpses of Long Island Sound across the tidal grass plain of the Poquonock River. This productive 100-acre salt marsh attracts resident and migratory birds.

At the 3-pronged junction (1.1 miles) bear right for the loop. The trail passes a pair of privies set back from the trail before arriving at the beach below Bluff Point. Tidepool rocks string off the point, while pebbles, cobbles, and sun-bleached shells compose the coastal shore. Snowfences help prevent the loss of sand and vegetation.

Views pan Long Island Sound from Groton Heights to Bluff Point and include New York's Fisher's Island and Rhode Island's Watch Hill. An attractive tombolo beach (spit) arcs west to Bushy Point. Journeying west along the 200-foot-wide spit, hikers may divide their time between the Sound and Poquonock bay shore; midway a battered boardwalk allows easy passage between the two.

Walkable at low tide, the bay shore records the tracks of wading birds and deer. Along the seashore, tide-deposited strings of seaweed, sea lettuce, bladder-floated algae, skate eggcases, periwinkles, horseshoe crab shells, and flotsam and jetsam excite beachcombers. About two-thirds of the way, stable sands replace the shifting gravels. At 1.9 miles, Bushy Point (a vegetated rock island at high tide) signals the turnaround point. Pine Island lies farther offshore, while a scenic brick lighthouse blinks to the west.

Next, return to the base of Bluff Point (2.7 miles) to top the 20-foot bluff. Mount it from the beach or from the main dirt road rounding behind it. Views broaden, straining east; a wooden bench invites pause.

Where the trail departs the east side of the bluff, a right turn leads to rocky Mumford Point. For the loop, follow the woods road bearing left. A dwarfed woods with a dense, thorny understory now enfolds the tour. As the road mildly climbs, side paths branch to the rocky shore.

Beyond a study enclosure to measure the impact of deer on area vegetation, rock walls again appear. Cardinal, blue jay, hawk, and vulture draw eyes skyward. Passing through an open area of tall grasses, keep to the main road.

At 3.9 miles, look across the rock wall to the right to discover ruins—a stone foundation, chunks of red brick, and a hard-to-see well now filled with stones. Here stood the home of Governor Fitzjohn Winthrop (grandson of the famous Massachusetts Bay governor). Circa 1700, the Winthrop house had a 300-foot tunnel connecting it to the barn, a safeguard against Indian attacks. Beware of poison ivy, when exploring.

Past the Winthrop site, keep to the main woods road; a smaller track journeys right. Tall forest enfolds the trail for the close of the loop (4.7 miles). Return to the trailhead, 4.8 miles.

RHODE ISLAND TRAILS

While small in geographic territory and well populated, Rhode Island remains 60 percent forested and boasts some fine natural spaces. Find mildly rolling lowland forests, sandy Atlantic Ocean beaches, and rocky shores. Retired military bases now serve as vital wildlife lands, with gulls using the abandoned runways to break open shellfish. Elsewhere, stone walls, pens, and cellars hint at a time when the forest was tilled and partitioned for pasture. Rocky realms, meadows, ponds, and swamps complete the discovery. Enjoy bird watching and some fine vistas, despite the low-elevation landscape.

68 GEORGE WASHINGTON MANAGEMENT AREA

OVERVIEW

In northwest Rhode Island, this extensive management area incorporates George Washington Memorial State Forest and the adjoining Casimir Pulaski Memorial State Park. Within the management area, find a burgeoning color-coded trail system, with the Walkabout Trail and Angell Loop being prized examples of the available hikes. Tour lakeshore, woodland, and wetland, finding solitude and wildlife discovery.

General description: Designed with two cut-over trails, the Walkabout Trail allows hikers to customize both tour length and difficulty. Angell Loop offers a comfortable lakeshore-woodland circuit, passing an Indian gravesite.
General location: 10 miles east of Putnam, Connecticut; 5 miles southwest of Pascoag, Rhode Island.
Special attractions: Bowdish Reservoir and Wilbur and Peck ponds; mountain laurel; hemlock, pine, and hardwood forests; wetland habitat; wildlife sightings; fall foliage.
Length: Walkabout Trail, 2-, 6-, or 8-mile loop, with a still longer tour possible, adding the Peck Pond spur (1.2 miles round-trip). Angell Loop, 1.6-mile loop.
Elevation: Walkabout Trail, 200-foot elevation change; Angell Loop, 75-foot elevation change.
Difficulty: Walkabout Trail, easy to moderately strenuous. Angell Loop, easy.
Maps: Walkabout Trail flier.
Special requirements: User fee area. In spring and following rains, wet

GEORGE WASHINGTON MANAGEMENT AREA

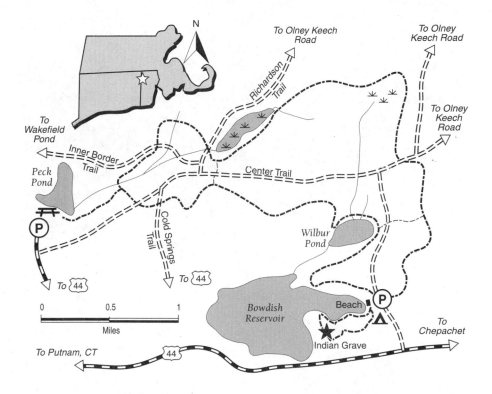

conditions on the Walkabout Trail increase the difficulty of the tour.

Season and hours: Year-round, generally spring through fall for hiking. Sunrise to sunset.

For information: George Washington Management Area.

Finding the trailhead: From the junction of Rhode Island 100, Rhode Island 102, and U.S. Highway 44 in Chepachet, Rhode Island, go west on U.S. 44 for 4.2 miles and turn north for George Washington Memorial State Forest and campground. Pass the campground, finding the Walkabout trailhead on the northeast shore of Bowdish Reservoir near the picnic area, beach, and boat launch (0.4 mile). Find Angell Loop south of the launch.

The hikes: Built by Australian sailors awaiting the repair of their ship, the H.M.A.S. *Perth*, the **Walkabout Trail** traces its name and intent to the aborigines, who coined the name for a compelling need to wander, a "walkabout."

Start at the marked trailhead, rounding the northeast shore of Bowdish

Wilbur Pond, George Washington Memorial State Forest, RI.

Reservoir, touring a hemlock-hardwood forest. A tri-color blazing indicates the start. Keep to the blue blazes for a 2-mile loop, red for a 6-mile loop, and orange for the full 8-mile loop.

Canada geese sometimes ply the water or plod along the reservoir's edge. Rocks and tangled roots erupt in the trail. Find soggy drainages and fragments of boardwalk, before turning away from the reservoir at 0.3 mile, where a flattish granite outcrop affords a farewell view.

The meandering woods trail skirts a private campground on Wilbur Pond. At 0.8 mile, the blue-blazed trail breaks away, briefly touring the state forest road, before turning to close its loop. Continue ahead along the forest rim of Wilbur Pond for the longer tours.

The limited openings allow only glances at this good-sized pond, but its mountain laurel rim engages the eye. At 1 mile, access a few large boulders and a 50-foot shoreline for unencumbered pond views. Ahead find a merry chase across the spreading inlet drainages; some require ingenuity to devise a dry crossing.

While the blazing may appear excessive during the main hiking season, once the leaves drop they are necessary. With a final look at a scenic reflecting bay-water, ascend away from Wilbur Pond (1.5 miles). Beyond the pond, find a mostly deciduous forest with occasional pine. At 2 miles, the red-blazed trail departs to the right to complete its loop. Follow the orange blazes for the full tour.

As fewer obstacles riddle the trail, enjoy a relaxing wander through woods. Changes in lighting, bird songs, and a whisper of breeze contribute to the tour's soothing message. At 2.9 miles, cross a drivable dirt road (Cold Spring Trail), then cross a grassy woods road and a second dirt road with a trailside bench at 3.2 miles. Now hike a time-healed woods road, passing through a dark hemlock grove, coming to a sign and red arrows for Pulaski Park (3.5 miles).

Detour left for Pulaski Park, Peck Pond, and the Pulaski Park trail system, ascending amid rich forest and enjoying cushiony footfalls on the wood-chip softened lane. At 4 miles, come out at an isolated pine-shaded picnic ground above Peck Pond. Pass through the park to reach the open beach access.

Multi-colored pastel blazings hint at other hiking tours. Large parking areas suggest a bustling site in summer; off-season visitors share the area with wildlife. Find flush toilets and water during the summer months.

Backtrack to the Walkabout Trail, retracing the red arrows to the orange-blazed trail. There resume the clockwise tour, bearing left (4.7 miles). Tour amid beautiful pines and cross a hemlock-lined brook, coming to a junction. The red arrows straight ahead lead back to Pulaski Park; the Walkabout Trail now heads right. By 5.1 miles, tour a skunk cabbage bog via board-walk, and at 5.5 miles, cross the dirt road of Inner Border Trail, remaining in wetter woods.

At the Richardson Trail (a road) crossing, find a bench seat. Now round a snag-riddled wildlife pond and marsh, crossing the earthen dam. Ascend away through woods, soon to be rejoined by the red-blazed trail (6.9 miles) as snags open the forest to mountain laurel.

Next cross Center Trail road and tour a rustic corduroy section through a marshy area, before the blue-blazed trail rejoins the tour at 8.5 miles. End the hike, returning to Bowdish Reservoir along the access road to the boat launch (9.2 miles).

For the purple-blazed **Angell Loop**, round the south shore of the boat launch cove, passing amid eastern hemlock, mountain laurel, white pine, oak, birch, and beech. The campground occupies the woods above the trail.

In 300 feet, reach the loop junction and bear right, keeping to shore. Bowdish Reservoir, large with an irregular shoreline, has a posted boat speed of 10 miles per hour for relative quiet. Cross a small boggy inlet, finding gaps in the trees to view the reservoir or cast a line. Huge rocks suggest taking a seat to admire the water and its mostly wild shore. Laurel abounds.

By 0.6 mile, gain over-the-shoulder looks at the beach area, before the trail curves away left, passing some large rocks. Now travel pine-oak woods, enjoying full shade and a slow ascent. Deer, chipmunk, woodpecker, and other woodland creatures enliven a tour.

At 0.85 mile, a 30-foot-long spur on the left leads to the Indian grave; be alert to spot it. A faded wooden sign and arrangement of stones alone mark the site.

Find a gently rolling forested return, traveling a time-healed woods road and footpath. Forgotten natural history signs indicate an American chestnut and a blueberry bush. Descend to close the loop and return to the trailhead 1.6 miles.

69 GEORGE B. PARKER WOODLAND

OVERVIEW

At this Audubon Society of Rhode Island property, find rich hardwood forest, moist bottomland, peaceful brooks, and early American history. The Isaac Bowen House, a central-chimney colonial located at the wildlife area headquarters, is on the register of National Historic Places. Across the property find foundations, stone walls, quarry sites, and inexplicable cairns that harken to the past. According to legend, Biscuit Hill traces its name to the Revolutionary War, when a food wagon of biscuits overturned en route to General Rochambeau's troops.

General description: The Paul Cook and Milton A. Gowdey memorial trails, two loops joined by a connecting trail, travel the Coventry and Foster tracts of Parker Woodland, exploring the natural and cultural wealth.
General location: 2 miles east of Vernon, Rhode Island; 4 miles northwest

of Coventry Center.

Special attractions: Solitude, bird and wildlife watching, historic sites, rich woods, spring and summer wildflowers, fall foliage.

Length: 7 miles round-trip, traveling both loops. Hikers may explore the loops individually, when the parking lot east of the headquarters is open.

Elevation: Find less than a 100-foot elevation change.

Difficulty: Moderate.

Maps: Wildlife area map, generally available at parking lots.

Special requirements: Obey all posted Audubon rules, including no pets, no bicycles, no smoking, and no collecting. For this color-coded trail system, blue marks the loops; orange, the access trail; and yellow, the connecting spurs.

Season and hours: Year-round, generally spring through fall for hiking. Sunrise to sunset.

For information: George B. Parker Woodland c/o the Audubon Society of Rhode Island.

Finding the trailhead: From Interstate 95, take exit 5, go north on Rhode Island 102 for 8.3 miles, and turn right (east) on Maple Valley Road. Go 0.2 mile to find the headquarters parking lot for Parker Woodland on the left. Find a second parking lot east on Maple Valley Road.

   The hike: From headquarters parking, follow the mowed swath along the fence to a sign: to the left lies the Nature Center; to the right, find all trails.

Boardwalk, George B. Parker Woodland, RI.

Go right and in 100 feet, follow orange blazes to the left, passing through a beautiful mixed woods of red cedar, pine, beech, birch, maple, oak, dogwood, and hickory. The groundcover likewise displays diversity, with Canada mayflower, club moss, Virginia creeper, poison ivy, and hog peanut. At 0.25 mile, reach a T-junction; left takes you to the Nature Center. Continue right, gently descending to reach the loops.

Travel a moist bottomland with a half-dozen fern varieties, sweet pepperbush, trillium, wood lilies, false Solomon's seal, nettles, and azalea. A scenic boardwalk crosses the soggier reaches. At 0.4 mile, cross the footbridge over Turkey Meadow Brook, a slow, thin waterway adorned by drooping boughs and vegetation. A sawmill once operated alongside the brook.

At 0.5 mile, reach the **Paul Cook Memorial Trail** (marked in blue), and turn left for a clockwise tour of Coventry Tract. Stones stud the trail; oak and hickory are the "big guys" of the woods. Sassafras, highbush blueberry, and huckleberry add a midstory layer. Rock walls grace the tour.

At 1 mile, cross Biscuit Hill Road, a grassy, narrow woods road. On both sides, find ruins from the Vaughn farmsite, including dry-laid fieldstone foundations, the cellar to a central-chimney colonial home, stairs, and a stone-lined well with its capstone ajar. A sign explains the lay of the farm buildings that date to the mid-18th century. Trees now pierce the cellar floor.

A slow ascent follows, passing amid pine and crossing lichen-mottled outcrop. At 1.4 miles, descend, ducking a protruding rock. Cross an unnamed woods road and resume the descent, touring a mixed hardwood forest riddled by outcrop and boulders. Expect to do some high-stepping in this obstacle course terrain.

The Paul Cook Memorial Trail then rolls, coming to a junction at 2 miles. The yellow-blazed trail to the left leads to the **Milton A. Gowdey Memorial Trail** and Foster Tract; the yellow-marked trail to the right leads to Biscuit Hill Road and parking lot 2. For the Paul Cook Memorial Trail alone, proceed forward, hiking past a room-sized boulder, following the blue blazes.

Go left for the full 7-mile tour, traveling a rocky trail through beech-hardwood forest. Pass an even bigger boulder than the one at the 2-mile junction, and follow Pine Swamp Brook upstream, contouring the slope some 20 feet above the drainage. Mosses darken the brook's boulders.

Cross the footbridge at 2.25 miles. A root-ribbed foot trail now ascends to the blue-blazed Gowdey Trail (2.45 miles). Go left for a clockwise tour, and watch for poison ivy. Find a gentle incline for a relaxing stroll. At 2.95 miles, descend back toward Pine Swamp Brook. Sweet pepperbush ushers the way, and more rocks riddle the trail.

Soon pull away from the brook, passing through another historical farmstead (3.25 miles). Rock walls, stone pens, and a 5-foot-deep foundation mark the site. Next descend a low rise amid white pine and hardwoods to cross Pig Hill Road at 3.5 miles.

Pines drop from the mix as you continue the slow descent. Where the trail passes between offset rock walls, find a boulder-dotted landscape. On

GEORGE B. PARKER WOODLAND

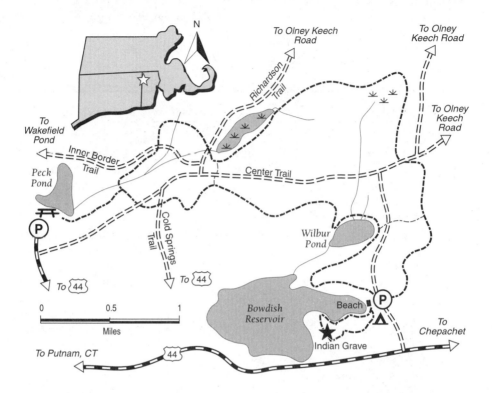

the right, at 4 miles, a disturbed area with displaced rock and reclaiming vegetation signals an old quarry site.

Advance via long, sleepy trail undulations, cross Pig Hill Road a second time, and pass through a (usually gated) parking lot. Keep left when rounding the sanctuary entry post to avoid the worst of the poison ivy. At 4.95 miles, close the loop and backtrack along the yellow-blazed trail to the Coventry Tract. Return to the 2-mile junction at 5.4 miles and bear left to resume the blue-blazed Paul Cook Memorial Trail.

Descend amid outcrops, briefly passing near Pine Swamp Brook. Find showings of mountain laurel, pass another foundation on the left, and cross Biscuit Hill Road to contour above Turkey Meadow Brook at 5.9 miles. At the 6.1-mile junction, continue ahead on the blue-blazed trail. The blue markers heading to the left lead to parking lot 2. The yellow ones to the right reach Biscuit Hill Road and Foster Tract.

Just ahead find a number of cairns, some 4 feet tall, others broad and squat. While their origins are unknown, one theory attributes them to colonial field clearing, another describes them as pre-colonial Celtic or Narragansett Indian sacred monuments. Pass a white-blazed trail on the right to close the loop at 6.5 miles. Retrace the 0.5-mile orange-blazed trail to the headquarters parking lot.

70 PACHAUG-TIPPECANSETT LOOP

General description: This 2-state circuit beginning and ending in Rhode Island's Arcadia Management Area tags the shore of Beach Pond, travels mixed woods and rocky hilltops, passes Escoheag Fire Tower (closed to the public), and concludes with a woodland meander. Travel foot trail and woods roads; a spur to Stepstone Falls extends the tour.

General location: On the Connecticut-Rhode Island border, 7 miles northwest of Hope Valley, Rhode Island; 16 miles northeast of Norwich, Connecticut.

Special attractions: Beach Pond views and access, mountain laurel and sweet pepperbush, intriguing rocky hilltops and slots, varied woods, wildlife, fall foliage, Stepstone Falls.

Length: 11.1-mile loop, with an optional 2.4-mile round-trip spur to Stepstone Falls.

Elevation: Find a 250-foot elevation change.

Difficulty: Strenuous.

Maps: Arcadia Management Area map; Nehantic and Pachaug trails map, *Connecticut Walk Book.*

Special requirements: The beach parking lot on the north side of Rhode Island 165 is a fee site; the fishing access on the south side is not. Keep to the trail where it tours along and through the private land of the South County Gun and Rod Club; travel is at your own risk. October 1 through February 28 Rhode Island requires hikers as well as hunters to wear a fluorescent orange hat or vest.

Season and hours: Year-round, generally spring through fall for hiking. Sunrise to sunset.

For information: Arcadia Management Area, Rhode Island Department of Environmental Management.

Finding the trailhead: From the junction of RI 3 and RI 165 (0.3 mile east of U.S. Highway 95), go west on RI 165 for 6.6 miles to reach Beach Pond parking on either side of the road. Arriving from Voluntown, Connecticut, from the junction of Connecticut highways 49 and 138/165, go east on CT 165/RI 165 for 4.3 miles, reaching Beach Pond. Find yellow and blue paint blazes marking the hike's start on the north side of RI 165, east of the parking lot entrance.

The hike: Follow the dual blazes of the **Tippecansett Trail** (yellow) and **Pachaug Trail** (blue), ascending stone steps and passing over a rise toward Beach Pond. Travel amid hemlock and red oaks, briefly contouring above shore, before curving away to reach the loop junction (0.5 mile). Adequate blazes guide hikers through the maze of woods roads and footpaths, leading to the junction.

At 0.5 mile, go left on the **Pachaug Trail** for a clockwise loop. The trail veers to and away from shore, dodging private land holdings; keep to the blazed trail. Along shore, find lush mountain laurel, sweet pepperbush, and highbush blueberry. Rocks and wet areas mark the rolling tour where it draws away from the pond. The drone of RI 165 accompanies the early distance.

By 1.25 miles, overlook a pretty, rounded cove with a gravelly bottom and a scattering of reflection rocks. Across the way, view a private dock; phragmites (plumed reeds) occupy the cove curvature.

Round above an inlet spring, find a trail register, and begin encountering stone walls. At 1.6 miles, stay left as a blue-blazed cut-off trail journeys right for a shorter loop option. Tour alternating hemlock flats and areas of oak, discovering more wet pockets. At 2.2 miles, pass a scenic boulder jumble that deformed the trunk of a hemlock growing alongside it.

At 2.25 miles, round a hillside of boulders and cliffs, cut up through a draw, circle the back of the hill, and push on to the next bouldery rise. Find

Tippecansett Trail, Arcadia Management Area, RI.

PACHAUG-TIPPECANSETT LOOP

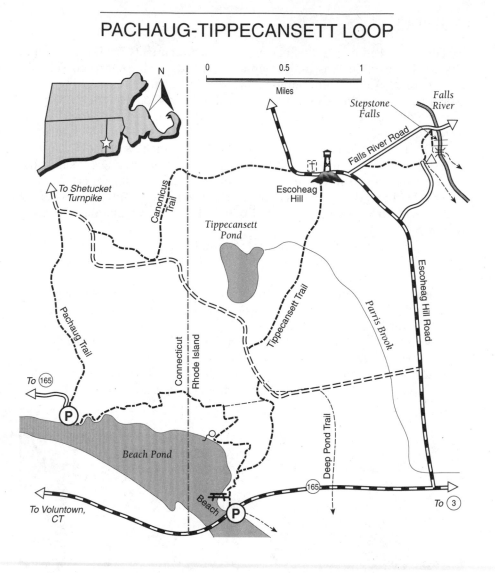

overhangs, shelters, and short passageways. After resuming a mixed-woods tour, cross a dirt road at 3.2 miles.

Return to the shore of Beach Pond, now in Connecticut, finding a boulder overlook before reaching the launch area (3.5 miles). Shadowy perch move through the water. Keep to the right-hand side of the access road, heading uphill through the boat launch parking area. There resume the hike, passing north through a dark hollow in the pine border. At the parking area, find chemical toilets.

Again tour woods and top outcrops, crossing a road. At 3.9 miles, descend a slot through massive boulder cliffs. The bouldery hillsides truly recommend this tour. Ascend and meander through the rocky realm, leaving the area at 4.7 miles, now touring a maple-mountain laurel passage. Locate stone walls and stone pens, hinting at a former pasture. Alternately tour pine and hardwood habitats.

At a lightly used dirt road (5.4 miles), the Pachaug Trail heads left. For the loop, go right now following the white blazes of the **Canonicus Trail.** Stay on the road for 0.3 mile, and then turn left on a woods road enfolded by young pines. Wetter areas host sweet pepperbush and brier.

Upon reaching a drivable dirt road at 6.2 miles, follow it left for 200 feet. There turn left onto a second woods road, similar to the first, although lacking the cushiony needle-strewn bed. Hardwoods replace pine, bringing with them an understory of laurel and shrubs.

Where the route forks at 6.8 miles, continue forward on the same woods road, avoiding a side road to the left. By now, the blazes have grown scarce. Again keep right at 7 miles, passing between the South County Gun and Rod Club and a private residence; keep to the woods road. At paved Escoheag Hill Road (7.75 miles) turn right following the road.

Opposite the historic cemetery of West Greenwich at 7.9 miles, find a blazed junction. Here end the Canonicus Trail, and follow the **Tippecansett Trail** right for the loop. To add a visit to Stepstone Falls, follow the Tippecansett straight.

For the falls detour, follow the yellow blazes along Escoheag Hill Road for 0.1 mile, turn left on Falls River Road for 0.3 mile, and turn right on a foot trail entering the hardwood-pine forest. As the trail passes through woods and the Stepstone Falls Backpack Area, blue blazes merge with the yellow ones, and hikers find the junction with the **Ben Utter Trail**.

Reach the falls area parking turnout (1.2 miles from the cemetery junction), and hike a few feet downstream along the scenic black water of brook-sized Falls River to find the four cascades of Stepstone Falls, a true Northeast charmer. The cascades spill over bedrock ledges and overhangs, with the largest cascade showing a 4-foot drop. Return to the junction opposite the cemetery (10.3 miles) and follow the Tippecansett Trail left past Escoheag Fire Tower, a traditional multi-story steel cage enclosed by fence.

From the tower, follow the well-blazed foot trail through oak-birch habitat, crossing outcrops and descending. At 10.9 miles, travel gun club land, heeding posted rules. Mountain laurel abounds. Cross Parris Brook and angle left across a woods road, touring a gentle landscape and relaxing woods.

Stay with the blazes, leaving the gun club at 11.8 miles. Soon after, turn left on a rocky woods road. At 12.3 miles, turn right as the white-blazed **Deep Pond Trail** proceeds along the road.

After skirting a gate, find the blue-blazed cut-off trail arriving on the right (12.5 miles). Continue forward on the Tippecansett Trail, meandering through pleasant mixed woods. Turn right to close the loop at 13 miles; return to the trailhead at 13.5 miles.

71 BREAKHEART POND-MOUNT TOM LOOP

General description: In Rhode Island's Arcadia Management Area, this woodland loop unites several named trails, passing an abandoned observation tower, reaching Breakheart Pond, crossing rivers and brooks, and touring the rocky ridge of Mount Tom. Travel foot trail and woods roads.

General location: 5 miles north of Hope Valley, Rhode Island; 22 miles northeast of Norwich, Connecticut.

Special attractions: Limited pond access; rich, varied woods; mountain laurel and sweet pepperbush; intriguing rocky hilltops; some views; wildlife; fall foliage.

Length: 13.5-mile loop.

Elevation: Find a 250-foot elevation change.

Difficulty: Moderate to strenuous.

Maps: Arcadia Management Area map; find trail maps generally stocked at the kiosk at the John B. Hudson Trailhead.

Special requirements: Permits required for camping; contact the Rhode Island Department of Environmental Management. Keep dogs leashed from April 1 through August 15. On Mount Tom, keep to the trail to avoid straying onto private lands. October 1 through February 28, all hikers must wear a fluorescent orange hat or vest per Rhode Island regulations.

Season and hours: Year-round, spring through fall best for hiking. Sunrise to sunset.

For information: Arcadia Management Area, Rhode Island Department of Environmental Management.

Finding the trailhead: From the Rhode Island 3 - Rhode Island 165 junction (0.3 mile east of U.S. Highway 95), go west on RI 165 for 2.5 miles and then right (north) 0.1 mile on a dirt road to reach the John B. Hudson Trail and off-road parking for 8 or 9 vehicles. Look for a small sign and yellow blaze.

The hike: Follow the yellow-blazed **John B. Hudson Trail** north from the road closure, strolling amid mixed oaks, maple, white pine, birch, sassafras, hickory, and beech. Fern, sweetfern, and huckleberry dress the forest floor. At 0.25 mile, a spur heads left 150 feet reaching a 30-foot wooden tower, now about the same height as the trees and no longer safe to mount. Despite its deteriorated state, the tower with its central pole and bird's nest platform offers a scenic detour.

Continue north finding bigger trees and a midstory of mountain laurel exploding in June blooms for an exceptionally pretty passage. Cross a small brook and the woods road of Tripp Trail, coming to a 3-way junction. The white trail to the left leads to a backpack shelter, the center prong is the John B. Hudson Trail, and the right prong offers hikers a wet-season pass to Breakheart Pond.

Continue forward on the John B. Hudson Trail, descending along and crisscrossing a small brook to reach fast-flowing Breakheart Brook with its stepped cascades and green banks, at 1 mile. This drainage tour often requires hopscotching from rock to root and may result in wet, muddy feet. Find sweet pepperbush and skunk cabbage. Where the trail tours a laurel flat, a white trail arrives from the camp shelter. Continue upstream to the dam and spillway for open views of Breakheart Pond (1.5 miles).

A thick deciduous rim and backset pines frame circular Breakheart Pond, with its lily pad mosaic, population of geese, and an eerie morning mist. Follow the dirt road to the right for 0.2 mile and turn left, staying the yellow blazes, as the trail meanders the woodland east of Breakheart Pond, a glimmer in the distance. Mountain laurel wanes from the mix, leaving an open understory beneath the beautiful big trees. Cross the footbridge over Breakheart Brook, passing between two beaver-dammed pools, and bear right.

Encounter multiple unmarked routes; keep to the blazed trail unless you carry a detailed map. A slow steady ascent leads to Matteson Plain Road (3.3 miles); angle left across the road for a rolling descent weaving amid and rounding over rocks. Yellow pollen from the pines sometimes dusts the forest plants.

From the pine flat, cross the footbridge over East Fork Flat River, a broad dark stream (4.1 miles). Here turn left on a more overgrown track as indicated by the blazes; the way soon clears after the initial log step-overs, ducking, and mild bushwhacking.

Pass through pine plantation and mixed woods, coming to a rickety footbridge spanning the West Fork Flat River (4.6 miles); assess before crossing:

White pine, Arcadia Management Area, RI.

wading may be necessary. Keep to the blazed route, making an occasional direction change. A corduroy aids in the crossing of a small wetland before the trail ascends to cross the shoulder of Penny Hill.

At 5.75 miles, bypass the **Penny Cutoff** as it heads left to the **Shelter Trail**. A sunnier oak-huckleberry complex and open rock outcrops characterize travel on Penny Hill.

Now descend through semi-open woods, with pitch pine and a few aspen joining the oaks, to cross Austin Farm Road (6.3 miles). Look for some quick direction changes before meeting Austin Farm Road a second time at 6.9 miles. Follow it left crossing the bridge over Falls River.

Hike past the yellow-blazed **Ben Utter Trail**, which hugs the upstream bank of Falls River, and stay on the roadway another 200 feet. There take the white-blazed **Escoheag Trail**, heading left to continue the loop. The blue-blazed **North-South Trail** briefly merges with it.

As the trail enters a mature pine plantation, look for the Escoheag Trail to ascend away right, reaching a leafy woods with a sporadic appearance of mountain laurel. At Barber Road (7.9 miles), the Escoheag Trail bears right; for the loop though, turn left, now following the **Mount Tom Trail** (also blazed white).

Travel a scenic flat-ridge straightaway, exploring a forest of small-diameter trees, interrupted by arborways of laurel. At the fork (8.9 miles) bear right, descending through a fuller forest with rock ledges to cross RI 165 at a rocky road cut.

Resume slightly to the left, still following the white blazes, stone-stepping up the slope to tour the rockier reaches of Mount Tom Ridge. Again find low oaks and sunny pockets as the trail rolls between outcrop and ledge, with filtered views seasoning the tour. After 9.8 miles, top outcrops for open views panning southwest at an opposite wooded ridge and marshy woodland basin. The vista holds great autumn appeal.

Descend past balanced boulders with fern-filled seams, touring pine-oak woods to reach paved Mount Tom Road (10.4 miles). Cross the road just north of Parris Brook and parallel the tannin-darkened water downstream, briefly hiking left on Blitzkrieg Trail (a dirt road).

Just ahead, white blazes point the way through a pine plantation; be careful of the many growing ant mounds, especially should you decide to sit in the shade. This piney stretch can be particularly hot and dry, so carry plenty of water.

At 11.5 miles, round a gate coming out at a Quonset hut (check station) and large parking area. Hike past the station to cross Wood River on the RI 165 bridge. Resume on the opposite side of the river, following the blazes east into the woods, paralleling but drifting away from RI 165.

Stay mainly amid pine or pine-oak woods, finding sheep laurel along a small brook before crossing it. Ascend one last ridge before dipping to cross Summit Road (12.6 miles). The rolling foot trail now parallels a scenic stone wall.

Next bypass the **North-South and Dove trails**. A wetter rock-studded

BREAKHEART POND-MOUNT TOM LOOP

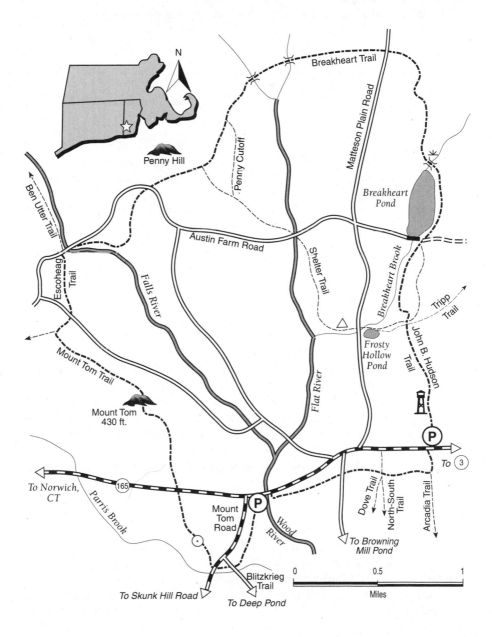

N

Penny Hill

Ben Utter Trail

Escoheag Trail

Penny Cutoff

Austin Farm Road

Matteson Plain Road

Breakheart Trail

Breakheart Pond

Breakheart Brook

Falls River

Shelter Trail

Tripp Trail

John B. Hudson Trail

Frosty Hollow Pond

Mount Tom Trail

Mount Tom 430 ft.

Flat River

P

To 3

To Norwich, CT

Parris Brook

165

Mount Tom Road

Wood River

Dove Trail

North-South Trail

Arcadia Trail

P

To Browning Mill Pond

To Skunk Hill Road

Blitzkrieg Trail

To Deep Pond

0   0.5   1

Miles

woods precedes the **Arcadia Trail** (13.2 miles). Follow the Arcadia Trail left for a soggy passage, touring via stepping stones and rustic corduroy. Reach RI 165 at a small parking turnout and angle right across the highway to return to the **John B. Hudson Trail**, closing the loop at 13.5 miles.

72 NORMAN BIRD SANCTUARY

OVERVIEW

At this 450-acre privately held Aquidneck Island sanctuary find north-south trending craggy ridges parted by linear marshes, abandoned pasture, and rich woodland. Inland freshwater ponds expand the wildlife habitat and enrich area views, which pan a dramatic rocky coastline to Rhode Island Sound. Eight miles of interlocking trail probe the property offering a variety of tours; the selected three hikes serve as an example of the sanctuary offering.

General description: Three hikes of varying difficulty examine woodland, field, pond, and ridge.

General location: In Middletown, 5 miles northeast of Newport, Rhode Island.

Special attractions: Wildlife watching; coastal, pond, and marsh panoramas; craggy ridges and puddingstone outcrop; wildflowers; fall foliage; historic visitor center barn.

Length: Woodland Trail, 1.1-mile loop; Hanging Rock Trail, 2 miles round-trip; Gray Craig Trail, 2 miles round-trip.

Elevation: The Woodland Loop is nearly flat; Hanging Rock and Gray Craig trails show a maximum 70-foot elevation change.

Difficulty: Woodland Loop, easy; Hanging Rock and Gray Craig trails, moderate.

Maps: Sanctuary map.

Special requirements: Per-person admission fee. Obey posted sanctuary rules; no pets.

Season and hours: Year-round, trails and center: 9 a.m. to 5 p.m. Tuesday through Sunday. Open daily in summer.

For information: Norman Bird Sanctuary.

Finding the trailhead: From the junction of Rhode Island 138A (Aquidneck Avenue) and Green End Avenue in Middletown, go east on Green End Avenue for 1.5 miles and turn right on Third Beach Road. Go 0.7 mile to enter the sanctuary on the right. Start the chosen trails, hiking southwest past the visitor center to a color-coded mapboard near the sheep pen.

The hikes: All three hikes share a common start and may be joined into a single long tour.

From the mapboard, follow the wood-chip trail straight ahead, skirting the sheep pen. At 0.1 mile, where the **Quarry Trail** journeys left through fields to an old slate quarry, bear right for the selected hikes. A mowed track advances the tour, passing along rock walls and through mixed woods.

At 0.2 mile, go left as the **Woodcock Trail** heads right touring shrubland and woods. Deciduous trees and planted evergreens now shade the tour, with sweet pepperbush, wild rose, and poison ivy amid the understory. At 0.25-mile junction, go right; the **Indian Rock Trail** heads left, passing a quartzite outcrop thought to have been used by the early Narragansett Indians for making tools.

In 200 feet, again go right as a spur branches away to link up with the Quarry Trail. Pass a beautiful multi-trunked maple and an outcrop sporting a memorial plaque, to reach a small wildlife pond (0.3 mile). Here find the three selected hikes: Bear left for the sanctuary ridge trails, including Hanging Rock and Gray Craig; to the right lies the Woodland Trail.

The **Woodland Trail** skirts the wildlife pond, traveling a red maple and black gum corridor, but the thick shrub understory denies pond views. Spurs to the right connect to the **Woodcock Trail**. Pass rock walls and some 10-foot-high humped-back outcrops of puddingstone. Boardwalk segments span the soggier reaches.

By 0.8 mile, the Woodland Trail curves back toward the visitor center, touring a tall shrub corridor. Bypass an owl box and traverse a field of waist-high grasses, clover, and milkweed. Again pass the Woodcock Trail on the right, returning to the visitor center near the mapboard and animal pen at 1.1 miles.

Forgoing the Woodland Trail option at 0.3 mile, bear left for the ridge trails. A bench seat overlooks the open snag-pierced pond adorned by duckweed, cattail, and aquatic grasses. Look for ibis, heron, frog, and turtle. Cross the footbridge, coming to a boardwalk junction at 0.4 mile. Here the **Hanging Rock Trail** heads left, **Gray Craig Trail** heads right.

Take the popular **Hanging Rock Trail**. The **Nelson Pond and Red Fox trails** quickly branch away to the right. Beyond the boardwalk find a root-riddled woods path. At 0.5 mile, an unsigned blue-dot trail heads left; keep right, touring amid beautiful gnarled red maple and ribbed and cobbled outcrops. The sanctuary trails narrow away from the visitor center.

Top Hanging Rock Ridge via a spur to the right at 0.65 mile or via the main trail at 0.75 mile, and follow the crest south to the nose of the ridge (1 mile). Ridge views feature Gardiner Pond, Second Beach, Sachuest Bay and Point, Rhode Island Sound, triangular Nelson Pond, and the fingery marsh isolating Hanging Rock and Red Fox ridges.

Serviceberry, dwarf juniper, oak, and wind-shaped pine vegetate the tiered and canted ledge; watch your footing. The tour halts atop Hanging Rock. Here find a plunging 30-foot cliff and an inspiring coastal view. Return to the visitor center for a 2-mile round-trip.

NORMAN BIRD SANCTUARY

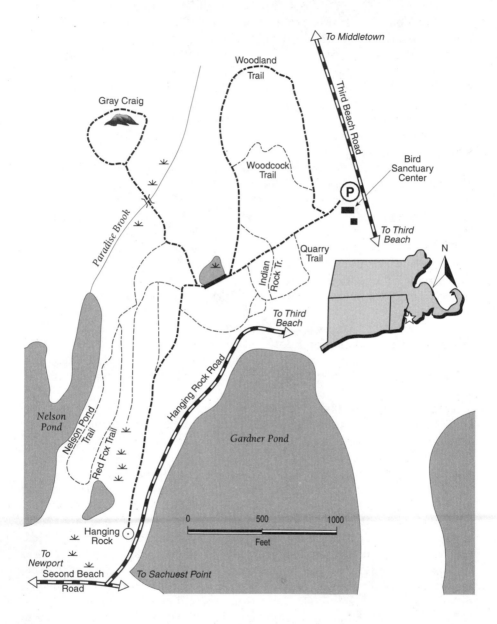

If you choose the **Gray Craig Trail** at 0.4 mile, travel amid dogwood, sweet pepperbush, fern, highbush blueberry, and red maples. In 0.1 mile (0.5 mile from the visitor center), a left spur leads to the **Nelson Pond and Red Fox trails**; keep to the Gray Craig Trail. Where the canopy opens up, find more shrubs.

Drop to the marshy flat of Paradise Brook, touring a boardwalk amid skunk cabbage, fern, and wildflowers and afterward return to forest. Intriguing, gnarled maples still grace the tour.

Ascend, coming to a loop junction at 0.8 mile; go left for a clockwise tour passing through an attractive forest that alternately shows boulders, patchy groundcover, and vine-entangled shrubs. Next, top the ridge (1 mile). Clad by red cedar and oaks, it affords only seasonal views overlooking the sanctuary toward Sachuest Point. Descend, returning to the loop junction at 1.2 miles. Retrace the first 0.8 mile to the visitor center.

73 SACHUEST POINT NATIONAL WILDLIFE REFUGE

OVERVIEW

At this 242-acre former naval communications station, visitors explore a jagged rocky peninsula, overlooking Sachuest Bay, the broad Sakonnet River mouth, and the open waters of Rhode Island Sound. From October to mid-April, wintering harlequin ducks with their striking plumage draw spectators; storms can crowd nearly a hundred of these birds onto the shoreline rocks. September flocks of tree swallows feeding on bayberry, fall migrating osprey and hawks, snowy owls hunting the peninsula's bursting winter rodent population, and the influx of spring-heralding songbirds, can each make a tour special. Occasionally, harbor seals haul out on the rocks.

General description: An easy perimeter loop travels the shoreline and upland habitat of Sachuest Point.
General location: 5 miles east of Newport, in Middletown, Rhode Island.
Special attractions: Bird and wildlife watching, rocky shores, coastal vistas, spring-flowering shrubs, surf fishing.
Length: 2.5-mile loop.
Elevation: The trail remains virtually flat.
Difficulty: Easy.
Maps: Refuge map, available at visitor center during hours, or request in advance from Ninigret National Wildlife Refuge.
Special requirements: No pets. Beware of poison ivy, and as biting insects can annoy, bring repellent.
Season and hours: Year-round. Grounds: a half hour before sunrise to a half hour after sunset. Visitor Center: 8 a.m. to 4 p.m., Saturday and Sunday.

For information: Seek information in care of Ninigret National Wildlife Refuge.

Finding the trailhead: From the junction of Rhode Island 138A (Aquidneck Avenue) and Green End Avenue in Middletown, go east on Green End Avenue for 1.5 miles. There turn right on Third Beach Road and stay on it for 1.8 miles, bearing right at 1.5 miles. Turn left (south) on Sachuest Point Road to reach the visitor center and parking lot in 0.7 mile.

The hikes: A perimeter loop explores the foot of this boot-shaped peninsula, visiting both Sachuest and Flint points. For a shorter tour to a single point, take either the east or west loop from the information board near bus parking.

For a counterclockwise perimeter tour, begin at the southwest corner of the parking area near a sign "Walking Your Dog?". Follow the paved path skirting the side of the visitor center, heading toward Sachuest Bay. Angle left on footpath to reach the bayshore bluff and journey south to Sachuest Point.

Views sweep the rocky refuge shore, the cliffs and historic buildings of Middletown, and the mansions of Newport across the way. Beach plum, bayberry, poison ivy, shore roses, and tangled vines weave a dense rich border, while daisy and clover accent the tour. In early summer, enjoy a fragrant intermingling of sweet and salt air.

By 0.4 mile, the bluff flattens allowing access to the rocky shore. In selecting a path to the rocks, beware of poison ivy. Huge gray rockweed-clad

Rocky shoreline, Sachuest Point National Wildlife Refuge, RI.

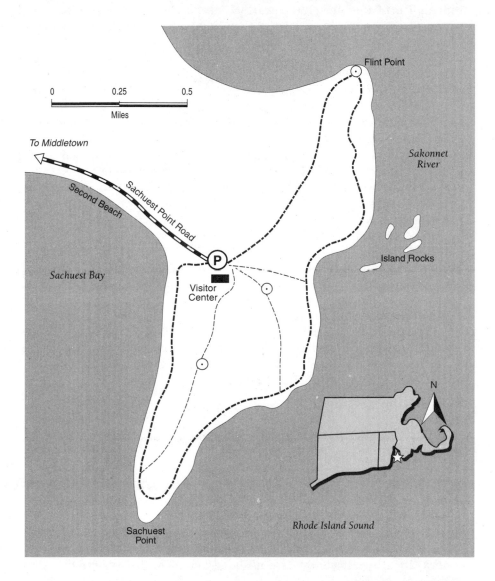

boulders with white quartz seams shape the shore. Look for mussel, crab, barnacle, and starfish amid the jumble.

The trail forks at 0.5 mile; stay right at all junctions to tour the perimeter. Spurs heading left travel the upland habitat reaching observation towers and eventually the visitor center. The untamed shrub-grassland offers chance sightings of red fox, weasel, and eastern cottontail.

A few interpretive plaques mark the perimeter tour; find the first at Sachuest Point (0.6 mile). Viewing includes a lighthouse island off Sakonnet Point and surf fishermen on the nearby rocks, casting for blacks, blues, and stripers (bass). An unexpected wave slapping the point calls one back to the wildness.

Resume the bluff stroll, heading north away from Sachuest Point. Edge a field, snaring coastal glimpses over the top of the thick seaward shrubs. At 0.8 mile, overlook a small scenic cove with rocky tongues extending to the water. Keep to the perimeter tour; birdhouses dot the field to the left. At 1 mile, find another trail fork, a bench, and interpretive sign— this one about ducks, which are best viewed November through March.

Coastal views now come like rapid fire, with looks at the scalloped shore, sun-bleached spits, straggled rocks, and dark waters gliding to shore. At 1.3 miles, a mowed swath travels inland. On the perimeter tour, come upon more benches; views now include the offshore fishing boats and Island Rocks—long, low gray outcrops piercing the water close to shore. Ahead, the shrubs again grow taller and thicker, blocking views.

At 1.9 miles, on Flint Point, take the spur heading right to reach a 1-story observation platform overlooking a bay cove on the Sakonnet River and Third Beach. Looks across the neck of the peninsula find Second Beach on Sachuest Bay. Cormorants often crowd a tiny rock island between Flint Point and Third Beach, capping the view.

From Flint Point, the perimeter loop swings southwest, returning to the visitor center. Pass through shrub corridor and shrub-field complex, where yellow warbler and swallows contribute to the finale. End at the parking lot, coming out near the information station and bus parking (2.5 miles).

74 VIN GORMLEY TRAIL

General description: This circuit travels the outlying forest, wetland, and rock habitat enfolding Watchaug Pond, with views of the pond reserved for the end of the hike. Travel public roadway, Burlingame State Park, and Kimball Wildlife Refuge, a property of the Audubon Society of Rhode Island.
General location: In southwestern Rhode Island, at the western outskirts of Charlestown.
Special attractions: A scenic boardwalk; mixed forest; azalea, sweet pepperbush, and both mountain and sheep laurel blooms; wildlife; fall foliage.
Length: 8.5-mile loop.
Elevation: Find a 150-foot elevation change.
Difficulty: Moderate.
Maps: Trail map; request a copy at the fee station or at campground office (west of Prosser Trail off U.S. Highway 1).

Special requirements: Parking fee. Expect some muddy, wet stretches in spring.

Season and hours: Year-round, spring through fall best for hiking. Open 8 a.m. to sunset.

For information: Burlingame State Park.

Finding the trailhead: Find access off U.S. 1 South only. From the junction of Rhode Island 2/Rhode Island 112 and U.S. 1 in Charlestown, go west on U.S. 1 South for 2.4 miles and turn right (north) on Prosser Trail for Burlingame State Park Picnic Area and Beach. On U.S. 1 North, go 3.4 miles east from RI 216, take the formal U-turn onto U.S. 1 South, and turn north on Prosser Trail in 0.4 mile. Reach day-use parking on the left in 0.7 mile.

The hike: Named for John Vincent Gormley, a dedicated trail-smith, this 8.5-mile hiker circuit offers a relaxing woodland stroll. Yellow paint and plastic blazes mark the tour.

From the day-use fee station, follow the blazes east out the access road and north (left) on Prosser Trail, a tree-lined 2-lane lightly trafficked road. In 0.6 mile, turn left on Kings Factory Road, hike another 0.3 mile, and turn left entering the woods for the natural portion of the tour. Chestnut, white, red, and black oaks, birch, pine, and cherry enfold the trail; beware of poison ivy near the start.

Find an enjoyable 4-foot-wide meandering trail. Mayflower, starflower, club moss, wild geranium, sassafras, huckleberry, and fern variously make up the understory vegetation. Deer, toad, fox, or neighborhood dog may

Colonial rockwall, Burlingame State Park, RI.

VIN GORMLEY TRAIL

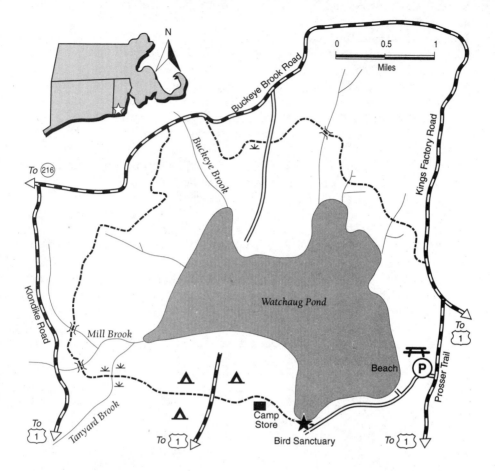

briefly divert attention.

At 1.1 miles, angle right across a quiet paved lane, touring a moister habitat with a thick congestion of shrubs, including sweet pepperbush, mountain laurel, azalea, highbush blueberry, and greenbrier. Ahead cross an inlet drainage.

The comfortable, obstacle-free trail allows eyes and thoughts to roam. At 1.6 miles, pass below a lichen-etched outcrop where mountain laurels find a niche. From a clearing, turn right on an attractive narrow woods road overlaced by hemlock-hardwood forest, with its shoulders dressed in mountain and sheep laurel.

At 2.2 miles, bear left, paying attention to the blazes and arrow markers for direction changes. Bird songs emanate from the leafy canopy, while Indian pipe pushes up through the forest duff. Small footbridges span a pair of slightly larger brooks. Cross a dirt road at 2.6 miles to tour a bog habitat via a rustic boardwalk of paired hewn logs. Afterward, turn left touring atop a flat outcrop.

Where the trail again rolls up and over rock outcrops, find 15- to 20-foot cliffs with showy fern seams. At 3.6 miles, depart the rocky area, again touring amid low shrubs, especially pretty when the sheep laurel parade their dark pink blooms. Turn left on Buckeye Brook Road to cross the bridge over the scenic wide slow water, accented by pond lilies and arrowhead; then resume the hike on the left. Oak, tall sassafras, and pitch pine frame the narrow woods path; find stone walls, patchy shade, and mountain laurel.

At 4.4 miles, turn left, remaining in a more open woods, with poison ivy becoming common. At 4.9 miles, again turn left, hiking an old woods road alongside a brook screened from view. A fuller canopy overlaces the trail. At 5.4 miles, cross the footbridge, near a scenic big maple. Soon after, tour more of the scenic boardwalk laid by Vin Gormley.

At 5.9 miles, cross the hewn-log bridge over Mill Brook, a meandering, tranquil tannin-tinted water overhung by green grasses, ferns, and branches. Dragonflies and frogs animate the setting. Bog boardwalks resume, passing amid red maple woodland, skunk cabbage, azalea, and sweet pepperbush. Watch for a couple of direction changesx before entering the state park campground (7 miles), restrooms and water available.

Hike through the open campground, following blazes, for a sunny walk. At 7.5 miles, past the playground but before the camp store, descend along the edge of a field, entering the woods at the far right corner of the field. A hardwood forest leads to Kimball Wildlife Refuge for the next leg of the tour. Obey rules.

At the refuge, side trails branch left to Watchaug Pond, while the blazed routes from the Audubon trail system arrive and depart on the right; keep to the yellow-blazed Vin Gormley Trail. At 7.8 miles, leave the Audubon refuge, hiking left on a dirt road passing a few lakeshore residences; keep to the road.

At 8.3 miles, find Watchaug Pond Fishing Access, for open viewing of the huge recreational water. At 8.5 miles, complete the loop returning to the picnic area parking at Burlingame State Park.

75 NINIGRET PARK, BEACH CONSERVATION AREA, AND NATIONAL WILDLIFE REFUGE

OVERVIEW

On the coast of Block Island Sound, this Charlestown town park, state beach conservation area, and 400-acre federal wildlife refuge offer prized recreation within a former U.S. Naval Air Station. Today's wildland features areas of upland grassland, shrubland, and woodland; marsh and pond habitats; and barrier-beach dunes, swale, and shore. The site provides a rich and varied wildlife habitat for native and migrant species.

General description: Two nature trails, a network of abandoned runways, and a stretch of barrier beach welcome hikers.

General location: In Charlestown, Rhode Island.

Special attractions: Wildlife watching, with nesting piping plover (April-August), woodcock courtship flights (dusk, mid-March through June), and wintering waterfowl; crystalline sand beach; Rhode Island's largest coastal pond (Ninigret Pond).

Length: Foster Cove Trail, 1.1-mile loop; Grassy Point Trail, 1.4 miles round-trip; East Beach Hike, 7-miles round-trip.

Elevation: The terrain is gentle, virtually flat.

Difficulty: Nature trails, easy; beach hike, moderate.

Maps: Refuge map; attain a copy at the office for Ninigret National Wildlife Refuge (NWR) in Shoreline Plaza or at the Charlestown Visitor Center, both off Route 1A.

Special requirements: Ninigret Park, Ninigret Beach Conservation Area, and Charlestown's Blue Shutters Town Beach all charge a vehicle admission fee. Cross dunes only at designated accesses, and respect closures for nesting piping plover and habitat protection. From mid-September through March, expect to encounter some beach vehicles (beach driving allowed by permit only). Carry insect repellent, leave pets at home, and beware of poison ivy and ticks.

Season and hours: Year-round. Ninigret Park: 7 a.m. to sunset. Ninigret Beach Conservation Area: 8 a.m. to sunset. Ninigret NWR: dawn to dusk. Blue Shutters Town Beach parking area: 8:30 a.m. to 5 p.m.

For information: Ninigret NWR or Ninigret Conservation Area.

Finding the trailhead: Find direct access off U.S. Highway 1 North in Charlestown; U-turns required for southbound traffic.

From the U.S. 1 - Rhode Island 216 junction, go east on U.S. 1 North, reaching the right-hand turns for East Beach Road in 0.8 mile, western Ninigret NWR (Foster Cove) in 2.6 miles, and U.S. 1A in 2.8 miles. U.S. 1A leads to Ninigret Park in 0.4 mile; reach the eastern refuge and Grassy Point trailhead at the end of the park road, past Frosty Drew Nature Center.

Southbound U.S. 1 traffic, locate the left-lane U-turns west of RI 212: Take the U-turn in 2.8 miles for Ninigret Park and both NWR nature trails. Take the one in 4 miles for the East Beach Hike.

For the East Beach Hike, park at either Blue Shutters Town Beach or Ninigret Beach Conservation Area.

The hikes: At the west access to the NWR, **Foster Cove Trail** leaves the southwest corner of the parking lot at the information board. Go right on the wide mowed lane enclosed by tall shrubs, maple, oak, willow, cedar, and cherry. Poison ivy, grape, and brier entwine the sides. Springtime showers the corridor with pink and white blooms. By 0.2 mile round Foster Cove, isolated by a thick shrub border. An occasional gap provides a view of the cove.

At 0.4 mile, an overgrown spur ventures right through a gauntlet of poison ivy, best to forgo. Deer, fox, rabbit, red squirrel, and songbirds accompany travelers. Next, take the mowed track heading left just prior to reaching a broad runway strip. Cracks riddle the runway. A sharp crash explains the strange dispersal of shells. Gulls circling 20 feet above the runway drop clams, breaking open the shells for easy eating.

Return, traveling a shrub corridor parallel to the runway. Find numbered panels from yesteryear semi-buried in the vegetation. At 1 mile, emerge on the runway near the rock barrier at the parking lot and close the loop.

For the NWR's **Grassy Point Trail** start near the information board at the southeast corner of the east-access parking area. Hike left following the hiker symbol and arrow toward Ninigret Pond, a 1,700-acre brackish coastal pond breached to the ocean.

Travel a shrub passage with wild plum, rose, poison ivy, and coastal scrub, quickly gaining access to a quiet, rocky cove and side pond rimmed by phragmites (plumed reeds). A scull may cut the water of Ninigret Pond, gulls clamor atop the rocks, and colored buoys mark crab pots. Cross-cove views locate Grassy Point and the observation platform. Round the cove to the left, closing loop back at the information board (0.25 mile).

This time, take the path to the right of the information board, again marked. Travel the now familiar shrub corridor with abundant sumac. At 0.4 mile (continuing the mileage), go left on an unmarked path for Grassy Point; a hiker symbol marks the path to right, which completes a second loop.

En route to the point, edge a cove of Ninigret Pond, passing a bench; beach pea and poison ivy grow along shore. Reach the 1-story platform at 0.7 mile to spy a low estuarine island and brushy points, a jungle of phragmites, and egret, cormorant, osprey, and gulls.

Return to the 0.4-mile junction at 1 mile, and bear left, coming out at another abandoned runway 1.1 miles. Go right to end the hike at the parking area (1.4 miles); left extends the tour along the upland of Ninigret Pond.

For **East Beach Hike**, start at Blue Shutters Beach for the full 7-mile hike, or start at Ninigret Beach Conservation Area to shorten the tour. Blue Shutters has a bathhouse/restroom; find chemical toilets at the conserva-

NINIGRET PARK, BEACH CONSERVATION AREA, AND NATIONAL WILDLIFE REFUGE

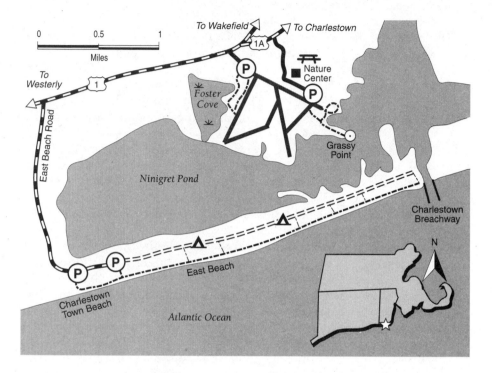

tion area. Bring drinking water for the sun-baked hike.

Hike east toward the Charlestown Breachway that opens Ninigret Pond to the ocean. At the west end of the tour, crowds linger close to the beach facilities. Drifting east, the tour grows more and more wild. Pass the entrance to Ninigret Beach Conservation Area at 0.25 mile. Behind the dune, primitive camping areas serve self-contained 4-wheel-drive vehicles, dispersing a few more beach-goers along the barrier beach.

A gentle cant greets the close-breaking waves, and orange flecks contribute to the beauty of the crystalline sand. Capped by dune grass and beach pea, four-foot-high dunes back the strand. Dips in the dunes reveal a shoreline swale and Ninigret Pond to the north. Black, purple, and green seaweed, whelk and skate eggcases, pebble patches, and a few shells complement the tour.

Offshore view the long, flat profile of Block Island, and fishing and leisure boats. Find designated dune accesses between the camp areas and beach at 1.2, 1.5, 2.2, 2.5, 2.8, and 3.5 miles. The jetty of Charlestown Breachway

East Beach, Ninigret Conservation Area, RI.

gradually becomes more obvious.

At the toe of the seaward dune, piping plovers nest; grant the birds a wide safety margin. Snowfences help preserve the dune. At 2.8 miles, pass from conservation land to national wildlife refuge. East of the refuge, private parcels back the beach, so keep toward the ocean shore.

Reach the Charlestown Breachway shaped by riprap jetties at 3.5 miles. A glorious aqua-green water surges in and out of Ninigret Pond, while overhead an osprey commonly patrols. Views sweep Block Island Sound, the breachway, Ninigret Pond, and the far marshy shore. Seasonally, seaweed overwhelms the waves curling to shore. Turn back, enjoying a fine hike or wade.

APPENDIX A — HIKER'S CHECKLIST

Use this list to minimize planning and packing oversights, adding items that you find critical to a successful trip.

Not every item will be needed for every trip, so customize the list to meet your (and your hiking companions') needs.

Consider the duration of the outing, the terrain, and the season. Check (but don't count on) the weather forecast. Expect the unexpected.

Ten Essentials
- ❏ extra food
- ❏ extra clothing
- ❏ sunglasses
- ❏ knife
- ❏ fire starter
- ❏ matches in waterproof container
- ❏ first-aid kit and manual
- ❏ flashlight
- ❏ map(s) for the trail
- ❏ compass

Clothing
- ❏ light-weight underwear
- ❏ long underwear
- ❏ under socks
- ❏ wool boot socks
- ❏ long pants
- ❏ shorts
- ❏ long-sleeve shirt
- ❏ T-shirts
- ❏ wool sweater or shirt
- ❏ wool hat and gloves
- ❏ visor or cap
- ❏ raingear
- ❏ warm coat or parka
- ❏ belt
- ❏ bandanna
- ❏ swimsuit or trunks
- ❏ hiking boots
- ❏ sneakers or camp shoes

Personal Items
- ❏ contacts or eyeglasses
- ❏ comb
- ❏ toothpaste and brush
- ❏ biodegradable soap/towelettes
- ❏ towel
- ❏ nail clipper and tweezers

- ❑ facial tissue or handkerchief
- ❑ toilet paper and trowel
- ❑ sunscreen and lip balm
- ❑ insect repellent
- ❑ wallet and keys
- ❑ emergency medical information
- ❑ watch

Gear

- ❑ water bottles
- ❑ pack(s)
- ❑ tent, with required poles and pegs
- ❑ ground cloth
- ❑ sleeping bag and foam pad
- ❑ stove and fuel
- ❑ pots and eating utensils
- ❑ can opener
- ❑ rope
- ❑ stuff bags
- ❑ large trash bags for emergency shelter for self or
- ❑ plastic bags for trash
- ❑ zip-seal bags for foodstuffs
- ❑ aluminum foil

Food

- ❑ three meals, plus snacks for each day out
- ❑ extra food for delays
- ❑ salt/pepper
- ❑ vegetable oil
- ❑ drink mixes

Health and Safety Items

- ❑ essential prescription medications
- ❑ emergency blanket
- ❑ water pump or purification tablets
- ❑ whistle
- ❑ pencil and paper
- ❑ picture wire for emergency repairs

Miscellaneous

- ❑ mosquito netting
- ❑ binoculars
- ❑ camera and film
- ❑ guidebooks—your FalconGuide
- ❑ identification books
- ❑ fishing gear and valid license

APPENDIX B — FURTHER READING

Appalachian Hiker II by Ed Garvey. Appalachian Books.

Appalachian Trail Guide to Massachusetts-Connecticut, Ninth Edition,
Norman Sills and Robert Hatton, Field Editors.
Appalachian Trail Conference.

Backpacking One Step at a Time, Fourth Edition by Harvey Manning.
Random House.

The Basic Essentials of Map and Compass by Cliff Jacobson. ICS Books.

Be Expert with Map and Compass by Bjorn Kjellstrom.
Charles Scribner's Sons.

Canoeing Massachusetts, Rhode Island and Connecticut by Ken Weber.
Backcountry Publications.

A Child's Introduction to the Outdoors by David Richey.
Pagurian Press Limited.

The Complete Walker III by Colin Fletcher. Alfred A. Knopf.

Connecticut Walk Book, Seventeenth Edition edited by John S. Burlew.
Connecticut Forest and Park Association, Inc.

Country Walks in Connecticut: A Guide to the Nature Conservancy Preserves
by Susan D. Cooley. Appalachian Mountain Club Books.

Eastern Forests: An Audubon Society Nature Guide
by Ann and Myron Sutton. Alfred A. Knopf, Inc.

A Field Guide to the Birds by Roger Tory Peterson. Houghton Mifflin Co.

Fifty Hikes in Connecticut by Gerry and Sue Hardy.
Backcountry Publications.

Finding Your Way in the Outdoors by Robert L. Mooers, Jr.
E.P. Hutton Co., Inc.

Forest Trees of Southern New England.
Connecticut Forest and Park Association, Inc.

A Guide to New England's Landscape by Neil Jorgenson.
The Globe Pequot Press, Inc.

A Guide to the Properties of The Trustees of Reservations.
The Trustees of Reservations.

Massachusetts and Rhode Island Trail Guide, Seventh Edition edited by
Jeff Wulfson. Appalachian Mountain Club Books.

Mountaineering First Aid, Third Edition by Martha J. Lentz,
Steven C. Macdonald, and Jan D. Carline. The Mountaineers.

Mountaineering Medicine by Fred T. Darvill. Wilderness Press.

Nature Walks in Eastern Massachusetts by Michael Tougias.
Appalachian Mountain Club Books.

Short Nature Walks on Cape Cod and the Vineyard, Third Edition by
Hugh and Heather Sadlier. The Globe Pequot Press, Inc.

The Shrub Identification Book by George W.D. Symonds.
William Morrow and Company.

The Sierra Club Naturalist's Guide to Southern New England by
Neil Jorgensen. Sierra Club Books.

Sixty Selected Short Nature Walks in Connecticut, Third Edition by
Eugene Keyarts. The Globe Pequot Press, Inc.

Travel Light Handbook by Judy Keene. Contemporary Books.

Trees and Shrubs of New England by Marilyn J. Dwelley. Down East Books.

Twenty-five Walks in Rhode Island by Ken Weber.
Backcountry Publications.

*Wild Country Companion: The Ultimate Guide to No-trace Outdoor
Recreation and Wilderness Safety* by Will Harmon.
Falcon Press Publishing Co., Inc.

*Wilderness Basics: The Complete Handbook for Hikers and Backpackers,
Second Edition* by the San Diego Chapter of the Sierra Club.
The Mountaineers.

APPENDIX C — WHERE TO FIND MAPS

For trail maps produced by the managing agencies, contact the information source named in the trail summary; turn to Appendix D for the complete address and phone number.

For copies of United States Geological Survey topographic quadrangles (USGS quads), check libraries, backpacking and mountaineering stores, or specialty map and outdoor publications stores. A state index will help you identify the name of the quad(s) that cover the area you are seeking.

Or contact the United States Geological Survey Map Distribution Center, Box 25286 Federal Center, Building 41, Denver, CO 80225. Ask for Massachusetts, Connecticut and Rhode Island indexes, and a price list for the maps.

In Connecticut, USGS quads, the *Atlas of Connecticut Topographic Maps*, and other state maps and profiles may be purchased at the Department of Environmental Protection Publications Store, Store Level, 79 Elm Street, Hartford, CT 06106-5127.

The *Connecticut Walk Book: A Trail Guide to the Connecticut Outdoors* published by the Connecticut Forest and Park Association contains both verbal trail descriptions and simple line-drawing maps done to scale, that locate the trail, key routes and towns, side trails, and major landmarks. Purchase current editions in area book stores and outdoor stores.

For information on ordering The Trustees of Reservations maps, contact The Trustees of Reservations, 572 Essex Street, Beverly, MA 01915-1530; 508-921-1944. With the purchase of a membership in this nonprofit organization, hikers not only promote the preservation of unique areas within Massachusetts Commonwealth, but they receive a 100-page guidebook to The Trustees properties and free or reduced-fee admission to the sites. Send a self-addressed envelope to the above address to receive information about becoming a member.

Maps produced by the New York-New Jersey Trail Conference or Appalachian Mountain Club typically are available at backpacking and mountaineering stores or directly from the organization. For an order form and price list, contact the respective organization:
New York-New Jersey Trail Conference, 232 Madison Avenue, New York, NY 10016; 212-685-9699
Appalachian Mountain Club, P.O. Box 298, Gorham, NH 03581; 1-800-262-4455 (for mail orders).

APPENDIX D — LAND MANAGEMENT LISTINGS

Appalachian Mountain Club
Bascom Lodge
P.O. Box 1800
Lanesborough, MA 01237
413-743-1591

Appalachian Mountain Club
617-963-9856 for cabin
reservations at Ponkapoag Pond,
Blue Hills Reservation.

Appalachian Trail Conference
P.O. Box 807
Washington and Jackson Streets
Harpers Ferry, WV 25425-0807
304-535-6331

Arcadia Management Area
Rhode Island Department of
Environmental Management
Division of Forest Environment
1037 Hartford Pike
North Scituate, RI 02857
401-647-3367

Beartown State Forest
P.O. Box 97
Blue Hill Road, Monterey,
MA 01245
413-528-0904

Bigelow Hollow State Park
c/o Quaddick State Park
Quaddick 818 Town Farm Road
Thompson, CT 06277
860-928-9200

Blackstone River and Canal
Heritage State Park
287 Oak Street
Uxbridge, MA 01569
508-278-7604

Blue Hills Reservation
Headquarters
Metropolitan District Commission
695 Hillside Street
Milton, MA 02186
617-698-1802

Blue Hills Trailside Museum
1904 Canton Avenue
Milton, MA 02186
617-333-0690

Bluff Point State Park and
Coastal Reserve
c/o Fort Griswold Battlefield
State Park
57 Fort Street, Groton, CT 06340
860-445-1729

Borderland State Park
257 Massapoag Avenue
North Easton, MA 02356
508-238-6566

Boxford State Forest
c/o Harold Parker State Forest
1951 Turnpike Road
North Andover, MA 01845-6326
508-686-3391

Breakheart Reservation
177 Forest Street
Saugus, MA 01906
617-233-0834

Broadmoor Wildlife Sanctuary
Massachusetts Audubon Society
280 Eliot Street
South Natick, MA 01760
508-655-2296 or 617-235-3929

Burlingame State Park
1 Burlingame Park Road
Charlestown, RI 02813
401-322-8910

Burr Pond State Park
Burr Mountain Road
Torrington, CT 06790
860-482-1817

Cape Cod National Seashore
Park Headquarters
99 Marconi Site Road
Wellfleet, MA 02667
508-349-3785

Caratunk Wildlife Refuge,
udubon Society of Rhode Island
301 Brown Avenue
Seekonk, MA 02771
508-761-8230

Cockaponset State Forest
Ranger Road
Haddam, CT 06438
860-345-8521

Connecticut Department of
Environmental Protection
Bureau of Outdoor Recreation,
State Parks Division
79 Elm Street
Hartford, CT 06106-5127
860-566-2304

Conservation Commission
Berlin Town Hall
240 Kensington Road
Berlin, CT 06037
860-828-7000

D.A.R. State Forest
Route 112, Goshen, MA
413-268-7098.
Mailing address: 555 East Street
Williamsburg, MA 01096

Devil's Den Preserve
The Nature Conservancy
Box 1162
Weston, CT 06883
203-226-4991

Devil's Hopyard State Park
c/o Cockaponset State Forest
Ranger Road
Haddam, CT 06438
860-345-8521

Essex County Greenbelt
Association
82 Eastern Avenue
Essex, MA 01929
508-768-7241

Friends of the Wapack
P.O. Box 115
West Peterborough
New Hampshire 03468

Gay City State Park
c/o Eastern Headquarters
209 Hebron Road
Marlborough, CT 06447
860-295-9523

George B. Parker Woodland
c/o Audubon Society of
Rhode Island
12 Sanderson Road, Smithfield
Rhode Island 02917-2600
401-949-5454

George Washington
Management Area
2185 Putnam Pike
Chepachet, RI 02814
401-568-2013

Goodwin Conservation Center
23 Potter Road
North Windham, CT 06256
860-455-9534

Hancock Shaker Village
P.O. Box 927
Junction of Routes 20 and 41
Pittsfield, MA 01202
413-443-0188

Hartman Park Manager
26 Foxtown Road
East Haddam, CT 06423
860-873-9319

Kettletown State Park
175 Quaker Farms Road
Southbury, CT 06488
203-264-5169

Laughing Brook Education Center
and Wildlife Sanctuary
Massachusetts Audubon Society
789 Main Street
Hampden, MA 01036
413-566-8034

Macedonia Brook State Park
159 Macedonia Brook Road
Kent, CT 06757
860-927-3238

Mashamoquet Brook State Park
RFD 2, Wolf Den Drive
Pomfret Center, CT 06259
860-928-6121

Massachusetts Audubon Society
Berkshire Sanctuaries,
472 West Mountain Road
Lenox, MA 01240
413-637-0320

Massachusetts Department of
Environmental Management
Division of Forests and Parks
100 Cambridge Street, 19th Floor
Boston, MA 02202
617-727-3180
For regional headquarters:
413-442-8928 (Berkshires)
413-545-5993 (Connecticut
River Valley)
508-368-0126 (Central Region)
508-369-3350 (Northeast)
617-727-3180 (Greater Boston)
508-866-2580 (Southeast)

Metropolitan District Commission
20 Somerset Street
Boston, MA 02108
617-727-5250

Metropolitan District Commission
Quabbin Park Visitors Center,
Quabbin Administration Building
485 Ware Road
Belchertown, MA 01007
413-323-7221

Mohawk Trail State Forest
P.O. Box 7
Charlemont, MA 01339
413-339-5504

Monroe State Forest
P.O. Box 7
Charlemont, MA 01339
413-339-5504

Mount Greylock State Reservation
P.O. Box 138
Lancsborough, MA 01237
413-499-4263

Mount Tom State Reservation
P.O. Box 985
Northampton, MA 01061
413-527-4805

Mount Washington State Forest
RD 3 East Street
Mount Washington, MA 01258
413-528-0330

Nehantic State Forest
c/o Rocky Neck State Park
Box 676
Niantic, CT 06357
860-739-5471

Ninigret Conservation Area
c/o Burlingame State Park
1 Burlingame Park Road
Charlestown, RI 02813
401-322-8910 or 401-322-0450
(May to September)

Ninigret National Wildlife Refuge
Shoreline Plaza
Route 1A, P.O. Box 307
Charlestown, RI 02813
401-364-9124

Norman Bird Sanctuary
583 Third Beach Road
Middletown, RI 02842
401-846-2577

Northeast Utilities
Northfield Mountain Recreation
and Environmental Center
99 Millers Falls Road
Northfield, MA 01360-9611
413-659-3714 or 1-800-859-2960

Norwottuck Rail Trail
136 Damon Road
Northampton, MA 01060
413-586-8706

Pachaug State Forest
P.O. Box 5
Voluntown, CT 06384
860-376-4075

Parker River National
Wildlife Refuge
Northern Boulevard
Plum Island, Newburyport,
MA 01950
508-465-5753

Paugussett State Forest
c/o Southford Falls State Park
175 Quaker Farms Road
Southbury, CT 06488
203-264-5169

Penwood and Talcott Mountain
State Parks
c/o Farmington Headquarters
178 Scott Swamp Road
Farmington, CT 06032
860-242-1158

Peoples State Forest
P.O. Box 1
Pleasant Valley, CT 06063
860-379-2469 or 860-379-6118

Pittsfield State Forest
Cascade Street
Pittsfield, MA 01201
413-442-8992

Purgatory Chasm State
Reservation
Purgatory Road
Sutton, MA 01590
508-234-3733

Sessions Woods Wildlife
Management Area
P.O. Box 1550
Burlington, CT 06013-1550
860-675-8130.

Sharon Audubon Center
National Audubon Society
325 Cornwall Bridge Road
Sharon, CT 06069
860-364-0520

Skinner State Park
Route 47, Box 91
Hadley, MA 01035
413-586-0350 or 413-253-2883

Sleeping Giant State Park
200 Mount Carmel Avenue
Hamden, CT 06518
203-789-7498

The Sleeping Giant Park
Association
P.O. Box 14,
Quinnipiac College
Hamden, CT 06518

South Cape Beach State Park
Great Neck Road
Mashpee, MA 02649
for information phone:
Waquoit Bay National Estuarine
Research Reserve 508-457-0495

Southford Falls State Park
175 Quaker Farms Road
Southbury, CT 06488
203-264-5169

The Trustees of Reservations
Central Regional Office
325 Lindell Avenue
Leominster, MA 01453
508-840-4446

The Trustees of Reservations
Northeast Regional Office
Castle Hill
P.O. Box 563
Ipswich, MA 01938
508-356-4351

The Trustees of Reservations
Western Regional Office
P.O. Box 792
Stockbridge, MA 01262
413-298-3239

University of Massachusetts -
Amherst
Department of Forestry
and Wildlife Management
Holdsworth Natural
Resources Center
University of Massachusetts
Box 34210
Amherst, MA 01003-4210
413-545-2665
or phone the Connecticut River
Valley Headquarters,
Division of Forests and Parks,
Massachusetts Department of
Environmental Management,
413-545-5993

U.S. Army Corps of Engineers
Cape Cod Canal Field Office
P.O. Box J
Buzzards Bay, MA 02532
508-759-4431

Wachusett Meadow Wildlife
Sanctuary
113 Goodnow Road
Princeton, MA 01541
508-464-2712

Wachusett Mountain State
Reservation
Mountain Road
P.O. Box 248
Princeton, MA 01541
508-464-2987

Walden Pond State Reservation
915 Walden Street (Route 126)
Concord, MA 01742
508-369-3254
or phone the site's visitor
information center/shop
508-287-5477

Waquoit Bay National Estuarine
Research Reserve
P.O. Box 3092
Waquoit, MA 02536
508-457-0495

Wellfleet Bay Wildlife Sanctuary
P.O. Box 236
291 State Highway Route 6
South Wellfleet, MA 02663
508-349-2615

West Rock Ridge State Park
c/o Sleeping Giant State Park
200 Mount Carmel Avenue
Hamden, CT 06518
203-789-7498

White Memorial
Conservation Center
80 Whitehall Road
P.O. Box 368
Litchfield, CT 06759-0368
860-567-0857

Windsor State Forest
River Road
Windsor, MA 01270
413-684-0948

ABOUT THE AUTHORS

Over the past fifteen years, the Ostertags, Rhonda (a writer) and George (a photographer), have collaborated on six outdoor guidebooks; produced hundreds of published articles on nature, travel, and outdoor recreation; and helped develop environmental impact studies.

George was born and raised in Connecticut and brings to this book his childhood enthusiasm tempered by a reflective eye. Find the passion he holds for the region reflected in his photography.

Rhonda writes with the fresh perspective and enthusiasm of a westerner new to this area.

Having hiked more than 1,500 miles in Southern New England this past year, the foot-sore couple has become well acquainted with the trails of Massachusetts, Connecticut, and Rhode Island. This book represents first-hand information gleaned from their experience.

Other titles by the team include *Hiking New York* (1996), (Falcon Press), *California State Parks: A Complete Recreation Guide* (1995) and *100 Hikes in Oregon* (1992), (both published by The Mountaineers, Seattle, Washington).

FALCONGUIDES

HIKE it

HIKER'S GUIDES

Hiker's Guide to Alaska
Hiking Alberta
Hiking Arizona
Hiking Arizona's Cactus Country
Hiking the Beartooths
Hiking Big Bend National Park
Hiking California
Hiking Carlsbad Caverns
   and Guadalupe National Parks
Hiking Colorado
Hiking Florida
Hiking Georgia
Hiking Glacier/Waterton Lakes National Park
Hiking Hot Springs
   in the Pacific Northwest
Hiking Idaho
Hiking Maine
Hiking Michigan
Hiking Montana
Hiker's Guide to Montana's
   Continental Divide Trail
Hiking Nevada
Hiking New Hampshire
Hiking New Mexico
Hiking New York
Hiking North Carolina
Hiking Oregon
Hiking Oregon's Eagle Cap Wilderness
Hiking Olympic National Park
Hiking Tennessee
Hiking Texas
Hiking Utah

Hiking Vermont
Hiking Virginia
Hiking Washington
Hiking Wyoming
Hiking Wyoming's Wind River Range
Hiking Northern Arizona
Trail Guide to Bob Marshall Country
Wild Montana

ROCK CLIMBER'S GUIDES

Rock Climbing Colorado
Rock Climbing Montana
Rock Climbing New Mexico & Texas

DENNIS COELLO'S
AMERICA BY MOUNTAIN BIKE SERIES

Mountain Biking Arizona
Mountain Biker's Guide to Central Appalachia
Mountain Biker's Guide to Colorado
Mountain Biking the Great Lake States
Mountain Biking the Great Plains States
Mountain Biking the Midwest
Mountain Biking New Mexico
Mountain Biker's Guide to
   Northern California/Nevada
Mountain Biking Northern New England
Mountain Biker's Guide to Ozarks
Mountain Biking the Pacific Northwest
Mountain Biking the Southeast
Mountain Biker's Guide to Southern California
Mountain Biking Southern New England
Mountain Biking Texas and Oklahoma
Mountain Biker's Guide to Utah
Mountain Biking the Midwest

■ *To order any of these books, or to request an expanded list of available titles, including guides for viewing wildlife, birding, scenic driving, or rockhounding, please call* **1-800-582-2665**, *or write to Falcon, PO Box 1718, Helena, MT 59624.*

FALCONGUIDES

Watch IT

THE WATCHABLE WILDLIFE SERIES
Alaska Wildlife Viewing Guide
Arizona Wildlife Viewing Guide
California Wildlife Viewing Guide
Colorado Wildlife Viewing Guide
Florida Wildlife Viewing Guide
Idaho Wildlife Viewing Guide
Indiana Wildlife Viewing Guide
Iowa Wildlife Viewing Guide
Kentucky Wildlife Viewing Guide
Montana Wildlife Viewing Guide
Nevada Wildlife Viewing Guide
New Mexico Wildlife Viewing Guide
North Carolina Wildlife Viewing Guide
North Dakota Wildlife Viewing Guide
Oregon Wildlife Viewing Guide
Tennessee Wildlife Viewing Guide
Texas Wildlife Viewing Guide
Utah Wildlife Viewing Guide
Vermont Wildlife Viewing Guide
Virginia Wildlife Viewing Guide
Washington Wildlife Viewing Guide
Wisconsin Wildlife Viewing Guide

BIRDER'S GUIDES
Birding Arizona
Birding Minnesota
Birder's Guide to Montana

SCENIC DRIVING GUIDES
Scenic Driving Alaska & the Yukon
Scenic Driving Arizona
Scenic Driving California
Scenic Driving Colorado
Scenic Driving New England
Scenic Driving Georgia
Scenic Driving Montana
Scenic Driving New Mexico
Scenic Driving Oregon
Scenic Driving the Ozarks
Scenic Driving Texas
Scenic Driving Utah
Travel Guide to the Lewis & Clark Trail
Traveling the Oregon Trail

ROCKHOUND'S GUIDES
Rockhounding Arizona
Rockhound's Guide to California
Rockhound's Guide to Colorado
Rockhounding Montana
Rockhound's Guide to New Mexico
Rockhounding Texas

FALCON
1-800-582-2665
P.O. BOX 1718
HELENA, MT 59624